# CATHOLIC RECORD SOCIETY
# PUBLICATIONS

## RECORDS SERIES
## VOLUME 86

Portrait of Mannock Strickland (1683–1744), school of John Closterman.

# Mannock Strickland

## (1683–1744)

### Agent to English Convents in Flanders

## *Letters and Accounts from Exile*

Edited by

RICHARD G.WILLIAMS

PUBLISHED FOR

THE CATHOLIC RECORD SOCIETY

BY

THE BOYDELL PRESS

2016

First published 2016

ISBN 978-0-902832-30-5

A Catholic Record Society publication
published by The Boydell Press
an imprint of Boydell & Brewer Ltd
PO Box 9, Woodbridge, Suffolk IP12 3DF, UK
and of Boydell & Brewer Inc.
668 Mt Hope Avenue, Rochester, NY 14620-2731, USA
website: www.boydellandbrewer.com

A CIP catalogue record for this book is available
from the British Library

The publisher has no responsibility for the continued existence or
accuracy of URLs for external or third-party internet websites referred to
in this book, and does not guarantee that any content
on such websites is, or will remain, accurate or appropriate

This publication is printed on acid-free paper

Printed and bound in Great Britain by
TJ International Ltd, Padstow, Cornwall

# CONTENTS

# ILLUSTRATIONS

# ACKNOWLEDGEMENTS

On 13 February 1790 all monastic orders in Revolutionary France were dissolved. The convents considered in the present volume lost most of their archives when they were driven out in 1793 and 1794. The letters and papers presented here come from the business papers of the Roman Catholic counsellor-at-law Mannock Strickland (1683–1744); they are the only known complete surviving business papers of any eighteenth-century lawyer, and survived because they were retained in England. They were brought in 1752 from a London garret where they had been stored since Strickland's death, tantalisingly shorn of one-and-a-half hundred-weight of 'waste paper', and they remain in the care of his descendants. I am most grateful to the Eyston family, and particularly to J. J. Eyston and The Mapledurham Trust, for their permission to publish them; their encouragement to do so has been wholehearted and most welcome. I am particularly grateful for advice, discussions and practical aid from Dr Francis Young (who, among other support, solved the problem of presenting the parallel synchronised elements of Strickland's accounts), to Dr Caroline Bowden of Queen Mary University of London, Director of the 'Who were the Nuns?' project (to which acknowledgment is also due), and to Dr James E. Kelly of Durham University, Dr Gabriel Glickman and Professor Paul Kléber Monod; special thanks go to Dr Hester Higton, editeur extraordinaire. Very brief extracts from the Louvain letters were published in Caroline Bowden et al. (eds), *The English Convents in Exile, 1600–1800, Part 2, Volume 5* (London: Routledge, 2014) with a brief explanatory essay; the accounts and the bulk of the letters appear here for the first time.

Letters sent in the reverse direction, from Mannock Strickland to these convents, can no longer be traced and must be presumed lost: Strickland rarely kept copies (although he almost always annotated letters with dates of his replies). All of his letters seemingly perished at the French Revolution when the convents were suppressed.

My wife has tolerated with good grace the virtual presence of the nuns – strong characters all – in our lives for rather a long time, and I am grateful for her advice and forbearance.

Richard G. Williams

Mapledurham, January 2016

# ABBREVIATIONS

| | |
|---|---|
| Anstruther 3 | Anstruther, Godfrey, *The Seminary Priests: A Dictionary of the Secular Clergy of England and Wales, 1558–1850. III. 1660–1715* (Great Wakering, Essex: Mayhew-MacCrimmon, 1976) |
| Bellenger | Bellenger, Dominic Aidan, *English and Welsh Priests 1558–1800: A Working List* (Bath: Downside Abbey, 1984) |
| BL | British Library, London |
| *Blount MSS* | Blount manuscripts (including Strickland Papers), Mapledurham House. References with a single letter (*C*, *D* or *E*) followed by numbers are the archival call references (e.g. *C* 98/42, *E* 39) |
| *C* | *Blount MSS*, Series *C* 1–212 |
| *D* | *Blount MSS*, Series *D* 1–70 |
| *E* | *Blount MSS*, Series *E* 1–121 |
| CRS | Catholic Record Society |
| *DNB* | *Dictionary of National Biography*, 63 vols (London: Smith, Elder and Co., 1885–1900) |
| *ECIE* | Bowden, Caroline (ed.), *English Convents in Exile, 1600–1800*, 6 vols (London: Pickering and Chatto, 2012–13) |
| ESTC | English Short Title Catalogue |
| Gillow | Gillow, Joseph, *A Literary and Biographical History, or Bibliographical Dictionary of the English Catholics*, 5 vols (London: Burns and Oates, 1885–1902) |
| Guilday | Guilday, Peter, *English Catholic Refugees on the Continent, 1558–1795. I: The English Colleges and Convents in the Catholic Low Countries* (London: Longmans, Green and Co., 1914) |
| *HoP* | *The History of Parliament* (Cambridge: Cambridge University Press), online version http://www.historyofparliamentonline.org |
| Hornyold | Hornyold, Henry, *Genealogical Memoirs of the Family of Strickland of Sizergh* (Kendal: T. Wilson and Son, 1928) |
| Kirk | Kirk, John, *Biographies of English Catholics in the Eighteenth Century* (London: Burns and Oates, 1909) |

| NS | New Style (Gregorian Calendar) |
| *ODNB* | *Oxford Dictionary of National Biography*, 60 vols (Oxford: Oxford University Press, 2004); online edition http://www.oxforddnb.com |
| OP | Dominicans (Order of Preachers) |
| OS | Old Style (Julian Calendar) |
| OSA | Augustinians (Order of St Augustine) |
| OSB | Benedictines (Order of St Benedict) |
| SJ | Jesuits (Society of Jesus) |
| STC | Short Title Catalogue (see also ESTC) |
| WWTN | 'Who Were the Nuns?' online database, http://wwtn.history.qmul.ac.uk. The database reference numbers are given after names and dates for each nun; they have a code made up of two letters and three numbers, as follows: |
| BB | Brussels, Benedictines |
| BD | Brussels, Dominicans (Spellikens) |
| DB | Dunkirk, Benedictines |
| LA | Louvain, Augustinians (St Monica's) |
| PA | Paris, Augustinians |

The full list of convent codes may be found on the WWTN database

*Abbreviations used in the letter headings*

| CT | Cecily Tunstall |
| MS | Mannock Strickland |
| MXE | Margaret Xaveria Ellerker |

# EDITORIAL PRINCIPLES

Mannock Strickland kept his accounts, in his own hand, in two series of vellum-bound cash day books, arranged so that receipts are on the left-hand page and the payments 'Per Contra' run in a synchronised sequence on the facing, right-hand, pages. The main series of four working books covers all his business; some entries are coded to show the banker used for particular transactions (*Blount MSS, E* 49, 1726–33; *E* 50, 1733–39; *D* 33, 1739–43; and *D* 34, 1743–44).

The second series contains fair-copy accounts for individual clients. Those for three convents are in one of these books (*Blount MSS, D* 31):

Louvain 1733–41 and 1742–44, fols 51–71 and fols 82–88
Spellikens, fols 71–78
Dunkirk 1728–44, fols 20–36, and, under the name of Lady Fleetwood, 1727–29, fols 16–18

This volume also contains accounts held by Phebe Brailsford, Charles Bodenham, Lady Mary Radclyffe and her executors.

A third volume (*Blount MSS, D* 30) contains accounts held by William Petre junior, the Petre estates, Jarrard Strickland, Lettice Wybarne, John Wybarne and Anne Viscountess Carington; it also contains the opening entry for Lady Crispe of Brussels for a similar account for the English Benedictines at Brussels.

Account books were kept for Edward Paston in the years 1720–44 (*Blount MSS, D* 32), for Roger Strickland (*Blount MSS, E* 48), and for his sister Mrs Stafford, for his nephew Edward Stafford and for Mrs Betty Molyneux in the years 1718–43 (*Blount MSS, E* 45).

## Dates and currency

It has proved less confusing to retain the original very clear dating in the accounts. The nuns in Flanders always followed the New Style (NS) Gregorian dating in use in their host countries. Strickland always used English Old Style (OS) Julian dating, while noting the NS dating of the letters to which he was responding. His usage is so clear that confusion is unlikely, despite the oddness of his appearing to send a response before the receipt of letters.

Both Strickland and the nuns retained the old practice of observing New Year on 25 March (Lady Day). Where applicable, the editor has added both years for dates falling between 1 January and 25 March.

Unless otherwise indicated, currency is shown in sterling as entered.

No attempt has been made to correct any arithmetical errors in the original documents.

## Spelling of place names

The anglicised form 'Dunkirk' is used throughout the Introduction and notes for the French town of 'Dunkerque', but where the French spelling occurs in the original documents it is left unaltered. The French forms 'Louvain' and 'Bruges' are used in the Introduction and notes in preference to the Flemish forms 'Brugge' and 'Leuven' (or, indeed, the now obsolete anglicised 'Bridges'); these forms are left unaltered (but explained in a footnote) in the documents themselves. The Flemish spelling of 'Spellikens' is adopted in the Introduction and notes in preference to the gallicised 'Spelicains'.

## Biographies

Individuals have been included only where information is otherwise available (often from other unpublished material in Strickland's papers). This particularly affects the inclusion of the large number of individuals named in the cash day books and not elsewhere, about whom nothing further can be added.

# INTRODUCTION

These documents – letters, account books and other papers of the Catholic counsellor-at-law Mannock John Strickland (1683–1744) – are a rare survival against the odds. According to the National Register of Archives, they form part of the only complete set of an English lawyer's papers of any period known to have survived. That they have done so is little short of a miracle in the face of political upheavals. They are equally unusual in that they reveal the human and organisational side of religious communities. They have survived the turmoil of the French Revolution which closed the convents in Flanders whence they originate. This expulsion occurred at very short notice in most cases – so short that the nuns were unable to rescue most or all of their archives. However, although one side of the correspondence is missing, the remainder of the documents have remained intact because the letters addressed to Strickland were kept by him as business records.

Strickland had no successor in practice after his death in 1744, although some of the deeds held for the convents were returned in 1745–46 to the new legal advisers, particularly to John Maire of Lartington, Yorkshire, who can with some reason be regarded as Strickland's successor, just as Strickland succeeded Henry Eyre and Edward Bedingfeld, both of Gray's Inn. In 1752 all of the remaining papers were transferred to Strickland's son-in-law Michael Blount II (1719–92), who removed them from London to his country home at Mapledurham, where they have remained ever since.

They could not have fallen into better hands, since Michael II was a hoarder (over 3,000 letters to and from him and a wealth of documents – some held by Strickland for clients – survive in the archives of his descendants). This archive is the source for the letters and documents printed here and is a rare survival of documentation concerning an area of growing interest to historians, but where few reliable records survive.

The documents – particularly the letters – speak for themselves about a side of monastic life not often seen. Above all, they speak of isolation, and of the helplessness of exile. The nuns were in a war zone, where the basics of food were scarce and expensive,[1] and at the mercy too of supposedly supportive families who were under financial stress. Their more generous donors were tardy in the extreme in their supply of funds,

---

[1] Although the Thirty Years' War of 1618–48 (during which Louvain had been besieged) had ended, sporadic warfare continued in Flanders for many more years.

while the nuns were powerless to enforce the law and claim what was due to them from a foreign land.

Strickland was one of a select group of English Catholic lawyers, along with the barrister Nathaniel Pigott (1661–1737) – the last Roman Catholic to be called to the Bar for the next century and a half – the brothers Henry (c. 1677–1719) and John Eyre (d. 1739) of Gray's Inn (Strickland's pupil-masters), John Maire (1703–71), conveyancer, and Matthew Duane (1707–85), conveyancer and numismatist. Between them, these lawyers did much to safeguard the estates and finances of Roman Catholic owners. A good lawyer and adviser, capable of raising and managing funding, could nullify all the worst effects of penal taxation and ensure the safe transition of estates from one generation to the next.

The Catholic establishments for English men and women in northern France and the northern Low Countries formed a feature of English Catholic life for two centuries. For boys there were schools at Douai, Bornhem and St Omer, for general education and as preparation for the priesthood which was supposed to re-convert the British Isles, a training undergone by three of Mannock Strickland's sons. Priests either completed their studies at the English College, Douai, or proceeded to another college – perhaps to St Gregory's, Paris – before returning to the mission field in England. For women, the choice was different and more final.[2] There were no formal schools, but a number of convents took in young women in their mid to late teens, for education and, in many cases, to provide permanent homes for daughters with either a vocation or no marriage prospects.

All of these religious houses, together with others in France, Germany, Spain and Portugal, derived monetary support from the English families whose members formed their community; that financial basis was often hand to mouth. Mannock Strickland, the leading Catholic counsellor-at-law and conveyancer of his day, met the need of some of these institutions for a resource channel, although he was not an open advocate on their behalf.

The collection of documents edited for this volume focuses on the financial arrangements of four convents of English nuns in Flanders in the first half of the eighteenth century and, in particular, on the work of

---

[2] There were a few choices for girls on the English mainland: Mary Ward's Institute at York, Mrs Cornwallis's school at Brook Green, Hammersmith, where Pope's friend Martha Blount was educated (see Valerie Rumbold, *Women's Place in Pope's World* (Cambridge: Cambridge University Press, 1989)), and its short-lived outpost of 1781–90 at Grove House near Henley on Thames, which was the misguided creation of Strickland's third son, Dr Joseph Strickland (see *Blount MSS*, C 64/1–41, correspondence between Eleanor Bayly of Brook Green, charged with setting up the Grove House school, and Dr Joseph Strickland, its chief promoter). The leading Catholic gentry families maintained chaplains (in defiance of the law), who may have done some tutoring.

their agent, Mannock John Strickland (1683–1744). The documents also shed light on the daily life of the inmates of the convents in all sorts of ways. It should be made clear that the documents from these four convents kept by Strickland are here published complete, without any omissions. The letters, especially, are well written, telling and entertaining and are supplemented by the complete cash day books kept by Strickland for each convent, a list of deeds held by Strickland as loan security for clients and returned to their owners after his death in 1744, and some miscellaneous related papers.

The convents were notorious hotbeds of Jacobitism, sustained by their hopes for a glorious reinstatement of the Catholic faith and the Stuart line of kings – the nuns needed that hope alongside their religion to maintain their resolve through times that were often both physically and spiritually harsh. The convents employed one or more agents to advise on and deal with business and legal matters; some used lawyers, others secular priests. All agents had a team of couriers and other helpers, male and female; in these particular cases, most seem to have been involved in the export cloth trade. The opportunity has also been taken to put into the public domain the papers concerning the campaign in the 1740s to rescue the failing Carthusian monastery at Nieuport and to draw certain comparisons and contrasts between this and the convents of nuns.

Consideration is given to the necessary background, not least to the workings of the financial system of this period. The reader will find, however, that, by and large, these letters provide their own explanation as they stand: clear and, it has to be allowed, entertaining. Biographical data has been provided for most of those named in the letters, where details beyond those given in the letters are known.

Two obsolete terms need explanation. The first is the function of the counsellor-at-law, still used in the United States but not in the United Kingdom. Essentially, the counsellor-at-law was a barrister who had never been called to the Bar but had the highest form of legal training; he acted for his clients as a general business and financial adviser able to source finance from lenders, scriveners and other funding providers. Strickland could not be called to the Bar, Catholics being debarred from such office by the penal legislation, but he could provide the full services of a barrister, though without the right of audience in court; he got round this problem by his employment as his clerk of a Protestant solicitor, Henry Rogers Trubshaw, who did have right of audience.

The other term that needs explanation is the title Procuratrix, one of the three elected principal officers in the convents, together with the Prioress and Sub-Prioress. The modern equivalent of this post would be that of a bursar, managing finances and premises. It was a key post in enclosed convents since this person was the one who acted as a contact with the outside world.

## The Strickland family

The convents could not have chosen better for their agent when four Flemish communities of English ladies selected Mannock John Strickland. Although his Catholicism prevented him from practice at the Bar, it did not preclude membership of the Inns of Court – he was a member of Gray's Inn from 1704 to 1732 and thereafter belonged to Lincoln's Inn (a particular base of Catholic support in an area of London heavily settled by Catholics[3]). A discreet Jacobite whose family had been part of the Stuart royal court in England and in exile was an ideal choice for institutions such as these, committed as they were to restoring James II and his lineage to the English throne. It was particularly important that they had family, business and marriage connections with so many Catholic gentry families – the Andrews, Arundells, Bedingfelds, Biddulphs, Blounts, the Earl Fitzwilliam of the Irish peerage and his sister (the titular Countess of Shrewsbury), the Giffards, Heneages, Herberts, the Marquises (Jacobite Dukes) of Powis, the Howard Dukes of Norfolk, the Jerninghams (Jernegans), Mannocks, Nevils of Holt, the Lords Petre, the Salkelds, Salvins, Scropes, the Talbot Earls of Shrewsbury, the Lords Stafford, the Stonors, Stricklands, Tichbornes, Timperleys, Towneleys, Waldegraves and Widdringtons, and many more, together with their networks of marriage connections – a readymade clientele and source of investors. Moreover, Strickland's legal training and his work saw him well placed to seek out necessary finances such as mortgages, loans and gifts.

Mannock Strickland himself wrote his own best sales pitch for attracting clients:

> It's possible you may remember my father Mr. Robt. Strickland and mother, the one vicechamberlain, the other of the Bed Chamber to King James's Queen Mary, my uncle Sir Roger Strickland Vice-admiral and Sir Thomas Strickland of the privy Counsel in King James the 2d's time. I hope you will not think that a branch of the family that has sufferd so much for Loialty, can be Guilty of any thing that's unjust, or asking an unreasonable favour of you ...[4]

Mannock John Strickland belonged to the junior branch of the prominent Catholic Stricklands of Sizergh, Westmorland, Catterick and Thornton Bridge, Yorkshire. The head of the family was Sir Thomas (1621–94). In 1674, he married, as his second wife, Winifred Trentham (1645–1725), a member of the household of Queen Mary of Modena. In 1688 Lady Strickland was sworn in as sub-governess to the newborn Prince of Wales. She and the Prince's governess, the Marchioness of Powis, were

---

[3] Geoffrey de C. Parmiter, *Elizabethan Popish Recusancy in the Inns of Court* (London: Institute of Historical Research, 1976).

[4] *Blount MSS, C* 41/203, 31 December 1741, copy letter, MS to Sir Henry Tichborne.

in charge of him when, following the arrival in England of the Prince of Orange, they escaped in secret with the Prince to Calais, before going on to St Germain-en-Laye, where the French king had offered James II and his family refuge. She became the young Prince's governess in 1693, following the death of Lady Errol, who had succeeded Lady Powis, and remained in post until 1696.

Strickland's parents were also at the heart of the Jacobite court: his father, Robert (1639–1709), entered the service of James, Duke of York (later James II) before the Exclusion Crisis of 1679, going with him to Brussels.[5] Robert's brother Roger (1640–1717) was briefly James II's Admiral of the Blue Squadron and was knighted for his performance at the Battle of Sole Bay, before demotion to the rank of Vice-Admiral for tactlessly attempting to have Mass said publicly aboard his flagship.[6] Strickland's mother was Bridget Mannock (d. 1736); she and her husband were both in the service of Queen Mary of Modena. Their youngest son, Francis (Frank) (1681–1745), was the most overtly Jacobite in the family, the only Englishman among the 'Seven Men of Moidart' who accompanied the Young Pretender on his second Jacobite rebellion. He had been the childhood companion of Charles Edward Stuart, on whom the Old Pretender regarded him as a bad influence.[7] Two of Mannock's aunts, Anne and Catherine, became nuns, as did his sister and daughter.[8]

---

[5] Robert was a cousin of Sir Thomas Strickland of Sizergh. For Robert and his family, see Hornyold, pp. 270–2.

[6] For Sir Roger Strickland, see Hornyold, pp. 264–7 (including his knighthood in 1672), and *HoP*, http://www.historyofparliamentonline.org/volume/1660-1690/member/strickland-sir-roger-1640-1717, accessed 20 December 2015.

[7] Frank Strickland was arrested at Carlisle, suffering from dropsy, of which he died two days later, on 1 January 1746 (Hornyold, pp. 272–3).

[8] The statement concerning Anne is made by Hornyold, p. 276, but not corroborated by the 'Who Were the Nuns?' database. Catherine (1681–1748)'s membership, at Dunkirk as a choir nun (name in religion Mary Catherine), where she was eventually joined by her mother, Bridget, is confirmed in her father's pocket-book, (Hornyold, pp. 268, 274; WWTN DB 169). Strickland's third daughter, Henrietta (1729–89; WWTN DB 170), was a Benedictine nun at Dunkirk and 'almost the last nun who died there before the suppression of the convent by the French Government in 1793, her death taking place on October 24th, 1789' (Hornyold, p. 271). She held various offices: clothed 1749, professed 1751; Sacristan, Guardrobe and Novice Mistress until 1789; Dean and Prioress until 1789. The life-size full-length portrait of a nun in the private chapel at Mapledurham is probably of her, given her seniority in office, rather than a member of the Blount family (whose nuns were Cecily (1626–42; WWTN PA 0180), Isabelle (Frances Henrietta (1717–40); WWTN BB 020), Jane (clothed 1641; WWTN PA 020) and Mary (1626–84; WWTN PA 019). Two of Strickland's sons, John (1723–1802) and Joseph (1724–90), became priests: John's career was relatively low-key, culminating in tenure of the Archdeaconry of Berkshire, not to mention eccentricity and binge-eating, while Joseph obtained a doctorate from the Sorbonne, but his argumentative nature caused his candidature for the presidency of St Gregory's, Paris, to be rejected. He spent his final decade as chaplain to the Stonor family,

Another sister, Theresa (1687–1778), continued the family's link with Queen Mary of Modena, becoming a maid of honour to the Queen, and by her first marriage in 1708 to John Stafford (d. 1714), son of the heir to the viscountcy of Stafford and her father's successor as Vice-Chamberlain to the Queen. Mannock Strickland grew up at the court in exile at St Germain-en-Laye with the third Earl of Derwentwater, generally regarded as having almost the status of Jacobite martyr. Strickland's standing would have been further enhanced by this proximity.

## Catholic lawyers

Penal laws prohibited Catholics from practising the law: as Charles Butler, a contemporary, saw it, Catholics were disabled from holding offices or employments, from keeping arms in their houses, from maintaining actions or suits at law or in equity, from being executors or guardians, from presenting to advowsons, from practising in the law or physic, and from holding offices, whether civil or military.[9] No calls to the Bar of Catholics were made between that in 1668 of Nathaniel Pigott and 1791.[10] Pigott worked with the third Earl of Derwentwater's lawyer and Strickland's pupil-master Henry Eyre (c. 1667–1719) on the defence of Derwentwater and other leaders of the 1715 Jacobite rebellion.[11] Pigott's advice that Catholics should give 'assurance both in conscience and law for our obedience to the government', in return for protection, saw him joining Eyre in persuading the two rebel earls to plead guilty to high treason as the only practical course. Lord Kenmure afterwards regretted that their lawyers had not mounted a more spirited defence.

There were Protestant lawyers willing to undertake work for Catholic clients: men such as Thomas Bramston (1658–1737) of the Six Clerks Office and of Skreens, Essex, and Richard Moreton (active 1732–33[12]), who were part of dynasties of lawyers and who undertook mortgages, assignments and leases for clients of Strickland between 1726 and 1743.[13] Other lawyers used by Strickland included Richard Rudyard, a Holborn lawyer, and Benjamin Muchall, also of the Six Clerks Office, and William Morland, of Old Southampton Buildings. These names betray a substantial

---

constantly arguing and litigating, against all good advice, over payment of his share of his parents' by then severely shrunken provision for their sons and daughters.

[9]   Charles Butler, *Historical Account of the Laws against the Roman Catholics of England* ([London]: Printed by Luke Hansard & Sons, for Keating, Brown, & Co., 1811).

[10]   Richard G. Williams, 'Nathaniel Pigott (1661–1737)', in *ODNB*, http://www.oxforddnb. com/themes/theme.jsp?articleid=92738, accessed 2 July 2010.

[11]   Strickland inherited Eyre's practice on the latter's death in 1719.

[12]   The National Archives, Kew, PROB 11/682/124.

[13]   Muchall was used by the Rookwood family (see Francis Young (ed.), *Rookwood Family Papers, 1606–1761* (Woodbridge: Suffolk Records Society, 2016), pp. 23–6, 35)).

hidden support base for the Catholic community in the various levels of the legal establishment.[14]

In fact, Catholics could defy the penal laws most of the time with relative impunity, as Paul Langford says: 'it was a matter of commonplace observation that the laws in question were rarely executed'.[15] Strickland got round the prohibition of Catholics from pleading in court by employing Henry Rogers Trubshaw (d. before 1770), a Protestant solicitor who could plead cases, as his clerk. Trubshaw was, however, kept at a distance from Strickland's work with the convents, and Strickland's scriveners (such as Henry Cranmer and Samuel Mabbat) were, as always, figures in the background, even when they sourced funds for loans and mortgages. His practice was condoned by no less a person than Sir Robert Walpole, who appointed him one of the commissioners charged with the recovery of that part of the Derwentwater estates charged with the portion of the third Earl's daughter, the wife of Strickland's patron Lord Petre.[16] In Catholic recusant circles it did one no harm to be so closely associated with Derwentwater.[17]

---

[14] Further lawyers sympathetic to Catholic clients include Richard Graham of the Inner Temple and his father and son of the same name (e.g. assignment of an outstanding debt from Graham to Mrs Mary Wiseman and Jabez Collier of Symonds Inn (*Blount MSS, C* 98/67, 1728)), and Henry Dry of Lincoln's Inn (e.g. assignment of a 1,000-year term held by Dry's late father, also of Lincoln's Inn, through Strickland's clerk Henry Trubshaw to Sir Robert Abdy (*Blount MSS, C* 98/73, 1741)). Other dynasty members include Anthony Bramston and Richard Moreton, both of the Six Clerks Office in Chancery Lane.

[15] Paul Langford, *A Polite and Commercial People: England 1727–1783* (Oxford: Oxford University Press, 1989), p. 294.

[16] The principal documents held by Strickland and now at Mapledurham concerning the settlement of the Derwentwater (Radclyffe) estates, in which the Louvain convent had a vested interest, are: *Blount MSS, C* 145/47, Rental of Derwentwater estates (1732?); *C* 145/35–45, Accounts relating to settlement of Lord Derwentwater's forfeited estates and payments due nevertheless under his marriage settlement (1721–31); *C* 145/47, Rental of Derwentwater's estates; *C* 145/48, Draft case of Lady Mary Radclyffe concerning effects on her inheritance of the Earl's attainder and execution (1732); *C* 145/49–50 and *C* 212/61, Letter of attorney appointing Strickland as Lady Mary Radclyffe's attorney to claim outstanding debts (1723); *C* 145/46, Memorial of Lord Petre and his wife (Derwentwater's daughter) claiming her portion under her parents' marriage settlement, with related documents and the assent of Walpole and Dodington to settlement and instructions to Strickland and others to attend to it (1732); *C* 212/43 and *C* 212/84, Sir John Webb's memorial to the Commissioners of Greenwich Hospital (1732); *C* 212/52, Draft of Lord Petre's memorial to the Lords of the Treasury (1732); *C* 212/60, Sir John Webb's memorial to the Lords of the Treasury (1732); *C* 212/40 and *C* 212/87, Draft assignment of £1,000 part of £20,000 from Mr Mostyn to Mr [Thomas] Bramston by Lord Petre's direction [in the hand of Henry Trubshaw with alterations and additions by Strickland] (January 1738); *C* 212/51, Associated draft of defeasance from Mr Bramston to Lord Petre as to £3,000 part of £20,000 charged on the late Earl of Derwentwater's estate [in the hand of Henry Trubshaw with amendments by Strickland] (27 January 1738).

[17] F. J. A. Skeet, *The Life of the Right Honourable James Radcliffe Third Earl of Derwentwater, (Co. Northumberland), Viscount Radcliffe and Langley & Baron Tynedale (Co.*

## Clients

Strickland's clientele bears out and provides evidence for Gabriel Glick-man's view that the real strength of the recusant community at this time lay not so much in the nobility or the religious but in a strengthened rule by the gentry.[18] There is, however, one striking aspect of it that cannot be passed over: the proportion of female clients is unusually high – predominant even – and Strickland's reputation for the care of his women clients may account for the interest taken by the convents in him as an agent. His business network included a number of overseas clients and linked to the ways in which he came to assist the convents: through reputation and recommendations. The Louvain connection and that with the Spellikens in Brussels came through recommendations by other agents such as Gilbert Haydock, and well as through family con-nections – his mother and sister were resident at Dunkirk.

Patrons additionally strengthened the connection with Louvain, which was dominated by the Radclyffe family, Earls of Derwentwater, who included the daughter of the executed Jacobite third Earl, and her husband, Robert James, eighth Baron Petre, one of Strickland's two chief patrons.[19] The links with the Spellikens and with Dunkirk were strengthened by Strickland's other chief patrons, the Herbert family, Dukes of Powis, in particular Lady Lucy Herbert. The connection with the Spellikens started in 1728 and with Louvain and Brussels in 1733, continuing to Strickland's death or to the death or retirement of a friendly procuratrix.

There was another motivation for the convents to choose Strickland: he was the leading Catholic conveyancer of his day, and conveyancers had a reputation for having their fingers on the sources of money:

> [Conveyancing] is the most profitable Branch of the Law; for to that of Drawing Deeds, they comonly [*sic*] add the Trade of a Money-Scrivener; that is, they are employed to find out Estates to purchase, or have Money to lay out for some, and borrow for others, and receive Fees from Borrower and Lender; and of course are employed to draw the Securities … This Business is engrossed in the Hands of a few; who suddenly make Estates.[20]

---

*Cumberland), and Fifth Baronet of Dilston; with an Account of His Martyrdom for the Catholic Faith & Loyalty to his Rightful King* (London: Hutchinson and Co., 1929).

[18] Gabriel Glickman, *The English Catholic Community 1688–1745: Politics, Culture and Ideology* (Woodbridge: Boydell, 2009), pp. 54–5.

[19] Strickland's papers contain a very large number (seventy-three documents) relating to the Radclyffe family – the earls, Lady Catherine, Lady Anne, Lady Mary, Arthur and Thomas (*Blount MSS, C* 145).

[20] R. Campbell, *The London Tradesman. Being a Compendious View of all the Trades, Professions, Arts, both Liberal and Mechanic* (London: T. Gardner, 1747), pp. 79–80.

## The convents and their financial affairs

A voluminous correspondence survives between Strickland and the four convents that he served in Flanders (an area where he already had clients).[21] These institutions were the English Augustinian Canonesses of St Monica's at Louvain; the English Dominicans of the Spellikens ('Pin House') in Brussels; the English Benedictine dames at Dunkirk; and the English Benedictine dames of Brussels. St Monica's was founded in 1609 by English members of the Flemish Augustinian Convent and was a notorious hotbed of Jacobitism; the canonesses were driven out in 1794 by the approaching French army. The Spellikens was founded by Cardinal Philip Howard at Vilvorde near Brussels in 1661, moving to Brussels itself in 1669.[22]

Mannock Strickland's mother and sister retired in 1718 to the Benedictine house at Dunkirk, founded in 1662 as a daughter house from Ghent. They made this move after the death of Bridget Strickland's mistress, James II's exiled Queen. From 1728, well before his mother's death there in 1736, Strickland acted on behalf of these *Dames Anglaises*. His sister Catherine (1681–1748) preceded their mother into the convent and spent her adult life there. The nuns were ejected in 1793 by the Jacobins and imprisoned with the Poor Clares of Dunkirk and Gravelines before being given permission to leave for London in 1795.

The earliest foundation of the four was the Convent of the Glorious Assumption in Brussels, founded in 1597/8 by Lady Mary Percy and flourishing in Strickland's day under its Abbess Lady Mary Crispe.[23] It remained there until forced to decamp to Winchester ahead of the revolutionary wars in 1794.

Strickland was regarded, because of his family connections and his professional reputation, as an unusually good 'catch', as the letters show.[24] Gilbert Haydock (1682–1749), a priest missioner go-between for these communities and chaplain of St Monica's convent from 1716, who 'was but a poor little Boy when he had the honour to know you at Dowey,'

---

[21] *Blount MSS, C* 64/70–240. Letters from Strickland to these convents can no longer be traced, all correspondence from their archives seemingly having perished at the French Revolution when the convents were driven out.

[22] The Spellikens was, if anything, more Jacobite than Louvain: 'Some of them [were] actually carrying out by correspondence active intrigues in favour of "James III"' (Basil Whelan, 'Our Historic English Convents: English Cloisters in Flanders in the Penal Times. VI – The Seventeenth and Eighteenth Centuries', *The Tablet*, 5 November 1921, p. 24).

[23] Guilday, pp. 256–65; Michael Blount, *A Congratulatory Poem presented to the Right Reverend Lady, Lady Mary Crispe of the Isle of Tenet, Abbess of the RR. Benedictin Dames at Brussells. On the Occasion of celebrating her Jubilie, the fifth day of June, 1737* (Brussels, 1737), reprinted in *ECIE*, vol. 3, pp. 361–5.

[24] *Blount MSS, C* 64/71: CT to MS, 18 August 1733 (NS).

had recommended Strickland to Louvain.[25] A similar recommendation appears likely with the Spellikens, while family connections accounted for his work for Dunkirk and Brussels, the latter of whose affairs he took over from his uncle, the banker Daniel Arthur.[26] Cecily Tunstall at Louvain thought Strickland tardy and neglectful at times but was terrified of losing his services: to an exasperated suggestion that she find someone else, she was 'sorry to find you think I have any one in my eye that I shall ever think will be to be compaired to you Sr'.[27] When the Catholic barrister Nathaniel Pigott died in 1737, Tunstall hoped that Strickland would get all of Pigott's practice (which he did not) but feared that such a resolution would give him less time for matters of 'less importance' – an ironic reference to their own affairs.[28]

The convents varied in size. The Spellikens was the smallest, with thirty-nine nuns in residence at some point or other between 1728 and 1737 (the years of Strickland's service to this convent) and just eleven professions in these ten years. The other three were bigger. Between 1728 and Strickland's death in 1744, Dunkirk had forty nuns resident at some point and had sixteen professions (varying in number per year between none and four). The English Benedictine ladies in Brussels had a similar total of residents between 1733 and 1744 (forty-one), with ten professions in twelve years. Louvain was the largest, with fifty-nine professions and sixty nuns resident at some time between 1733 and 1744.[29]

Convent life fostered longevity in the community: at the Benedictines in Brussels, life expectancy from profession to death ranged from five to seventy years, with five nuns living over sixty years from profession and nineteen living over fifty years. At Louvain, nine lived for over sixty years after profession and twenty-nine for over fifty years. At Dunkirk, between 1728 and 1744 there were five nuns who lived for over sixty years after profession and fourteen who lived for over fifty years; twenty nuns were then living in the convent. Even the smaller convent of the Spellikens could produce two nuns who lived for over sixty years following profession and twelve who did so for more than fifty years; the resident population was twenty-nine. This was the size of the ageing community

---

[25] *Blount MSS, C* 64/71: CT to MS, 18 August 1733 (NS). For Haydock see Kirk, pp. 117–18; Anstruther 3, p. 96.

[26] 'Records of the Dominican Nuns of the Second Order, Brussels (Vilvorde and Brussels), 1661–1697', in *Dominicana*, Catholic Record Society 25 (London: Catholic Record Society, 1925), p. 206.

[27] *Blount MSS, C* 64/90: CT to MS, 22 August 1734 (NS).

[28] *Blount MSS, C* 64/148: CT to MS, 19 August 1737 (NS).

[29] These numbers have been calculated by the editor on the advice of Dr Caroline Bowden from the WWTN database, using the *Lists* feature under *Publications*. The data are not complete and should be treated as provisional, as the means of deeper analysis have not yet been developed. Nevertheless, they give some idea of the size of the community.

which Strickland served. By way of comparison, Julian Hoppit gives an average English life expectancy of thirty-seven years at the start of the eighteenth century, rising to forty-two by 1750–59; the nuns appear to have been moving in the wrong direction, for life expectancy at birth in France in the 1740s was only twenty-five.[30]

It is difficult not to see these mostly elderly women as representatives of a slowly dying cause in both politics and religion, although a deeper analysis of the now available data would be necessary to confirm or confute that proposition. The professions – the act of taking the vows as a nun – during Strickland's service to them are sparse, except at Louvain. Their age profile is higher than that of the general population, and they have chosen or been forced into exile.

## IDENTITY

There is currently great interest in the lives of English nuns in exile, especially in Flanders and northern France. Particularly important in fostering this interest has been the 'Who were the Nuns?' project led by Dr Caroline Bowden, with support from Queen Mary University of London and the Arts and Humanities Research Council; the biographical notes in this publication (which use data from the archives at Maple-durham House and other sources) include the reference numbers to the database. Out of that project sprang the major six-volume collection of studies and sources *English Convents in Exile, 1600–1800* (*ECIE*) to which the present editor contributed a brief annotated selection of the Louvain letters. That work speaks to two particular interests, the one in women's studies and the other in the history of spirituality. The present volume takes a different slant on these communities, looking particularly at the workings of the finances and the everyday human struggle for these women and their supporters to live and to survive.

One cannot escape the glaring evidence that the convents were a means of keeping financially embarrassed families afloat (or those claiming to be so). Settlements have been mentioned where the provision for daughters and for younger sons was reduced if they entered religious houses – or, as the euphemism tactfully put it, they were 'absent beyond sea'. We have noted an example of a fifty per cent reduction in such cases. Worse could happen to disrupt the overriding aim of passing Catholic estates on to Catholics: if a family member was born abroad, as was Alexander Pope's friend Teresa Blount (1688–1759), who was born in Paris and therefore an alien unlike her brothers and sisters, then that fact would

---

[30]  Julian Hoppitt, *A Land of Liberty? England 1689–1277* (Oxford: Oxford University Press, 2000).

debar her from ever inheriting an estate should it need to pass through such a female line as a last resort. She hid her bitterness behind the remark that 'ours is not a wedding family'.[31]

One must wonder why the corresponding male communities were – with the exception of the schools at Douai, St Omer, Bornhem and Esquerchin – less successful than the convents of nuns. Take, for example, the English Carthusian establishment at Nieuport in Flanders, for which Michael Blount II tried unsuccessfully to raise funds between 1745 and 1748. There was at this time a family acceptance of the monastic vocation for the one younger son, Walter Maurus Blount (1727–46), who became a monk in Brussels at the age of eighteen and died before fulfilling his vocation, a rare younger son in a family with hardly any such surviving into adulthood until the nineteenth century. Documents relating to the attempted rescue of the Nieuport community are set out in Appendix 3 below.

Strickland's fundraising text speaks of the difficulties under which both female and male communities tried to establish themselves.[32] Michael Blount II corresponded widely in the Catholic community, as the supporters of the nuns must also have done, and a certain amount of this correspondence survives. More importantly, Strickland's extant account books detail the names and amounts of contributions. It is worth noting, however, that the male and female communities seem to have attracted largely different configurations of donors: for instance, the donors to the male community attracted a fair number of priests (whether on their own account or as channels from their lay communities cannot be ascertained), some Protestants and a notable number of legacies. Unfortunately it still was not enough, and the attempt the rescue the Carthusians sadly failed.[33]

The sums donated to the male communities, if this example is taken as typical, were almost all small, unlike many of those to the female communities – typically a matter of only a few shillings at most, with few larger gifts. The target audience seems to have been more varied, extending beyond Strickland's clientele and including a marked number of priests and a few Protestants (as can be ascertained from the coding against the names). All this suggests that the convents were seen as having a different purpose from the male communities, whose focus was mainly missionary.

---

[31] *Blount MSS, C* 63, Packet J: Teresa Blount to her brother Michael I [1737?]. It is ironic that the marriage under objection is that of Strickland's daughter Mary Eugenia to Michael Blount's I's son and heir, Michael II (1719–92).

[32] *Blount MSS,* unnumbered volume, pp. 1–3.

[33] *Blount MSS, D* 9/7–8: list of subscribers to the fund for the relief of the English Carthusians at Nieuport; collection organised by Michael Blount II and total received by Diana Winstanley, 1745/6, and booklet with list of subscribers, 1747/8.

## THE CLIMATE – FINANCIAL AND OTHERWISE

The first half of the eighteenth century was a time of agricultural depression in England, with a high degree of fluctuation in rents, and in northern Europe generally. Bad weather peaked in the winter of 1739/40, one of the severest winters ever, following one of the disastrous growing seasons which plagued this era. It was cold enough for the ink to freeze even by the fireside.[34] On 2 May 1740 this harshest of winters culminated unexpectedly:

> As I'm writing this & all yesterday & the night past there has fallen so great a snow that none in our House tho' several past 70 has ever seen so much fall in so short a time[.] we've had now 8 months of winter it beginning in September & ever since weve had snow & frost so that we are in great danger of loosing the fruits of the Earth god give us patience.[35]

Landlords had difficulty collecting rents,[36] and the effect on those whom the landlords funded could be passed on to the convents they funded in the event of late payments or even non-payments. Strickland's patron Lord Petre was a typical example. On his western estates in Devon, Somerset and Gloucestershire, rents were in arrears by £574 19s 6d at Lady Day 1734, compared to a rental income in 1731 of £1,643 1s 3¼d ; the arrears generally ran at about one-third.[37]

Funding was further at risk from the vagaries of the currency markets, and the nuns were forced to become experts in financial dealings and the day-to-day fluctuations of the currency market. Here, too, were the players in the complex support network – from bankers and financial dealers to couriers. There were villains – intentional or just incompetent – who failed to honour agreements. Mr Fell annoyed the Louvain canonesses by having made a bad investment on poor advice and lost them precious money. Even worse in their eyes were the Brent sisters, particularly the notorious Jacobite Lady Lytcott, guilty in Tunstall's eyes of nothing short of fraud.[38]

There were strict rules for management of finances and annual submission of accounts to superiors and bishops, and the nuns were forbidden to advance money to anyone, however desperate the need. This was in line with canon law's general prohibition of usury, defined by the *Oxford English Dictionary* as 'The fact or practice of lending money at interest'. The nuns appear to have observed this prohibition to the letter, although

---

[34] *Blount MSS, C* 64/190: CT to MS, 27 January 1740 (NS).

[35] *Blount MSS, C* 64/197: CT to MS, 3 May 1740 (NS).

[36] Langford, *Polite and Commercial People*, p. 442.

[37] *Blount MSS, C* 103/61–105.

[38] See the repeated references to Fell in the Louvain correspondence. For Sir John and Lady Lytcott (also spelled Litcott and Lithcot) and her sisters Margaret Brent and Mrs Throckmorton, see Glickman (2009), *passim*, and the Louvain letters.

it is clear that a reasonable interest charge seems to have been generally observed in mortgage and other loans of this period at four or five per cent at the very most.

## RECRUITMENT OF WOMEN AND RAISING OF FUNDS

The dispatch of offspring to religious houses on the Continent could tempt families – and not just the hard-pressed – to use this as a means of saving money. The 1737 marriage settlement of Thomas Markham of Claxby, Lincolnshire, mortgaged for £5,000, was intended to take the financial pressure off while still providing generously 'in order to keep the whole estate … united and settled in the blood name and family, so long as it shall please God'. Although generous provision was made (£3,000 for one child, £4,000 for two and £5,000 for three and more), there was a sting in the tail: portions for any children entering a religious order were to be reduced to a maximum of £500.[39]

The case of Lady Catherine Radclyffe (discussed in detail below) shows how precarious the support base was.[40] Long life (which we have seen to be unusually prevalent in these convents) had its extra perils for a woman in exile in an enclosed order, where the very old had somehow to find a way of being seen to prove every year their continuing life, where mistiming the process could lose them more than they could afford, and where some were totally dependent on the funding brought by others. Panic could and did ensue when a nun was described in error as a non-religious resident. And then there were those who could not make their profession because their funding was late or never came.

The ambition of the convents is plain – expansion. Louvain was seeking to raise funds for a large extension to its church, anticipating a growth which never came and was therefore badly mistimed. These particular convents were hotbeds of Jacobite support. The optimism and the political ambition went hand in hand.

## NETWORK AND RELATIONSHIPS

Financial arrangements at Louvain and the Spellikens were in the hands of a single officer, who bore the title of Procuratrix. Procuratrices held office for a lengthy fixed term or until death. At Dunkirk and the Brussels

---

[39] *Blount MSS, C* 130/22. This settlement is unusual in its reference to religious orders; the usual euphemism is 'living beyond sea'. Strickland was responsible for the tight financial control of the drafting of this and other settlements.

[40] For an example of the certificates of her life – in other words, proof that she was still alive at an unusually advanced age for the period – see Appendix 2. The wording differs slightly from one certificate to another.

Benedictines, financial dealings appear to have been in the hands of the prioresses. The network of individual agents with which all worked is apparent, even if the agents are shadowy; some were priests, others merchants, and there were a number of women to whom the escorting of postulants and pensioners was entrusted. The nuns would often call the tune in getting money ready for transfer at the best market rates. It is a curious and unexplained fact that many of the intermediaries used were in the export cloth trade – the lace merchant John Brussell, and others. We know little, however, of Mme Broeta of Antwerp beyond her name, that of her deceased husband and her address, but she was a major player in getting money exchanged as it went to and fro.[41]

Strickland took a risk in providing foreign exchange services: Sr Mary Young, Prioress of Brussels,[42] issued a bill of exchange for £100 in 1741 drawn on Strickland which was endorsed in French by the banker John Nettine for payment. It was duly presented with a notarial certificate issued in London by Benjamin Bonnet for the London merchants Levy and Ruben Salomon and was protested on its presentation at Strickland's house, where a woman to whom Bonnet spoke informed him that Strickland was out of town and that she could not say anything about the bill. The bill was then passed to Spellerberg and Metzner for clearance at a total cost for the bill, protest, recharge, commission and postage of £102 3s 0d.[43] The extra sum of £2 3s 0d may not seem of moment to today's reader, but in the currency of the time it was enough to cause significant problems, such as the summary halting of a nun's progress to her clothing and admission.

Strickland's relationship with the wealthy house at Dunkirk was a straightforward banking relationship, involving the collection of substantial income with little evidence of problems, and honouring the drafts drawn on Strickland by the Abbess, Lady Anne Benedicta Fletewood.[44] His relationships with Brussels and the Spellikens were more personal, and that with Louvain would have tried the patience of a saint. The letters from Cecily Tunstall, Procuratrix at Louvain, are fussy, demanding and occasionally tart. A network of priests and agents worked on behalf of the Louvain canonesses – Gilbert Haydock; another priest called Thomas Brown who lived close to Strickland and was better known by the alias of Thomas Day (1665–1748), Treasurer of the English Chapter and its

---

[41] She is unknown to the Municipal Archives in Antwerp.

[42] Not on the WWTN database.

[43] *Blount MSS, C* 129 (1741). The reason for its being protested is unclear; other bills drawn by her presented no problems.

[44] *Blount MSS, D* 7/16–102: bank drafts, Benedicta Fletewood to various persons, drawn on MS (1730–44). Abbess Anne Benedicta Fleewood [also Fletewood] (1665–1748), WWTN DB 061.

Dean from 1732;[45] Derwentwater's agent Henry Rodbourne; the woollen draper Thomas Tancred of Red Lion Square;[46] and various couriers, notably Alexander Burgis, Peggy Cholmeley and John Collingwood – with all of whom Strickland was expected to liaise. Strickland's role was the simple but important one of banker, holding and investing money and answering notes drawn upon him, the correspondence being full of notifications of drafts issued and drawn on him for payment.[47] He was also used as a supply channel for such things as lace sent from Bruges, and in reverse for the supply of devotional books.[48]

On occasion, the tightness of finances made it very hard for the nuns to lay in basic provisions at a difficult time.[49] Another problem for them was communication back to England, which could be uncertain.[50] Strickland was expected to manage their financial affairs in the home country. This became all the more important to the nuns if they received money abroad which they had difficulty investing, in this case because of the threat of war. Low Country rates were below the prevailing four or five per cent then general in England. At the Spellikens, Ellerker on occasion expressed further unhappiness about rising interest rates: in late November 1734 she wrote that, in Bruges, 'the charges goe high above seven pound in the hundred' for exchange rate transactions (suggesting an unstable and volatile capital and exchange market in semi-war conditions).[51] The prevailing conditions of foreign exchange transactions were generally poor:

> We have had lately paid us here 6 or 700 pound sterling and am much at a loss how to get it put out; Intrist is Reduced so low here. If you Charitably can find an occation of putting it out there tho' wee shou'd loose by the return, it wood in my opinion be better, than to let it ly dead sum time perhaps, and after, all that can here be hoped for, is three and a halfe per ct. or four Curant as wee call it, which is 6 pence exchange pd us for 7d.[52]

## BANKING

Strickland used three main sources for banking on behalf of the nuns. Payments were made using the Bank of England, coded by him in the set of four master day books with the letter 'B', and through three gold-smith-bankers, notably his wife's cousin Anthony Wright (d. 1782?) at

---

[45] Anstruther 3, p. 28 (s.v. 'Brown, Thomas (2), al. Day').
[46] *Blount MSS, C* 64/91: CT to MS, 28 September 1734 (NS).
[47] *Blount MSS, C* 64/70–247: letters, CT to MS, 1733–44.
[48] *Blount MSS, C* 64/71: CT to MS, 18 August 1733; *C* 64/74: CT to MS, 25 September 1733 (NS).
[49] *Blount MSS, C* 41/174: MXE to MS, 7 November 1733 (NS).
[50] *Blount MSS, C* 41/171: MXE to MS, 4 February 1728 (NS?).
[51] *Blount MSS, C* 41/178: MXE to MS, 27 November 1734 (NS).
[52] *Blount MSS, C* 41/176: MXE to MS, 24 August 1734 (NS).

the sign of the Golden Cup in Henrietta Street, Covent Garden. From 1729 Wright was the head of the firm which was – until its crash with debts of £1 million in 1840 – to be the leading English Catholic banking firm (coded 'Wr'). the others were, perhaps deliberately, more shadowy firms: Peter Wyke (coded 'W'), a goldsmith based at Gray's Inn Gate in Holborn, and Edward Peirson (coded 'P'), who traded at St Dunstan-in-the-West and went bankrupt in 1729. Another firm often used was that of the goldsmith Benjamin Pyne, who underwrote several mortgages for Strickland. The metamorphosis of goldsmiths into bankers forms part of the transition started late in the previous century from the primary use of specie to the modern forms of deposit banking and paper instruments. For the rest, it is clear that Strickland himself acted as his own banker, as was increasingly true of scriveners such as Thomas Gyles, one of the Proctors of the Prerogative Court of Canterbury, and Samuel Mabbat of Gray's Inn, used by him as lenders.

## COURIERS AND FOREIGN EXCHANGE

Foreign exchange was often referred to as 'returning'. The exchanges were handled by agents such as Mme Broeta, who aggregated sums from various clients; large sums seem to have attracted better rates, constantly monitored by the exchange agents, who would often demand sums in hand from the convents. The convents transferred money to and fro (even across the Channel) as a form of negotiable instrument or document called bills of exchange, which survive for Dunkirk and the Brussels Benedictines, while for Louvain Cecily Tunstall sent separately the bills of exchange of which she gave notice in her letters. Bills of exchange were documents guaranteeing payment of a specific amount of money, either on demand or on a particular date. They did not attract interest but they could be traded as a cash equivalent, in whole or in part, to third parties. Payment went to the holder of the bill.[53] Parallel to these were Strickland's four detailed cash day books, which are particularly revealing of the resident convent population.

It may come as a surprise to see how much time Sisters Tunstall and Ellerker spent in watching closely the exchange rate to get the best return; less surprising, perhaps, is the intensity of the scrutiny the procuratrices received from their fellow nuns. The most tiresome part of Strickland's dealings with the Louvain convent concerned money due to Lady Catherine

---

[53] These bills do not survive. Bills of exchange belong to the history of the development of modern deposit banking from the late seventeenth century onwards, under such figures as the merchant banker and Lord Mayor of London Sir Robert Clayton (1629–1707). See F. C. Melton, *Sir Robert Clayton and the Origins of English Deposit Banking, 1658–1685* (Cambridge: Cambridge University Press, 1986).

Radclyffe, already mentioned. However, Tunstall's regrets expressed at the death from smallpox of Lord Petre in 1742 show a sincerity totally unclouded by any ulterior reactions of frustration at further problems getting the money due to St Monica's.[54] The money mattered a great deal to them and not just to the nominal recipient of the annuity or portion, since such funding supported several mums or postulants; Tunstall said that '[If] Lady Catherins [annuity] fails I shall not be able to pay the expences of the House without new suply's'.[55]

## SECURITIES

Lawyers still often held deeds on behalf of clients until recent regulatory changes, many from a much earlier date. We know of some of these from the records (not reproduced here) kept by Strickland's widow and by his clerk Henry Trubshaw of the deeds returned to clients or their representatives following Strickland's death. The mortgages, bonds and other financial instruments certainly do not represent the fluctuating record of securities on which Strickland drew for his clients, but they give substance to the financial basis of donors and their estates that were central to the support of these convents.

## ACCOUNTS

This volume also features the detailed day book accounts that Strickland kept for Louvain and the Spellikens. For them, as for a number of other key clients, he kept throughout his career a main set of day book records of payments and receipts (four volumes span his entire working career) and a number of others hold duplicated details of up to four clients each. Their existence has allowed the editor to cross-check the accounts for Dunkirk from Dame Benedicta Fleetwood's many demand notes. The Benedictines in Brussels cannot be treated the same way: few transactions are identifiable with certainty, since the fundraising model seems to have been different and not dependent on a single individual. These accounts are quite unlike the published benefactors' books,[56] and much more like a daily financial record; nor are they the annual accounts (which do not survive) that the convents were required to submit to their bishop and which Strickland provided.

The Augustinian Rule required each convent to submit annual accounts to the bishop or 'chief superiour'. Although at Louvain Cecily Tunstall

---

[54] *Blount MSS, C* 64/238: CT to MS, 7 August 1742 (NS).
[55] *Blount MSS, C* 64/166: CT to MS, 17 July 1738 (NS).
[56] *ECIE*, vol. 5.

kept her own accounts, she also required Strickland to furnish annually a more official version, which was often not forthcoming as promptly as she desired.[57] His accounting was meticulous and 'very exact'.[58] Tunstall also asked even more frequently for an account with any payment giving origins and intended recipients of the separate sums, with dates of payment, all of which she had to show in accounts and 'particular letters of advice'; without this information she refused to pay anyone.[59] She therefore required Strickland, when he wrote, to mention each sum received, 'because I neither can pay others their money nor draw a Bill till I have it from you that so much is p[ai]d & from such persons'.[60]

## LEGAL ADVICE

Strickland's specifically legal advice was rarely asked for, although many of the affairs in which he dealt for the convents had a clear legal dimension. One case was that of Miss Stapylton, whom the Louvain convent was forced to send to Brussels

> to chuse her sister there for her guardian she being minor herself in hopes to have her share of her uncle Eyre's will. Pray let us have your oppinion of this matter whether there's any likelyhood of gaining or whether the will is valid in favour of the widow.[61]

Strickland was asked to obtain a copy of Eyre's will for the nuns.

### The convent of St Monica's, Louvain

Most of the extant letters in the archive were received from the procuratrices at two of the four convents: St Monica's and the Spellikens. It is therefore possible to assess their particular financial concerns in more detail. At St Monica's, the issues that appear to have occupied the mind of Cecily Tunstall, the convent Procuratrix, most urgently revolved around debt collection, late arrival of payments for inmates, and ensuring the best use of the foreign exchange in Brussels.

## DEBT COLLECTION

Debt collection was a major requirement placed on Strickland. This was a particularly difficult one, since to the normal difficulties of collection

---

[57] *Blount MSS, C* 64/134, 142, 151 and 155: CT to MS, 10 February, 5 May, 5 November and 29 December 1737 (NS).
[58] *Blount MSS, C* 64/107: CT to MS, 2 September 1735 (NS).
[59] *Blount MSS, C* 64/76: CT to MS, 18 November 1733 (NS).
[60] *Blount MSS, C* 64/87: CT to MS, 29 May 1734 (NS).
[61] *Blount MSS, C* 64/148: CT to MS, 19 August 1737 (NS).

were added those caused by attitudes of indifference or even contempt from the debtors to persons and communities strictly illegal under English law, and who therefore might use the illegality of the convents as a pretext for evading payment. Some debts were very long-standing, one even referring to a pensioner who had been in the house thirty-six years before.[62] Three debts to Louvain were particularly troublesome – a bad investment of £300 by Mr Fell resulting in loss of their money, which included a bond debt from the notoriously Jacobite Lady Lytcott of Paris. This, one suspects, she was unlikely to repay and, after her death in 1735 (reputedly penniless in spite of her rumoured marriage to 'the famous Mr Ward who in all the news papers is now so famous and follow'd by all'[63]), her son certainly had no intention of repaying it.[64] Mrs Throckmorton, who owed a related debt, just ignored all pressure.[65] Strickland was variously instructed to try to claim the money owed by Lady Lytcott from Mr Ward, from the son or from her sisters, Mrs Brent ('who is lyable to pay our debt'[66]) and Mrs Conquest. All three debts were interrelated.[67]

The debt from Fell, one of the network of trusted agents on whom the English continental religious houses depended, pained them particularly, since the money was 'a foundation for one here who can not proceed till tis recovered' – a comment that betrays, as so frequently in other cases, how inflexibly Tunstall managed finances related to individuals in the convent.[68] Different approaches were demanded, depending on the relationship with the debtor. The nuns trusted Fell, even though they blamed him, and one of their number, Mrs Johnson, wrote to him 'to see if he who has been wholy to blame for putting our money out so can't at Least bring them to some reason or assist you in bringing such proofs as may help to gain our right'.[69] In his case they had hopes of at least recovering outstanding interest, and possibly more, and Strickland was asked what he had done and was doing about 'the £300 Mr Fell lost

---

[62] *Blount MSS, C* 64/147: CT to MS, 19 July 1737 (NS).

[63] *Blount MSS, C* 64/104: CT to MS, 12 July 1735 (NS): they heard that she 'dyed not worth a grote'.

[64] *Blount MSS, C* 64/107: CT to MS, 2 September 1735 (NS).

[65] *Blount MSS, C* 64/77, 97, 104, 113, 134, 148, 151, 156, 159, 171, 176, 180, 181, 184, 186, 188, 205, 242, 244, 246 and 247: CT to MS, 12 December 1733, 1 February, 12 July and 23 December 1735, 10 February, 19 August and 5 November 1737, 25 February, 18 April and 24 November 1738, 31 January, 14 April, 2 June, 11 September, 3 November and 30 December 1739, 11 October 1740, and 3 February, 10 April, 29 July and 6 October 1744 (NS).

[66] *Blount MSS, C* 64/104 (for Ward) and *C* 64/107 (for the others): CT to MS, 12 July and 2 September 1735 (NS).

[67] *Blount MSS, C* 64/153: CT to MS, 5 December 1737 (NS).

[68] *Blount MSS, C* 64/113: CT to MS, 23 December 1735 (NS).

[69] *Blount MSS, C* 64/142: CT to MS, 5 May 1737 (NS).

us for the persons friends who is to be taken on that said £300 has writ latly that they hear it may yet be recover'd?'[70]

As the nuns were understandably reluctant to have recourse to law, Strickland advised them to pursue the debts directly with Fell, which they did through correspondence involving Mrs Johnson and Mr Day and with continuing advice from Strickland. Eventually they reached a point where they heard that Fell had sufficient money left him to pay the remaining principal and interest on £202 15s 5d, and thought he should do so without their having to sue Mr Lytcott for it, at which point they turned back to Strickland in the hope that this was enough information to enable him to act for them.[71] Strickland seems to have prevailed with Lytcott over his mother's debt to the extent of extracting a promise from him that the debt would be repaid as soon as part of her estate was sold.[72] Or he may not have prevailed: Tunstall instructed Strickland to tell him that they would go to law for their money, 'which he has owned to be a just debt'.[73] Success still eluded them, for even in 1743 Tunstall's successor as Procuratrix at Louvain, Christina Towneley, was asking about progress and relayed the Superior's instruction that 'if faire means would not do, she desired you would try rigour'.[74] Strickland then first advised that Fell had enough in hand to cover the Lytcott debt, and that it should be recovered through Fell, but he changed his mind in his final letter to Louvain, feeling that the matter needed timely resolution, 'Mr Lythcoate being a bad manager'.[75]

Strickland was expected to deal particularly harshly with Mrs Throckmorton: 'we know from good hands that she is a very tricking woman & will do what she can to make us loose the rest as we've done Lady Lithcote's part'.[76] Or again, 'Please to see also if nothing is to be done to Mrs Throckmorton for we're credibly informed that she's a mear tricking woman who seeks only to put of those she deals with so pray use her accordingly & alow her no more time to shuffle'.[77] The subject of Mrs Throckmorton and the community's other debtors becomes an ongoing litany in correspondence, and Strickland eventually instigated legal proceedings, which did not move fast enough to satisfy Tunstall.[78]

---

70 *Blount MSS, C* 64/151: CT to MS, 5 November 1737 (NS).
71 *Blount MSS, C* 64/247: Christina Towneley to MS, 6 October 1744 (NS).
72 *Blount MSS, C* 64/188: CT to MS, 30 December 1739 (NS).
73 *Blount MSS, C* 64/212: CT to MS, 28 April 1741 (NS).
74 *Blount MSS, C* 64/240: Christina Towneley to MS, 27 August 1743 (NS).
75 *Blount MSS, C* 64/249: Christina Towneley to Mrs Strickland, 18 May 1745 (NS).
76 *Blount MSS, C* 64/134: CT to MS, 10 February 1737 (NS).
77 *Blount MSS, C* 64/137: CT to MS, 26 March 1737 (NS).
78 *Blount MSS, C* 64/142, 148, 151, 165, 169, 170, 176, 180, 181, 184, 186 and 205: CT to MS, 5 May, 19 August and 5 November 1737, 7 July, 14 October and 7 November 1738, 31 January, 14 April, 2 June, 11 September and 3 November 1739, 11 October 1740 (NS).

She reminded him that she could not bear to see debts outstanding when they were short of money and that he had written, eighteen months before, on 30 June 1738, 'I have been suing Mrs Throckmorton for her debt & I think we now have good bail for the payment of it so that I expect both Principal & Interest next Mich[ael]mass term'.[79]

Pushing him hard, Tunstall then stated that she would expect payment of Mrs Throckmorton's money next term, although nearly two years later she was again asking when she would have the money due from her and other outstanding debtors.[80] By this time, Mrs Throckmorton was dead and Tunstall was wistfully hoping that 'her heirs are able to do some thing'.[81] Strickland finally reclaimed for the nuns a total of £165 6s 10d principal and interest in February 1740/1.[82]

Tunstall was unforgiving about Strickland's failure to put St Monica's at the top of the queue in payments from the estate of Lettis Wybarne and again following her son's intestate death, considering that Strickland had failed in his duty as Mrs Wybarne's executor. A sum of £36 11s 6d was owed to the convent as payment of pension (i.e. board and lodging) and travelling for her daughter Charity in 1700–02, which Strickland promised on 15 July 1737 to recover for the nuns,[83] and a flood of comments and recriminations followed.[84] First, he was accused of having given Wybarne's son (whom they expected not to honour his mother's debts to a foreign Catholic community) money which was theirs by right, as Strickland had

> given him money that should have paid old debts you'll best get it of him for we shall not apply to him but to you as being Exec[uto]r to his mother & we have your promise that you would take care we should be paid & we know as I had the honour to tell you before that since you've paid others that were after us you can't deny to see the same justice done to us.[85]

The Wybarne family, having asserted that Strickland had 'a considerable sum' left in his hands to settle all debts, stirred up trouble by writing repeatedly to Elizabeth Smith. Strickland expressed surprise at non-payment of the debt, and Tunstall wrote sharply to him that the nuns disliked the lack of any positive answer and objected to being the

[79]  *Blount MSS, C* 64/188: CT to MS, 30 December 1739 (NS).
[80]  *Blount MSS, C* 64/205: CT to MS, 11 October 1740 (NS).
[81]  *Blount MSS, C* 64/184: CT to MS, 11 September 1739 (NS).
[82]  *Blount MSS, C* 64/247: Christina Towneley to MS, 6 October 1744 (NS?).
[83]  *Blount MSS, C* 64/188 and 190: CT to MS, 30 December 1739 and 27 January 1740 (NS).
[84]  *Blount MSS, C* 64/163, 167, 169–71, 176–9, 187, 190, 195, 197, 205, 211, 215, 219, 227, 231, 236, 244 and 246: CT (the last two from Christina Towneley) to MS, 20 June, 22 July, 14 October, 7 and 24 November 1738, 31 January, 6, 20 and 26 March and 17 November 1739, 27 January, 19 April, 3 May and 11 October 1740, 18 April, 6 June, 4 August and [November] 1741, 24 January and 1 June 1742, 10 April and 29 July 1744 (NS).
[85]  *Blount MSS, C* 64/187: CT to MS, 17 November 1739 (NS).

last paid when their debt was one of the oldest. They would not 'expect nor consent to be left to the mercy of the young Esqr: but must require this of you as having power to raise it if you have no more of that said money in your hands now'.[86] Strickland wrote back immediately and forcefully, making it clear that the Wybarne family's version was incorrect and unfair to him, forcing an all too brief lull in the ongoing skirmish in the form of an apology from Tunstall.[87]

The nuns then complained of having to rely too much on Strickland's word and that they had found that they had reminded him of it 'too late', as he had paid others who had not had to wait so long.[88] Tunstall claimed that others were pressurising her but was still willing to be blunt with Strickland, even though she was making it clear that they were alarmed at his belief that they intended putting their business in other hands. There was, however, a certain method and logic in Tunstall's tactics:

> all our house has a great esteem & value for you & 'tis our opinion that our business can't be safer but at the same time they often blame me for not putting you in mind oftener of your promise Concerning Mrs Wybourne's debt &c because they know you've such a multiplicity of business on your hands that unless each concerned solicites for dispatch first come first served.[89]

Nevertheless, the nuns were only too conscious that they could neither expect nor compel the son to pay and were therefore entirely dependent on Strickland in this matter, even telling him so. Real alarm set in when Lettis Wybarne's son died intestate with no-one to look after his affairs, with a fear that if they did not get payment of their debt then Wybarne's widow would take letters of administration, to their disadvantage. Tunstall was very sharp:

> If you'd been pleas'd to have paid us while you had the sum design'd for that end in your hands we should not have needed either to have applyed to the Heirs or anyone else. Our Honoured Lady had a Letter from the late Mrs Wybourn with a promise to pay that debt the very first money she touched which only death hinder'd her from performing pray Sr let no more delays be made but see that we are satisfied soon or else we shall loose it.[90]

Two years later Tunstall was still needling Strickland with claims that she knew that the Dominicans had received the money due to them, even though their claim was in respect of a time seven or eight years later, and demanding that

---

[86] *Blount MSS, C* 64/177: CT to MS, 6 March 1739 (NS).
[87] *Blount MSS, C* 64/179: CT to MS, 26 March 1739 (NS).
[88] *Blount MSS, C* 64/188: CT to MS, 30 December 1739 (NS).
[89] *Blount MSS, C* 64/190: CT to MS, 27 January 1740 (NS).
[90] *Blount MSS, C* 64/195: CT to MS, 19 April 1740 (NS).

as soon as money can be raised to pay debts we ought to come first as being the first that can claim a right to be paid for Mrs Charity Wybourn was here in 1700 1701 1702 & that money which I want was for her pension & lent for her Journey.[91]

In 1744 the money was still unpaid. Young Mrs Wybarne was now married; Christina Towneley, the new Procuratrix at Louvain, presumed that affairs in that family were 'regulated and that Mrs Charity [Wybarne] will think of paying the debt here she was so solicitous about, till it Came to her turn to pay it'.[92]

In another case of outstanding debt, Strickland was asked to confer with Morgan Hansbie, another of the network of agents serving English continental houses, as to 'what is to be done in order to oblige Mrs Winefrid Hyde either to give sufficient security for our £150 or refund it she being the only one of the 3 now living who was bound for it[?]'.[93] Hansbie was to be consulted in his role as executor to a Mrs Thorold as he still retained a power to act. The convent had accepted Mrs Hyde's offer of a £100 East India bond, 'but now she will not own 'tis her debt[.] yu'll see plainly by the Copy of the bond I here send you that she can't justly refuse payment'.[94]

Mrs Hyde also owed the nuns more than three years' interest. They had accepted four per cent on promise of prompt payment and had only done so because Mrs Hyde's aunt had borrowed or taken it 'to do a charity to a poor gentleman who could not give any security himself', and on whom she now wished to throw the debt. As prompt payment had not occurred, the nuns wanted five per cent interest (£24, or £19 10s 0d if she paid the whole amount immediately). Pressure was to be kept up on her too: in 1737 Strickland was to do what he could to get money out of her before Morgan Hansbie came over to Louvain again, for 'when he's once out of her way she'll do nothing'.[95] Presumably this did not succeed, since he was soon being asked whether Mrs Hyde could be forced to pay them, and whether what they had already done was sufficient to empower him to act against her.[96] Strickland also received a splendid reminder from Tunstall to the effect that patience (surely a desirable virtue in a religious) only renders such people more unwilling to pay.[97]

---

[91]  *Blount MSS, C* 64/231: CT to MS, 24 January 1742 (NS).
[92]  *Blount MSS, C* 64/246: Christina Towneley to MS, 29 July 1744 (NS).
[93]  *Blount MSS, C* 64/137: CT to MS, 26 March 1737 (NS).
[94]  *Blount MSS, C* 64/137: CT to MS, 26 March 1737 (NS).
[95]  *Blount MSS, C* 64/142: CT to MS, 5 May 1737 (NS).
[96]  *Blount MSS, C* 64/159: CT to MS, 18 April 1738 (NS); *C* 64/161: CT to MS, 13 May 1738 (NS).
[97]  *Blount MSS, C* 64/171: CT to MS, 24 November 1738 (NS).

As if this were not enough, Strickland then received a pointed reminder that Mrs Hyde lived at Weston, beyond Bath, followed closely by another letter conveying Morgan Hansbie's information that she had been in London all the time and an instruction to Strickland to take legal action against her either in the Superior's name as sole heir to Mary Worthington or in his own and asking him what he needed to empower him to do so.[98] The nuns were sure that the Superior could not appear in person (although they did subsequently ask if this was correct) but were worried that something different from a letter of attorney would be needed 'if it should be a woman that is to represent Mrs Mary Worthington',[99] until reassured by Hansbie that 'either man or woman may pass for Mrs Worthington's representative'.[100] Strickland then proposed that the Dominican Provincial, Thomas Worthington, should act for his late sister Mary's interests in this affair of Mrs Hyde; Tunstall did not like this at all and lobbed the delicate problem back to Strickland. She objected to Worthington's involvement, saying that

> he's not so proper a person in his judgment as his nephew who for reasons known to us we don't care to employ & we having a neece of the Lady Mrs Worthington in our house why can't the Letters be taken out in her name, or as is thought in our House Mrs More is intitled the best to it.[101]

Tunstall made clear that they wanted no dealings at all involving either uncle or nephew. If the employment of Thomas Worthington was, however, unavoidable and 'must need be imploy'd we must get the Consent of his masters on this side the Sea, but will not have to do with his nephew'.[102]

Mrs Hyde continued to evade the nuns until 1740, when Strickland was again informed that she was in Hammersmith and that he was to tell her that they would sue if she did not pay up immediately.[103] He was asked to try every tack; Morgan Hansbie suggested a 'kind letter' to her might do the trick, so they asked Strickland to forward one in the very letter in which they asked his advice on this,[104] and asked him in the next letter and one further time to confirm that he had sent it.[105]

---

[98] *Blount MSS, C* 64/163: CT to MS, 20 June 1738 (NS); *C* 64/165: CT to MS, 7 July 1738 (NS).

[99] *Blount MSS, C* 64/167: CT to MS, 22 August 1738 (NS).

[100] *Blount MSS, C* 64/167, 169 and 184: CT to MS, 22 August and 14 October 1738 and 3 November 1739 (NS).

[101] *Blount MSS, C* 64/186: CT to MS, 3 November 1739 (NS).

[102] *Blount MSS, C* 64/187: CT to MS, 17 November 1739 (NS).

[103] *Blount MSS, C* 64/197: CT to MS, 3 May 1740 (NS).

[104] *Blount MSS, C* 64/211: CT to MS, 18 April 1741 (NS).

[105] *Blount MSS, C* 64/212 and 215: CT to MS, 28 April and 6 June 1741 (NS).

## CHASING LATE PAYMENTS

Payments, although known to be due, were often tardy, and Strickland had to confront any number of expedients and excuses to avoid or delay payment from relatives or friends in England of the members of the religious orders, who could not easily be forced by law to pay money to such destinations. In January 1734 he was informed that Miss Sheldon's pension was due and that of Miss Stapylton would shortly be so; for the latter Strickland received orders to contact her father, who 'has [the money] always ready', and who would not pay until asked, but who got angry if not asked to pay at the appropriate time.[106] Four years later a substantial sum of £450 became due to this young lady, in return for some deeds which the Louvain convent held as security which were to be delivered back to Strickland's colleague Edward Webb only on payment of the money and some extra due from her father.[107]

Nine months later Strickland was ordered to pursue Mr Belson[108] of Winchester and Stokenchurch for non-payment of £42 6s 0d arrears for his sister's board in Louvain.[109] Then again, he was told that 'many has heard of money', in the second of two letters full of such details.[110] The chain of requests was sometimes lengthened: Strickland had to inform Peggy Cholmeley, one of the nuns' go-betweens, that Mr Willoughby expected £20 from her on a particular date.[111] Similarly, he had to report on a small sum due from Lady Shrewsbury for Anne Talbot and £3 promised by Lord Langdale for a poor man in Louvain.[112] Almost all of these names are of people with whom Strickland dealt in other capacities; there can be little doubt that the likelihood of his having some leverage in obtaining payment from them, in spite of conflicts of interest, was one of the reasons for which he was employed. The January 1735 letter from Mr Trapps to his sister at Louvain to inform her that he would pay her money as soon as he knew to whom to pay it in London sounds like yet another excuse for tardiness, particularly as Strickland was requested to give him a discharge in full 'for his sisters share due beyond sea for the year 1733'.[113]

---

[106] *Blount MSS, C* 64/79 and 99: CT to MS, 8 January 1734 and 29 March 1735 (NS).

[107] *Blount MSS, C* 64/163, 165 and 169: CT to MS, 20 June, 7 July and 14 October 1738 (NS).

[108] John Belson (c. 1625–1704), son of Augustin Belson; Catholic historian and controversialist.

[109] *Blount MSS, C* 64/91: CT to MS, 28 September 1734 (NS).

[110] *Blount MSS, C* 64/92–3: CT to MS, 12 and 26 November 1734 (NS).

[111] *Blount MSS, C* 64/84–5: CT to MS, 20 April 1734 (NS); CT to Mrs Strickland, 26 April 1734 (NS).

[112] *Blount MSS, C* 64/88: CT to MS, [7 August 1734 or 1735 (NS)].

[113] *Blount MSS, C* 64/97: CT to MS, 1 February 1735 (NS).

This was not the only tardy payment for Mr Trapps's sister: Mr Tunstall was to pay her 50s 0d for the first year's interest on rents on property in Paris due in September 1733 for the 'Legacy left Mrs Trapps here by her sister Nanny' and had to be given a receipt for it, as with all his payments to the house at Louvain.[114] One wonders about other possible expedients to avoid payment, such as the case of the friends of Miss Green at Louvain, who wrote as soon as they knew Strickland to be the person to whom to pay her pension, assuring him of its full payment but only paying one year out of the three years due.[115] In extreme cases of non-payment Strickland was expected to sue for debt, as with two ladies named to the Louvain convent by Mr Day.[116]

Such sagas could be long-running. Mr Dillon, who lived next to the church of St Peter Le Poer in Broad Street, sent his daughter to Louvain in 1734, where she quickly settled well.[117] Cecily Tunstall seems to have been surprisingly less than sure of the precise identity of 'Banker Dillon', and Strickland was required to pursue an outstanding promised payment by him for his daughter of £26 11s 0d in late 1735.[118] This money was, according to Miss Dillon, to be paid under orders from her father by a merchant of the same name, whom Strickland was asked to trace and from whom he was to demand the money.[119] Tunstall assumed four months later that he would have had it.[120] When Dillon failed to pay the correct amounts of £15 per annum to the house and 21 guineas for the daughter's use, it was not Tunstall who put him right but Strickland who was ordered to do so.[121] Dillon appears to have separated from his wife, who became very agitated when her husband failed to pay the sum, Strickland of course being required to demand it.[122]

Tunstall may have been less than helpful to her confidential adviser: there were two merchants named Dillon, and the one whom Strickland approached refused to admit he had money for his daughter, whereupon Tunstall instructed:

> I must beg you'll desire Mr Day to get it out of him that paid him for the 2 boys at Dowey for as there are 2 marchants it may be that he who has it for her will not pay it but to Mr Day.[123]

---

[114] *Blount MSS, C* 64/97: CT to MS, 1 February 1735 (NS).
[115] *Blount MSS, C* 64/100: CT to MS, 15 April 1735 (NS).
[116] *Blount MSS, C* 64/97: CT to MS, 1 February 1735 (NS).
[117] *Blount MSS, C* 64/92: CT to MS, 12 November 1734 (NS).
[118] *Blount MSS, C* 64/111: CT to MS, 25 November 1735 (NS).
[119] *Blount MSS, C* 64/101: CT to MS, 17 May 1735 (NS).
[120] *Blount MSS, C* 64/107: CT to MS, 2 September 1735 (NS).
[121] *Blount MSS, C* 64/110: CT to MS, 15 November 1735 (NS).
[122] *Blount MSS, C* 64/133 and 135–8: CT to MS, 4 and 20 February, 15 and 26 March and 9 April 1737 (NS).
[123] *Blount MSS, C* 64/142: CT to MS, 5 May 1737 (NS).

Communication was not, however, the Dillons' *forte*: Day discovered that the real problem was that Strickland did not know how much to demand from Dillon, although Tunstall had mistakenly been under the impression that Mrs Dillon had told him; Tunstall told Strickland how much was due and sent him back to demand it.[124] Dillon then made a partial payment only, to the further annoyance of Tunstall.[125] Meanwhile Mrs Dillon made full payment, leaving Tunstall to instruct Strickland to pay back any surplus, apparently oblivious to any embarrassment it might cause him.[126]

Questions concerning the receipt of payments notified to members of the convent run as a theme through the correspondence. There were further recriminations on this theme. In a back-handed thanks for a set of accounts, Tunstall noted that two payments about which she had written to Strickland several times had long been paid, tartly commenting to Mrs Strickland: 'this shows how necessary 'tis to let me know who pays money to him & for whom'.[127]

## LADY CATHERINE RADCLYFFE

The most tiresome part of Strickland's dealings with the Louvain convent concerned money due to Lady Catherine Radclyffe, sister of the second Earl of Derwentwater and a long-time resident of the convent, who died shortly before Strickland, in June 1744, at the very advanced age of ninety-three. She was entitled to a £100 annuity out of the family estates, which were sequestered following the execution of her nephew the third Earl and only restored following the success of his daughter in reclaiming from Greenwich Hospital (to which Walpole had given the forfeited estates) her entitlement to £20,000 of his estates, with Strickland's help following her marriage to his patron the eighth Lord Petre.

The first mention of the annuity occurs in 1733, when Tunstall asked Strickland to pay Henry Rodbourne (a fellow lawyer and the agent for the Derwentwater estates in Northumberland) his fees for recovering one and a half years of the annuity;[128] Rodbourne was apparently pressing for payment, and Tunstall had no compunction about asking Strickland to pay this even though there was insufficient money in the convent's account with Strickland. By the end of 1733 two years' payment was outstanding to the then seventy-eight-year-old Lady Catherine, and the convent was

---

124  *Blount MSS, C* 64/145: CT to MS, 15 June 1737 (NS).
125  *Blount MSS, C* 64/148: CT to MS, 19 August 1737 (NS).
126  *Blount MSS, C* 64/150: CT to MS, [7 October 1737 (NS)].
127  *Blount MSS, C* 64/85: CT to Mrs Strickland, 26 April 1734 (NS).
128  *Blount MSS, C* 64/73: CT to MS, 11 September 1733 (NS).

getting very restive.[129] The trustees in England kept demanding regular proof that she was still alive in the form of notarial certificates of her life, which Strickland had to obtain through the Louvain convent.[130]

At one time anyone who had seen her could provide the certificate: a Mr Wisely, who brought over Tunstall's nieces, was in 1733 willing to provide this, but the convent then heard nothing further of him and became distressed by the consequent further delay in payment.[131] The trustees then began to want something more official, and most subsequent certificates were provided by a local imperial notary. By 1742 certificates were being asked for more frequently, Lady Catherine being over ninety, and Tunstall, doubtlessly correctly, surmised that the agent 'suspects she's dead but on what account we can't guess for she's now better than she's been this many years'.[132] The process often proved less than straightforward and frequently failed to result in the payment of the annuity.[133] Strickland was therefore required to 'hasten' Walton over the payment in December 1734,[134] with some success, since his announcement of its receipt led to hasty clamour from Lady Catherine to draw the money.[135] Annual certificates were forthcoming in January 1734 (which Tunstall vainly hoped would 'prove more effectual than that we sent last year at this time'[136]), and early in 1735 (when the notary in Brussels was slow in getting it executed).[137] The nuns thought that Rodbourne had managed to do away then with the need for further certificates:

> Mr Rodbourn writes that with much adoe he has secured her annuity for her so that we shall not need to renew the certificate of life as we supose any more[.] she sais Mr Watson can't now refuse the payment.[138]

George Walton (mistakenly referred to as Mr Watson), the Petres' Essex agent, then puzzled the nuns by demanding a new certificate in September 1735, causing offence because no payment had been made since 1733.[139] By November 1734 Lady Catherine was demanding that Strickland 'solisite' Walton urgently for nearly three years of her money, and in September 1735 he was instructed to tell Walton on handing over yet

---

[129] *Blount MSS, C* 64/77: CT to MS, 22 December 1733 (NS).
[130] See Appendix 2 for an example of a certificate and an English translation.
[131] *Blount MSS, C* 64/75–7: CT to MS, 6 and 18 November and 12 December 1733 (NS).
[132] *Blount MSS, C* 64/234: CT to MS, 11 May 1742 (NS).
[133] *Blount MSS, C* 64/75: CT to MS, 6 November 1733.
[134] *Blount MSS, C* 64/95: CT to MS, 17 December 1734 (NS).
[135] *Blount MSS, C* 64/97: CT to MS, 1 February 1735 (NS).
[136] *Blount MSS, C* 64/80: CT to MS, 22 January 1734 (NS).
[137] *Blount MSS, C* 64/97 and 99: CT to MS, 1 February and 29 March 1735 (NS).
[138] *Blount MSS, C* 64/101: CT to MS, 17 May 1735 (NS).
[139] *Blount MSS, C* 64/107–8: CT to MS, 2 and 6 September 1735 (NS); *C* 64/91: CT to MS, 28 September 1734 (NS).

another certificate that Lady Catherine 'expects a year & half at least else: why a new certificate'.[140] Even when payment did occur, as in May 1734, Strickland faced further questions, since only one year's annuity out of two overdue was paid just as a third was becoming due.[141]

Tunstall delayed taking out a next certificate at Lady Day 1736 on the vain grounds that payment might be more speedy if Lady Catherine were seen to be alive after that date.[142] What the certificate said was very sensitive; Daniel, the notary, alarmed Tunstall by describing Lady Catherine (accurately) as 'a nun at Louvain' in the 1737 certificate, leaving the nuns unsure whether his doing so was accidental or deliberate – an act which 'may make it worse by giving the Government notice of her being so'.[143] While Strickland did not request that the certificate be drawn afresh, Tunstall agonised repeatedly over the mistake and got it drawn anew.[144] But perhaps Daniel the notary was just careless: he made a mistake in the date of the Lady Day 1738 certificate which Tunstall hoped would be of no consequence.[145] When Tunstall sent the Lady Day 1739 certificate she started to get anxious about future payments, especially in view of Lady Catherine's extreme old age and their dependence on the annuity, and asked whether the certificate should now be renewed half-yearly as under the previous Lord Petre.[146]

Six months later Tunstall was worrying again, asking whether she should get a new certificate for Lady Catherine's life for the half-year, 'in case she dyes before the whole year be so'.[147] As Strickland did not answer this enquiry, Tunstall instructed him to arrange the certification from 1742.[148] By February 1744 Lady Catherine was taken ill with a cold and the nuns were fearful for her life and asking precautionary guidance as to whether the will she had made, sealed up by a notary, should be proved in Louvain before being sent to Strickland.[149] One final certificate was sent in April 1744;[150] less than two months later she was dead, at the age of ninety-three, although that final certificate was expected by Strickland to bring the nuns one final payment, to which they still hoped

---

[140] *Blount MSS, C* 64/92: CT to MS, 12 November 1734 (NS); *C* 64/108: CT to MS, 6 September 1735 (NS).

[141] *Blount MSS, C* 64/87: CT to MS, 29 May 1734 (NS).

[142] *Blount MSS, C* 64/119: CT to MS, 1 May 1736 (NS).

[143] *Blount MSS, C* 64/140: CT to MS, 16 April 1737 (NS). Daniel had 'had no occasion to know her for such, so that if he should come here, she may go to him in secular'.

[144] *Blount MSS, C* 64/144: CT to MS, 28 May 1737 (NS).

[145] *Blount MSS, C* 64/159: CT to MS, 18 April 1738 (NS).

[146] *Blount MSS, C* 64/180: CT to MS, 14 April 1739 (NS).

[147] *Blount MSS, C* 64/185: CT to MS, 12 October 1739 (NS).

[148] *Blount MSS, C* 64/234: CT to MS, 11 May 1742 (NS).

[149] *Blount MSS, C* 64/242: Christina Towneley to MS, 4 February 1744 (NS).

[150] *Blount MSS, C* 64/245: Christina Towneley to MS, 21 April 1744 (NS).

and expected money due to her from her brother Arthur's estate to be added.[151] Henry Rodbourne was responsible for requesting the early certificates, which he did directly, although the certificates themselves had to be returned to Strickland, who passed them on to the trustees of the Petre family for payment by Walton. Rodbourne, who also had to pursue payment in England, often with difficulty,[152] found the duty irksome and passed it to Strickland at the earliest opportunity.[153]

Lady Catherine was further entitled to parts of the estates of her sister Lady Mary Radclyffe of Old Elvet, Durham, and her brothers Arthur Radclyffe and Colonel Thomas Radclyffe, all of which proved hard to reclaim, even though they included money left to the convent by Lady Mary and (through her and her brothers) money from another sister, Lady Anne Radclyffe. In 1735 Strickland sent for her execution an Act of Renunciation to permit an administration of Arthur Radclyffe's estate to be taken out in the Low Countries in order to empower Mrs Dacres and Lady Mary Petre to receive £2,000 due from the late Earl of Derwentwater's executors to Arthur Radclyffe and to enable Sir John Webb safely to pay Lady Catherine her one-fifth share (£400) of this. In 1740 Sir John Swinburne still had in his hands a further £200 belonging to the Louvain convent from this source, and Tunstall typically refused, whatever the renunciation may have meant, to allow Strickland to give up any claim for money on their behalf.[154] Later in the same month she gave Strickland full power of attorney to claim her entitlement.[155] Tunstall also asked her brother Constable – a notorious non-correspondent – to take up the matter of Lady Mary's affairs with her great-niece Lady Petre: she had 'writ of our intentions to my Br Constable but never has heard a word since from him which I wonder at'.[156]

This lack of response from Constable over a period of more than nine months produced an offer of further help in the matter from Strickland, which was gratefully accepted. Tunstall was fearful of any concessions that her brother had made, especially since she knew that he had deducted from an account given to Lord Petre a £10 debt owed by Lady Mary to the Louvain house for an annuity to her attorney Robert Ashmall. Strickland was not to make any concessions on the recovery of what was indeed a considerable sum: £943 5s 0d in all by 1736, mostly consisting of life rents. Lady Mary had redeemed the estate of her brother Colonel Thomas Radclyffe in 1718 for £1,100 and had continued paying interest on ten

---

[151] *Blount MSS, C* 64/247: Christina Towneley to MS, 6 October 1744 (NS).
[152] *Blount MSS, C* 64/101: CT to MS, 17 May 1735 (NS).
[153] *Blount MSS, C* 64/75: CT to MS, 6 November 1733 (NS).
[154] *Blount MSS, C* 64/204: CT to MS, 30 September 1740 (NS).
[155] *Blount MSS, C* 64/102: CT to MS, 21 May 1735 (NS).
[156] *Blount MSS, C* 64/120: CT to MS, 15 May 1736 (NS).

annuity bonds until her death. Tunstall had all the deeds and bonds in Louvain, all of them attested by Mr MacNenny, an Irishman whom she called 'a very able Counsellor to the Arch Dutchess'.[157] She was willing to arrange copies for Petre to inspect, though she was unsure whether the copies would need to be notarised, but flatly refused to hand the originals over to Petre until the debt was settled.[158]

Tunstall may indeed have been right about the likelihood of her brother making concessions, since he told her in November 1736 that he had 'given up the Colls [Thomas Radclyffe's] estate wholy to Lord Petre' and instructed her to apply to him for it now that another year's payment was due. The nuns asked Strickland's advice, both on whether Lady Catherine should write to Petre and on whether he would now pay without prompting; they did not want to importune him, but

> as 'tis in a great measure for the maintenance of several persons in our house & our Rents here are so Low & ill pay'd & we've had a sad sickly time on't having the small pox in our House & has this 3 months besides many other illnesses it would be a vast help if we could get this old Debt or part paid at least. The partys think me to blame not to write oftener about it but I asure 'em of your kind promise to do all in your power in it.[159]

The Louvain ladies felt betrayed by all the refusals and the references to others. While there is every sign that Strickland never shrugged off the responsibility on to others, they still got no nearer their money, and Tunstall talked of asking her cousin Hanford if he had had resort to Chancery or some other means to get what was due to him and his brother and sister twelve years before from Lady Ann Radclyffe's estate: 'Thus you see Sir we are driven from pillar to post & none will own the Debt. we must seek to do our Selves right some other way if you can tell us any safe & quick'.[160]

Lady Petre eventually wrote 'a very kind letter' to her great-aunt, promising to pay 'as soon as things are settled' (whatever that might mean) all that Lady Mary would have given to the Louvain convent. Tunstall, however, instantly raised another possible obstacle about which the nuns had known for five years, without telling Strickland, and on which they wanted his advice:

> My Cousen Haggerstone told us 4 or 5 years ago that then an Estate was sold & the mony received by Lady Mary's Executors which might have paid all or a great part of the debts but whether t'was the Coll's or Lady Mary's own I can't tell.[161]

---

157  *Blount MSS, C* 64/122: CT to MS, 15 June 1736 (NS).
158  *Blount MSS, C* 64/124: CT to MS, 27 July 1736 (NS).
159  *Blount MSS, C* 64/129: CT to MS, 16 November 1736 (NS).
160  *Blount MSS, C* 64/233: CT to MS, 13 February 1742 (NS).
161  *Blount MSS, C* 64/135: CT to MS, 20 February 1737 (NS).

If this is not loading the scales against one's confidential adviser, nothing else is. In spite of all this, nothing happened, and Tunstall asked Strickland to confer with her brother Constable about the debt ('the best secured demand we have on his Lordship'[162]) now due from Lord Petre, even though Constable had relinquished responsibility for pursuing it.[163] Then she asked if a letter from her to her brother would help,[164] even two years after he had given up dealing with the affair; in so doing, she was trying to pressure Strickland into obtaining from Petre payment of at least the yearly sums due, especially the sum due to her cousin Barbara Crathorne, left her by Tunstall's aunt Lady Anne Radclyffe long before the Colonel's payments to several others in the house, which was her only maintenance for life and had not been paid since 1730.

Tunstall believed that Lord Petre would pay if he knew the situation and wanted the money immediately, which was one of the nuns' best sources of income after the problematical annuity to Lady Catherine Radclyffe, as 'we've had great Expences & Law Suites this year & shall have in all Likelyhood still greater the next'.[165] Lady Petre wrote to Lady Catherine in April 1738, hoping that matters would soon be settled so that she and others would be paid.[166] At the same time, Constable and Lord Petre asked Strickland to arbitrate on accounts not yet settled between them. Constable hoped that Strickland would then be able to get payment at least of Barbara Crathorne's annuity, unpaid since 1729 and presumed indisputable since given by Tunstall's aunt Lady Anne Radclyffe in her lifetime; both Colonel Thomas Radclyffe and his brother Frank were bound for its payment. Strickland was asked to discuss the matter with Constable.[167]

Every little bit that the nuns discovered was added on to the debt, as when they found out that Mrs Swinny, a poor woman in receipt of a Radclyffe annuity, had lived on until 5 May 1721.[168] Tunstall repeated at every opportunity her belief that the nuns' claim to at least some of the debt was so good that Lord Petre could not refuse payment.[169] This did not stop Lord Petre refusing to pay, and one has to wonder whose side Strickland was on in this particular case. The longer the affair dragged on, the more concerned Tunstall became; by the time Barbara Crathorne's £20 annuity had been outstanding for eight years Tunstall was concerned

[162] *Blount MSS, C* 64/166: CT to MS, 17 July 1738 (NS).
[163] *Blount MSS, C* 64/152: CT to MS, 11 November 1737 (NS).
[164] *Blount MSS, C* 64/155: CT to MS, 29 December 1737 (NS).
[165] *Blount MSS, C* 64/153: CT to MS, 6 December 1737 (NS).
[166] *Blount MSS, C* 64/159: CT to MS, 18 April 1738 (NS).
[167] *Blount MSS, C* 64/163: CT to MS, 20 June 1738 (NS).
[168] *Blount MSS, C* 64/167: CT to MS, 22 August 1738 (NS).
[169] *Blount MSS, C* 64/168: CT to MS, 25 September 1738 (NS).

that it would be harder to pay 'all at a clap', especially as they had heard that Petre was 'dipd in vast Buildings &c so that we fear we shall be the last payd'.[170]

Hardly two months after this Strickland found himself required to remind his patron that many of the rents due were life rents and that a lot of interest would be due if not paid annually.[171] Tunstall was beside herself with anguish, expecting Strickland to fulfil the nuns' expectations and not knowing where to turn if this source of money, so long expected, failed: 'Else we can't tell what to do having relied so many years on the payment & get nothing but hopes given'.[172] The nuns even naïvely believed that if Strickland ensured that Lord Petre knew they desperately needed money for a church building project he would pay up immediately.[173] Likewise, the nuns automatically assumed, when Strickland unwisely revealed to Elizabeth Smith at Louvain that he had been to Petre's (then secondary) seat at Ingatestone, that the prolonged affair of this debt would consequently be resolved. They could not contain their frustration and disappointment when Strickland said not a word about it.[174]

The nuns took the view that the Derwentwater money, forfeit originally on the conviction for treason of the third Earl, and only restored in part to his daughter Lady Petre, ought to be paid regularly to its intended recipients such as Barbara Crathorne, 'who ought to have it yearly & no body can hinder her of it tho it had been in the Go[vernme]nts hands much less should Lord Petre be so long behind hand'.[175] Tunstall's regrets at the death from smallpox of Lord Petre in 1742 show, however, a sincerity totally unshadowed by any ulterior reactions of frustration at further problems getting the money due to the nuns:

> We're very sensible of your loss of Lord Petre & are also more in pain for Poor Lady who we have a most tender concern for not hearing whether her Ladyship has also had the same fatal disease being left with child as we heard[.] but since we can't tell how it goes for God's sake if you hear let us know.[176]

A further sum became due from the executors of another brother, William Radclyffe, following his death in Rome in 1732. Strickland was twice told to contact Sir Ralph Radclyffe to let him know that the deceased had

---

[170] *Blount MSS, C* 64/171: CT to MS, 24 November 1738 (NS). This refers to Lord Petre's grand rebuilding of Giacomo Leoni's Old Thorndon Hall and its Palladian rebuilding after a fire by James Paine, and to the extraordinarily lavish estate planting.

[171] *Blount MSS, C* 64/176: CT to MS, 31 January 1739 (NS).

[172] *Blount MSS, C* 64/179: CT to MS, 26 March 1739 (NS).

[173] *Blount MSS, C* 64/181 and 184: CT to MS, 2 June and 11 September 1739 (NS).

[174] *Blount MSS, C* 64/186: CT to MS, 3 November 1739 (NS).

[175] *Blount MSS, C* 64/188: CT to MS, 30 December 1739 (NS).

[176] *Blount MSS, C* 64/238: CT to MS, 7 August 1742 (NS).

left his estate to a Mr Draper, whom Strickland was required to identify and trace with the assistance either of Sir Ralph or a Mr Fenwick who was a likely source of information (Tunstall did not know the address of any of these individuals). Draper was a trustee for Lady Catherine and also for Lady Newburgh, both of whom were 'in great want of money', but information was to be obtained by Strickland from Sir Ralph, who would be unlikely to pay it without better security.[177] Four years later, the nuns were anxiously asking Strickland if he knew whether it was true that William Radclyffe had left a will or if they would have to ask in Rome.[178] They thought that he had made one in England and altered it in Rome, cutting them out by leaving everything to his nephew, Lord Derwentwater's son,

> which will we learnd Lord D[erwentwate]r got canceld & recover'd all at Law from his son & spent the Campain he kept in Italy 3 years ago £9000 as one that comes from spain tells us.[179]

Strickland was therefore to attempt to recover what appears to have been a substantial sum of money which the Louvain convent believed its own. They seem to have regarded this as a right, since the fifth Lord Derwentwater had prevailed on them to lend them money without any more security than a bill drawn on Henry Rodbourne, which the latter protested as he had no moneys of Derwentwater's in his hands.[180]

Money was also overdue from young Lady Petre's grandfather Sir John Webb, who had paid her just £13 of some £60 due two years before.[181] Further money due to her had to be reclaimed from other sources, the urgency being driven by Lady Catherine's age. Lady Catherine asked Strickland to take what he felt appropriate for his trouble, hoping that she would live long enough to have another dividend from the effects of 'Mr Aurthur' (Daniel Arthur, the Paris banker?), which could have been obtained long ago 'if the family of the Swinbourns [Swinburnes] had pleased'.[182] Strickland was not the only victim of such side-swipes!

It is difficult to say with certainty who drove the community's impatience over the certainly unsatisfactory payment of the annuity. Tunstall made the most of recounting Lady Catherine's frequent complaints that she was 'in pain to know how her afaires stands' and was 'not pleased to have it so long a doing'.[183] She recalled with relish an enquiry about

---

[177] *Blount MSS, C* 64/93 and 96: CT to MS, 26 November 1734 and 4 January 1735 (NS).
[178] *Blount MSS, C* 64/130–2: CT to MS, 5 and 31 December 1736, 1 February 1737 (NS).
[179] *Blount MSS, C* 64/131: CT to MS, 31 December 1736 (NS).
[180] *Blount MSS, C* 64/134: CT to MS, 10 February 1737 (NS).
[181] *Blount MSS, C* 64/77: CT to MS, 12 December 1733 (NS).
[182] *Blount MSS, C* 64/104: CT to MS, 12 July 1735 (NS).
[183] *Blount MSS, C* 64/81, 105 and 106: CT to MS, 5 March 1734 and 19 and 30 August 1735 (NS); *C* 64/187: CT to MS, 17 November 1739 (NS).

Walton's identity: was he 'a Steward for the Family or the government[;] Lady Cat: wants to know'.[184] The pain was not entirely or principally personal: the annuity was depended on not just for Lady Catherine's support but also for that of several other inmates. The money mattered a great deal to the nuns; Tunstall expressed her nervousness that

> it will be the last we shall have for her for she decays fast & has lived a fair time. We shall have a very great loss of her for money put out here is at very small interest & that ill paid & with great trouble to those that are to collect it if I may use that term for 'tis as hard to get our own money as to raise a tax.

She went on to say that 'if Lady Catherins fails I shall not be able to pay the expences of the House without new suply's'.[185] A certain naïveté or innocence, as well as helplessness, was certainly evident in Tunstall's recounting of Lady Catherine's constant asking if Strickland had received her 'so long due' £100, knowing at the time that another payment was due in a few days and believing in all innocence that Walton and his masters could not refuse payment if it was demanded: 'She wonders what excuse they can make for not paying the year last past since 2 certificats of Life were required for it & not yet paid'.[186]

## PLAYING THE FOREIGN EXCHANGE MARKETS

Tunstall could be very demanding about the sending of money at a particular time. Money was short, rents were 'ill paid' and grossly insufficient to 'pay the expences of the year without surplus from England', and there were desperate shortages in what was effectively a war zone.[187] The way the nuns lived was not the cheapest, 'for we're in great want all things excessive dear especialy lent dyet & all people here so poor they can't pay their rents'.[188] Prices for corn and other basics had doubled in ten years, and widespread poverty put the rents on which part of their income was based severely in arrears.[189] Tunstall reckoned that they could not survive without their 'suplys out of England'.[190]

> We're forc'd to lay out what they [Tunstall's nieces] want & can't well spare it at this time Corn growing still dearer every day by reason of the war &

---

[184] *Blount MSS, C* 64/111: CT to MS, 25 November 1735 (NS).

[185] *Blount MSS, C* 64/166: CT to MS, 17 July 1738 (NS).

[186] *Blount MSS, C* 64/114: CT to MS, 10 January 1736 (NS).

[187] *Blount MSS, C* 64/153: CT to MS, 6 December 1737 (NS); *C* 64/75: CT to MS, 6 November 1733 (NS).

[188] *Blount MSS, C* 64/192: CT to MS, 3 March 1740 (NS).

[189] *Blount MSS, C* 64/194r, CT to MS, 5 April 1740 (NS).

[190] *Blount MSS, C* 64/205: CT to MS, 11 October 1740 (NS).

we want money to lay in a provision for they tell us there will be none to be had in a very short time. 'tis all to be transported.[191]

There were two aspects to this urgency: firstly Tunstall's desire to play the foreign exchange markets (where rates of return could be much higher than ordinary interest rates of four or five per cent) to maximise the community's income, and secondly her belief that when she was notified of payment Strickland had invariably got it.[192] In many, possibly most, cases, payment was made in the form of promissory notes payable at a later date, and there is evidence of Strickland being out of pocket at times in order to remit funds.[193] All too often, Tunstall took at face value information about payments promised: in January 1736 she wrote that in November 1735 Mr Crathorn paid money to a Mr Brigham in York to procure bills for £92 13s 3d to pay his sister through Strickland,[194] in addition to £30 already left by Crathorn with him in London, only to receive a swift and forceful rejoinder from Strickland that he had not received the bills. This elicited an apology for the sister's impatience.[195]

War did indeed break out in April 1744, declared by the French, and Tunstall's successor, Christina Towneley, had to ask Strickland to use the channel provided by Mme Broeta in Antwerp for contact:

> At this Juncture people are not content to have their money Lye in London … Our Garisson encreases dayly, but none of our Countrey folks[.] those at Bruxells have received great Honnours from Prince Charles who Came out of his Coach to Compliment the hors gards, which has a little affronted the troops of this Countrey, who he bid march on.[196]

This comment on the Young Pretender is the sole extant one which expresses an opinion on the Stuart royal family; it is plain that Towneley was not impressed.

Tunstall demanded the presence of someone to pay bills even if Strickland were not there. However, her apologies for keeping Mrs Strickland in town to ensure her bills were paid instantly sound most unconvincing, especially when one realises that Strickland had not yet at that time agreed to represent St Monica's.[197] She also asked him to permit his wife or someone else to write for him at any time when pressure of other affairs prevented him from doing so, and to receive payments in his absence which otherwise would not be left.[198] A particularly tart rejoinder followed

---

[191]  *Blount MSS, C* 64/75: CT to MS, 6 November 1733 (NS).
[192]  *Blount MSS, C* 64/109: CT to MS, 30 October 1735 (NS).
[193]  *Blount MSS, C* 64/79: CT to MS, 8 January 1734 (NS).
[194]  *Blount MSS, C* 64/114: CT to MS, 10 January 1736 (NS).
[195]  *Blount MSS, C* 64/115: CT to MS, 21 January 1736 (NS).
[196]  *Blount MSS, C* 64/244: Christina Towneley to MS, 10 April 1744 (NS).
[197]  *Blount MSS, C* 64/70: CT to MS, 24 July 1733 (NS).
[198]  *Blount MSS, C* 64/84: CT to MS, 20 April 1734 (NS); *C* 64/87: CT to MS, 29 May

complaints about his failure to answer instantly, requesting him as he was 'so taken up with affairs of greater weight that you will order your clerk or some one you can trust to let us know what different sums & from & for whom in our house you may have received'.[199] Finally, Tunstall expected Strickland to send to other agents such as Fell for money paid to them for the convent,[200] even inside Lent (when, as she said, 'we don't write in Lent but upon business'[201]).

Cecily Tunstall watched the Flanders exchange markets closely, and most of her currency dealings were with the widow of the merchant Charles Broeta in Antwerp. She was always especially keen to garner as much money as possible when rates were high, and Mme Broeta on occasion pushed her to do so, by letting her know that the exchange was good at Antwerp:[202] 'our old marchand Broeta at Antwerp is in great hast to have Bills from us in order to pay her correspondants in England'.[203] Clearly, such transactions benefited both parties.[204] The case in January 1734 was one of those in which Tunstall left Strickland out of pocket by drawing £100 on him: 'at present the exchange is very high and therefore a great advantage to us & perhaps if I stay till you've more money it may fall'.[205]

Strickland was asked, in effect, to put himself out more than this, in two ways: he was requested to try to obtain more money for the convent while the exchange was high and also to set himself at further disadvantage by paying himself back out of the next income received (which was always hard to gather in). We should not, however, be too critical of Tunstall over her attempts to play the market, since the political situation was so precarious. As she herself wrote, 'at present the exchange is very high but if we have war here t'will not last so long'.[206] She was plainly terrified of catastrophic exchange swings, talking of 'the considerable loss not to be able to draw money while the exchange is so high as it has been, but fear t'will not last'.[207]

If the rate dropped before money arrived from Strickland for which she had been clamouring, she did not fail to rebuke him: 'but also 'tis now too late for the great advantage of the exchange which has fallen

---

1734 (NS).

[199] *Blount MSS, C* 64/175: CT to MS, 27 January 1739 (NS).
[200] *Blount MSS, C* 64/73: CT to MS, 11 September 1733 (NS).
[201] *Blount MSS, C* 64/83: CT to MS, 30 March 1734 (NS).
[202] *Blount MSS, C* 64/75 and *C* 64/165: CT to MS, 6 November 1733 and 7 July 1738 (NS).
[203] *Blount MSS, C* 64/89: CT to MS, 17 August 1734 (NS).
[204] *Blount MSS, C* 64/75: CT to MS, 6 November 1733 (NS).
[205] *Blount MSS, C* 64/79: CT to MS, 8 January 1734 (NS).
[206] *Blount MSS, C* 64/82: CT to MS, 9 March 1734 (NS).
[207] *Blount MSS, C* 64/84: CT to MS, 20 April 1734 (NS).

considerably lower than 'tis been several months'.[208] The concerns were
practical and nothing short of life and death matters, when Tunstall could
ask in desperation whether there were any further old debts which Strickland could pursue, since 'corn is now excessive dear & without some
supply I can't provide for our great family'.[209] Tunstall believed that
exchange rate swings were seasonal, wanting in January 1739 to draw
on Strickland 'before the fall of the exchange w[hi]ch I fear if I don't
hear soon will certainly as usual at this time a year [fall] to our great
loss'.[210] She had a long-term perspective on such transactions, quibbling
to Strickland in 1739 about their costs, which she knew to have been
cheaper two years earlier.[211]

## INVESTMENT

Strickland's services were similarly required in the matter of investment
of the nuns' money, for which in general they preferred land security. In
1735 he was asked to invest some money belonging to Lady Catherine
Radclyffe.[212] He was expected to give good advice on sound securities,
being pointedly reminded by Tunstall of the £300 lost by Mr Fell on
unsound ones.[213] The houses could generally only invest money belonging
to the house itself, not normally that of individuals, in spite of the request
to invest money belonging to Lady Catherine. At one stage the Louvain
house dithered over the investment of either £300 or £400, eventually
leaving it to Strickland's judgement from his knowledge of the circumstances. He advised the higher sum, and this was what he eventually
placed, although Tunstall made clear that they preferred the lower sum,
as they wanted 'the rest very much for to satisfy each one for whom 'tis
sent so can only put out what is belonging to the house'.[214] This sounds
like a classic situation in which whatever was done would fail to please
the client. The nuns had, however, another reason for preferring the lower
sum: 'some in our House had found by experience the D[uke] of Powis
a very bad pay master'.[215]

It appears that Strickland had suggested the investment in a mortgage
on the Northamptonshire estates of his patron. Tunstall wanted quick

---

[208] *Blount MSS, C* 64/175: CT to MS, 27 January 1739 (NS).

[209] *Blount MSS, C* 64/168: CT to MS, 25 September 1738 (NS).

[210] *Blount MSS, C* 64/174, CT to MS, January 1739.

[211] *Blount MSS, C* 64/187: CT to MS, 17 November 1739 (NS).

[212] *Blount MSS, C* 64/105: CT to MS, 19 August 1735 (NS).

[213] *Blount MSS, C* 64/104: CT to MS, 12 July 1735 (NS).

[214] *Blount MSS, C* 64/107: CT to MS, 2 September 1735 (NS).

[215] *Blount MSS, C* 64/111: CT to MS, 25 November 1735 (NS).

investment so that money was not lying idle, however briefly, and suggested English land security or East India bonds.[216]

Strickland seems in the final event to have proposed something different, having made a £400 investment offer of his own on land in Kent, which the Louvain canonesses certainly accepted even though it pushed them slightly beyond the limits of what the house could raise and obliged them to draw on private money from Lady Catherine Radclyffe and other inmates.[217] The nervous Tunstall, knowing of Strickland's poor health, asked him to place the deeds in the hands of their agent Thomas Day when all was settled, 'least as God forbid you might come to dye sudenly or such unforseen accidents may happen, we having nothing to shew for't could have no claim to our money'. The deeds would then presumably have been delivered by Day to the convent in Louvain, as their 'uper superiours' allowed them to invest only 'with good securitys in our hands or those we order to take care of it'.[218]

Smaller loans also occurred, but deals were often unsatisfactorily performed. Even the trusted Morgan Hansbie transgressed by tardy repayment of interest on a £150 loan agreed direct with him at four per cent, 'which we were content with only on promise of exact payment otherways at 5 per cent so he knows that is far from all due to us'.[219] Strickland had to do the dirty enforcement work.

## ELIZABETH SMITH'S SETTLEMENT

Tunstall again showed nervousness over Elizabeth Smith's settlement, which was unusual in that it had been drawn by Strickland himself in his own name, presumably with some declaration of trust to make clear that it was undertaken for her: 'we also here you have the Bond or deed of trust for Mrs Smiths Portion or Settlement which being drawn in your name must be deposited in some other hand as the custom is'.[220] This was to be deposited with Day, since they did not want Strickland's heirs to imagine it to be theirs in the event of his death.[221] It was one of a number of documents proving money due to Mrs Smith or to the

---

[216] *Blount MSS, C* 64/201: CT to MS, 26 August 1740 (NS); *C* 64/111: CT to MS, 25 November 1735 (NS). The latter makes mention of 'usury', which is regarded today as excessive interest charges. In the seventeenth and eighteenth centuries, however, it was defined as any profit on a loan, regardless of the size of the loan. As will be seen below, the nuns could not spend the principal of a loan, meaning that the only money available for spending consisted of rents and gifts.
[217] *Blount MSS, C* 64/113: CT to MS, 23 December 1735 (NS).
[218] *Blount MSS, C* 64/124: CT to MS, 27 July 1736 (NS).
[219] *Blount MSS, C* 64/107: CT to MS, 2 September 1735 (NS).
[220] *Blount MSS, C* 64/184: CT to MS, 11 September 1739 (NS).
[221] *Blount MSS, C* 64/201: CT to MS, 26 August 1740 (NS).

Louvain house which they expected Strickland to deposit with Day. Since they did not appear with Day as expected, they reminded Strickland that they thought he had

> drawn out of the writings what belonged to our House & they being drawn in your name you should have given a Deed of trust to a 3d Person who we have chosen, which was Mr Day. the settlements being but one writting you can't have that but might have had an abstract of what belonged to us. this she thought was done long ago but since 'tis not she will write to Mr Hide about it.[222]

Mrs Smith then heard that Hyde had left a copy of the settlement for the Louvain house with Strickland the previous year. Telling him how to do his job, she declared that it would show him how to make the deed of trust and that she would send him another copy if he had lost it (which he had, thereby losing them a year and a half's income which they would otherwise have had, or so they contended[223]). Tunstall warned him further that it must not be made out for or in the name of Elizabeth Smith, but 'to our house or our present Lady and her heirs &c … this you know Sir I doubt not better than we but some times one does not reflect of things'. If this were not done they would have been unable to claim it after Mrs Smith's death, a presumably common ploy by houses such as these to extend their income.[224]

Smith seems to have been as demanding as Tunstall; after informing Strickland that he should receive her annuity from Rowland Bellasis and Lancelot Kerby, the Winchester attorneys of Mr Sheldon and Mrs Wells,[225] Smith and her sister Isabella bullied the Louvain 'chief Ladys' into authorising Strickland to demand the whole £1,000 principal for their annuities from those legal representatives, 'for we are convinced that we shall not be paid regularly or even at all'.[226] They may, of course, have been right. Elizabeth Smith then capriciously asked Strickland to change tack and to write to Bellasis and Kerby stating his full authority to proceed against them at law in the event of non-payment of the annuity,

> for she desires us to secure the principal that she may have no more trouble about it[.] they seemd at first rather to wish we'd take it all in but we thought it in safe hands but now we find there is no hope of payment since the first fails only please to warn 'em of it that they may not be surprised.[227]

[222] *Blount MSS, C* 64/209: CT to MS, 9 January 1741 (NS).
[223] *Blount MSS, C* 64/211: CT to MS, 18 April 1741 (NS).
[224] *Blount MSS, C* 64/210: CT to MS, 17 February 1741 (NS).
[225] *Blount MSS, C* 64/207: CT to MS, 8 November 1740 (NS).
[226] *Blount MSS, C* 64/212: CT to MS, 28 April 1741 (NS).
[227] *Blount MSS, C* 64/213: CT to MS, 16 May 1741 (NS).

Further vacillation by Mrs Smith followed: since no word came of any payment, the Louvain convent decided that they

> can't be any longer without our money & if they refuse to pay the Interest we must Sell the land that is ingaged for it, this Mrs Elizabeth Smith much desires her self, else I had not writ it before, she said what could she expect hereafter if the very first 2 years they refused payment. So pray press it hard upon them for Mr Sheldon writ he'd given orders long ago to Mr Bellase.[228]

Before the letter had even been sent, Tunstall heard that a £50 payment had been sent to Strickland on the instructions of Mr Sheldon and Mrs Wells, so he was told not to write if he had not already done so, but to wait until the second year of the annuities was out.

## STRICKLAND AND TUNSTALL: AN UNEASY RELATIONSHIP

Cecily Tunstall was highly impatient in her business dealings, not even being able to wait a few days when Strickland was out of town on business and drawing a short-notice bill at three days' sight for £120 which she sent to Mrs Strickland, claiming that she would not have drawn so much 'but that the Exchange is very high & may not be so long'.[229] On another occasion she pointedly drew on him for a lesser sum than she would have otherwise done, remarking acerbically: 'for many wants there money & have got sevaral Bills another way because they could not stay for your return'.[230]

Tunstall feared the financial consequences when she did not have the reply she expected (that the money was there and would be transmitted immediately), since the community lost heavily on the foreign exchanges when individuals had smaller sums transmitted, and it was clearly in their interest to have larger remittances.[231] If Strickland failed to send over sums fast enough, then inmates of the convents became desperate and the losses (and Tunstall's anguish) became palpable, for 'several will procure Bills an other way as some does already which is a considerable loss in the exchange for the less sum's gains much less by exchange'.[232]

Tunstall could become agitated, too, over the slightest delay, as when she failed to hear from Strickland for fifteen days about £35 which Mrs Ledger informed her sister at Louvain was to be paid to him by the Duchess of Cleveland's banker, which was needed on 'an urgent occasion'. She wanted to know what else he had in hand for them: 'at present

---

228  *Blount MSS, C* 64/216: CT to MS, 29 June 1741 (NS).
229  *Blount MSS, C* 64/85: CT to MS, 26 April 1734 (NS).
230  *Blount MSS, C* 64/111: CT to MS, 25 November 1735 (NS).
231  *Blount MSS, C* 64/84: CT to MS, 20 April 1734 (NS).
232  *Blount MSS, C* 64/114: CT to MS, 10 January 1736 (NS).

the exchange runs very high but will soon alter so must again iterate the petition to hear from you instantly'.[233] He did not reply until 16 January; he had been seriously ill.[234]

Strickland was frequently accused of not informing Tunstall of payments received for members of the convent. Mrs Smith's sister Frances was said to have paid Strickland money at Christmas 1733 for transmission onwards, but at the end of March 1734 Mrs Smith complained that she had heard nothing of it (or was it subsumed in other payments which he had notified?).[235] The clamour could get loud: Mr Collingwood and Mr Darcy were supposed to have made payments for their sisters; the two Misses Jones were expecting four guineas from friends; Miss Stapylton didn't know whether her father had paid her pension; and Mr Ward's sister, expecting £20 from him, 'stays in expectation ont & can't go forward in her intended purpose till she hears you have it or at least a Bill for't'.[236]

Mrs Knight's mother promised two guineas for her daughter at Louvain in September 1734. In February 1735 Tunstall mistrustfully asked whether it had come,[237] whereupon Strickland pursued the outstanding sum, paid just after this.[238] Mrs Orm had money for her niece in Louvain, and it is somewhat bizarre to read that not only did she not know Strickland's address to make the payment but that the convent in Louvain did not know her address either, especially as in a letter three months later Tunstall certainly knew that the lady lived in Greenwich.[239] Whole letters could be filled with nothing but demands for information about receipt of expected moneys.[240] We do not know what answer Strickland gave to Tunstall's over-optimistic suggestion that he should give a note to persons paying money for the convent which they could then send on to Louvain so that the house would be able to draw the money sooner.[241]

Mention has already been made of Tunstall's tendency to overdraw on the account with Strickland to gain foreign exchange advantages. This habit was more generally prevalent, she frequently raising a note upon him for money supposedly paid to him without the knowledge that funds to cover the note were there.[242] Although, on occasion, others protested

---

[233] *Blount MSS, C* 64/173: CT to MS, 4 January 1739 (NS).

[234] *Blount MSS, C* 64/176: CT to MS, 31 January 1739 (NS).

[235] *Blount MSS, C* 64/ 83–4: CT to MS, 30 March and 20 April 1734 (NS).

[236] *Blount MSS, C* 64/84: CT to MS, 20 April 1734 (NS).

[237] *Blount MSS, C* 64/97: CT to MS, 1 February 1735 (NS).

[238] *Blount MSS, D* 31: Strickland's account book with St Monica's, Louvain, fol. 55, receipt entry for 17 February 1735 (OS).

[239] *Blount MSS, C* 64/99: CT to MS, 29 March 1735 (NS); *C* 64/103: CT to MS, 21 June 1735 (NS).

[240] *Blount MSS, C* 64/101: CT to MS, 17 May 1735 (NS).

[241] *Blount MSS, C* 64/182: CT to MS, 23 June 1739 (NS).

[242] *Blount MSS, C* 64/81: CT to MS, 6 March 1734 (NS).

the notes and refused payment, Strickland himself seems always to have obliged, even at disadvantage to himself, as his wife was most eager to point out:

> [even if he had been out of town] nothing would have been neglected in your affairs for he is a Person of such strict Justice & Honour that I am sure no body ever sufferd through his fault, and I believe Madam very few to be found if any that duse as he has often dun to do Honour to your Bills paying Money out of his one [own] Pocket when you have drawn before he has receved the Sumes you have drawn for Peoppel often send you word the[y] have paid Mr Strick[land] when those payments are in Bills & not be receved some times in thurty days after & then with a great deal of trouble this I know becaus I have after Mr Strick[land] has been out of town severall times Payed your bills before I have had Monny such care he has allways taken not to disopint you I wish our Payments would be payd when due but mony in some Peopels hands is hard to be got out I must do Mr Strick[land] this justis as to say his Character was before I was Married just as I see & those that know him have always found the advantage of being in his hands & the diferance of his usage from others. I have been 17 years his Wife & his Merits dayly increase my admiration & respect for him & tho he dont writ Madame so often as you would have him I am sure I may say he writts as often as he can do you any service.[243]

Although Strickland seems in almost all cases to have honoured bills from these convents there is evidence of at least one case when he did not, only to receive a repeated request from Cecily Tunstall to honour a bill not quite covered by funds which she believed in his hands, for

> I'm in great want of money & am dun'd on all sides & know not what way to turn me to get supplys corn Butter flesh & all things are so excessively dear that if we have not ready money we can't live on credit … I don't hear the like scarceity from any Letter out of England except my 2 Cousen Willowbeys who of all others I fancy have the least reason to complain who are single women & have good fortunes & I only look on it as an excuse for their not having paid theyr Cousen's pension in time.[244]

Strickland had to lecture Tunstall on the drawing of bills. He complained to her about those drawn at two days' sight, particularly those predicated on funds which he might have received on longer dates, and she agreed to draw on him at least at eight days' sight. She demurred, however, at the drawing of really long-dated bills, for the specific reason that they 'may not sell so well … for they desire always speedy payment'.[245] As proof of her point she cited Mr Wollascott's bill, given to her at twenty

---

[243] *Blount MSS, C* 64/143: copy reply, Mrs Strickland to CT, in CT to Mrs Strickland, 19 May 1737 (NS).
[244] *Blount MSS, C* 64/206: CT to MS, 25 October 1740 (NS).
[245] *Blount MSS, C* 64/167: CT to MS, 22 August 1738 (NS).

days' sight, '& it is now a month since it was presented & no payment so that 'tis in danger to be protested'.[246]

A mixture of different days' sight of bills was particularly attractive in the context of foreign exchange transactions when exchange rates were good, and for this reason Tunstall ignored Strickland's instructions on one occasion, sending a mixture of bills at three, ten, twelve and twenty days' sight in the belief that this would give them the best return.[247]

## OVER-REACHING AMBITION

Strickland set a low value on the level of administrative competence in these communities and was openly critical of the succession at Louvain following the death from a stroke of the Prioress in November 1733; Tunstall expressed surprise that he had 'so mean an opinion of our family to think we are not better provided with one fit to succeed our D[ea]r deceased Lady'.[248] The choice of this much-vaunted successor fell on the cousin of the previous Prioress, Cecily More of Kirklington in Yorkshire, sister of the Dominican Provincial Thomas Worthington, of a Heneage cousin of Tunstall and of a nun in Rouen – narrow circles indeed. Nothing in the correspondence gives a clear indication of More's competence, but she would appear to have been the source of a most ambitious and unrealistic venture, a substantial building project for a church which the community wanted to pursue even without adequate resources, justifying it by the shortage of space in their existing buildings.[249] In November 1738 they tried hard to call in all outstanding debts urgently as they had 'begun a work in our Church which requires ready money' and 'we want money very much at present towards building, or rather repairing our Church'.[250]

The Louvain canonesses were forbidden to spend their principal, leaving them with no other means of raising funds than to collect arrears. They made the desperate need of funding for the church the main reason for their frantic efforts to get their hands on Lettis Wybarne's legacy. When they realised that this was not immediately forthcoming, they applied pressure to Strickland to recover other long-standing but problematic debts:[251] 'some way or other we must have money or else we can't go forward with the Church which occasion when lost can't be recovered

---

246 *Blount MSS, C* 64/167: CT to MS, 22 August 1738 (NS).
247 *Blount MSS, C* 64/185: CT to MS, 12 October 1739 (NS).
248 *Blount MSS, C* 64/77: CT to MS, 12 December 1733 (NS).
249 *Blount MSS, C* 64/181: CT to MS, 2 June 1739 (NS).
250 *Blount MSS, C* 64/170–1: CT to MS, 7 and 24 November 1738.
251 *Blount MSS, C* 64/179: CT to MS, 26 March 1739 (NS).

without immense cost'.[252] The ladies of Louvain, having got themselves
into a fine mess over this ill-conceived project, expected Strickland to
get them out, blaming all their troubles on Lord Petre's failure to pay (or
that of Strickland to extract from him) money due on Radclyffe family
support for the convent. They had rashly depended on these particular
sources of funding so far as to have run themselves considerably into
debt on the work on the church. They should not have done this, as they
were strictly forbidden to spend any principal and their annual revenues
were too small. They had compounded their troubles by buying wood for
which they were unable to pay and needed to raise over £200 towards
more than £300 lent them by a friend in order to pay the workmen.[253]

## OTHER ISSUES

Other problems could occur in the convent on which Strickland's advice
was crucial. When Isabella Smith fell ill with smallpox at Louvain, she
was due for payment of a bill from Mr Eyre drawn on the goldsmith-
banker Anthony Wright of Covent Garden, money for which she and the
convent were, as usual, desperate. Strickland was asked to resolve the
dilemma: the convent would not let her endorse the bill for health and
hygiene reasons, and he was to ask either Eyre or Wright if they would
permit Mrs Tunstall to do so on her behalf.[254]

Dealing with executors was regarded as Strickland's responsibility.
Thus Tunstall forwarded orders to contact the executors of a Mr Green
whose daughter was a member of their order, so that she could receive
her legacy.[255] On another occasion he was instructed to ask Morgan
Hansbie in their name for £150, for 'which he as Executor to the late
Mrs Thorald has power to act for us', they being fearful that any delay
would caused them to lose the legacy.[256] He was also asked to act for
executors, as for Dame Cecily More, Superior at Louvain, who was
named as executrix to Mrs Mary Worthington and empowered him to
act for her after advice taken from Morgan Hansbie.[257]

The sheer volume of trivial matters loaded onto Strickland, especially
by Tunstall, was clearly irksome to him, but he was often the only means
by which certain things could be arranged or certain information obtained.
Tunstall wanted information on the whereabouts of her nieces (daughters of her brother Cuthbert Constable), who were due to come over

---

[252] *Blount MSS, C* 64/184: CT to MS, 11 September 1739 (NS).
[253] *Blount MSS, C* 64/190: CT to MS, 27 January 1740 (NS).
[254] *Blount MSS, C* 64/126: CT to MS, 19 September 1736 (NS).
[255] *Blount MSS, C* 64/86: CT to Mrs Strickland, 1 [10?] May 1734 (NS).
[256] *Blount MSS, C* 64/106: CT to MS, 30 August 1735 (NS).
[257] *Blount MSS, C* 64/153: CT to MS, 6 December 1737 (NS).

to Louvain; she also wanted Thomas Day, the messenger who appears particularly to have overseen movements of Catholics between England and the Continent, informed of their coming and wanted the nieces to bring over various impedimenta required by the convent, including a French grammar.[258] Day further had to take steps to recover a coffee mill abandoned by a Mrs Primer in Bruges for unclear reasons, she 'not daring to bring it'.[259]

Strickland was required to ensure that precise rules were followed in order to satisfy customs regulations. In 1735 Mr Burgis failed to send the books for Louvain with exact itemised prices and to do so via the London corresponding merchant Samuel Grimes to Louvain's broker-merchant contact Mme Broeta in Antwerp. Having heard that the books had been put into the 'Children's Box' unpriced and unannounced, along with children's clothes (for which the individual prices were given), the nuns had good reason to fear that if more was put in a box 'than the marchands has notice of', the senders forfeited 'their veracity'; a previous consignment with an extra knife and fork had caused trouble at Antwerp. If these things were not declared at Antwerp with prices, they could all be confiscated, to the convent's loss, for which they made it abundantly clear that Strickland would be held to blame.[260]

Even favours could become burdensome. The sending to Strickland of some cambric which his wife wanted produced endless complications.[261] Tunstall was still asking many months later if Mrs Strickland had yet received it.[262] It did not stop him, however, hazarding a request to Louvain for some lace, which he mistakenly believed they made but which they promised to order for him from the lace merchant in Brussels.[263] Nor was he dissuaded from asking Tunstall for a further delivery of black cambric for his wife for deep mourning late in 1737, about a year after the death of his mother[264] (and therefore presumably either for a close relative of his wife or for one of his Mannock kin).[265] He should, however, have known better, since it never came. Tunstall arranged that it would be sent through their regular merchant contact, Mme Broeta in Antwerp, and for customs dues to be paid on it.[266] Broeta did not send it until February, to her London contact Samuel Grimes, whereupon it

[258] *Blount MSS, C* 64/71–4: CT to MS, 18 and 21 August, 11 and 25 September 1733 (NS).
[259] *Blount MSS, C* 64/64: CT to MS, 25 September 1733 (NS).
[260] *Blount MSS, C* 64/100: CT to MS, 15 April 1735 (NS).
[261] *Blount MSS, C* 64/88: CT to MS, 7 August 1734 or 1735 (NS).
[262] *Blount MSS, C* 64/121: CT to MS, [18 May 1736 (NS)?].
[263] *Blount MSS, C* 64/152: CT to MS, 11 November 1737 (NS).
[264] *Blount MSS, C* 64/128–9: CT to MS, 2 and 16 November 1736 (NS); letter of condolences followed by an announcement of masses to be said for her soul.
[265] *Blount MSS, C* 64/154: CT to MS, 16 December 1737 (NS).
[266] *Blount MSS, C* 64/155: CT to MS, 29 December 1737 (NS).

disappeared.[267] By the time Grimes found it, it was too late to be of use to the Stricklands.[268] It remains clear, however, that the Stricklands never got it and that probably Grimes never did either, since in July Tunstall wrote complaining to Mme Broeta of the failure, which she eventually ascribed to theft.[269]

Other orders in reverse for fabric sent through Strickland were obviously connected with crafts practised in the convent to earn it money. The making of lace has been mentioned above; Strickland was also asked to accept and pass on to the canonesses via Peggy Cholmeley a parcel of old cambrics for making flowers promised to Mrs Crathorne by her aunt Cockaine.[270] The route taken by some items, via Strickland, was sometimes surprising: a parcel of sheets was sent from Bruges to him for Mrs Ledger, and he was asked to forward it to Mrs Johnson in Louvain.[271]

Medicines were also ordered through Strickland. Mrs Orm was procuring for the Louvain community a salt bottle, which Strickland was to send at the very first opportunity.[272] Mrs Johnson asked him to get and send over a salve 'or something of that nature'.[273] And he was asked to pay a Mr Williams for 'drugs & Gumbs he sent' via the Louvain convent's servant Nicolas, and Mr Collingwood for some indigo.[274] Strickland cannot have been pleased by requests to sort out confusion over orders for spectacles for Tunstall and Mrs Johnson, sent out by him (having received them from Mr Burgis and having in turn passed them on to Peggy Cholmeley for dispatch) to a Mr Porter in Bruges under instructions passed through him; they took six months to arrive, and then they could not tell which of two orders they represented.[275] Strickland then received instructions for the order of two more pairs, one for each of the two ladies.[276] On another occasion, a watch was ordered through him for Mrs Eyre.[277]

---

[267] *Blount MSS, C* 64/156: CT to MS, 25 February 1738 (NS); *C* 64/157: CT to MS, 27 March 1738 (NS).
[268] *Blount MSS, C* 64/158–9 and 161: CT to MS, 4 and 18 April and 13 May 1738 (NS).
[269] *Blount MSS, C* 64/164–6: CT to MS, 4, 7 and 17 July 1738 (NS).
[270] *Blount MSS, C* 64/157 and 161: CT to MS, 27 March and 13 May 1738 (NS).
[271] *Blount MSS, C* 64/116: CT to MS, 7 November 1741 (NS).
[272] *Blount MSS, C* 64/119: CT to MS, 1 May 1736 (NS).
[273] *Blount MSS, C* 64/214–15: CT to MS, 19 May and 6 June 1741 (NS).
[274] *Blount MSS, C* 64/226 and 231: CT to MS, 7 November 1741 and 24 January 1742 (NS).
[275] *Blount MSS, C* 64/117: CT to MS, 6 March 1736 (NS).
[276] *Blount MSS, C* 64/120: CT to MS, 25 May 1736 (NS).
[277] *Blount MSS, C* 64/217: CT to MS, 17 July 1741 (NS).

**The Spellikens**

One of the most troubled convents was that of the Spellikens, the Dominican nuns in Brussels. Strickland's correspondent was the Yorkshire-born Procuratrix, Sr Margaret Xaviera Ellerker, who wrote to him on financial matters from the time of his succeeding the secular priest Morgan Hansbie in February 1727/8 until her death in 1736.[278] The connection was cemented by Strickland's sending his son Thomas there to be educated.

## INVESTMENTS

The correspondence with the convents has two main themes. As demonstrated above, the most frequent is that of obtaining money due to members of the communities who were being supported at the convents' expense. This was why they employed Strickland. In theory, the main financing of the convents was effected through investment of the portions of the women entering these institutions, an activity which Strickland took over in 1733 from his banker uncle Daniel Arthur, though he was advising the Spellikens as early as 1730 when he found an investment at five per cent for them for the £200 portion of Sr Mary Cecily Polhampton (1707–46).[279] Sr Ursula Coleman (1667–1733) had 2,000 guilders of her portion of 3,500 guilders invested through Arthur with the Duke of Powis until the Duke paid the principal in 1734, when it realised £1,040; Strickland then invested £1,000 of this money with Lord Petre from 1737 to 1739 at four per cent, which he then transferred to Lord Arundell at the same rate. Of the remaining money, 500 guilders (the usual sum) went on her clothing and pension, and, in her case, 600 guilders was invested elsewhere and the convent was forced to use 400 guilders for clothing for Sr Isabella Hansby (1662–1734).[280]

Catherine Thorold, aunt of Sr Catherine Winefrid Hyde (1698–1752), left her niece £125 to bring her complete fortune up to £295, this final sum being invested by Strickland on Mr Paston's estate at five per cent.[281] From the portion of Sr Margaret Mary Agnes Short, 3,000 guilders were

---

[278] 'Hansbie, Morgan Joseph', in *DNB*, vol. 8, p. 1193; Gillow, vol. 3, pp. 112–13. Hansbie (1673–1750) was a Dominican friar and chaplain to the Spellikens in 1708 (Gillow has 'Benedictine', surely in error). In 1712 he was vice-rector and in 1717 rector of the Dominican College, Louvain, provincial in 1721, prior of Bornhem in 1728, vicar-provincial for Belgium in 1728, and then 1738–42 and in 1747 vicar-provincial in England, chaplain to Lady Petre at Cheam 1743. He was 'a hearty Jacobite' (Gillow), 'an ardent Jacobite' (*DNB*).
[279] 'Records of the Dominican Nuns', pp. 213 and 231. It is uncertain whether the proposal was followed, since the records also refer to its investment at 3.5% in the City of Brussels.
[280] Ibid., p. 206.
[281] Ibid., p. 212.

also invested in Paston's estate at the same rate in 1736.[282] Part of the smaller portion of her younger sister Sr Mary Ursula Short was drawn over to Brussels to form part of an investment placed at four per cent at Hainault by the nuns through their local banker John Nettine.[283] The portion of Sr Mary Francis Segrave was split, 2,100 guilders being invested at four-and-a-half per cent with Mrs Kingsdon in 1735 and 590 guilders on Lady Carington's estates at four per cent in 1738.[284]

All of these investments were made in the properties of Strickland's existing clients. Not only were portions invested, but 'actions' (shares) were occasionally assigned as a source of income on the arrival of newcomers, and investments were more commonly in English land than in that of the Low Countries. One portion (that of Sr Ellerker herself) consisted in part of a stock of 700 copies of a book entitled *The Reformation Judged* and the brass plate for printing copies of *The Tree of Life*, which were to be sold.[285]

Other money was due to the community as a whole and also proved difficult to obtain. In the first surviving letter, Sr Ellerker refers to problems over a bond intended to secure a 'perpetual rent' which they wished to increase in size to achieve a greater income by adding in arrears due for several years, to bring the bond value up to £1,000 (Strickland himself contributed £5 3s 11d to make the total up to £1,040).[286] This may have been due from the Duke of Powis – the bond being referred to as 'at 5 per: Cent in his Graces hands'[287] – since there are several subsequent mentions of difficulties in obtaining money due from him. The nuns preferred 'to continue the Money in the same Famely; if Mrs Attmoors is added to the Capitall of the Bond', but Strickland was to satisfy himself that he had 'security to your likeing'.[288]

The overriding concern was that 'the Income be regularly paid up every halfe year';[289] small wonder, when the last income from this source had been received in March 1715, apart from £100 in 1720 and £20 in 1725. Ellerker calculated that fourteen years' interest at £40 per annum were then due (March 1727/8) – £560 in all. The nuns' difficulties in obtaining this money had forced them into using capital.[290] The go-between in these dealings was their long-standing intermediary Morgan Hansbie,

---

[282]  Ibid., pp. 213–14 and 232.
[283]  Ibid., p. 214.
[284]  Ibid.
[285]  Guilday, p. 418 (where she is not named).
[286]  *Blount MSS, C* 41/172: MXE to MS, [October? 1728] (Strickland answered it 11 October 1728).
[287]  Ibid.
[288]  *Blount MSS, C* 41/171: MXE to MS, 4 February 1728 (NS?).
[289]  Ibid.
[290]  *Blount MSS, C* 41/172: MXE to MS, [October? 1728].

who was closely familiar with their financial arrangements. But it was mainly Strickland who had to prise out recalcitrant debtors.[291] There was also an implied rebuke to Strickland in a later letter, showing that Sr Ellerker was well informed about Powis's finances and maybe even implying that Strickland was not being firm enough with the Duke.[292]

Instances of investments in bonds are common. For example, Miss Segrave had an annuity from Mr Shevereux (presumably Devereux) payable half-yearly and secured by bond:[293]

> I have orders from our Governes to enquire what Money hath been paid to your hand for Mrs Segrave's use (who's Grandmother Lady O'Neal I believe you might know) Mr. Mening [Melling?] last post writ to the young Lady saying he had paid a sum of Money to you for her, but never mentioned what it was; our agreement for Mis's fortune was 350 pound sterling and 25 for her weding close exchange and if you've reced: I shall be glad to draw a bill for the 25. the 350 we all desire you will endeavour to place at Intrist if you have prospect off doing it soon if not we eare advised to draw it over the Change going well.[294]

Strickland placed Miss Segrave's fortune within two months of the request on advantageous terms, as the next letter reports,

> so quickly and at so high intrest which indeed is a great service to us; Mr Hansbie thinks it best to be Declared in Trust for Mrs: Ann Chilton Residing at Bruxelles in the Par[ish] of St: Gudelay [Gudule].[295]

Strickland also managed to place Mrs Chilton's fortune with some speed; indeed he was asked to add some other sums to it to make a more attractive investment (it is possible that he may have suggested such a tactic). He was involved in transactions intended to circumvent the prevailing high interest rates on foreign exchange:

> 'twas most agreeable news to Mrs: Chilton … that you'l have so soon a good occation of putting out the Money which is a very great Kindness to us: you may be sure of 600 pound before Chrismas this is to advertize you, when you please, you may Receive 380 pounds of Mr: Samuel Grimes Banker in London: it must be demanded in the name of Mr: John Baptist Vannuffle Merchant of Lace in Brussels he having given his order this post to Mr: Grimes to pay the said Summ to you, or your order; when you have acqua[in]ted me with the Receit of it, I shall pay the equivalant to Mr: Vannuffle here.
>
> Wee have a Capitall that was paid inn at Bridges in the hand of Lady Lucy Herbert of 220 pound, which I have writ this post to desire her Ladyship it might be returnd [i.e. paid as foreign exchange] to you as soon as possible. These 2 Som's [I] mention makes up six hundred. and if Mrs Andrew pays

---

[291] *Blount MSS, C* 41/173: MXE to MS, 12 June 1733.
[292] *Blount MSS, C* 41/188: MXE to MS, 23 June 1736 (NS).
[293] *Blount MSS, C* 41/183: MXE to MS, 16 February 1735 (NS).
[294] *Blount MSS, C* 41/175: MXE to MS, 30 June 1734 (NS).
[295] *Blount MSS, C* 41/176: MXE to MS, 24 August 1734 (NS).

you 50 you may add that to the six hundred. if you shood prevail with the Duke [of Powis] for all the Arrears (which is more than to be hoped for) wee might add 50 more and make it up to 700.

However, even when such agreements had apparently been success-fully made, they did not always work effectively, and Strickland was then required to chase them:

> I think [Mr Hansbie] told me he advised Sir with you about a life Rent of 10 pound a year that hath three years in arrears Left by Mr: Coalman to his Daughter, that Setled here; and gave us some hopes of your geting the Money for us.[296]

Investments often had to be made up from a large number of small elements to achieve a sum which Strickland could usefully place. A lot of work was involved, as well as considerable uncertainty as to whether the money to be invested would all materialise to match the client seeking such an investment. Some idea of the amount of work involved can be gained from a statement such as this:

> A letter ten days agoe from Mr: Hansbie gave account he had pd you £20: and said he had 25 more (that he prevaild to have for our Sister Catherin Hide) at our appointment I answerd without loosing a post, desird he wood turn all the Plat Rivers to Run into your hand; he had yours writ to Mrs Andrews for £30 she shood a paid long agoe, least that shoud not do: R[everend] Mo[ther] writ to her this post & desird without delay the 30 p[ounds] might be paid to you or Mr: Hansbie I believe it won't fail nor the 10 from Mrs: Hide, if so, with the £10 you had from Mr: Paston as I take it makes 195 p: added to the 380 comes to 575. If Mr: Hansbie hath any to return perhaps you may have of him 25p: to make up the £600.[297]

Strickland appears to have been particularly successful in raising invest-ment money, unless Sr Ellerker has misunderstood him when expressing her puzzlement:

> [I] can't comprehend how you have so much money of ours as you mention to put out viz first to Mr: Kingsdon 291 the 3d of March laste. Secondly yours of the 12 of September, just before you went out of Town, Acquants us, with your puting out for us 400 (upon the same security of the 1040) at 5 p cent, the securety you mention to take date the 14 of June 1735: accordingly I Regestered those tow in our Rentall, according to your computation then, there was due to you for balance £32 4s 2d. In your last you speak of £200 to Mr. Paston the 4 of June, and £200 to Mr. Warpole, the 4 of September, and mark to your selfe only £58 16s 10d for Balance: tho' you'v Received neither of the £50: belonging to Mis Nutte Short, nor the Intrist from his Grace; nor

---

[296] *Blount MSS, C* 41/177: MXE to MS, 20 November 1734 (NS).
[297] *Blount MSS, C* 41/179: MXE to MS, 23 December 1734 (NS).

do you mention £10 Mrs: Andrews was to pay October last; give me leave to repeat again I can't Imagin where you had so much Money of ours.[298]

Ellerker stated baldly that 'I hate publick funds'.[299] The preferred loan targets were Catholic gentry and nobility, through loans and mortgages upon land and property. It would appear, however, that Strickland did not always choose them, and that the convent expressed their desires in such matters on occasion:

> Last June wee Lent 500 pound to Edward Dicconson Esqr of Rightington in Lankeshire, a worthy Catholick and good Estate for four per cent exchange, wee had a writing drawn here, our security is upon a farm he boat [bought] for 12 pound, which is not in any Setelment, he's now in England and designs to be back before Chrismass in his return promised to waite upon you to have our Security drawn as you judge proper: if you have any papers or Coppyes to send over to us, he's a very secure hand.[300]

Unfortunately, such unilateralism could result in bad law, and Strickland appears in this case to have issued something of a rebuke to Sr Ellerker, who replied: 'I've not yet seen Mr. Dicieson; but will be sure to observe your kind advice, and press for the Deeds being sent to you to draw securety according to agreement'.[301]

## INCOME FROM ADMISSIONS

One further source of income was from the admission of new ladies to the convent: '[I] hope e'r long Sir to repay what we are indebted [to you], being to receive 40 pound this month, for a Lady that hath put on our Livery a few days agoe'.[302] Indeed, the convents appear to have taken on members only if finance were promised or available to support them:

> A deserving young gentlewoman that's engaged wth us in the Novit[iate] hath the mismortune [misfortune] to hear of her Father's Death, Mr. Short of Berry [i.e. Bury St Edmunds]. Her fortune £300, was Left her by her Gran Mother Short, Conditionally, if she live to be of Age, if not 'twas to fall among her brothers and sisters; and the Intrist 15 a year, to be paid her, till she posess the Capital; upon this Condition, wee received her with the promiss of our having Sufficient Security, before her Prof[ession] which now draws near. If you please Sir to discover this Affair with Mr: Bostock Merser that maryed her Aunt, and procure such Security as you judge proper, with which all here will be well Satisfied, if the said Security is not Setled in six weeks, she will

---

[298] *Blount MSS, C* 41/187: MXE to MS, 25 January 1736 (NS).
[299] *Blount MSS, C* 41/188: MXE to MS, 23 June 1736 (NS).
[300] *Blount MSS, C* 41/186: MXE to MS, 9 November 1735 (NS).
[301] *Blount MSS, C* 41/187: MXE to MS, 25 January 1736 (NS).
[302] *Blount MSS, C* 41/172: MXE to MS, [October? 1728].

be forced to defer her wedding day, which she's very worthy off, and it will be a great mortification to the ferverous young Lady to have it put off.[303]

## Non-payment of funds

Personal suffering and hardship to sisters appears to have followed non-payment of funds to individuals such as Mrs Power Daly, for whom Strickland was pursuing arrears of payment and of whom it was said that 'shee hath sufferd much with great patience, Humillity and Christian Currage'.[304] Strickland was able to report success in obtaining Mrs Daly's arrears, although he and the convent clearly expected that he would have to find means to pursue it whenever the annuity became due.[305] She continued to be harassed by her nephew in Ireland, John Coleman, who asked her to assign to him the money she expected for her arrears in the belief that she had some control over Irish funds which Coleman could not get but wanted her to depend on, presumably as an alternative to English funds to which he was looking for relief. Sr Ellerker, in asking Strickland on Mrs Daly's behalf to 'put a stop to her nephew Coalman takeing that money', sent a copy of both Coleman's latest letter to his aunt and the postscript of another related letter, which offers some perspective:

> Dear Aunt,
> I received your letter, not much to the purpose. For what I writ is true; and if you won't consent, must take some. But as I told, you shall have it out of Ireland. But that you shan't want shall have a hundred here at present, and the rest soon, if you will send me an answer if you will agree,
> From your affectionate Nephew J. Coleman.
> Postscript: If you don't answer to what I write, must stop all. For charity begins at home.
> A Copy of the Postscript of Mr. Edmond Flanagan's Letter, dated Carrowreague, Jan: the 13th. 1734–5.
> I can assure you, Mr Greene, in the Memory of the oldest Man on Earth, Mony was not seen so scarce in this nation, as now it is. No Buying of any Thing, excepting Eatables. All Farmers are broke. All the poor People daily going a begging, God knows where to find it. Estated Men daily pressed by their Creditors. In short no Mony.[306]

Strickland was to prepare a letter of attorney authorising him to act for Mrs Daly, and was sending it to her for signature, so that he could deal with the matter, of which nothing further is mentioned.

---

303 *Blount MSS*, C 41/174: MXE to MS, 7 November 1733 (NS).

304 *Blount MSS*, C 41/179: MXE to MS, 23 December 1734 (NS).

305 *Blount MSS*, C 41/181: MXE to MS, 29 December 1734 (NS).

306 *Blount MSS*, C 41/184: copy letter, John Coleman to Madam Power Daly, 17 February 1735, in MXE to MS, 9 March 1735 (NS).

Miss Short's money, part of which was in East India Company bonds, was to prove particularly troublesome, not to mention money due for her two sisters, who also entered the convent and had similar expectations and for whom Strickland was asked in due course to make similar agreements to that here requested for the elder sister:[307]

> we have not heard from Mr: Hansbie since the 27 of May. He then told us you and Mr: Bostock was agreed about the £300 for Miss Short we understood you to have dominion off. We have a third, in order to setle here, a Lady of your Acquantance Mrs Andrews, in part provides for; which money she may pay you for us you'l pleas to Receive; I believe she will pay 50 pound for Sr Yates before the Middle of August, another 100 she's to give; that will I think be paid yearly till 'tis out.[308]

The agreement was formally drawn up, doubtless prepared by Strickland himself, as a later letter shows:

> I was favour'd with yours of the 25 p[en]ult and the 6th instanter with the Copy of the Agreement with Mr. Bostock which seems very Consciencious and clear both as to him and us: we are much oblig'd to you for it ...[309]

The money for Sr Ann Coalman proved similarly difficult to obtain. She had died on 7 February 1733, with the legacy from her father, in the form of a lifetime annuity, unpaid. The convent wanted Strickland to claim this on their behalf, but such a situation was particularly unlikely to result in payment from the father's executors.[310] The Grimes–Vannuffle transaction presented further difficulties, as Strickland reported. There was clearly little he could do short of referring the whole matter back to the originator:

> Mr: Vannuffle seem's as much Concernd and Surprizd as I, that Mr. Grimes did not pay the 380 pound upon your demand. He hath repeated his orders to him this post warmly, not to fail the payment of the said sum to you. Am sorry for the trouble it gives you.[311]

Some idea of the complications which Strickland was expected to handle is revealed in the subsequent history of this transaction. Vannuffle appears to have been unconventional in his dealings, and the nuns called the transaction off for a while after a second round of difficulties:

> I was ... heartily Mortified at the trouble you had in twice demanding the Money of Grimes and the Confusion to you and my self in the disapointment of puting it out: I never had such a blunder in all the time we had done

---

[307] *Blount MSS, C* 41/185: MXE to MS, 4 June 1735 (NS).
[308] *Blount MSS, C* 41/175: MXE to MS, 30 June 1734 (NS).
[309] *Blount MSS, C* 41/176: MXE to MS, 24 August 1734 (NS). The agreement does not survive.
[310] *Blount MSS, C* 41/182: MXE to MS, 26 January 1735 (NS).
[311] *Blount MSS, C* 41/179: MXE to MS, 23 December 1734 (NS).

> business; Mr: Vannuffle is the person above this 20 years wee always have recourse to in all our Affairs for Assistance or advise, but I always thought there was in this some sort of shouffleing, and wondered why he did not according to the Common way of exchange he gave me a Bill to send to you …: the Change is now so high the Banqueers here Mr: Decleve, and likewise Mr: Nettine I've try'd em both now demand for the returning £380 thirty five pounds 12 shill 10d, which is so prodigious a loss upon that sum, as wood take two years income of the said sum to make good …[312]

The nuns then decided, when interest rates on foreign exchange dropped sharply the following month, that they wished Strickland to invest the money, which they transmitted.[313]

## EMERGENCY FUNDRAISING

The finances of the convent were not proof against sudden emergencies, and at such times the pressure on Strickland to raise resources increased beyond its usual already considerable level:

> Wee have an unexpected expence come upon us by the late great Tempest wee have an incloster wall bloun doun to the ground, and another Incloser wall a great breach in it few escaped some damage, many have much greater than wee, thank God tho' it fell in the Street no body was hurt wee got it made up with deal and Post, till the season to Build.[314]

Strickland was expected to support the nuns' efforts at fundraising in such a crisis, although their ideas of a source of such income were hardly encouraging in the light of all too familiar previous experiences: 'Wee writ to [the] D[uke of] P[owis] very very pressingly upon the fall of our walls, & L[a]d[y] Lucy the same, and I'm shure your endeavours & Mr: Hansbies will be added'.[315] For once, all this persuasion worked:

> I was … exceeding glad to find the D[uke] had cleard all the Intrist. The great expence of Rebilding our Incloser wall, that was bloun down by the great wind last January, forces me to draw upon you for 125 pound I gave a bill in favour of Mrs: Broeta of Antwerp.[316]

## STRICKLAND AND ELLERKER

Strickland's services to the community appear to have depended solely on the personal connection of a member with himself. By June 1736 Ellerker had held the office of Procuratrix for fifteen years, had been ill

---

312 *Blount MSS, C* 41/182: MXE to MS, 26 January 1735 (NS).
313 *Blount MSS, C* 41/183: MXE to MS, 16 February 1735 (NS).
314 *Blount MSS, C* 41/182: MXE to MS, 26 January 1735 (NS).
315 *Blount MSS, C* 41/183: MXE to MS, 16 February 1735 (NS).
316 *Blount MSS, C* 41/185: MXE to MS, 4 June 1735 (NS).

for seven months and was due, if she lived that long, to come to the end of her period of office in September of the following year.[317] The letters abruptly stop after a scrawled final letter from Sr Ellerker, which reads:

> please to pay to Mr: Hansbie three Gynney: and at the time most proper to take out the 300 out of the Bank of England Mrs Andrews hath promised £50. I am so ill I can't write but always
>
> Sir
>> your most humble servant
>> Margaret Xa Ellerker[318]

The handwriting, always that of an elderly woman, has disintegrated, and one must assume that she was dying. With her died Strickland's business for the convent of the Spellikens, always problematic and scarcely financially rewarding, but only ever conceivable on the basic premise that his clientele and the supporters of the convent were one and the same. It is unlikely that, given the circumstances clear from the correspondence, any representative would produce results which could ever be regarded as successful.

How successful was Strickland? Was Ellerker truthful or flattering when she wrote:

> Mr: Ha[n]sbie told me in his last you was out of Town he wanted to give you more money for us, that he had in his hand, and had more to Receive then, wee never had so good fortune in our lives; and Atribute a great part of it to your Charitable kind care and Conduct in puting out Money for us, which other ways wood lye dead; wee are so helpless in such Affairs; wee can never sufficiently pray for you, and yours, nor express how Infinitly wee are obliged to you.[319]

### 'Doubly dead'

The Flanders religious houses were in a precarious position, and not just financially. When Michael Blount II attempted in 1748 to raise funds for the English Carthusians, his petition on their behalf (although not successful enough to save them) typified the problems under which these houses laboured – problems evident in Strickland's dealings too.

English religious all suffered from both legal and physical isolation, which was even more acute in the case of the women than the men. Ellerker said: 'You know wee are dubbly Dead to the Law: being pa[pists] & R[eligious]'.[320] They were unable to have recourse to English law, being

---

[317] *Blount MSS*, C 41/188: MXE to MS, 23 June 1736 (NS).
[318] *Blount MSS*, C 41/193: MXE to MS, 21 December 1736 (NS). See Fig. 5.
[319] *Blount MSS*, C 41/185: MXE to MS, 4 June 1735 (NS).
[320] *Blount MSS*, C 41/172: MXE to MS, [October? 1728].

debarred from suing in the courts to obtain redress as both Catholics and exiles. Both the penal laws concerning Catholics and the principle of the geographic extent of the applicability of English common law put them beyond the pale, and those who sent their offspring abroad to be educated were breaking the law.

Communication with England further sharpened their sense of isolation. Tunstall frequently complained about Strickland's failure to answer letters or, when he did, of his failure to give her the information for which she had asked.[321] There were also frequent worries whether letters had miscarried, sometimes coupled with anguished insistence that she must know the contents of any letters during a period of suspected loss.[322] This sense of the fragility of communication was rife: a failure in the arrival of expected goods from Mr Burgis led to the fear that they had been lost 'in the last storm' and a frantic demand that Strickland contact him.[323] Or again, when she asked whether her last letter had reached him or was 'dip'ed in the sea as several we have had out of England has been of late Ostende having been almost drown'd?'[324]

Although he did not answer every letter, there is nothing to justify the criticism that Strickland hardly wrote or that he was tardy in replying – indeed, the evidence (from his own indications of his replies) is very much to the contrary. Tunstall could be an obsessive correspondent; Strickland only replied when he had something to communicate.

All of the convents held securities, some negotiated by Strickland, which were supposedly the basis of regular income. In 1743 £3,000 was held for the Spellekens (Duke of Powis: £1,000; Mr Kingdom: £291; Mr Paston: £200 and £500), nearly £10,000 for the ladies at Dunkirk (Mr Thornton: £7,000; Powis: £400; Mr Caryll: £200; Richard Jones: £350; Matthew Swinburne: 5,000 livres), and a set of hard-to-quantify securities for Louvain (Elizabeth Smith's settlement; Mr Spelman's security for £400; Strickland's declaration of trust to Elizabeth Smith; Mr Worthington's order; Winifred Hyde's bond; Mr Lythcot's bond and judgment; and securities for the lives of Isabella Smith, Winifred Bartlett and Charlott Stapylton).[325] All were a source of trouble for Strickland, since interest tended to be paid erratically or not at all and had to be chased.

---

[321] *Blount MSS, C* 64/81: CT to MS, 5 March 1734 (NS).

[322] *Blount MSS, C* 64/84 and 95: CT to MS, 20 April and 17 December 1734 (NS).

[323] *Blount MSS, C* 64/97: CT to MS, 1 February 1735 (NS).

[324] *Blount MSS, C* 64/118: CT to MS, 23 March 1736 (NS).

[325] *Blount MSS, D* 31, loose undated note to Henry Trubshaw, partly in Strickland's hand [1743].

## The nuns' tastes in reading

Books were frequently in request. Various people, including the Catholic booksellers Thomas Meighan and Francis Needham, bought them to order,[326] and Strickland had to arrange for them to be carried over by Thomas Day or by other less regular travellers with individually priced lists, both for customs purposes and for charging to those who had ordered them.[327]

There is some evidence of the nuns' preferred choices in the Louvain letters. The evidence is of course limited, but some hints may be given of the type of reading most popular with them. All the titles mentioned are in English; these titles in many cases survived in substantial numbers, suggesting widespread popularity of the works collected and used by the nuns; if they bought titles in other languages they are not mentioned in the letters. The range and identity of titles mentioned mirror the content of the Catholic gentry libraries known to the editor.

Bruges seems to have been a place for the abandonment of goods: not only a coffee mill but also books which Mrs Towneley was forced to leave there, with the loss of two primers which went missing. Strickland was required to instruct Day to find or replace them and obtain another devotional book.[328] Other instructions for book purchases were frequent, such as one for an 'Eye catechism for a little child' (price one shilling).[329]

Works of spiritual guidance were the most popular genre; several messages demanded a search for a second-hand copy of the hugely popular but out-of-print *Guía de Pecadores* (*Sinner's Guide*), first published in 1555 by the Dominican friar Luis de Granada (1505–88), a work marked by its elegant use of the Spanish language.[330] St Teresa of Avila claimed that Granada's *Guía* had converted over one million souls in her lifetime, and it was counted among their favourite spiritual books by her and such prominent figures as St John of the Cross, St François de Sales, St Charles Borromeo, St Vincent de Paul and St Rose of Lima. There were numerous editions in many languages. The first English translation, by Richard Meres, was published in 1614; it was printed in London by

---

[326] *Blount MSS, C* 64/174 CT to MS, January 1739 (Meighan); *C* 64/230 and 238: CT to MS, 8 January and 7 August 1742 (NS) (Needham).

[327] *Blount MSS, C* 64/74: CT to MS, 25 September 1733 (NS).

[328] *Blount MSS, C* 64/80, 81, 83 and 89: CT to MS, 22 January, 6 and 30 March and 17 August 1734 (NS).

[329] *Blount MSS, C* 64/85: CT to MS, 26 April 1734 (NS).

[330] *Blount MSS, C* 64/100, 107, 109, 120, 128, 144 and 150: CT to MS, 15 April, 2 September and 30 October 1735, 15 May and 2 November 1736, and 28 May and [7 October] 1737 (NS).

Richard Field for Edward Blount (STC S106491). Banks's *Art of the Love of God* appears to have been a work of similar character.[331]

Popularity would seem to be indicated by an order for two sets of Mr Dorrell's books,[332] and of the ubiquitous John Gother's *Books for the Sick*,[333] Bishop Richard Challoner's new *Think well on 't*,[334] a volume of *Litanies and Prayers*,[335] the *Pocket Manual* and *The Litanies of Jesus* (1720),[336] and one or two copies of *Bona Mors*, 'not the little Book but one made by a Jesuit which is as big as a Manuel but not so thick', which Tunstall thought was subtitled *A Pious Association for the Obtaining a Happy Death*.[337] Also ordered was a new *Life of Bishop Fisher*, presumably that by Thomas Bayly (for which Strickland was requested to subscribe on the nuns' behalf),[338] three sets of *Church Annals* due to be delivered to Strickland by the Catholic publisher Thomas Meighan,[339] three copies of St Augustine's *Confessions*,[340] the two-volume *Gospels and Epistles, Lessons, Collects and Graduals for all Sundays & Feasts in the whole Year*, in English,[341] a set of two English dictionaries ordered by different ladies,[342] and a list of ten books which Strickland was to inform their servant Nicolas where to buy (together with some cauliflower seed!),[343] besides many other mentions of parcels of books being sent or to be sent.[344]

Robert Persons (1546–1610), an Elizabethan Jesuit and the companion of Edmund Campion, was strongly influenced in his writings by Luis de Granada, and it is no surprise to see the nuns requesting his *Christian Directory, or Persons Resolutions* (otherwise known as *A Christian Directory, guiding Men to Eternall Salvation, Commonly Called the Resolution*), first published at St Omer by the English College Press

---

[331] *Blount MSS, C* 64/112: CT to MS, 30 November 1735 (NS). This title cannot so far be identified.

[332] *Blount MSS, C* 64/118: CT to MS, 23 March 1736 (NS). These are also unidentifiable.

[333] *Blount MSS, C* 64/150: CT to MS, 17 October 1737 (NS).

[334] *Blount MSS, C* 64/138, 144 and 156: CT to MS, 9 April and 28 May 1737 and 25 February 1738 (NS).

[335] *Blount MSS, C* 64/144: CT to MS, 28 May 1737 (NS).

[336] *Blount MSS, C* 64/141: CT to MS, 23 April 1737 (NS); *Pocket Manual* requested again in *C* 64/156: CT to MS, 25 February 1738 (NS).

[337] *Blount MSS, C* 64/156: CT to MS, 25 February 1738 (NS).

[338] *Blount MSS, C* 64/172: CT to MS, 9 December 1738 (NS).

[339] *Blount MSS, C* 64/180: CT to MS, 14 April 1739 (NS).

[340] *Blount MSS, C* 64/201: CT to MS, 26 August 1740 (NS).

[341] *Blount MSS, C* 64/208: CT to MS, 2 December 1740 (NS).

[342] *Blount MSS, C* 64/95: CT to MS, 17 December 1734 (NS).

[343] *Blount MSS, C* 64/222: CT to MS, 6 October 1741 (NS).

[344] *Blount MSS, C* 64/95: CT to MS, 17 December 1734 (NS).

in 1582 and subsequently much enlarged, as in the 1622 edition cited here (STC S114106).[345]

The convents were well informed of new publications: Tunstall was quick to criticise when her cousin and supplier Peggy Cholmeley sent John Gother's old *Practical Catechism* in place of a new one of the same title by her cousin Will Crathorne, which Strickland was required to get from him in Hammersmith since it was not yet with the booksellers.[346] In that same letter she refers to catalogues of books (presumably booksellers' lists), making it clear that this was their tool of selection. The influence of other communities made itself felt, as in the case of a Dublin publication of 1711, *A Short Treatise of the Antiquity, Institution, Excellency, Privileges, and Indulgences of the Famous Confraternity of our B. Lady of Mount Carmel. Commonly Called the Scapular* (ESTC T95185).[347]

As one might expect, requests for books of prayer and for liturgical works such as collects, epistles and gospels are frequent, but inaccurate citation makes some difficult to trace.[348] Some, such as *An Introduction to the Celebrated Devotion of the Holy Rosary*, a London publication by John Clarkson and sold by Thomas Meighan (ESTC T112630), were requested hot off the press in 1737 at one shilling a copy and sold in quantity (Louvain ordered six copies). Catechisms were also required; the similarity of this type of publication confused the nuns, who then asked for them by names of authors who had not even published them but whose other works they supported. The nuns' devotional regime is illustrated by requests for morning and night prayers and litanies, and some awareness of new publications of these is evident.

Classics such as the *Confessions* of St Augustine, the soon-to-be-classic first publication by Richard Challoner, *Think well on't* (London: Thomas Meighan, 1736, ESTC T118429), and *Spiritual Combat, a Guide to the Spiritual Life*, by Lorenzo Scupoli, appear alongside one-off requests such as the *Pratique du Sacrament de Pe* (1728) by Antoine Godeau (1605–72), in the original French.[349] The request for *A Pious Association for the Obtaining a Happy Death* could have been for any one of a type of publication popular in Catholic circles of the time.

Requests for exegetical works do not appear; that may have been the province of the convents' chaplains. A request for an English dictionary does, however, occur. Non-religious titles are even less frequent. One

---

[345] *Blount MSS, C* 64/172: CT to MS, 9 December 1738 (NS). Forty editions of this work had been published by 1640.

[346] *Blount MSS, C* 64/156: CT to MS, 25 February 1738 (NS).

[347] Cited, slightly inaccurately, as *The Garden of the Confraternity of our Blessed Lady of Mount Carmel.*

[348] For example, *The 30 Days Prayers to our Blessed Lady.*

[349] This is presumably the work cited as *The Scripture Penitents.*

such is the popular 1723 work (also published in an edition in the Hague in 1727 as well as in several London issues), *A Short View of the History of England* by Bevill Higgons (1670–1735), which cost five shillings and suggests a desire on the part of the nuns to preserve a sense of their Englishness (ESTC T108391).

## Other services

There are many human touches to be found in the documents – the supply of medicines and spectacles, of books and other items; the arrangements for escorting pupils and postulants to and fro across the Channel; the all too human suffering in a time of cold winters; and the poignant last letter of the dying Sr Margaret Ellerker. One learns from these letters something of the physical conditions in which the nuns lived, although one will learn little of their devotional lives.

Some of the requests for information made to Strickland can be surprising. Tunstall asked repeatedly about her brother Constable's talk of marriage, wanting to know the identity of the intended bride and whether he had consulted Strickland about a marriage settlement.[350] She hoped 'he's now about weding in good earnest',[351] and Strickland was expected not only to ensure that he did so but also to assure Tunstall of the suitability of the match. He was asked to confirm or deny rumours they had heard that the intended bride was a daughter of Mrs Heneage (a lady with very close connections with their convent).[352]

A sense of isolation is repeatedly marked in the nuns' correspondence, not just by their pursuit of such matters as the above, but also by their total dependence on their agents and the sheer vulnerability which comes through at every turn. They did not even trust English newspapers that came their way on matters affecting their co-religionists, as when Tunstall asked Strickland for authoritative confirmation (presumably derived from his close association with Jacobite circles) of whether Lord Derwentwater had got his pardon, as stated in those papers.[353] However, there can be little doubt that they had an ulterior motive on this occasion, since such a pardon would have immeasurably assisted their efforts to claim Radclyffe money.

Strickland and the network of agents were expected to work together as a bureau for the tracing of addresses and persons. He was required to get £5 to Mrs Ann Saville for her journey over to Louvain; after a

---

[350] *Blount MSS, C* 64/75, 89, 99, 100, 101 and 106: CT to MS, 6 November 1733, 17 August 1734, and 29 March, 15 April, 17 May and 30 August 1735 (NS).
[351] *Blount MSS, C* 64/100: CT to MS, 16 April 1735 (NS).
[352] *Blount MSS, C* 64/103: CT to MS, 21 June 1735 (NS).
[353] *Blount MSS, C* 64/166: CT to MS, 17 July 1738 (NS).

letter asking him to make the payment came another, saying that Mrs Saville would find neither Day nor Strickland without the help of Mr Haydock.[354] He was even asked to remedy the omission by Mrs Heneage's sister at Louvain who had forgotten to inform her 'who has care of our afaires',[355] so that she could pay him some money for transmission. The most splendid commission of all was the request for money which Strickland was asked to forward to someone whose name appeared only in the enclosure and whose address the ladies at Louvain did not know and of whom they said: 'we're resolved to teze him with letters to try what we can get that way'.[356]

The Stricklands were also expected to act as a staging post for women and girls on their way to and from the convents: thus Gilbert Haydock's niece Jenny was ordered by her father to stay at their house on the way to Louvain and her departure to be notified to him.[357] In 1737 a girl from Lancashire was ordered by Tunstall to report to the Stricklands for directions to either Hugh or Gilbert Haydock, who was to bring her over with him.[358] The Stricklands seem to have been key figures in the passing on of girls to these convents. In May 1737 Tunstall asked Strickland to forward a letter to

a Lady who has her Daughter at hammersmith & waits for an occasion to send her here to us which I fear will be too late to come with Mr H[ugh]: Haydocke if so please to put her in mind of Mr Hansby who designes for these parts soon as they tell us.[359]

Strickland was also told that Mrs Knight of Kingerby, near Market Rasen in Lincolnshire, wanted to be informed when someone was bringing over young ladies to Louvain from England, although it was unclear whether she yet intended to send her daughter. His involvement in this work appears to have been covert: a Mrs Parry, who had not met him, did not know of 'good Mr Hansby, who has brought Grace Lathouse very soon & safe & is very gratfull to you & your Lady for the care you had to send one to the wagon for her'.[360]

Not only was hospitality required; when Tunstall's niece stayed with the Stricklands, Mrs Strickland was asked to buy her a pair of stays,[361] and the same service and much more was asked for another Constable niece who was returning from Louvain to her home at Burton Constable.

[354] *Blount MSS, C* 64/72 and 74: CT to MS, 21 August and 25 September 1733 (NS).
[355] *Blount MSS, C* 64/81: CT to MS, 6 March 1734 (NS).
[356] *Blount MSS, C* 64/95: CT to MS, 17 December 1734 (NS).
[357] *Blount MSS, C* 64/106 and 108: CT to MS, 30 August and 6 September 1735 (NS).
[358] *Blount MSS, C* 64/141: CT to MS, 23 April 1737 (NS).
[359] *Blount MSS, C* 64/142: CT to MS, 5 May 1737 (NS).
[360] *Blount MSS, C* 64/144–5: CT to MS, 28 May and 15 June 1737 (NS).
[361] *Blount MSS, C* 64/215: CT to MS, 6 June 1741 (NS).

The young lady was due to make only a short stay in London and had asked for the company of either Mrs Strickland or her daughter, during which time Mrs Strickland was asked to 'procure her the best Taylor to take mesure of her for a pair of stays & what ellse she wants for she has no cloths fit to appear in'.[362] The nuns had heard of a smallpox epidemic in London and said anxiously that they would not have her 'go into any publick place either for divotion or diversion if posible'.[363] The young lady's father was adamant that her Cholmeley cousins 'have the Government of her'.[364] The young lady herself had 'a great dislike to be with my Cousen Cholmeleys & for a young creature to be in common lodgings would not have been proper'.[365] On account of the smallpox epidemic they did not want the girl to stay long in town; Mrs Strickland was asked to make suitable arrangements with Lady Clifford (a relative) for an appropriate companion and a coach.[366] It did not even occur to Tunstall that Mrs Strickland might have been out of town – she was, and had to come back specially, only to find that the girl did not even turn up at the Stricklands' house, so that they had to find her.[367]

Letters were frequently enclosed for forwarding in correspondence to Strickland;[368] one was even to be placed in Lloyd's Coffee House for sending to Antigua.[369] Since Strickland was reluctant to charge the nuns for his services, he would have borne the costs of this traffic himself, a change from his normal practice of leaving open to his clients the question of remuneration (with heavy hints of the great and deserving extent of his work). On another occasion, in order not to breach the rules of the order that they should correspond during Lent only on business matters, he was asked to forward a letter from Mr Melling, the chaplain at Louvain, to his cousin John Shepherd, a seminary priest who had been staying with Mrs Heneage but had moved on and needed to be traced.[370] Tunstall once forwarded a letter through Strickland to Lord Montgomery,

[362] *Blount MSS, C* 64/221: CT to MS, 22 September 1741 (NS).

[363] *Blount MSS, C* 64/220 and 224: CT to Mrs Strickland, 5 September and 13 October 1741 (NS).

[364] *Blount MSS, C* 64/221: CT to MS, 22 September 1741 (NS).

[365] *Blount MSS, C* 64/223: CT to MS, 13 October 1741 (NS).

[366] *Blount MSS, C* 64/221-222: CT to MS and Mrs Strickland, 22 September and 6 October 1741 (NS).

[367] *Blount MSS, C* 64/222 and 224: CT to MS and Mrs Strickland, 6 and 13 October 1741 (NS).

[368] *Blount MSS, C* 64/99, 100, 110, 125, 126, 129, 131, 133, 137 and 138: CT to MS, 29 March, 15 April and 15 November 1735, 14 August, 19 September, 16 November and 31 December 1736, 4 February, 26 March and 9 April 1737 (NS) (among others).

[369] *Blount MSS, C* 64/78: CT to MS, 23 December 1733 (NS).

[370] *Blount MSS, C* 64/116, 118 and 120: CT to MS, 21 February, 23 March and 15 May 1736 (NS). John Shepherd (1678–1761), ordained 1706. Bellenger SHEP02.

the heir to the Duke of Powis, and it would appear that he was expected to be the return channel for correspondence too.[371]

The dependency of these communities on lawyers and advisers was always a personal one, fragile and subject to loss of continuity in the event of an adviser's death: the demise of the attorney Mr Culcheth was described as a misfortune to the nuns, since he had business of theirs in his hands for Mrs Magrath, which they hoped that his executor and clerk, Mr Chorley, would handle, as indeed he promised.[372]

## Convent Jacobitism

Guilday described the Louvain convent as 'perhaps of all the English communities in Belgium the most intensely loyal to the House of Stuart … In its list of professions nearly every name prominent in the Jacobite cause is represented'.[373] The convent of the Spellikens in Brussels had a guest-house built next to it with money from the sale of their previous house at Vilvorde; this guest-house 'soon became the rendezvous of the Jacobite leaders who were on the Continent'.[374] The convent was full of ardent Jacobites, such as Sr Mary Rose Howard (1677–1747), Prioress from 1721 to 1724. Elizabeth, Duchess of Gordon (niece of Cardinal Howard, who moved the convent to Brussels, and daughter of the 6th Duke of Norfolk), lived in the guest-house, and she and the Prioress became the recognized intermediaries between James III in Rome, Bishop Atterbury of Rochester (then in exile at Brussels) and the Jacobite party in England. An active correspondence was carried on between the Chevalier and his friends, and the Dominican Convent was the point of departure and arrival for all letters going to England and coming from the Jacobites at home.[375]

The Benedictine convent in Brussels was also 'one of the Jacobite centres on the Continent', and Charles II's royal foundation of the Benedictine convent at Dunkirk was full of ladies from families politically important in the Jacobite cause.[376] The true significance of the many letters enclosed for forwarding in correspondence from some of these convents to Strickland becomes abundantly clear in the light of this knowledge, as does his role in keeping track of the whereabouts of the recipients. Although he seldom crossed to France and the Low Countries, leaving most of the journeys to others, notably Day and Burgis (both of whom

---

[371] *Blount MSS, C* 64/148: CT to MS, 19 August 1737 (NS).
[372] *Blount MSS, C* 64/75 and 77: CT to MS, 6 November and 12 December 1733 (NS).
[373] Guilday, p. 382.
[374] Ibid., pp. 416–17.
[375] Ibid., pp. 417–18.
[376] Ibid., pp. 264, 273.

seem to have been able to move across the Channel with great freedom), one can be left in no doubt whatsoever by his dealings with precisely these arch-Jacobite communities that Strickland was a willing, safe and regular channel for Jacobite intelligence and a committed and highly discreet agent for the cause. Such affiliations are most difficult to prove because of the secrecy required, but no possible room for reasonable doubt concerning Strickland's role as a Jacobite agent can exist in the light of his work with these convents.[377]

### Strickland's Remuneration

One odd feature of Strickland's relationship with these convents is that he did not take any fees from them for his dealings. Indeed, they constantly reminded him to do so, even down to the assessment of postage costs, as well as his salary (a term used once, rather surprisingly, when one would have expected mention of fees).[378] Thus yet another reminder from Louvain:

> you've now twice sent our accounts & has not so much as deducted for all the letters I've writ. I've complaind of this to 2 worthy persons of your acquaintance & hope by their means to prevail on you to do as you are so obliging to act for the Black Ladys at Bruxells or on what terms you think fit we can comply with.[379]

And yet, in the main series of four account books that cover his entire career we can see that he paid himself a salary and that he billed for items such as carriage hire, postage and writing of accounts, that he regularly paid his clerk for his work, and that he charged for legal work according to his copy of the published 1730 edition of the Chancery guide.[380] It is difficult to reconcile the contradictions, though it has to be said that one suspects some source of covert funding. How else does one square his much-vaunted 'magnificence' of manner of living with his more limited lifestyle, or the considerable scale of his money-lending (even with guarantors) with a lower than expected financial balance?

### Success?

Ultimately the best measure of Strickland's success is financial. Between March 1728 and September 1744 he raised a total of £10,475 9s 5d for

---

[377] Paul Kléber Monod, *Jacobitism and the English People 1688–1788* (Cambridge: Cambridge University Press, 1989).

[378] *Blount MSS, C* 64/85 and 99: CT to MS, 26 April 1734 and 29 March 1735 (NS).

[379] *Blount MSS, C* 64/90: CT to MS, 22 August 1734.

[380] *Tables and Fees of the Officers and Servants belonging to the Lord Chancellor and Judges* (1730) (listed in the sale catalogue of Strickland's library, 1745).

Dunkirk and £10,454 11s 9¼d for Louvain. He achieved the considerable feat of keeping the Louvain canonesses' account in credit during every single reporting period (usually by a margin of £100–£140 but on one occasion by as little as £7). He dramatically transformed the finances of the smaller Spellikens after 1733 to the tune of £5,570 3s 6½d. Because of their different funding arrangements, it is not possible to give a comparable total for the Benedictines at Brussels. These totals look impressive to our eyes, and all the more so when one realises that in modern terms Strickland's agency raised the equivalent today of almost £3 million. While his management may not always have been popular with the convents, it was sound and effective. Some income was for the house, some for particular ladies. It would be oversimplifying to state that sums intended for individuals were generally larger than those for the convent's general use, since the realisation of a particular investment occasionally produced a large sum – such as £235 as proceeds of a mortgage assigned to the Dunkirk convent in 1734 by the Duke of Powis.

## Tribute

One final manifestation of the relationship between donors and convent dwellers is not included in this volume: a jubilee poem composed by Michael Blount I in 1737, constituting a long congratulatory ode printed on a single large sheet in two columns addressed to Lady Mary Crispe, Abbess of the Benedictines in Brussels.[381] It serves to remind us of the support that these institutions thought they could enjoy from their supporters at home. Sadly, as the reader will see from these letters and documents, the reality of support received did not always match the nuns' imagined entitlements.

---

[381]  Reprinted in *ECIE*, vol. 3, pp. 361–5.

Fig. 1. Portrait of a nun from the chapel of Mapledurham House, identified
by the editor as Dame Henrietta Strickland OSB (1729–89), third daughter of
Mannock Strickland, Dean and Prioress of Dunkirk. Flemish School, eighteenth century. The portrait is inscribed *Elegi abiectus esse in domo Dei mei*
('I have chosen to be the least in the house of my God'). Reproduced by kind
permission of J. J. Eyston Esq. and the Mapledurham Trust

4 S
1755

Cejourd'huy dixhuitieme Jour du mois de
Janvier mille sept cent trente cinq nouveau
Stile de Brabant, et Septieme Jour dudit
mois de Janvier Stile d'Angleterre, pardevant moi Jaques Antoine Dusij notaire
admis par le Conseil Souverain de Sa
Majté Imperiale et Catholique ordonné
en Brabant résidant a Louvain
presens les temoins embas denommés
comparurent le Sieur Gilbert Haijdocke
et le sieur Jean Melling ambedeux
Anglois, lesquels jointement les ds
temoins embas denommés, Sous serment
preté es mains de moi led. notaire
ont declaré, attesté et affirmé, ainsi
que moi notaire, de bien connoitre
honorable Ladij Catherine Radclijffe
Seconde fille du tres honorable
François feu Comte de Darmenswater
decedé; que Lad. honorable Ladij
Catherine Radclijffe est actuellement
en vie pour S'être cejourd'huij
presentée en personne pardevant
nous en Sa demeure où nous nous

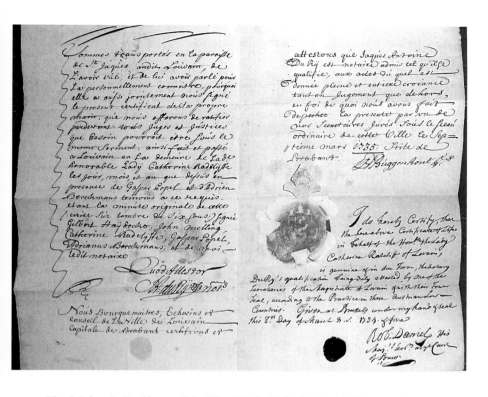

Fig. 3 (*above*). Certificate of the life of Lady Catherine Radclyffe, 1735 (inner pages). Reproduced by kind permission of J. J. Eyston Esq. and the Mapledurham Trust

Fig. 2 (*left*). Notarial certificate (in French) of the life of Lady Catherine Radclyffe, 18 January 1735 (NS), recording the appearance of Gilbert Haydocke and Jean [John] Melling to testify before Antoine Du Rij, imperial notary at Louvain, who then was taken to see Lady Catherine. *Blount MSS, C* 145/63, reproduced by kind permission of J. J. Eyston Esq. and the Mapledurham Trust

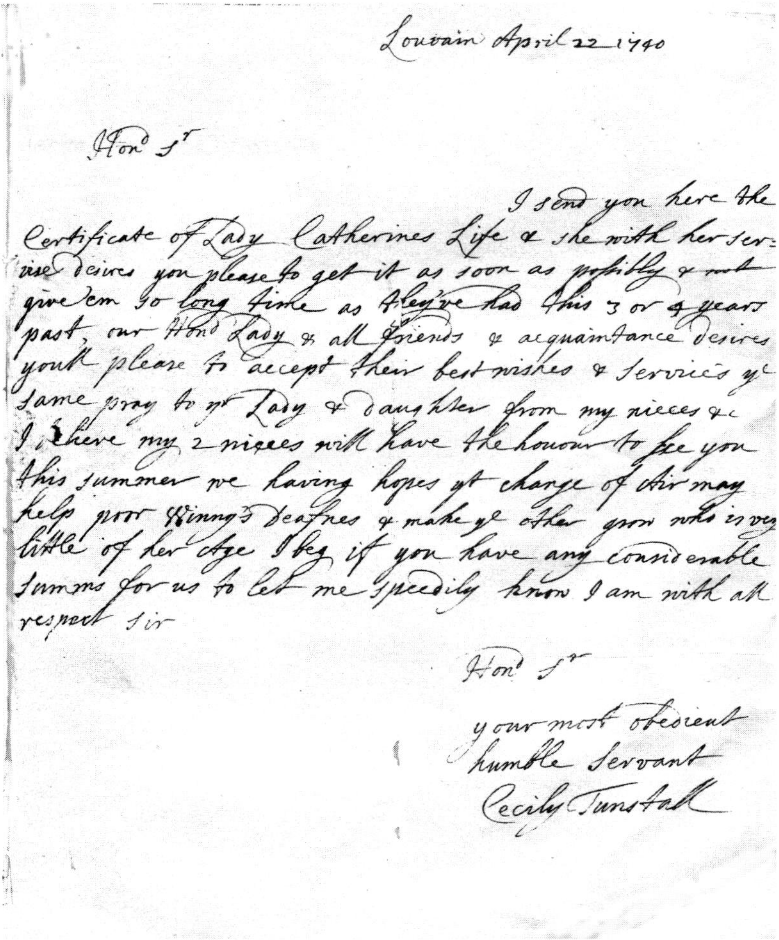

Fig. 4. Letter from Cecily Tunstall to Mannock Strickland, 22 April 1740, describing the verification of the life of Lady Catherine Radclyffe. Reproduced by kind permission of J. J. Eyston Esq. and the Mapledurham Trust

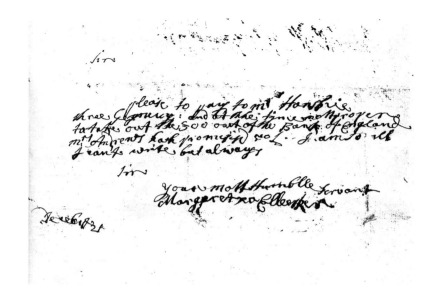

Fig. 5. Margaret Xavier Ellerker's final letter to Mannock Strickland, written while she was dying, 21 December 1736. Reproduced by kind permission of J. J. Eyston Esq. and the Mapledurham Trust

# PART I

# LETTERS

# LETTERS FROM ST MONICA'S, LOUVAIN, 1731–45

*Blount MSS, C 64/69–291*

**1.** *Bryan Tunstall to MS at Gray's Inn. 28 December 1731.* Blount MSS, C *64/69*

York Decembr the 28th 1731

Sir

Dr Carnabys sending you some Bills payable as he tells me the 7th of next month (of which moneys he has desired you to pay to my order eighty five pounds) gives me this favourable opportunity of saluting my old acquaintance with my best wishes of an happy new year:

I beg you will be so kind as to pay to Mr Tho Day fifty pounds of the said money to whom I have accordingly given a bill upon you and another for £35 to Mr Richard Brigham or order payable at 12 days after date when I suppose you will have received the money.

I should be glad of any occasion of serving you in these parts and of showing you with how much esteem & sincerity I am

Sir / your humble servt / Bryan Tunstall

**2.** *MS to Cuthbert Constable. 18 April 1732.* Blount MSS, B *25, fols 87–9*

London Apr. 18th. 1732.

Sir.

I have the favour of both your Letters and beg Leave to give you my Sentiment of what I Apprehend you are no wayes concernd in Interest in, but may be a Dispute of Right betwixt the present Earl[1] and his

---

[1]  Charles Radclyffe, 5th Earl of Derwentwater (1693–1746).

Niece.[2] The Collonel[3] by his Will after Subjecting his real Estate to the paymt of such of his Debts as his personal Estate would not extend to pay Devised the same real Estate to Lady Mary [Radclyffe?] for Life, Rent to James Earl of D. [Derwentwater] his heirs and Assignes for ever. By this Will which must be the Guide in this Dispute the personal Estate of which the Norham Tythes were part must first be Exhausted by payment of Debts before the real Estate can be Charged, and then the real Estate or so much thereof, as was not Disposed of for paymt. of Debts was to goe according to the Devise that is to Lady Mary for life Rem[ainde]r. to Ld. D. in Fee. If this Matter stood purely upon the Will (which I think it must doe notwithstanding the subsequent attainder of Ld. D.) there could be no Doubt but that the Rem[ainde]r. in Fee which was vested by the Will in Ld. D, did upon his death Discend to his son and heir the late Lord, and upon the Death of the late Lord it must be as free from doubt that the estate itself (Lady Mary being dead) Discended to his Sister and heir Lady Anne. This I say would certainly have been the Case had things gone in their naturall Course, so that now wee have onely to Consider whether my Lord's Attainder ought to vary it. I believe you and all of us agree that Attainder, tho legall, was still unjust and I think it full as Criminal to reap any Advantage by an Act of, what wee call, Injustice as to be Guilty of it ourselves. Neither doe I think the present Earl, who is a Man of so much honour, would ever Claim any Right but what he would have been intitled to had neither he nor his Br been attainted. This is my opinion of the Affair, and I hope my reasons will make it yours and be the Means of Settling this Matter to the Satisfaction of all parties. As soon as ever wee can get the Decree ag[ains]t Ridley[4] drawn up and perfected the same shall be put in Execution, and then I hope wee shall be able to free you from the Importunities of the Hanfords. you were very obligeing in thinking of me at my Brothers; I beg my Complimts to yours and am

Sr. / your most obedient humble Servant / M: S. Lady Anne is not yet Marryed, nor will be this Fortnight. / To Cuthbert Constable. Esqr.

---

[2] Anne Mary, Baroness Petre (1716–60), only daughter of James Radclyffe, 3rd Earl of Derwentwater and wife of Robert James, 8th Baron Petre of Writtle (1713–42), whom she married on 2 May 1732.
[3] Colonel Thomas Radclyffe.
[4] This appears to be part of a challenge to the 1716 Act for making over the Derwentwater estates to Greenwich Hospital, for which Nevill Ridley was one of the trustees, or possibly an attempt to reclaim forfeited Derwentwater estates at Newsham, Plessey, Shotton and Nafferton bought up by Matthew White and his business partner, Richard Ridley, both prominent figures in Newcastle, after the 1715 Rising.

**3.** *CT to Mrs [Mary] Strickland. 24 July 1733 (NS) (answered 27 July 1733 OS)*. Blount MSS, C *64/70*

Louvain 24 July 1733

Dear Madame

I find by yours that Mr Haydocke[5] is gone out of town tho' you don't say so, but I hope you'll see that the Bills I've drawn on him be paid till we hear that Counr: Strickland will do it. I have Drawn Bills for £330 dated July 18. one of them £200 & the other £130 so that you'll be pleased to send them to Mr Wyke or as you know for the money. I'm sorry you're forced to stay in Town on our account but hope it will not be long till we hear whether Mr Strickland will take the trouble or no. in the mean time

Dr / Madam / I remain your most obliged humble servant / Cecily Tunstall

Please to accept our Hon[oure]d Ladys best wishes & the most kind love from your Dr Br[other].[6] I leave your Dr Girl[7] to speak for her self

---

[5] Gilbert Haydock, priest.
[6] Either her own brother John Wright (d. 1760) of Kelvedon Hall, Essex, or, more likely, one of her brothers-in-law, Roger Strickland (1680–1749) or Francis (Frank) Strickland (1691–1745), youngest brother, one of the 'Seven Men of Moidart'.
[7] Strickland's eldest daughter, Mary Eugenia (1722–65).

**4.** *CT at Louvain to MS (as 'Counsellor Strickland') at Lincoln's Inn. 18 August 1733 (NS) (answered 21 August 1733 OS)*. Blount MSS, C *64/71*

Louvain August 18. 1733

Honoured Sir

This owns the honour of 2 from you of the 16 July & 27. I need not tell you how welcome they both were, & must needs own next to your self Sir, we are obliged to Mr Haydocke[8] for the unexpected favour of your Corespondance which we never durst have aim'd at had he not incouraged us: whom I would not have a loser by us, & so beg you'll please when you have any reason [of] seeing him, to let him have what is due to him since his quarterly accounts was even'd, for he has writ & done several little things since.

I beg Sir you'll please to pay Mr Burgis what he demands when he shews his note: & Mrs Towneley here has sent 3 pieces of Lace for her

---

[8] Gilbert Haydock.

sister Lady Mostyn which she directed to Brudges[9] to Mrs Marcham who was orderd to direct them for you Sir she is to tell you whether she paid the Dutty at Brudges or if not to desire you Sir to pay it out of our moneys in your hands, the number of yards is writ on a bit of paper & seald too the lace. If you hear any thing of our 2 poor little neeces be so good as to let us know for we've had no news of them since what you Sir was so good to let us know, only my Br[other][10] writ out of the Country & thought they might be here before his letter which we received a week ago. We fear they are sick at London if they are not set out yet please to send by them what was to have come by Mrs Savil of whom we can hear no news, I must needs add that if you see Mr Day you'll let him know of the Children's coming for he has things for us too, & that the Girls may bring a good french Gramer with them. I'm confounded to give you Sir all this trouble but hope you'll pardon the freedome of her who is & ever will remain

Honoured Sir / your most obliged humble Servt / Cecily Tunstall

———•◦•———

Please to accept the best respects of our Honoured Lady

Mr Haydocke with his humble service bids me tell you Sir you was but a poor little Boy when he had the honour to know you at Dowey.[11] We're all very proud that my Br Constable has the happyness of your friendship. My 3 Sisters desire your most humble service may be acceptable. I for my part am quite confounded to give you Sir so much trouble the very first time I've the honour to write to you but hope not to make a Custome out & will indeavour for the future not to trouble you but in money matters or what I can't avoid, so again I beg leave to subscribe my self Honoured Sir

your most obliged humble Servant Cecily Tunstall

———•◦•———

Please to forward the enclosed to Mr Day & let him know his article of postage was very plain in my accounts 5d.

---

9  Bruges.
10  Bryan Tunstall.
11  Douai.

**5.** *CT to MS ('Counsellor Strickland') at Lincoln's Inn. 21 August 1733 (NS).* Blount MSS, C *64/72*

Lovain Aug 21 1733.

Honoured Sir

Tho I troubled you but last post yet I'm obliged again to beg the favour of you Sir to pay on sight of a little bill that Mrs Anne Savil will bring you the sum of £5 of the money yet in your h[ands.] I shall not draw any more till I can hear of a large sum paid but this is what's needful for her Journey. I wish she could meet with my little nieces to come with for I can't yet hear of them 'tis strange no one at London can write a word to Cous: Cholmeley[12] & if at London yet, 3 of them & not one ever writes to their Aunt here. I hope Sir you'll excuse this freedom which I take knowing you are so obliging to my Br[other] as to take a part with us in his concernes, & will I hope give us some account of these poor little Children for we fear the worst that they are fallen sick at London. Please to accept the respects & service of our Honoured Lady, my 3 sisters Cous: Cholmeley who has had the honour to know you the same from

Honoured Sir / Your most obliged humble servant / Cecily Tunstall

---

Since my last to you Sir I've received one from Mr Haydocke who gives me an account of what he has disburs'd since his quarterly accounts of which I spoke in mine to yours so I [think] it requires no answer.

---

12 Margaret ('Peggy') Cholmeley, one of the most active of Strickland's couriers.

**6.** *CT to MS ('Counsellor Strickland') at Lincoln's Inn. 11 September 1733 (NS).* Blount MSS, C *64/73*

Lovain 11 of Sep: 1733

Honoured Sir

Tho' I've not had the honour to hear from you since yours of July 27: OS which I received Aug 12 NS: yet I must needs trouble you now to beg you'll please to pay Mr Rodbourne whatever he shall require to defray the Charges, & fees, he's been obliged to give in order to recover Lady Catherin Radclyffe's Pension; as also to requite him self for all the pains he's taken to procure it for us, which as he owns him self by his Daughter last December had been very great, & since I believe much more, at least more effectual for he says as soon as they have a certificate of her life since last Penticost, we shall have a year & a half due for her [*illeg. line*] will not suffice at least as far as it will go pray let him have it, & tho' he does not demand any fee for him self yet we desire he will demand it, not to have patience till you have sufficient. One Mrs Orm has paid some time ago 2 guineas or more for her neice here to Mr Fell & she desires you'll please send to him for it. Our Honoured Lady desires you'll please to accept her best wishes & service so does all my sisters & none mor[e *page cut away*]

We hear nothing yet of the Children whether they are set out or no; only Cous: Pegy Cholmeley writ they stayd to have their pictures drawn.

**7.** *CT in London to MS at Lincoln's Inn.* Blount MSS, C *64/74*

London Sep 25 1733

Honoured Sir

Not knowing whether you are still in London or no, I defferd sending this Bill of £20 wch as you see is drawn on Mr James Rokeby by his Br: & till I hear again from you Sir I shall not venture to draw any Bill, not knowing what the fees will come too, that Mr Rodbourne requires. I must beg the favour also to enquire & let us know whether Mrs Saville intends to come or no; & whether you've pd her the £5 for her Journey: if she comes soon pray let her bring the Packets that are in Mr Days hands for our house, & please to let him know I've received his of the 7 Sep: & that Mrs Primer left the Coffee mill at Bridges[13] not daring to bring it. The Children came the day after I writ that I'd heard nothing of them. I hear Sir you've a son[14] not far from Lovain but can't hear where.[15] If our Town lyes in his way I should be extreamly glad to shew him any civilety that lyes in my power, for I'm sorry to find so many ways of troubling you & none of serving so obliging a Friend. If Mr Day would be so good as to direct what he has in his hands to me, they would come better: for my neeces would not take them because they were not directed they are Books which I writ for to Mr Haydocke & are for several persons in our house so that I should be glad to know the prises of each appart, he only has put them in [*illeg.*] in his accounts to me if this could be done I should be glad; but he not being in Town I fear I can't obtain that favour: at least any Bookseller can tell what the 3 prayer books for Sundays &c come to : I fear also without Mr Haydocks help Mrs Ann Saville will not find you and nor Mr Day: if this finds you at home I hope Sir you find the most kind service & best wishes of our Honoured Lady my sisters & self that your Lady will be so good as to accept the same fro[m Honoure]d Sir your most humble servant

Cecily Tunstall

---

13 Bruges.
14 John Strickland (1723–1802).
15 At the Catholic school at Bornhem, near Ghent.

**8.** *CT at Louvain to MS at Lincoln's Inn. 6 November 1733 (NS).*
Blount MSS, C *64/75*

Louvain the 6 no. n:s: 1733

Honoured Sir

I've defer'd as long as I well could answering the favour of yours of sep: 22. o:s: not knowing whether you've return'd home or no but being in very great want of money makes me now trouble you to know what I may draw: for if you remember Sir that Mr Rodbourne was to have what he wanted or required for fees &c now since your going out of Town he writ again to have a new certificate of Lady Catherin Radclyffes life or if any one could answer before witnesses to have seen her Ladyship this Mr Wiseley who brought our Little ones here is able & willing to do: & who we have heard nothing of since he went from here a month ago or more, Reverend mother writ to Mr Rodbourne of your being out of Town & so beg'd the favour of him to forward this afair as soon as possible but we've no answer for he had a mind we found to put the affair in your hands. Cos Margret Cholmeley has writ to her Sir that she paid about £19 I think or thereabouts to you Sir we should be glad to hear you had it we also are in great want of some money for my 2 little neeces if yu hear from my Br about any; for we're forc'd to lay out what they want & can't well spare it at this time Corn growing still dearer every day by reason of the war & we want money to lay in a provision for they tell us there will be none to be had in a very short time. 'tis all to be transported. My Br[other] desired us to let him know our rates & he would order money to be paid but after we'd told him he says not a word in his answer to ours of that but speaks of his going to be maried but to whom we know not but wish he may have consulted so worthy a friend as you Sir about it. Our marchand at Antwerp[16] tells us the exchange is very good so that we should be very glad to know soon what we may draw. Tis a misfortune to us that Mr Culcheth died in your absence who had business in his hands that is for Mrs Magrath, but we hope Mr Chorley with whom he left all will take care to secure the writings, he has writ to her & promesis he will. I fear Sir I shall tire you with this long scrale so must conclude

Honoured Sir / your most obliged humble servant / Cecily Tunstall

Please to accept the best wishes of our Reverend Lady my sisters & self & 2 little nieces who oft speak of your daughter.

---

[16] The widow of Charles Broeta.

**9.** *CT to MS at Lincoln's Inn. 18 November 1733 (NS) (answered 23 November 1733 OS).* Blount MSS, C *64/76*

Louvain the 18th nov: o.s. 1733.

Honoured Sir

I doubt not but that you've had my answer to the favour of yours out of Devonshire. This owns that of oct: 30 & is to advise you that I've drawn a Bill of £100 on you this day at 3 days sight to the order of the Mademoiselle Broeta I hope I've not left you without some of our money in your hands, if I've tis your own fault but I hope at least you'll have more soon. I must beg you'll please to let me have an account from whom each sum of money came & for whom I hope your Lady kept the date of each payment for that is necessary in the general account but for particular letters of advice tis enough to have from you that so much for such a person is paid, without which I never pay any though they have had a letter from their friends of it, we wonder much we hear nothing of Mr Wisely who promised to answer for Lady Catherine Radclyffe's life so that we hoped this Martlemiss have received 2 years pension & am surprized that nothing & think the £42 7s 10d is a great deal for nothing for we fear you'll have as much to do again to get it as if nothing had been done. We're in the utmost trouble & grief for our honoured Lady who fell in a fit of an apoplexy last Saturday morning, all was & is done to help her she came to her self so as to have understanding but can only say one or 2 words now & then, we've little or no hope of her recovery please to let her Cous: Peggy Cholmeley know that we don't expect nor desire from my Br Constable a whole years of pension before hand so far from that all we desir'd was a sum of money for their little necessarys &c & now especially as we hear tis likely to be hard times in Yorkshire we desire she'll let my Br know this for her letters would sooner come to his hands than ours & we've writ very fully to him but forgot that point please to accept all service &c from my sisters & neeces & the same from

Honoured Sir / your most obliged humble servant / Cecily Tunstall

———•◦•———

Our Dr Honoured Lady[17] is dead since I writ this Letter, please to send the inclosed to Mr Burgis or if you don't know him Mr Day does.

---

[17]  Mary Worthington (1656–1733), WWTN LA 319.

**10.** *CT to MS at Lincoln's Inn. 12 December 1733 NS (answered 20 December 1733 OS).* Blount MSS, C *64/77*

London Dec: 12 1733

Honoured Sir

This comes to return you thanks for your accounts & compliments but am sorry that you have so mean an opinion of our family to think we are not better provided with one fit to succeed our Dr deceased Lady. & can with truth asure you Sir that she is to all our satisfaction (except her own [who] is chosen) succeeded by my Cousin Cecily M[ore] of Kirklington: sister to Cousin Henage & one more at Roan[18] who are all that remains of that family. I would draw a Bill of £30 on you now but that I'm in hopes you'll recover part at least of the £300 Mr Fell ow's us & Lady Catherins money. I should be glad to know in what case Mr Rodbourne left it to you & whether you must solicit anew for it she thinks it strange to have no more paid then £13 &c which as I writ before Sir John Webb might & as we think should have paid long ago for till my Late Lords death t'was due from him. so we hoped & expected that for the fees payd already we should hav had 2 years or at least a years & a half's pension. please to let us have these particulars as soon as you can; for Considering her great age of 78 or more t'will be scarce worth the money if more must be paid for it. Mr Wiseli who came with my nieces promis'd to answer he had seen Lady Cath: Rad: & since he went we've never heard word of him. As to our afaires we always have requir'd to have quarterly accounts, Ballanced by the Bills we drew & Salary letters Coach-hire &c, to which we gave a discharge in our next letter, but unless you find this convenient to you Sir we shall with thanks like whatever you please to do for us. Mrs Magrath in your absence address'd her self to Mr Chorley: & he has very obligenly offerd to act as his master Mr Culcheth had done in her afairs. So gives you many thanks Sir please to find here the best wishes of our new Honoured Lady my sisters &c & neeces the same in a very perticular maner from

Honoured Sir / Your most obliged humble servant / Cecily Tunstall

---

[18]  Rouen.

**11.** *CT to MS at Lincoln's Inn. 23 December 1733 (NS).* Blount MSS, C *64/78*

Lovain Dec: 23 1733

Honoured Sir

This is only to desire you'll put the enclosed into Loyds Coffee House in order to be sent to Antigua, & to wish you a most happy Xmass & many [more] please to accept the same from all who have the honour to know you I've just seen your son's master who asures me he is very well & gives most high commendations of him. Tis long since we've heard any thing out of Yorkshire, makes me fear things goes not well with our friends / in hast must conclude

Honoured Sir / your most obliged humble servant / Cecilia Tunstall

**12.** *CT in Louvain to MS at Lincoln's Inn. 8 January 1734 (NS).* Blount MSS, C *64/79*

Jan: 8 1734 Louvain

Honoured Sir

I hope you'll pardon my hast to draw a Bill of £100 this day on you when I tell you the reason is that at present the exchange is very high and therefore a great advantage to us & perhaps if I stay till you've more money it may fall. Therefore I hope you'll excuse me tho' yet you've not got enough to pay it. I must beg you'll pay your self out of the next that comes for we expect Miss Sheldons pension, & soon Miss Stapyltons will be due & Mr Stap: he's for being in town & not knowing your address I beg you'll take the means to sent to him about the middle of Feb: for it. I shall observe your orders about Lady Cath: Rad: when tis time, & when you have her money &c please to take what is due to you for your self for the accounts send as I told you in my last we shall not stand on those points with you, but once or 2 a year as you please when you have more money please to pay one guinea to Mr: Challoner who lent it to Mrs Savil he lives in Queens Square Devonshire Street, at Mrs Brets. I must again beg the favour if you can get us any more money now soon to let me know that we may have the advantage of the exchange so must conclude with my best wishes of a happy new year

Honoured Sir / your most obliged humble servant / Cecily Tunstall

———•—•—

Our Honoured Lady desires you may find her best respects & wishes the same from all who have the honour of your acquaintance.

**13.** *CT to MS at Lincoln's Inn. 22 January 1734 (NS) (answered 11 February 1733/4 OS).* Blount MSS, C *64/80*

Louvain Jan 22 1734

Honoured Sir

I hope this Certificate of Lady Cath: Radclyffe will prove more effectual than that we sent last year at this time. If you can easily see Mr Day please to let him know that we have but just now received the books which Mrs Towneley was to have brought & was forced to leave at Brudges but that the 2 primers they both deny to have had so I fear they are lost he has now one book yet to send. I should be glad he would also get one *think well on't*[19] when any occasion serves to send me here & you'll please to pay him out of what moneys you'll have, I hope before this you'll have had 2 or 3 little sums we have heard of which will pay the last I over drew &c so conclude with my best wishes &c from

Honoured Sir / your most humble & obedient servant / Cecily Tunstall

Our Honoured Lady desires you'll accept her best respects & service the same from my nieces & sisters &c.

---

[19] The first book of meditations published by Richard Challoner (first published 1728).

**14.** *CT to MS at Lincoln's Inn. 5 March 1734 (NS) (answered 7 March 1733/4 OS).* Blount MSS, C *64/81*

Louvain 5 March 1734

Honoured Sir

I can't impute your so long silence to any thing but miscarrige of letters for I've never heard one word from you since that with orders to have a Certificat of Lady Catherins Life which I got done & signed by Mr Daniel at Bruxells pray let me hear as soon as you get that for Lady C: R: is in pain to know how her afaires stands. I hope you've had wherewith all to pay the £100 Bill for we have heard of several little tokens paid. My Cous: Henage has writ to know who has care of our afaires, & her sister here forgot to tell her, so if you can let her know to pay it you, it will oblige our Honoured Lady, who presents you her humble service pray if you know any thing of Mr Burgis who said he would set out such a day for our parts let us know for the high winds make us fear for him, & if he is not set out I hope Mr Day will give him the Books &c he has yet to send & will let us know if he sent the 2 primers or no for no news have we of any thing t'will be time to put

Mr Stapylton in mind to pay Miss's Pension so conclude with my best wishes of a good Lent &c

Honoured Sir / your most obliged humble servant / Cecilia Tunstall

—•◦•—

I've seen your son John's master this day who gives him a high Carracter & sais he's well please to find here the best wishes of my sisters & all that have the honour to know you. If you've not had mine with the Certificate I [beg] you'll let me hear the moment you have it that I may get it r[eady]

**15.** *CT to MS at Lincoln's Inn. 9 March 1734 (NS).* Blount MSS, C 64/82

Louvain March 9 1734

Honoured Sir

At last Mr Burgis is arrived safe & as soon as I had Lady Catherin's Letter sign'd I here send it you, & hope soon to hear of the £200 being paid. Please to let me know for whom the rest of the money is for, that you have yet in your hands, & whether the £100 I drew on you is paid. I hope you'll have £20 of Mrs Willoughby[20] soon which with Miss Stapyltons pension &c may be soon drawn for at present the exchange is very high but if we have war here t'will not last so long. Lady Catherin orders me to put in this little bill to secure this letter please to forward the enclosed & you'll oblige

Honoured Sir / your most humble servant / Cecily Tunstall

—•◦•—

Please to accept the best wishes of our Honoured Lady &c

---

[20]  It is revealing that where female relatives (here sisters) were involved with the convents they fulfilled different roles: Cassandra Willoughby as courier, Elizabeth as nun. A similar assignment of roles occurred with the Cholmeleys.

**16.** *CT to MS at Lincoln's Inn. 30 March 1734 (NS) (answered 8 April 1734 OS).* Blount MSS, C 64/83

Louvain March 30 1734

Honoured Sir

I receiv'd yours of the 7: & hope before that you've answerd that about Lady C: Rad: which Mr Burgis brought safe, & I answer the same day. Mrs Smith[21] is concern'd she hears nothing of the money her Sister Frances sent her, & said she'd paid it you last Xmass. But since you don't name it in either of your last Letters I can't tell what to say, unless it be in the £50 you said you had & only names £31 from Mr How[ard][22] perhaps the rest is this [*illeg.*] be please to let me know as soon as you can, & how much I may draw I don't know the £100 is paid I drew on you last. I must beg when you see Mr Day you'll please to pay him for the 2 little Books Mr Burgis brought me & tell me what they are each, & desire him if he sees Mrs Ricardy to ask her if Mrs Savil left the 2 primers with her, for she thinks she went from him to Mrs Ricardy. If you've any occasion to write or see my Br Constable tell him we're in great trouble we've heard nothing of him since the midle of Decem last past tho' we've writ twice we hope only miscarrige of letters & no worse health is the cause

if you'd be pleased to tell my nephew to write to him if no other occasion serves for we don't write in Lent but upon business so conclude

Honoured Sir / your most obliged humble servant / Cecilia Tunstall

———•◦•———

Please to accept the best wishes of our Honoured Lady sisters & self

---

[21] Sr Elizabeth Mary Winefrid Smith.
[22] The Hon. Philip Howard.

**17.** *CT to MS at Lincoln's Inn, via Ostend. 20 April 1734 (NS).* Blount MSS, C *64/84*

Louvain April 20th 1734

Honoured Sir

I can't, or at least will not yet impute your long silence to any other cause than the miscarriage of Letters Lady Catherin is very uneasy till she hears whether you've had the letter I sent you above 6 weeks ago & several others has drawn their money another way because tis so long before we can hear whether you've had it or no. Mrs Smith as I writ you in my last paid money for her sister here & we've never heard yet tho' 'twas paid at Xmass whether you have it for you mend none but Miss Joness £31. I beg you'll please not to fail to let us hear as soon as ever Mr Ward pays £20 for his sister who stays in expectation on't & can't go forward in her intended purpose till she hears you have it or at least a Bill for't also Mr Collingwood for his sister & Mr Darcy for the same the 2 Mrs Jones has heard of 4 guineas from their friends but especialy Miss Stapylton wants to hear her pension & other money she expects from her papa is paid I hope if you've not yet gone to him for't you'll not fail now for I've heard he is very angry when noone comes to demand it when due it was our 24 feb: ns when your afairs will not permit you to let us have the honour to hear from you, I beg your Lady or some other by your orders will do me the favour, for 'tis a considerable loss not to be able to draw money while the exchange is so high as it has been but fear t'will not last please to find here the best wishes of our Honoured Lady & the same from

Honoured Sir / your most obliged humble servant / Cecily Tunstall

———•◦•———

Please to let Cous: Pegy Cholmeley know that Mrs Willoughby expects £20 from her the 5 April o.s.

**18.** *CT to Mrs Mary Strickland at Queen Square. 26 April 1734 (NS).*
Blount MSS, C *64/85*

Lovain April 26 1734

Madam

Mr Strickland being out of Town as I believe by his of the 8th instant I hope Madam I may adress these few lines to you to let you know that this day I've drawn a Bill of £120 on 3 days sight to the order of the widow Broeta I'm not sure whether I desir'd Mr Strickland to ask my Cous: Pegy Cholmeley for the £20 due the 5th of April to Cous: Willoughby: please if he has not had it to send for't. I find by the accounts that the £8 for Mrs Smith[23] has been long payd & also £10 for Mrs Wollascot which she has often writ about & never could hear it was paid this shows how necessary 'tis to let me know who pays money to him & for whom which I hope Madam you'll be so good to let him know & that I'm sorry to find he has not reckond what is due to himself neither for Letters nor sallary which I hope he will make up for the next money that is paid. I should not have drawn now so much but that the Exchange is very high & may not be so long please also to let Mr Burgis have what money he asks for & if you see him desire him to send what things is ready by a man that is to come over to fetch Miss Prudent very soon & that he will buy for me an Eye Catechism for a Little Child price 1 shilling. Be pleased to present our Honoured Lady's most humble service to Mr Strickland & mine, & accept the same from

Madam / your most humble servant / Cecily Tunstall

---

[23]   Sr Elizabeth Mary Winefrid Smith.

**19.** *CT to MS at Lincoln's Inn, but addressed internally to Mrs Strickland, since CT is unsure of MS's return. [10?] May 1734 (NS) (answered 10 May 1734 OS).* Blount MSS, C *64/86*

Lovain 10 May 1734

Madam

Not knowing whether Mr Strickland is return'd or no I make bold to trouble you one more [time] hoping you'll be so kind to let us know if the £30 for one Mrs Ward be payd or at least if you receive only a Bill for't to let us know as soon as possibly you can: & also we have had orders to send to some of the executors of the late Mr Green in order to receive moneys for Miss here they say Mr: Burgis who lives at Mr Beezly's in Panton Street can inform you who to address for it. I hope Madam you'll pardon this freedome & believe me

Madam / your most humble servant / Cecily Tunstall

**20.** *CT in Louvain to MS at Lincoln's Inn. 29 May 1734 NS (answered 28 June 1734 OS).* Blount MSS, C *64/87*

Louvain May 29. 1734

Honoured Sir

I hope you'll soon receive the other £100 of Lady Catherine's she desires to know why it is not paid as well as the other. & before this comes or soon after there will be an other half year due for pentecost I've this post drawn a Bill on you for £130 att 3 days sight to the order of Mr Turville at Antwerp I'm very sensible you can't write for every little sum you receive all I desire is that when you do me the favour to write you'll mention each sum because I neither can pay others their money nor draw a Bill till I have it from you that so much is paid for & from such persons Mr Shepherd has writ to his Cousin here that he has £5 for our Honoured Lady if he knew you were in town he would pay it for when he went you were not come up another time if your Lady would be so good to receive sums that come t'would be a great favour & add to the many received by

Honoured Sir / your most humble servant / Cecily Tunstall

———•◦•———

Please to find here the best wishes & service of our Honoured Lady sisters & nieces &c

**21.** *CT to MS at Lincoln's Inn. Attached bill [no longer present].*
Blount MSS, C *64/88*

[7 August 1734 or 1735]

Honoured Sir

This is only to desire you to get this Bill paid as soon as you can &
let us know when you have it Mr Wyke has the money ready so 'tis but
to call for it I hope you'll have had Lady Catherine's by this. I asked
the marchand woman about the Cambrick she said it was scarce 8 of
our ells so that I don't think any has been taken away for I till now did
not know how many ells was in it having bought it in a piece & was the
only one I could find at that time being in hast to send it for the deep
mourning but had very ill luck as you know please with my service to
let your lady know this please not to forget to let me know whether
you had the [£]2 10s 0d for Mrs Talbot[24] from Lady Shrewsbury & if
you've heard of the £3 Lord Langdale promised to pay us for a poor
man in Town that we advanced it to. This wth our Honoured Lady's &
all services where due is all from

Honoured Sir / Your obliged humble Servant / Cecilia Tunstall

---

[24]  Mrs Anne Talbot.

**22.** *CT to MS at Lincoln's Inn. 17 August 1734 (NS).* Blount MSS, C
*64/89*

Louvain August 17 1734

Honoured Sir

I hope you'll excuse my haste & allow me without further notice to
draw a Bill on you that is as soon as I hear from you what you have in
your hands for us & from whom for since yours of the 28 June we've
heard of several sum's paid to you as £31 from Mr Howard for Miss
Stoner & for Miss Crathorne & from Mr Day £27 15s 0d & because
our old marchand Broeta at Antwerp is in great hast to have Bills from
us in order to pay her correspondants in England. Pray Sir be so kind as
to let us hear either from you or your Lady as soon as you receive this
& if you hear any thing of my Br Constable's marriage let us know to
whom. Please to give the things you have in Louvain for us to Cous: Pegy
Cholmeley or Mr Collingwood to send us, & if you see Mr Day please
to tell him that Mrs Savil says that she thinks Mrs Ricardy may know
where she left the 2 primers for she's quite forgot that she ever had 'em.
Our Honoured Lady desires you'll find here her most kind service as well
as all my sisters & 2 little nieces & 2 Cous: Cholmeleys the same from

Honoured Sir / your most obliged humble servant / Cecily Tunstall

**23.** *CT to MS at Lincoln's Inn. 22 August 1734 (NS).* Blount MSS, C 64/90

Louvain the 22 Aug 1734

Honoured Sir

This answers the favour of yours [of] July 29th with your accounts where I find twice £20 for us & we don't yet know whether 'tis by mistake or not, having heard lately from Wicklife[25] & no mension of the 2nd £20 please to let us know as soon as you can; for we indeed writ for something for a poor Relation in these parts but has had no answer but that I've drawn a Bill on you yesterday on 3 days sight to the orders of the W[idow] Broeta for £170. I'm sorry to find you think I have any one in my eye that I shall ever think will be to be compare'd to you Sir but realy to tell you the truth I'm very uneasy to be obliged to trouble one of your merits so much & find no way to return the favours[.] you've now twice sent our accounts & has not so much as deducted for all the letters I've writ. I've complaind of this to 2 worthy persons of your acquaintance & hope by their means to prevail on you to do as you are so obliging to act for the Black Ladys at Bruxells[26] or on what terms you think fit that we can comply with for if I could chuse or had the choice of all London I should certainly prefer Mr Strickland to all the rest & could only wish to have the favour to hear oftener from you or any other you please to trust when you can't afford us that honour. I'm very sensible your Business &c makes it imposible to aford us so often as others have done that favour & when I've been importune on that head t'was to satisfy others in our family who are required by their friends to let 'em know when the money they've paid is acknowledged so that I hope you'll not impute that rudeness wholy to me who am the humble servant to all but yet would not for any thing in the world disoblige so worthy a friend. I hope you'll please to let us hear if you know any thing of Br Constables weding as I don't doubt but you do; whom can he better consult than so judicious & worthy a friend. I wish t'was as much in my power as his, to shew how much I am

Honoured Sir / your most obliged humble servant / Cecily Tunstall

———•—•—•———

Please to accept the humble service of our Honoured Lady my sisters & 2 Cousen Cholmelys & 2 little ones

---

[25] Wycliffe, Northumberland, a Tunstall family estate.
[26] The Spellikens.

**24.** *CT to MS at Lincoln's Inn. 28 September 1734 (NS).* Blount MSS, C *64/91*

Louvain Sep the 28 1734

Honoured Sir

This answers the favour of your Lady's letter which was very acceptable & hope when you can't afford me the pleasure she will. Please to let her know Miss Eyre is very well & much hers. Lady Catherine begs you'll urge Mr Wattson to pay the 2nd years pension & half more due at least it used to be paid at martmas & wisontide but since my Lord's death the whole 3rd year is not due till Xmass next. Mr Bellson[27] promised to pay arriars due for his sisters but we hear nothing on't if you could write a word to him he lives at Winshister & would be more than 20 from us he ows £42 16s 0d for his 2 sisters board here &c. Your son is very well at Burham[28] & most extremely praysed by all that know him we was in hopes to have seen him here but he did not come out this vacancy I hope the next to have the satisfaction to see him. I'm glad you've had £20 to make up for that 2ce put for us & hope the next will make up what is due to you for trouble & letters &c which we beg you'll please to take with many thanks to you Sir for we're very sensible of the favour you do us & heartily wish it in our powers to return tho we shall always fall short of your merits our Honoured Lady desires you'll please to find here her most humble service & best wishes ye same to your self & Lady from

Honoured Sir / your most obliged humble servant / Cecily Tunstall

---

Please to forward the enclosed by some marchand to Antigo.[29]

My sisters & neeces join with me in our most kind service to your Lady & self & cous: Cholmeleys both the same

I writ this Mrs Trapps desires you'll please to inquire of Mr Tankerd[30] a wollen draper in Red Lion square I think who always receives her money from her Brother if he [has] nothing for her of him.

---

[27] Probably a son of John Belson of Stokenchurch.
[28] The school at Bornhem.
[29] Antigua.
[30] Thomas Tancred (or Tanckred), of Red Lion Square, member of a dynasty of woollen drapers.

**25.** *CT to MS at Lincoln's Inn. 12 November 1734 (NS) (answered 8 November 1734 OS).* Blount MSS, C 64/92

Louvain novem 12 1734

Honoured Sir

I beg you'll let me know either by your self or Lady what money you've had since I drew my Last Bill & whether no hopes of any more for Lady Catherine she desires you'll please to solisite Mr Watson again & again for it. But that I daily hoped to have had the favour of an answer to my Last I should by her Ladyships orders have writ this long ago. Cousin Willoughby has heard of her money being paid to you but I not having had it from you can not be sure no more than of money paid for a poor Cousin of ours by my Br Constable & for the 2 Children as also £5 for Mrs Jonson from Mr Burgis. If you see him desire he'll give you what he has for our house & please to pay him what ever he shall demand for me or Mrs Hacon for whom pray sent the inclosed as directed & if you have these things from Mr Burgis or Mr Day please to give them to Cous: Pegy Cholmeley to send this when she sends any thing for the Children pardon this trouble & if too great Mr Burgis will do it himself please to accept the best wishes &c from our Honoured Lady my sisters &c

Honoured Sir / your most obliged humble servant / Cecily Tunstall

If Mr & Mrs Dillon are yet at London please with my humble service to tell 'em Miss is perfectly well & content here as po[*illeg.*] please also to let your Lady know [with my k]ind service that Miss [Aire?] is very well & much hers as also my 2 neeces.

**26.** *CT to MS at Lincoln's Inn. Address of Ralph Radcliffe Esq [sic] at Hitchin, Herts, noted on verso by Strickland. 26 November 1734 (NS) (answered 3 December 1734 OS).* Blount MSS, C 64/93

Louvaine no. 26 1734

Honoured Sir

Tho' I've long expected the favour of an answer yet I must again trouble you on the present occasion at the request of Dr Honoured Lady Catherine Radclyffe who's desir'd by her neece Lady Newburgh to write to one Sir Ralph Radclyffe to know how much mony he has in his hands due before Mr William Radclyffe's death & since his death (he's been dead 2 years) this month of November for she desires he may know that Mr William Rad[clyffe] left his Estate to Mr Draper so that the arears since his death becomes due to the said Mr Draper which he will

be pleased to pay him he will shew him the deed. Now Sir whether
this Mr Draper be some one in England who the Late Mr W[illiam].R]
adclyffe]. trusted or my Lord D[erwentwate]r him self Lady Catherin &
we all are in the dark unless you Sir know one Mr Rodger Fennick who
lived in London & may inform you for I know not whether Sir Ralph
Radclyffe may be informed from the first hands. Some years ago my
Lady Cat. had almost the same Comision & writ to Sir Ralph from her
Br then living but had no answer she sent the letter to Mr Fenwick but
now we've neither an address to Sir Ralph nor him so that unless you
Sir can inform us we're at a loss what to do & what I've writ is word
for word what Lady Newbourg[31] writt they're I fear in great want of
money so as soon as you can Sir pray let us hear from you not only of
this but other money: for many has heard of money but till I can have
it from you I can't draw for it so I hope you'll pardon my importunity
& believe me with all sincerity

Honoured Sir / your most humble & oblidged servant / Cecily Tunstall

———•◦•———

Please to let your Lady know with my service that Miss Eyre & Miss
D[illon] well with my neeces who are all her[e t]he servants

---

[31]   Lady Newburgh.

**27.** *CT to MS at Lincoln's Inn. 3 December 1734 (NS).* Blount MSS,
C *64/94*

Louvain Decem 3d 1734

Honoured Sir

This owns the favour of yours of no[vember]: 8 which came but this
day to my hands. I doubt not but by this you've had a £30 from Mr
Crathorn of Ness which we writ he had sent you October past so that
I venter this day to draw a Bill on you for a £130 hoping also that Mr
Burgis has paid you a £50 for Mrs Johnson & that he's taken out of it
what I owe him & whatever he demands any thing in our names I hope
you'll let him have it & that the things he gives you to send us you'll
give either Cous: Peggy Cholmley or Mr Collingwood to send us I'm
really asham'd to be so often troublesome to you but know not how to
help it. May your Lady find here my best wishes as also all friends here
as named & let her know Miss Eyre's is well & Miss Dillon if her Fr &
Mother are in Town I promised to let em know what I writ to you. Our
Honoured Lady's best wishes to you both with those of

Honoured Sir / your most obliged humble servant / Cecily Tunstall

———•◦•———

I must beg you'll pay Mr Shepherd what he layd out for 2 books & send the Books the next Box that comes for my neeces from Cous: Pegy &c

Since I writ this a fear came into my head that the mony from Mr Rowland Lacon is the same that was paid before if not let me know soon she had a promise of another but i['m] not sure please to forward the enclosed to Mr Burgis I've not his direction.

**28.** *CT to MS at Lincoln's Inn. 17 December 1734 (NS).* Blount MSS, *C 64/95*

Louvain De: 17: 1734

Honoured Sir

I had not so soon troubled you with this but to recomend the inclosed to your care to read & send it to him we having no direction now which if you'll get us & send as soon as possible for we're resolved to teze him with letters to try what we can get that way. I should be glad to know whether you ever writ to me between that of your Lady's of Aug 23 & that of no[vember]: 8 for I fear letters has been lost if so please to let me know the Contents I must also beg the favour of you if I did not in my last to send to Mr Shepherd who lives with Mrs Henadge[32] for a Book or Books he has for one in this town that we're obliged to & that you'll please to pay him for it & with all other things that Mr Burgis has for us or has given you or Cous: Marget Cholmeley: that he'll say (that is) Mr Burgis will pack all up in a Box & send 'em to one Mr Samuel Grimes a marchand in London in order to send em by the first ship that goes to Antwerp & direct em to Mademoiselle Broeta & give her an exact account of the value of each particular this I take the freedom to beg of him not to trouble you more than I must needs please to desire him to remember that Mrs Hacon says he's forgot her Book she bespoke that is an other English Dictionary the Box must be markd & figuered & he sent the mark &c to Mademoiselle Broeta for as he's her corespondant but I have not his direction. Lady Catherin has again spoke to me to desire you'll please to hasten Mr Watson (pray whether is he a Comisionary or a Steward for the Family) she says she's heard very latly that Sir John Web[b] has 2 stewards there please to find all our best wishes of a Happy Xmass to your self & Lady & let her know Miss Eyre is very well & my 2 neeces & much hers & so is

Honoured Sir / your most obliged humble servant / Cecilia Tunstall[33]

---

32 Heneage.
33 Note in MS's hand: 'Mr. Burgis at Mr Beezley's in Panton Street'.

**29.** *CT to MS at Lincoln's Inn. 4 January 1735 (NS) (answered 17 January 1734/5 OS).* Blount MSS, C *64/96*

Louvain Jan 4 1735

Honoured Sir

I sent a copy of Sir Ralph Radclyf's letter & your's to Lady Newburgh who in the mean time has writ a 2$^{nd}$ Letter to Lady Cath: Radclyffe to desire her to write again to Sir Ralph to beg him to be so kind as to send the money he has in his hands that was due to Mr William Radclyffe before his death to that Banker at Leghorn that he used to send the Bills of Mr Wm: Radclyffe upon, & the person who is heir to that money will give that Banker proof of his being so, & give a proper receipt for it; she adds [that] your Ladyship will let Sir Ralph know that Mr Radclyffe dyed the 7 of november 1732. the remainder of the money that is due since that time, Mr Draper will receive the Estate being left to him. This is word for word the Content of Lady Newburghs last Letter. I thought to stay till my Lady had received Sir Ralphs letter to you but my Lady Catherine Radclyffe presses me to write thinking they're in great want of the money; but I fear t'will be in vain, for that I don't think Sir or Mr Ralph Radclyffe will scarce pay any money without more security. I hope by this you've had the 2nd £100 from Mr Watson Lady Catherine desires to have it pressd more & more. I should be glad to know as I said in my last whether you've had twice £20 for Miss Green from Mr Lacon? Or is it the same your Lady own'd because her sister said they would pay another £20 very shortly after the first. Please to let me know what Little sum's you've had since your Last for Mr Trapps Wisiscote Bartlet Collingwood &c have paid or orderd money to be paid as they write this with my best wishes of a happy new year to your self & Lady the same from our Honoured Lady 2 sisters neeces Miss Eyre Miss Dillon to her papa & mama if in Town.

Honoured Sir / your most obliged humble servant / Cecily Tunstall

please to forward the inclosed as directed & desire Mr Burgis to let me know when the box sets out & the value of it either to me or that Mr Gryms will let Mademoiselle Broeta know that she may answer at the Compter of Antwerp for it.

**30.** *CT to MS at Lincoln's Inn. 1 February 1735 (NS) (answered 7 March 1734/5 OS).* Blount MSS, C *64/97*

Louvaine Feb: 1: 1735

Honoured Sir

This day I received the honour of yours of Jan 17: which Lady Catherine was very glad of & if she had not been in such hast to have me draw it I would have staid till her new Cirtificate of Life were legalized at Bruxells which is not yet done there though here it is drawn up so that [it] is for the next post. I've drawn a Bill on you for £120 as usual if I had not just now had yours I'd pen in hand to have desired you to write assuring my self that one [of your] mails has been lost in the last storm in which we apprehended the things we desir'd Mr Burgis to send might have been with a Letter from him for 'tis Long since his friends has expected to hear from him if you see him pray let him know it. Mrs Knight had a Letter from her Mother last September in which she says she had or would pay you 2 guineas for her daughter here of which we have had no notice from you Sir if you've had it please to let me know. Mr Trapps has writ to his sister to let her know he will pay her money as soon as he knows to whom in London to pay it to & then he desired as soon as you receive it that you will give him a discharge in full for his sisters share due beyond sea for the year 1733 & he says that at the same time he will pay you 50 shillings more for the first years interest being due out of the above rents (that is at Paris) due Sep 1733 for the Legacy left Mrs Trapps here by her sister Nanny for which he requires a receit he advancing this money to his sister before he has had it from Paris. This is what he always requires from all that have been our aggents but as you Sir have never had any money from the said Mr Trapps yet so I write this that you may know how to satisfy him according to his Letter to his sister. We've had a Letter this post from Mr Fell who gives me poor hopes of any thing but the Bonds. Pray Sir if any thing can be done wth the two Ladys that Mr Day named to us see what can be done or whether we can't sue 'em; also if Mr Watson will pay the last year now expired for Lady Catherine without a new Cirtificate let us know soon. We've had some news from Rome as if Lord Darwent:[34] was relapsed & either dead or dying if so which I'm not certain of because we've had no letter from Lady Newbourg but only Letters from some other hands to a Friend in our Town mentions it. I say if so, perhaps my Lady may take a step over into England to see what she can doe for her Children for whom it may be something may be recovered of their own Estate you say nothing of Sir Ralph Radclyffe so I must conclude

---

[34] The Earl of Derwentwater.

Honoured Sir / being always your most obedient & most obliged humble servant / Cecily Tunstall.

———◆◆◆———

Please to find here the best wishes & service of our Honoured Lady sisters & 2 neeces & Miss Eyre [&] Miss Dillon to your self & Lady Miss Dillon would be glad to know whether her papa & mama are gone down or in town yet.

**31.** *CT to MS at Lincoln's Inn. 29 March 1735 (NS)*. Blount MSS, C 64/99

Louvaine the 29 March 1735

Honoured Sir

This owns the honour of yours the Cirtificate of Lady Cath: Radclyffe's Life I've had long ready & only waited for your orders to send it. Pray in your next please to let us know more of the Sale of Lord Darwents[35] estate which I've heard nothing of but what you Sir writ. I've drawn a Bill of £50 on you by this post & for the rest you'll please to pay one Mrs Winefride Ireland £sixteen fifteen shilings & 2 pence which sum she left with us & now desires it at London she lived with Mrs Eyre here & is now with Miss Stapylton please also to send to Mr Stapylton for our miss's pension he has it always ready and is vex'd when we don't call for it in time, t'was due Feb: last. Mrs Orm has money to send her neece here but does not know yr lodgings nor I hers. Pray if you know any thing of my Br[other']s weding let me know. I beg Sir when you receive more money you'll deduct of what expences of letters &c & for these almost 2 years trouble which we could never have had the face to have given you but that we hoped you would have taken as others have done. I've often pressed this both to you Sir & to others in order to persuade you but yet in vain but pray believe me for we'd rather pay every half year or year than have so much run on so hope to find it in your next accounts please to forward the inclosed to Mr Burgis unless you know where Mr Hansby lives to whom 'tis address'd please to find here our best wishes to your self & Lady I remain

Honoured Sir / your most obliged humble servant / Cecily Tunstall

———◆◆◆———

Mr Trapp's account is the very same he gave us notice of so I send it you back

---

[35] The Earl of Derwentwater.

**32.** *CT to MS at Lincoln's Inn. 15 April 1735 (NS) (answered 29 April 1735 OS).* Blount MSS, C *64/100*

Louvain the 15 of April 1735

Honoured Sir

I hope before this you've had the £20 for Mrs Isabella Smith, & Miss Stapyltons pension besides several other little sums (as some thing for Mrs Jenings, if you see Mr Lacon please to tell him Miss Greens friends writ as soon as ever they knew who to pay her pension to [each] year they would not fail to pay all due he has only paid one year & she has been here next August 3 years please also if y[ou see] my Br to desire he'll give us orders about £15 we've had, whether 'tis for us & Cos: Crathorn or his Children, we writ to him twice & yet never heard a word of him but hope he's now about weding in good earnest. I'm very sorry Mr Burgis did not send the Books for our house as I desired he would with an exact price of each & to Mademoiselle Broeta instead of which they are as we hear put into the Children's Box without any value put on 'em or giving any notice of em when I'd expressly desird 'em to be given to Mr Grimes to send Mademoiselle Broeta & she has wated these 2 months for em & we are by this way like to endanger the loosing em all & the Children their cloathes too for if any thing be put in a Box more than the marchands has notice of they run the risk of forfeiting their veracity that sent 'em, as last Box which the Children had Mrs Prudent put only a knife & fork in that was not declared, & the Gentleman at Antwerp was extreamly mortified at it saying he would never get em any thing more that way if they abuse his friend's kindness so much, so I beg never more any thing be sent by a marchand without giving exactly the value that they may be declared at Antwerp in time where they are stoped as we supose for want so tho' late I yet must beg you'll let me know the value of each thing that was given to Cous: Cholmey for our Lady & me &c she's set the value on the Children's Clothes but not a word of any thing but that Mr Strickland has sent her 7 parcells of Books for Madam More & me & no value at all of the things please to forward the inclosed & when the person sends an answer please to send it us for she can't get a Letter to her Sister here by the post please to accept the best wishes of our Lady & self to you & your Lady with Miss Constables & Miss Eyre & Miss Dillon with all known & unknown I conclude

Honoured Sir / your most obliged humble servant / Cecilia Tunstall

If Mr Burgis comes in your way desire he will procure & send me Granado's *Siners Guide*[36] if the Last Edition be to be had either at second hand or better at first for I've heard the print is out & pay him if you please for it & Mr Shepherd for the 2 Great Books I'm afraid they've not been valued yet neither.

---

[36] Luis de Granada, *The Sinner's Guide (Guia de pecadores)*.

**33.** *CT to MS at Lincoln's Inn. 17 May 1735 (NS)*. Blount MSS, C *64/101*

Louvain May 17 1735

Honoured Sir

I hope you'll excuse my importunity when I tell you that Lady Catherine orders me to tell you Mr Rodbourn writes that with much adoe he has secured her annuity for her so that we shall not need to renew the certificate of life as we supose any more she sais Mr Watson can't now refuse the payment. Mrs Isabella Smith has heard long ago that her Br Sheldon or Mr Eyre (for I may mistake) has paid you a sum for her as also my Cous: Betty Willoughby has paid £20 for our Mrs Willoughby we hope also by this you've sent to Mr. Stapylton else he will be angry for he's always ready when the year is out Miss Green's friends has long ago promis'd her to sent mony & she wants it very much pray let us hear of these particulars & you'll much oblige

Honoured Sir /          your most humble servant / Cecily Tunstall

---

Miss Dillon says one of her name, a merchant has orders from her father to pay you money for her if you know him please to send to him for it & accept the most humble service of our Honoured Lady & all my sisters self to your Lady & you if you know any thing of my Brs weding please to let us know & of the above named sums & soon as you can & also if Mr Ward has yet paid any thing for his sister who must stay till she hears of it which will be no small disapointment to her

**34.** *CT in Louvain to MS at Lincoln's Inn. 21 May 1735 (NS)*. Blount MSS, C *64/102*

Louvaine the 21 May 1735

Honoured Sir

This day I received the honour of both yours & send you here Lady Catherine's renunciation with full power to act for her. I've also drawn a Bill of one hundred & 20 £ on you as usual this day. I hope by this you've had Miss Spapyltons [*sic*] pension for as I said in my last he's very angry when it lays by him & no one comes for it there are several other little sums expected which if paid we shall be glad to know Miss Dillon says one of her name a Banker or marchand has money in his hands for her & thinks you know him if so please to send to him for it & you'll oblige her who remains

Honoured Sir / your most humble servant / Cecilia Tunstall.

<hr />

Our Honoured Lady & self &c begs you & your Lady will accept her &c my most grateful thanks & service &c.

**35.** *CT to MS at Lincoln's Inn. 21 June 1735 (NS) (answered 23 June 1735 OS).* Blount MSS, C *64/103*

Louvain June 21 1735

Honoured Sir

I long to hear you've had the deed sign'd by Lady Cath: & must beg you'll pay Mr Hobbs the sum of £4 2s 4d which I've had here paid me for Knives &c due to the said Mr Hobbs in England he lives in Bedford Court b[y Red] Lion Square but as I've giv[en a] Bill so I hope he'll send for it. Mrs Orm lives at Grinnidge[37] in Kent if any occasion comes to send or to go there she would send her niece 2 or 3 guineas if she knew how to get them to her. Mr Howard has been here with his family & says he's paid you Miss Stoner's Pension. I beg you'll forward this to Mr Day & tell Mr Shepherd I would be very glad to know how much the 2 great Books cost for the man that has 'em would have paid me long ago for em if he knew what they cost if you've paid Mr Shepherd as I hope you have you can tell I hear my Br is going to be married to one of Mrs Henidge's Daughters. I hope Sir you'll tell us if 'tis true & that you've been busy in drawing & making setlements in order to it which is the reason as we hope we not had the honour of a line or 2 from you nor my Br to whom both we & his 2 little ones here writ to beg to see my nephew as he goes to paris but fear he's gone which his sisters will be very much troubled at. I must conclude for want of place

Honoured Sir / your most humble servant / Cecily Tunstall

<hr />

Please to pay Mr Day for some Books he got for us & accept the service of our Honoured Lady my sisters & all your friends &c.

---

[37] Greenwich.

**36.** *CT in Louvain to MS at Lincoln's Inn. 12 July 1735 (NS).* Blount
MSS, C *64/104*

Louvain July 12 1735

Honoured Sir

I've drawn a Bill on you this day for £100 because 'tis money I
must pay to others so can't put it out at interest we should like what
you propose very well if we could have good land security for it please
to let us know to whom & what security because we lost £300 of Mr
Fell's puting out very lately tho' I make no comparison & don't doubt
but you'll please to see we be not loosers by it & are very much obliged
to you for the kind offer Lady Catherin Leaves it wholly to you Sir, to
take what you please for the trouble you've had about her affaires & is
very sensible of the obligation she has to you for the goodness & pains
you've taken & will pray for your whole family & says she hopes to
live to have an other dividend of Mr Aurthur's Effects[38] which might
have been done long ago if the family of the Swinbourns had pleased &
hopes when you hear any thing of it you'll take care to claim her share.
As to the £300 we are like to loose by Mr Fell unless you Sir can do
any thing to the recovering any or all of it you know part of it was in
Lady Lithcots hands who we hear dyed not worth a grote but can scarce
believe it if 'tis true she was marryd to the famous Mr Ward who in all
the news papers is now so famous and follow'd by all so that we hope
if we could apply to him maybe some thing might be had? Please to let
us have your advice on this & Mrs Throckmorton is the other we should
be glad to know whether she's able to pay any thing I think Sir you have
Mr Fell's bond & rely on your goodness for the rest our Lady & all my
sisters & neeces &c are much yours but none more than

Honoured Sir / your most obliged humble servant / Cecily Tunstall

---

[38] Arthur Radclyffe, brother of Lady Catherine Radclyffe.

**37.** *CT to MS at Lincoln's Inn. 19 August 1735 (NS) (answered 15
August 1735).* Blount MSS, C *64/105*

Louvain Aug the 19 1735

Honoured Sir

Your last gave me hopes to hear again in 2 or 3 posts but finding none
in 2 months I'm press'd to beg you or your Lady will be so kind as to let
me know as soon as this is received whether yet Lady Cath: Radclyffe's
pension is yet paid & whether you've paid £30 to Mr Cuthbert Haydocke
which we owed him, & whether my Br Constable has not paid £20 for
us & which my Br Tunstall orderd him to pay 3 months ago as he says.

Several other small sums besides; we've expected long to know who the 2 young Ladys are your Honoured Lady writ to me about. But the chief thing that makes me give you this trouble is realy the money yet in your hands of Lady Cat: &c which if you can't get good land security for we beg to know very soon for I have not here sufficient to pay what I owe to several persons so beg a speedy answer 'tis strange we can't hear from my Br Constable we've writ 2 letters or more this with respects & service Miss Dillon begs you'll enquire of one of her name a Banquer who has money for her as she had notice from her mother when in Town since which she never hears any thing of em pray with her service to your Lady & self enquire for she is very uneasy till she hears my sisters & self are much your but none more than

Honoured Sir / your most obliged humble servant / Cecilia Tunstall

**38.** *CT to MS at Lincoln's Inn. 30 August 1735 (NS).* Blount MSS, C 64/106

Louvain Aug 30 1735

Honoured Sir

I would not have teis'd you again so soon but that my Cous: Witham[39] who went from hence this day has given me this Bill on Mr Day & had before an other of £6 as he suposed paid to you some time ago we've had much ado to prevail with him to let us keep your son[40] here a few day[s] whom all admire that know him. I'm truly glad he is in such good hands & heartily wish my nephew were in the same & am in no small concern that he is not Lady Catherine daily asked me if I've not heard from you about her Anuity & Miss Dillon still is in great pain she neither hears of her money nor from her friends so I must again intreat & beg you or your Lady will not fail on sight of this to let me have an accont of all I writ about in my last & this & whether my Br is yet marryd for we would fain know please to find here all that's kind & gratefull from our Honoured Lady my sisters neeces Cousen's Cholmeleys & in general all friends especialy your Son beg'd both your Blessings: for I told him this morning I was going to write & believe me ever

Honoured Sir / your most obliged humble servant / Cecily Tunstall

We've writ several times to Mr Hansby about a £150 which he as Executor to the late Mrs Thorald has power to act for us but since he will not answer we desire you in our name to require it of him for if we stay

---

[39]   Several identifications of this individual are possible (see further in Appendix 1).
[40]   John Strickland.

longer we're likely to loose it all so pray use your utmost in it. Mr Hay-docke with his service bids me tell you his neece Jenny sets out from hence the 5 of next m[onth] & that his brother orders him to send her to your house straight.

**39.** *CT to MS at Lincoln's Inn. 2 September 1735 (NS).* Blount MSS, *C 64/107*

Louvain Sep 2 1735

Honoured Sir

Though I writ but last post, yet having received the honour & favour of yours with the accounts which are very exact, we wonder much that Mr Watson can need a new certificate of Lady Catherin's life since we've had no payment on account of the last we had, for perhaps he does not know that 'twas due last decem: OS & our Jan 11 NS. the last was for the year 1733 which was paid a month or 2 before the last certificate was desir'd so that for the years promis'd he'll ha[ve] Certificates which is hard however this day w[*illeg.*] about it but as it was to be legalis'd at B[rux]ells we can't yet send it but I would not stay for that because of your most obliging offer we can't tell which to choose but can better spare the 300 than the 400 but as you know each circumstance better than we could we leave it wholy to your prudent management. We beg to know as soon as possible for we want the rest very much for to satisfy each one for whom 'tis sent so can only put out what is belonging to the house. As for Lady Catherins yearly pention is for her maintainance in part she bids me tell you with her most humble service that as she can't tell as well as you the trouble & pains you've had so she still begs that you'll demand what you think fit for in her present circumstances she's not able to reward you according to your merits nor her wishes before I have an answer I doubt not but you'll have had money for Miss Dillon &c so I believe I may draw £100 on you if I want it besides what you'll put out especially if 'tis the £300 which we as I said like better but if you don't we'll easily sie'd [?] here is a gentleman that asures us Lady Litcot has left a son who lives with his Aunt Conquest in Bloomsberry Square this I say because Mr Day writes me word that a share of her Estate is now in the possession of her sister Brent who is lyable to pay our debt. That son as I said in my last went from hence with my Cousin Witham the 29 of last instant; we should have been glad to have had more time to show our gratitude to you Sir in his person I doubt not but you'll have great comfort in him Mr Pre: [President][41] says he has great obligations to you on account of his nephew Witham at least I'm

---

[41]  Dr Robert Witham, President of the English College, Douai, 1714–38.

sure we have much greater on our own which dayly encreases which our Honoured Lady & we are all very sensible of but none with more sincere acknowledgment than

Honoured Sir / your ever obliged humble servant / Cecily Tunstall

---

Please to make our services acceptable to your Lady if Mr Burgis sends for any money please to let him have it I believe he's forgot I desird him to procure me of Granados *Siners guides*[42] if 'tis to be had Mr Hasby has only paid as I find £10.10s.0d the intrest of 150 is at 4 per cent £6 & 3 years was due last march which we were content with only on promise of exact payment otherways at 5 per cent so he knows that is far from all due to us.

---

[42] Luis de Granada, *The Sinner's Guide (Guia de pecadores).*

**40.** *CT to MS at Lincoln's Inn. 6 September 1735 (NS) (answered 12 September 1735 OS).* Blount MSS, C *64/108*

Louvaine Sep 6 1735

Honoured Sir

This is only to forward the inclosed Certificate, & pray tell Mr Watson that Lady Cath: expects a year & half at least else why a new certificate. I've drawn a Bill of one hundred pound on you the 4th Instant to the orders of the Widow Broeta this day Miss Haydocke sets out for you: as her Papa orderd her. Our Honoured Lady begs you'll accept her most kind service so does Mr Haydocke my sisters neeces Cousins &c I remain

Honoured Sir / your most humble servant / Cecily Tunstall

**41.** *CT to MS at Lincoln's Inn. 30 October 1735 (NS) (answered 4 November 1735 OS).* Blount MSS, C *64/109*

Louvain oc: 30 1735

Honoured Sir

I hope this will find you well returned home which will be a great pleasure to me to hear of for several as well as Lady Catherine has heard of money being paid for 'em but till I hear that you're come back & has received the money I can not draw a Bill which will be a great advantage now & will not be so if we stay till Xmass as we hear so please to let me know as soon as possible what I may draw & for whom which will much oblige

Honoured Sir / your most obedient Humble servant / Cecily Tunstall

Please to make our Honoured Ladys service with my neeces & sisters to you both with Miss Aire's[43] & all who have the honour of your & her acquaintance if you see Mr Burgis please to put him in mind he may sent the Siners Guide by 2 young Ladys that are to come to us soon

---

[43] Eyre?

---

**42.** *CT in Louvain to MS at Lincoln's Inn. 15 November 1735 (NS).* Blount MSS, C *64/110*

Lovaine Novem 15 1735

Honoured Sir

Though I writ very lately I can't help again intreating you to let the Banker Dillon know that the sum for our House is £15 a years pension & 11 guineas for her use. We suposed you had not found this Mr Dillon so I got Mr Mes[?] to write to Mr Day about it but still she nor we has not heard you'd have it we've had from several hands that you've come up to Town so again beg to hear as soon as possible about all the money & whether the £300 is yet put out & in whose name the writings runs. Mr Dillon lives by the Church St Peeters poor in Bread street London as Mr Day was so kind as to write we stay to hear from you about Mrs Primmers 20 guineas from Mrs Wells & she is in much expectation to hear of it as well as Mrs Hacon & Mrs Willescote[44] & many more so most humbly intreat to hear as soon as you can either from you or by your orders which will much oblige our Honoured Lady & also

Honoured Sir / your most obliged servant / Cecily Tunstall

Please to forward the inclosed it being to one in want.

---

[44] Mary Xaveria Wollascott.

---

**43.** *CT to MS at Lincoln's Inn. 25 November 1735 (NS) (answered 28 November 1735 OS).* Blount MSS, C *64/111*

Louvain Novemr 25 1735

Honoured Sir

I hope before this you'll have Received the £10 from Mr Wrights also £26 11s 0d from the Banker Dillon for she's long expected the like sum from him & I wonder I hear nothing of it in yours of Nor: 4. We leave to you Sir whether you think best the £300 or £400 security the reason why we inclyned to the £300 was because some in our House had found by experience the D[uke] of Powis a very bad pay master we should be very glad to put out our money in England if we could have good Land security but that's the fear if you think this the best way of puting out mony, pray act with all expedition in it for now it has layd dead several months we beg to have your opinion of East Indy Bonds several think that the best way for people of our sort for we may not alow of usury which is alowd in England so pray let us have your oppinion of these maters as soon as possible I shall draw a Bill on you in the usual form this day for £150 for many wants there money & have got sevaral Bills another way because they could not stay for your return Mr Day will soon have a small sum for Lady Cath: which he'll pay you so I hope this Bill I draw will not leave you very bare of mony but as soon as Mr Watson pays the arrears of Lady C Rad: Annuity you'll please to give me a speedy account for she & Mrs Dillon wanted it long pray let me know who Mr Watson is whether a steward for the Family or the government Lady Cat wants to know please satisfy me in all these points & you'll much oblige

Honoured Sir / your ever obliged & humble servant / Cecilia Tunstall

———•◦•———

Our Honoured Lady & all friends beg you'll accept their service as also your Lady

**44.** *CT to MS at Lincoln's Inn. 30 November 1735 (NS) (answered, no date).* Blount MSS, C *64/112*

Louvain no: 30 1735

Honoured Sir

The day after my last I received this Bill so would loose no time but send it by the first post pray please to desire Mr Burgis if you can conveniently to send what he has for us by the 2 young Ladys we expect if they be not already set out & please to pay him what soever he demands for things he gets for us if he would get me also Mr Jenks's *Art of the Love of God*[45] also I should be obliged to him so in hast I must conclude

Honoured Sir / your most humble servant / Cecilia Tunstall

---

[45] Silvester Jenks, *Essay upon the Art of Love: containing an exact anatomy of love and all the other passions which attend it* ([London?], 1702).

**45.** *CT to MS at Lincoln's Inn. 23 December 1735 (NS).* Blount MSS, C *64/113*

Louvain December 23 1735

Honoured Sir

This own's the favour of yours of nov: 28. I'm a little surprised that Mrs Wells's 20 Guineas are not yet receiv'd when I made so sure of 'em & found in your last of no: 4 that £26 was ow'd from her in which the 20 guineas is contained & £5 for Mrs Smith which I paid her, the 20 guineas was for Mrs Primer so I fancy you expected 20 more but that is all we expected. Mrs Wollascot wonders Mr Wright will not pay the 10 [£] her Br ow'd her & gave advice of long ago. Our Honoured Lady with her best wishes to you & your Lady of many happy Xmass's returns you many thanks for your kind offer & we asure you Sir of an intire trust & confidence in you & I tho't I had suffieciently assured you in my Last of it by leaving it entirely to your choice whether to take the £3: or 400 offered we all incline most to your own offer but would rather put out £400 than 300 if as good security for the 400 as the 3 you offer your self but beg you'll act speedily either yours in Kent or the £400 which we upon your assurance of its being unexceptionable liked very well & beg that without expecting any more letters from us about it you'll please to dispose as I said of either 3 or £400 which will be made out by Lady Catherines 9 guineas which I sent you a Bill of from Paris for the rest is all other peoples money so that we had not then fully £400 to put out I must still beg to hear soon from you because several expect little sums which I can't pay till I draw something more & till I know what you'll put out for us I can't tell what will remain & also beg you'll please to see what can be had or done in the business of Mr Fell's £300 which is a foundation for one here who can not proceed till tis recoverd this with our Best wishes & offers of service is all from her who is with all gratitude

Honoured Sir / your most humble & obedient servant / Cecily Tunstall

---

The 2 young Ladys are arived so that if Mr Burgis send me any thing let him give it to Mr Grimes for Mademoiselle Broeta.

**46.** *CT in Louvain to MS at Lincoln's Inn. 10 January 1736 (NS)*
*(answered 5 January 1735/6 OS).* Blount MSS, C *64/114*

Louvaine Janu: 10 1736 n.s.

Honoured Sir

Since my last wherin I pressd much a speedy answer Mr Crathorn writes to his sister here in the following words: I don't doubt but you've heard before now of your money. I can only tell you that I no sooner arrived here than thee next day I return'd your money to York to Mr Brigham, who was desired to procure Bills & return them to Counlr Strickland, accordingly on the 25ᵗh of novemr they were sent who has acknowledg'd the receipt of the moneys viz £92 13s 3d which was the sum total of your [*illeg.*]te, so that I persuade my self, you must have had notice before this, both of that, & the £30 I left in London to be deliverd to the same Mr Strickland in order to be return'd. The £30 you have own'd & I've paid it to Mrs Crathorn so that I can't pay, nor draw more, till I hear from you Sir, which favour I reiterate being much solicited to draw & pay several people their monys which I can't do you know, till I hear you have it also Mr Bartlet writes his sisters & his Bror this side the sea that he has paid you for their use the sum of £12 10s 0d. I hope Mrs Wolascote's £10 is received before this. Lady Cat: sends for me every post, to know whether I have not yet heard from you of the 100 so long due their is now another year will in a few days fall due to her. She wonders what excuse they can make for not paying the year last past since 2 certificats of Life were required for it & not yet paid which she thinks they could not refuse if soliscited for the said payment. Till Lady day is a very small time more to require a new certificate. Please to let me know whether I shall need to have another at the end of the year or from Lady day next to come t'morrow is my Lord's aniversary so a whole year will be due again & nothing yet for the last. I most humbly beg you'll please to let me have a line or 2 as soon as possible for otherwise several will procure Bills an other way as some does already which is a considerable loss in the exchange for the less sum's gains much less by exchange. Please to find here all that is kind & the best wishes of the time from our Honoured Lady & all that have the honour to know you & your Lady & chiefly from her who is & will still remain

Honoured Sir / your most obliged humble servant / Cecily Tunstall

**47.** *CT in Louvain to MS at Lincoln's Inn. 21 January 1736 (NS) (answered 23 January 1735/6 OS).* Blount MSS, C 64/115

Louvain Jan 21 1736.

Honoured Sir

T'was only to satisfy Mrs Crathorn that I was so hasty she thought her self sure by her Br[other']s Letter that you'd received the money. you don't mension yet whether Mrs Wollascotts £10 is yet received so that I can't draw it till I know also £5 for the 2 Mrs Jones's. I've drawn a Bill this post of £150 on you as usual because Mrs Crathorn &c was in some want of their money. I hope to hear from you soon that the Bill of Lady Cath: Rad: pension is received we former[l]y sent (as I'm inform'd) the Copys of our Bonds to Mr Carnaby or my Br Constable who promises to see us paid what Collonell Radclyffe or Lady Mary owed us so I think it not necessary to send any more but will agin press my Br to take care of our Interest when I have my Bros answer if he does not do it I'll with thanks let you know all particulars. Our Honoured Lady returns wth me her gratefull acknowledgment for your kindness in this & the putting out the £400 on good security for us. We wish you could in a more effectual maner acknowledge all favours Received by

Honoured Sir / your most obliged humble servant / Cecily Tunstall

———•◦•———

I hope your Lady will accept of my sisters & my kind service all her friends here are well my Cousin Pegy Cholmeley is to send a Box soon for my 2 neeces if Mr Burgis has any thing for us I should be glad he'd send em to her but she must write what they are before they come & for whom & the value if any of your family see him please to let him know this with my service.

**48.** *CT to MS at Lincoln's Inn. 21 February 1736 (NS).* Blount MSS, C 64/116

Louvain 21 Feb: 1736

Honoured Sir

I received the favour of yours of Jan: 23d & stay till I hear you have had Lady Catherins Bill paid wth Mr Wolascotes & £70 my Br Constable orderd Cous: Pegy Chol: to pay you for the Children which as I'm sure of I must needs draw of you for we want the money much & so beg you'll please to let me know as soon as possible what I may draw Mr Melling with his service begs you'll please to sent this Letter as directed by some one that can take the pains to inquire of him, since the Direction is not exact. Also I beg you'll please to pay what money Mr Shepperd shall demand upon Mr Mellings account. But if you have received or shall receive any money from Mr Day or any one else for Mr Melling, that money may be discounted. Please to put to our accounts the letter & the trouble of finding Mr Sheppeard for since he's gone from Mrs Henage's Mr Melling has not heard of him nor can direct right to him please to let Mr Burgis know if he's any Books or any thing else for us he may give them to Cous: pegy Chol: & let her know the price & that she may send em with the Childrens Box or the same way apard in a parcel & you'll be so good to let Mr Burgis have what money he's laid out for em which will much oblige

Honoured Sir / your most humble servant / Cecily Tunstall

most humble service a[ttend] your Lady with that of all your friends here & best wis[hes th]e time.

**49.** *CT to MS at Lincoln's Inn. 6 March 1736 (NS).* Blount MSS, C *64/117*

Lovain March 6 1736

Honoured Sir

Tho I had the Honour of yours of Jan: 23d yet I durst not venture to draw a Bill upon you till I had the favour of yours of Feb: 20 which now I do for £140 hoping you'll soon have something more else I would not Leave you without more in your hands than £4 10s 11d½ which is the remainder of the ballance the Bill is on Broeta as usual at 3 days' sight we have but now received the Box which was sent to Mr Porter at Brugis last sepr: o:s: in which was 2 pair of spectacles in a case directed to me which I think you had Sir from Mr Burgis & gave to Cous: Marget Cholmeley for me but Mr Burgis writ to Mrs Johnson that he'd sent her the spectacles she'd desired now whether these are for her or no is what we want to know & whether you paid him for em also with my service please to give him this note that if he can procure me these Books & can give em to Cousin Pegy Cholmeley time enough to send in the next Box or rather in a Box by 'em selves directed to Mademoiselle Broeta with her things to come from Mr Grimes as her chief correspondant they will come sooner & Better to me only for him to tell me the value or send it to her in time to declare it in the custom house please to accept the humble service of our Honoured Lady my sisters & Self the same to your Lady from all her acquaintance Miss Eyre & Dillon are both well so conclude

Honoured Sir / your most obliged humble servant / Cecily Tunstall

Please to pay Mr Burgis what he lais out for the Books &c as also if you have not had my last wherin I desired you to pay Mr Shepherd what Mr Melling ow'd him.

**50.** *CT to MS at Lincoln's Inn. 23 March 1736 (NS).* Blount MSS, C 64/118

Louvain March 23 1736

Honoured Sir

Least my last might have had the misfortune to be dip'ed in the sea as several we have had out of England has been of late Ostende having been almost drown'd to secure the timely notice of my drawing a Bill of £240 on you the 6 or 7 of this instant which I hope you had if not this will I believe come time enough to pay it. Please to let Mr Burgis know his friend had his so that now we know who the spectacles are for desire him to let you know what is to pay for what I desired last & that he'll send em to Mr Grimes in the citty for Mademoiselle Broeta he seems to think all has not been paid which was owing to him so pray what he demands let him have I had in your last account £2 11s 6d there was 2 sets of Mr Dorell's Books[46] he writ in his last he wanted to know, please to let him know as soon as you can for he sais he seldome comes to Town & had rather not stay so long for letters which we do to save him charge. This with our best wishes I was going to say a happy Easter but tho' ours is nigh you're but in the begineing of Lent so conclude

Honoured Sir / your most humble servant / Cecilia Tunstall

---

[46] Not identified.

**51.** *CT in Louvain to [MS at Lincoln's Inn]. 1 May 1736 (NS) (answered 26 April 1736 OS).* Blount MSS, C 64/119

Lovaine May 1 1736

Honoured Sir

I defer'd some Time after Lady day before we renew'd Lady Catherin's Certificate of life hoping the newer the date is the sooner you'll have the payment we've had notice that Cousin Willoughbys pension is paid to you & some other little sum's. I hope you've let Mr Burgis know what I writ that the Books may come at the same time with the Box tho' not in it for as yet Mademoiselle Broeta has had no notice of it Mrs Hacon has orderd Mr Burgis to address to you for money thinking that you'd had hers from her Br[other] but tho' she's heard since that tis not paid nor will be this long time yet please to let him have what he's laid out for her or us on any account if Mrs Orm sends you a salt Bottle please to send it by the first opertunity also if you know where Mr Shepard lives nor who lived with the Late Mr & Mrs Henage his Cousin Mr Melling has heard nothing from him since last August & is in great pain about him if you can inform him of him 'twill be a great favour this will come time enough I hope with our best wishes to your self & Lady & whole family of a most happy Easter & may so conclude

Honoured Sir / your most obedient humble servant / Cecily Tunstall

**52.** *CT to MS at Lincoln's Inn. 15 May 1736 (NS) (answered 28 May 1736 OS).* Blount MSS, C *64/120*

Louvain May the 15 1736

Sir

I receiv'd the favour of yours of April 26 o.s. & must draw a Bill this post of you for £60 it being all mony belonging to particulars I hope you'll have received £8 for Mrs Smith & 42 from Mrs Knight which will answer what will be owing to you & others as Mrs Talbote & others if you see Mr Burgis any time please to desire he'll get 2 pair of spectacles the very same he got & sent last sepr for Mrs Johnson of 40 & please to let him have mony for the same & any thing else he demands Mr Melling with his service desires to know whether you received a Letter inclos'd in mine for Mr Shepherd I sent it some time in lent but I can't just tell the date now our Honoured Lady & all my Sisirs & neeces &c begs your Lady & self will find here all their best respects & services the same from

Honoured Sir / your most obedient humble servant / Cecily Tunstall

If you know whether Lady Mary Radclyffe's affairs are settl'd with Lady Petre please to let me know for I writ of our intentions to my Br Constable but never has heard a word since from him which I wonder at. Since I writ you we hear from Mr Burgis that he's sent 3 Books for me but not the *Guide* I desired of Granada[47] please to tell him tho' 'tis at 2nd hand I'd rather have it than none & desire he'll direct the spectacles for me & distinguish em from those Mrs Johnson has writ for latly.

---

[47]   Luis de Granada, *The Sinner's Guide (Guía de pecadores).*

**53.** *CT to MS at Lincoln's Inn. [18 May 1736?]. Enclosed draft now detached and missing.* Blount MSS, C *64/121*

Honoured Sir

This comes only to let you know that as soon as I think you've had this I shall draw a Bill of £160 on you by the Widow Broeta I hope my Br[other] will have paid you some more money for the Children pray my humble service to you[r] Lady I hope she's at last receiv'd the Cambrick our Reverend mother & all friends joins in all that's kind to your Lady & self please to accept the same from

Honoured Sir / your humble servant / Cecily Tu[nstall].

**54.** *CT to MS at Lincoln's Inn. 15 June 1736 (NS).* Blount MSS, C *64/122*

Louvain June 15 1736

Honoured Sir

Yours of May 28 o.s. was as usual very acceptable; as for the last year's accounts send em when you please, the year's not out since your last till 1 of August o.s. but if you receive Lady Cath:s Annuity, or any other sum please to give me advice. I wonder you have nothing from Mrs Knight who owes me £42 your offer to help us concerning our demands upon Coll: Rad[clyffe']:s Estate is very kind, & we most willingly accept of [*illeg.*] I sent my Br Constable an account last January of our demands yet have had not answer as to that point, but I find by yours that my Br has given Lord Petre's an account & has deducted of the sum £10, which was a debt Lady Mary owed our house on account of Mrs Ashmall; but now since witsontide Lord Petre's must consider that the life Rents are again due so that the whole sum not to mention the foresaid £10 amounts to £943 5s 0d as you shall see after & if you know, whether my Br has wholy given up the Coll:s Estate to Lord Petre you'd oblige me to let me know so much: for Lady Catherine assured me Lady Mary gave £11000 to redeem the said Coll's Estate in 1718. now as to our securities & Bonds we shall not fail to deliver up all those that are not Life Rents on payment of each sum, & the Life Rents also for those who are Dead as soon as all the Arrears of these are paid, which we claim as their Heirs. If Lord Petres desires to see the Copys we will send em, or if that will not satisfy his Lordship, he may send some one he can trust to see the originals, which yet we shall not part with. We have 10 several Bonds the first is a Legacy or better it being sign'd & seald by my Aunt Anne Radclyffe in her lifetime as also by the Coll:[48] & besides expressly orderd in her Last Will both she & he obliges their Heirs Executors &c to pay the sum of £400 down or an Annuity of £20 a year to be duly paid Mrs Barbara Crathorn at 2 payments to wit Martinmas & Whitsontide her life during this has been paid till 1730 incluse the other are Gifts to his sisters & small annuitys to several persons signd & seald by the Coll before 3 witnesses attested by a very able Counsellor to the Arch Dutchess, and a great man at Bruxells by

---

[48]  Colonel Thomas Radclyffe.

name Mr MacNenny an Irish man who understands the English Law as well as ours. I'll put here in order the Arrears of each

| | |
|---|---:|
| In primis the Interest of Mrs Barbara Crathorns Life Rent for 5 years & a half is | 110-00-0 |
| 2 is a Deed of Gift to Lady Catherin Rad: from the Coll signd & seald as above | £100-00-0 |
| 3 a like Deed from him to Lady Eliz: Radclyffe her Heirs &c | 080-00-0 |
| 4 a Present to both his sisters or our House of | £100-00-0 |
| 5 a Bond in the same form given to our Late Lady Worthington of an Annuity of £10 per Ann her life during she died 1733 no 23 the arrears to her death come to | 170-00-0 |
| 6 A Deed in the same form given to Mrs Jane Worthington arrers amount to | 180-00-0 |
| 7 A Life Rent in the same form given by the said Coll to Cousin Barbara Crathorn of £6 per Ann the arrears of which for 19 years & half yet unpaid amount to | 117-00-0 |
| 8 A like deed given to Mrs Catherine Johnson the arrears for 19 years & half come to at £4 per an tho the principal is the same as the last but not the Annuity | 078-00-0 |
| 9 a smal Annuity given by him to a poor Cousin of his Mrs Ann Erington & her Heirs she dyed a few years after so only due at her death 2 years & half | £003-15-0 |
| 10 a like small Rent Rent given to one Mrs Swinny who died not long after so due only | £004-10-0 |
| Sum total | £943-5-0 |

The Collonel has obliged his Heirs Executors Assigns &c to pay all those to the said persons or their Heirs &c we have had some years of all these paid by him, & after his death by Lady Mary, and since her death by Br Constable: we have several letters to shew wherin Lady Mary promises to pay all her Brothers Debts to our house which was none but the foresaid also my Br Constable says Lady Mary orderd all Debts to be paid before all legacys &c please to let me have your advice upon this as soon as possible & pay Mr Cuthbert Haydocke my Bill of £20 & send or give this little Bill as soon as you can: please to make my Compliments to your Lady & accept the same from her [Ladyship] we remain with all Gratitude

Honoured Sir / your most humble servant / Cecily Tunstall

**55.** *CT in Louvain to MS at Lincoln's Inn. 5 July 1736 (NS) (answered 2 July 1736 OS)*. Blount MSS, C *64/123*

July 5 1736

Sir

I can't expect any longer for Lady Catherines £100 because Mr Witham &c wants their money I don't certainly remember whether I told you of Mr Haydocke's £20 due to him for which he has a Bill to shew you I hope e'er this you've had the money from Mrs Knight &c so that I may draw £40 in expectation of a greater sum for indeed we are in some want of money at present & begs you'll send Lady Catherins as soon as possible that is to let me know when 'tis paid & to press the payment if you can; it will much oblige Lady C: I have not heard this long time from my Br[other] Constable so I know not whether he had paid our money or no. I sent a Bill of 40 this day as usual not having to pay those I named without. Else I should have been very glad to've had the £100 with it suposing you have received some money since the Last I know I'd rather have wanted than have left you so bare had it not been others money & as I am not sure you have enough to answer the Bill because of Mr Haydockes & Mrs Talbots Bills yet I beg this time you'll allow it which will much oblige

Honoured Sir / your ever obliged humble servant / Cecilia Tunstall

Please to find here our Honoured Ladys &c most humble service the same to your Lady from all that have the honour to know her.

**56.** *CT in Louvain to MS at Lincoln's Inn. 27 July 1736 (NS) (answered 30 July 1736 OS)*. Blount MSS, C *64/124*

Louvain July 27 1736

Honoured Sir

We have long expected one Mr Cocks to carry over the eldest Miss Eyre's,[49] but hearing nothing yet of him, I think to send the Copys of the Deeds over by the Post: if you would the very first moment you receive this, let me know whether we must send all in whole sheets of large Paper, as they are now writ on, for fear of the wast paper: also if they must be attested by a Publick notery we having none that understands English, & they having been approved by Mr [Remy?] I should think it unnecessary: but let me know pray by the first post, as also if I may draw Lady Catherines money yet for she wants it, also if I may draw the last

---

49  Miss Betty Eyre.

[*illeg.*] desired on the deeds by themselves, or in a Letter? The £5 you ask about was own'd by Mrs Mary Talbout in my last. When all these afairs are settled we must beg the favour of you to put the Bonds or securities for the £400 in Mr Days hands, least as God forbid you might come to dye sudenly or such unforseen accidents may happen, we having nothing to shew for't could have no claim to our money, so beg you will nott take it ill of me, who has the greatest respect & esteem imaginable of you as all must that has the honour of your acquaintance, & can answer for all our family of the like, but tis an indispensable obligation laid on us by our uper superiours that we may not put out money but wth good securitys in our hands or those we order to take care of it. This is what our own father orderd us to do with a writing by which he orderd my 2 Brothers[50] to pay us each a small pension that writing was orderd to be kept by those we should choose but not to be left on my Brs hands & is now in Cousin Thomas Cholmeleys; this I say to shew 'tis not the least shadow of mistrust, but a reasonable care we must have for were it not for pensions &c out of England we could scarce live, at least very poorly I'm sure, our Honoured Lady & all our family are entirely yours, but none with more sincerity than

Honoured Sir / your most obliged humble servant / Cecily Tunstall

May our most humble service attend your Lady & whole family if Mr Burgis has given you a Book please to send it by this gentleman that comes for Miss Eyre & tell him the poor scotch man was robd in his journey to us so that I would not have him send us more that way tho he tr[*illeg.*]es little Books yet it comes more to help him than they come to.

---

[50]  Cuthbert Constable and Marmaduke Tunstall.

**57.** *CT to MS at Lincoln's Inn. 14 August 1736 (NS) (answered 7 September 1736 OS).* Blount MSS, C *64/125*

Louvain Aug: 14 1736

Honoured Sir

I beg the favour of your speedy forwarding the Inclosed by the penny post the very day you get it: it requiring a speedy answer as also to let me know by the very frst post whether I may draw Lady Catherine's money for she asks me every day about it. The President of Dowey College[51] is here, & gives me a most extraordinary Carrecter of your Son in his care

---

[51]  Dr Robert Witham.

for his piety diligence & chearful complyance with all that is required of him besides many other qualities he will or has acquainted you with as I don't doubt our Honoured Lady & all acquaintance begs you'll accept all Service's the woman is arrived out of England for Miss Betty Eyre's[52] but the gentleman is not yet come from Paris I think to send the papers by him it being too great a bulk to send by the Post so conclude as ever

Honoured Sir / Your most obliged Humble servant / Cecily Tunstall

---

[52] There is more than one person who could be identified by this name.

**58.** *CT to MS at Lincoln's Inn. 19 September 1736 (NS).* Blount MSS, C *64/126*

Louvain Sep 19 1736

Honoured Sir

I long to hear you've had the copys of deeds I sent by good luck by the post for the good old woman lost all her Bagage in London streets as I hear please to forward the inclosed & let me know as soon as you can well do it what money for Mrs Wisoscate[53] &c for they want to know my compliments attends your Lady & your self the same where due from

Honoured Sir / your humble servant / Cecily Tunstall

If you could without inconveniency let either Mr Eyre or Mr Antony Wright know that Mrs Isabella Smith is fallen ill of the small pox & tho' out of danger now yet we won't let her endorce the Bill on him so that if he would alow me to do it else she must stay for the money a great while.

---

[53] Probably Mary Xaveria Wollascott.

**59.** *CT to MS at Lincoln's Inn. 1 October 1736 (NS) (answered 15 October 1736 OS).* Blount MSS, C *64/127*

Louvain octo i: 1736

Honoured Sir

I had yours of the 7: of sep o:s. & have drawn a Bill of £100 on you the other day which I hope you'll be able to pay because Mrs Wollascot &c says that some mony has been paid for em. Mrs Willowby &c is due so that I hope there is no difficulty but please to let me know whether or no Mrs Williscotts[54] is paid to you she says her Br[other] said he had receiv'd your Bill for it but since you don't name it it must be a mistake. Our Lady bids me tell you she is obliged to you Sir for your ready Compliance with her desires to have the security's in Mr Day's hands, we heard nothing from my Br Constable but what you writ that he'd paid £20 which till I hear more I can't tell what it is for for we expect a greater sum from him if you know please to let me hear for I can't dispose of the mony till I know please to let Mr Burgis know what I writ of the Book I desired he would send to Mademoiselle Broeta for me that is to her Correspondant Mr Grimes in the Citty to be sent to her for me Mrs Collingwood expects to hear of some mony from her Brother when 'tis paid would please to let me know this with our Honoured Ladys best respects & service to your Lady & self with the same from

Honoured Sir / your most obliged humble servant / Cecily Tunstall

---

[54]  Wollascott.

**60.** *CT to MS at Lincoln's Inn. 2 November 1736 (NS) (answered 29 October 1736 OS).* Blount MSS, C *64/128*

Louvaine No: 2 1736

Honoured Sir

We all heartily Condole your loss & tho we doubt not of her happyness yet pray as much as if she wanted it I had the favour of yours the 1 instant so that as yet we could not have any publick service for any in particular but all in general but the first Conveniency we shall not fail to perform a Solemn Service for your Honoured Mother[55] as we do for our greatest benefactors in which rank we esteem you Sir I wish for a more & quite different occasion to shew the value & gratitude we owe you. Mrs Wolascote wth her service says her Br writ the 5 July o:s: that he'd your note for the receipt of £5 which she thinks you may have forgot to give me Notice of please to look in your Book at your conveniency & forward this inclosed to the person 'tis address'd to Cousin Pegy Cholmeley will send for the Tongs &c as her Sister desir'd her Mr Burgis has writ latly & says nothing of the *Siners Guide* &c so that I believe you have not yet sent to him about 'em as also the spectacles the same as the last which he got for Mrs Johnson 2 pair which I desire you'll pay him for & give to Cousin Peggy to be sent to Broeta at Antwerp by Mr Grimes one Mrs Gage has laid down 2 Guineas for Mrs Magrath which you'll please to send her back when she calls for 'em I hope you'll please to take out of

---

[55]  Bridget Strickland.

the money in your hands for the year's Letters coach hire or what ever expences & trouble you've had on our account this our Honoured Lady wth her best respects orders me to tell you May your Lady find here her service with all her acquaintance here as named I am

Honoured Sir / your most humble servant to command / Cecily Tunstall

---

Mrs Wolascott has brought me this note of her Brs Letter to [*word cut away*] Cousin:

I suppose we have received the five Pound for which I have had Mr Stricklands receipt now sometime so I remain with best services to all friends

Dr Sister / yor affect: Brother / Will: Wollascott [56]

---

[56] This is a fragment of a letter from William Wollascott to his sister Mrs Wollascott of 5 July 1736 (OS).

**61.** *CT to MS at Lincoln's Inn. 16 November 1736 (NS) (answered 16 November 1736 OS).* Blount MSS, C *64/129*

Louvain the 16 novem 1736

Honoured Sir

This owns the favour of yours oc: 29 & to asure you we've dubly perform'd our promise: & to beg you'll please to forward the inclos'd & also pay Mrs Eliz: Blevin the £3 15s 0d which you receiv'd for Mrs Mary Hacon as soon as you can she'll come for't as soon as she has Mrs Hacons orders for it. Lady Catherine Rad: with her service desir's to know whether you think t'would be proper for her to write again to Lady Petre about our demands she's once writ but had no answer tho 'tis 3 months ago. My Br Constable has asur'd me that he has given up the Colls Estate[57] wholly to Lord Petre & orderd me to apply to him for't now another year is fall'n at our Martlemass. Pray let us have your advice on this for if we thought Lord Petre would do it of him self we would not importune him but as 'tis in a great measure for the maintenance of several persons in our house & our Rents here are so Low & ill pay'd & we've had a sad sickly time on't having the small pox in our House & has this 3 months besides many other illnesses it would be a vast help if we could get this old Debt or part paid at least. The partys think me to blame not to write oftener about it but I asure 'em of your kind promise to do all in your power in it which will much oblige

Honoured Sir / your most humble servant / Cecily Tunstall

---

[57] Colonel Thomas Radclyffe.

May your Lady & self find her our Honoured Ladys & my most humble service as also my sisters neeces & Miss Aire's who are all well.

**62.** *CT to MS at Lincoln's Inn. 5 December 1736 (NS).* Blount MSS, *C 64/130*

Louvain Decem 5 1736

Honoured Sir

I've drawn a Bill of £70 on you the usual way because several persons want their little money. I've left about £13 4s 11d. yet till more comes. Lady Catherine with her most hearty thanks for all your care & concern in her affairs, leaves her self wholly to you to act for her as you see proper nothing has been writ to her on that subject either by Lord Dr[58] or Lady Newbrugh but we've highly disobliged my Lord by leting him know our out apartments were long before promis'd to Mr Wollascott so that we had no conveiniency's for his Lordsp & family upon which he writ to his Aunt that our Lady's rudeness hinderd him from the satisfaction of seeing her Ladyship but whether this had happen'd or not we asure our selves they would hinder us of all they can we only know by hearsay that Mr Will: Radclyffe left a Will but supose you may be better inform'd then we are yet but if you think it needfull we may inform our selves at Rome please to let us have your advice upon it for Lady Cat: will do nothing without it please to find here both hers & our Honoured Ladys best wishes & service the same from
Honoured Sir /your most obedient humble servant / Cecily Tunstall.

---

58  Lord Derwentwater?

**63.** *CT to MS at Lincoln's Inn. 31 December 1736 (NS) (answered 21 January 1736/7 OS).* Blount MSS, *C 64/131*

Louvain Decem: 31. 1736

Honoured Sir

This comes to wish your self & Lady a most happy new year also in case my Last of the 5: of this Instant may be lost to let you know I last post drew a Bill of £70 on you as usual also to forward this inclosed by the penny post for we've no address for Lady Newburgh & the same day I was favour'd with your Last of Novem: 16 o:s. she writ to Mrs Johnson to desire the titles of several writtings Lord D[erwentwate]r left here with her. I in my last asured you Lady Catherine would do nothing without your advice & had heard nothing of any such thing from Lord or Lady or anyone else of that family if you hear any more of it please to let me know for we thought he had made a will both in England &

after at Rome alterd it & left a [sum] to his little nephew Lord D—s son which will we learnd Lord D—r got canceld & recover'd all at Law from his son & spent the Campain he kept in Italy 3 years ago £9000 as one that comes from spain tells us. but whether true or no I know not but if you can't be informd in England we can write to one at Rome that may be able to inform us please to let us have your advice about this mater & whether you've not had some small money from Mrs Carew or Bostock 3 guineas or any other which will add to the many favours already conferd on

Honoured Sir /your most obliged humble servant / Cecily Tunstall

Our Honoured Lady hopes you'll please to find here her best wishes pleas to le[t me] know whether the Book I w[rote about] to Mr Burgis be in the Paket [for] the children.

**64.** *CT to MS at Lincoln's Inn. 1 February 1737 (NS).* Blount MSS, C 64/132

Feb: 1 1737

Honoured Sir

I'm much concern'd to be so long without hearing from you sometimes I fear miscarrige of Letters but we having heard from others in England almost every post makes me fear you're out of order or out of town I beg to hear as soon as you get this & to pay Mr Chorley the sum of £8.2s.5d. which Mrs Magrath ows him. I supose she'll order him to send for it my Br Constable writes me word he's paid £30 lately Mrs Bostock has also writ to s[ay] that she's sent 3 or 4 guineas to her girls beside several I can't think of I can't pay em till I hear we've had the same, besides we would be glad to know whether we need inform our selves at Rome about the will of the late Mr William Radclyffe & till we hear from you we can't tell what to do in it our Honoured Lady joyns in all due respects & services as also all your & Ladys acquaintances so must conclude still beging a speedy answer

Honoured Sir / your most obliged humble servant / Cecilia Tunstall

**65.** *CT to MS at Lincoln's Inn. 4 February 1737 (NS).* Blount MSS, C 64/133

Louvain Feb: 4 1737

Honoured Sir

This comes to beg the favour of you to forward the inclosed & to enquire after your health which I hear to all our great concern has been very bad had I had the least notice sooner we should have made it our chief petition to heaven to pray for your recovery. If you can send any one to Marchand Dillon for Miss's Pension &c I should be glad because her mother is much troubled she has not had it yet & I heard you was out of town but it must have been a mistake. I hope this will find you quite recoverd if not I beg the favour of your Lady or who you please to let us hear a word or two for we shall always be uneasy till we have the satisfaction to hear you'r well my Br Constable has paid Cholmeley we hope 'tis in your hands before this, our Lady &c desires you'll accept her most kind service all dues to your Lady from

Honoured Sir / your most humble servant / Cecily Tunstall

Mrs Galle thinks the Letter will cost less open so please to put it in a cover & direct it as 'tis at the bottom writ.

**66.** *CT to MS at Lincoln's Inn. 10 February 1737 (NS).* Blount MSS, C *64/134*

Louvain Feb: 10 1737

Honoured Sir

Tho I writ last post yet I must let you know that this day I've drawn £100 bill on you. You say the Balance amounts to £119 9s 1d but I fear the £20 from my Br Constable should not be counted because I had only one notice from him & you once before of £20 & now £30 but not twice £20 I fear the first was ownd by you Sir the 7 Sep: o.s. so you'll see whether the 2nd is paid we know nothing what Lady Newburgh does nor had she ever writ here but for her papers we had here, first to have the titles of each which was the packet I sent you & since she orderd us to send the whole Box to Gent[59] some here would have had us kept the writtings in place of a security we want for what my Lord D[erwentwater] Borowd of us & gave us only a Bill on Mr Rodbourne for £100 which Mr Rodbourne protested as having nothing of my Lords in his hands; he owes us almost 300. but most part of our House thought 'twould be to no purpose to keep those old writtings so we sent 'em to Gant[60] as my Lady desired I asure you Sir Lady Catherine neither has nor will do any thing but by your advice. As soon as your health will permit I beg you'll press Mrs Throckmorton to pay what she owes us of Mr Fell's debt of £300 for we know from good hands that she is a very tricking woman & will do what she can to make us loose the rest as we've done Lady

---

[59] Ghent.
[60] Ghent.

Lithcote's part we also beg you'll give us an account what we owe you both for general & particular trouble & Letters for once a year we must give an account of all expence's to the Bishop & 'tis 2 years we've had nothing of that from you Hon[oured Si]r which will oblige your very humble servant / Cecily Tunstall /

Pray let us know how you do.

Your most humble servant.

**67.** *CT to MS at Lincoln's Inn. 20 February 1737 (NS) (answered 25 February 1736/7 OS).* Blount MSS, C 64/135

Louvaine Feb: 20 1737

Honoured Sir

I hope this will find you quite recoverd & that you'll be so good as to forward the inclosed as soon as you can & please not to forget to send to Marchand Dillon for Miss's pention &c: her Mother is much concern'd that she has not yet had it we hear from Mr Bartlet that he's pay'd you a good sum for his 2 Sisters &c: I should be glad to know you have it & please to write or order somebody else if you can't conveniently about what I named in my last viz whether my Br has twice paid £20 since Sep: last besides the £30 also Mrs Talbot says she only expected £5 & you've writ 5 guineas so that I would not have you loose any thing thus I've given her the £5 5s 0d on your Letter. Lady Anne Petre has writ a very kind letter to her Aunt[61] & promises as soon as things are settled she'll perform all that Lady Mary [Radclyffe] was to have payd if she'd lived. I should be glad if you can inform me where the hinderance lyes: for my Cousen Haggerstone told us 4 or 5 years ago that then an Estate was sold & the mony received by Lady Mary's Executors which might have paid all or a great part of the debts but whether t'was the Coll's[62] or Lady Mary's own I can't tell I suppose you heard that poor Mr Wollascott has lost his son & heir I'm glad they were not here then but at Gant & durst not come here for fear of the smallpox the Child dyed of a feaver that rein'd them & they were all ill of it pray what was the illness that you & Mr Rodbourn had for he writ that you both had been ill & could not meet sooner our Honoured Lady & all friends are much your's & none more than

Honoured Sir / your obliged humble servant / Cecily Tunstall

---

Pray let us know what advice Lady Newburg takes or whether any but her own & her Lord.

---

61  Lady Catherine Radclyffe.
62  Colonel Thomas Radclyffe.

**68.** *CT to MS at Lincoln's Inn. 15 March 1737 (NS).* Blount MSS, C *64/136*

Louvain March 15 1737

Honoured Sir

I receiv'd with great pleasure the honour of yours Feb: 25 o:s. & must needs draw a bill on you for £100 this post because several wants their moneys. I hope before this you've had Miss Dillons money for she's long wanted it also from Mr Sheldon £30 or more which he says he's payd you I must beg you'll forward the 2 inclosed. I'm glad my Br paid twice £20 which I must let him know we've had for I was forced to write for it again so that if you can let him know before me I should be glad least he be in pain about it. I'm overjoy'd you are so well recoverd & wish the continuance our Honoured Lady & all here does the same but none more than

Honoured Sir / your most humble servant / Cecilia Tunstall

**69.** *CT to MS at his house at Queen Square, London. 26 March 1737 (NS).* Blount MSS, C *64/137*

Louvain the 26 March 1737

Honoured Sir

I beg you'll forward the inclosed & confer with Mr Hansbie what is to be done in order to oblige Mrs Winefrid Hyde either to give sufficient security for our £150 or refund it she being the only one of the 3 now living who was bound for it & heir to both the other 2 Mr Hansbie was Executor to Mrs Thorold but he's given up his trust still leaving him self a power to act Mrs W[inifri]d: Hyde offers to give us an East Indy bond of £100 which we accepted of but now she will not own 'tis her debt yu'll see plainly by the Copy of the bond I here send you that she can't justly refuse payment she owes us also 3 years Interest & more for one Pound ten shillings is yet due for the year 1734 & all for 1735 1736 1737 fallen due the 17 March new stile we were content to accept it at 4 per cent on Condition of exact payment but that being so far behind we expect the 3 years at 5 per cent so in all she owes £24 for the Interest which we will not abate unless she pays it imediatly all at once & then the debt will be only £19 10s 0d wch we only accepted on account her Aunt borrowed it or took it to do a Charity to a poor Gentleman who could not give any security himself she now would throw it on him but you'll see by the bond he's not named in it. Please to see also if nothing is to be done to Mrs Throckmorton for we're credibly informed that she's a mear tricking woman who seeks only to put of those she deals with so pray use her accordingly & alow her no more time to shuffle please to let me know as soon as possible if Miss Dillons money is paid for she wants it very much also if 'tis needful to get a fresh certificate of Lady Cath: Radclyffes Life now after Lady day is past o:s: this with all dues & offers of service attends you & your Lady from

Honoured Sir / your most obedient humble servant / Cecily Tunstall

**70.** *CT in Louvain to MS at Lincoln's Inn. 9 April 1737 (NS) (answered 8 April 1737 OS).* Blount MSS, C *64/138*

Louvain 9 April 1737

Honoured Sir

Mr Stapylton giving his daughter no direction but for him at one Mr Days in London makes me give you this trouble & to beg if you can tell us a more exact one to him for I'm confident that can't reach him so please to forward this to Miss Stapylton & get this Bill payd by Mr James Rokeby for us also to give Miss Haydocke or her father what they demand to lay out for several persons in our house before she comes hither again please also to let Mr Burgis know that I'd rather have him send what he has for me to Mr Samuel Grimes in the Citty to come over as merchandise for Mademoiselle Broeta at Antwerp than by Mr Haydocke because he will have difficulty to bring what his own friends has desired him for them selves tho that Mr Burgis will get me one or 2 of the new *Think well ont* written by Mr Chalenor[63] & send all as afore sayd & not by occasions please to give him money for all & fail not if you please to let me know if Miss Dillons money is not yet paid for it was ready ever since last October as she had writ by her Mother ever else is payd or due I beg to have notice which will much oblige

Honoured Sir / your most obedient humble servant / Cecily Tunstall

My best respects atends your Lady the same from all friends & be so kind as to let me know what would be acceptable to your self & her Ladyship I have an occasion to send any of our work by Mr Haydocke on his return who is to come here wth his daughter.

---

[63] Richard Challoner, Bishop of Debra and Vicar Apostolic of the London District.

**71.** *CT in Louvain to MS at Lincoln's Inn. April [1737].* Blount MSS, C *64/139*

Sir

I beg you'll do me the favour to send the inclosed down to Mr Hugh Haydocke it's for a friend of mine & pray pay for the letter upon our charge that he may be put to no expenses he's to bring a tea Kitching for one here if he desires the money of you to pay for it please give it to him it will be faithfully return'd here my humble service to your Lady who I hope is in good health accept the same from

Yours to Command / Cecily Tunstall

April the [*blank*]

**72.** *CT to MS at Lincoln's Inn. 16 April 1737 (NS).* Blount MSS, C 64/140

Louvain April 16 1737 n.s.

Honoured Sir

I've got Lady Cath: Radclyff's Certificate renewed but whether by chance or no I know not Mr Daniel has put in a nun at Lovain which we fear will spoil all pray as soon as possible let me have your advice whether we shall take notice to him of it for he seemed to be in a very obliging temper to our notary who carry'd it to him so that I believe he would change the phrase if needful but till I've had your advice I dare not take any notice of it least if he did it on set purpose he may make it worse by giving the Government notice of her being so: he has had no occasion to know her for such, so that if he should come here, she may go to him in secular this is all that presses at present only to know whether you've had £50 from Mr Sheldon for Miss which he writes he paid you the 8 of March please to find here our Honoured Ladys best wishes for a happy Easter 'tis very nigh with us but I can't tell whether it is with you however all our best wishes attend you & yours but none with more earnest wishes than

Honoured Sir / your most obliged humble servant / Cecily Tunstall

**73.** *[CT] to MS at Lincoln's Inn. 23 April 1737 (NS).* Blount MSS, C 64/141

Louvain April 23 1737

Honoured Sir

This is only to let you know that we orderd a young Girl out of Lancashire to address her self to you to find out Mr H: Haydocke who is to take her with him hither I had forgot to tell you this in my last & feard she might surprise you we've also heard that Cousen Willoughby's £20 is paid to you & £50 for Miss Shelldon I beg to hear whether you've had these sums & also Miss Dillons for they all want their moneys & till I hear you have em I can't give em any makes me itterate this request to hear as soon as you can possibly tho the accounts are not ready no mater for that only a word or 2 of advice concerning these points if not too late I should be glad of a very small Book by the young Girl whose name is Latchouse or Lattass who has 2 sisters here the one is a *Pocket manual*[64] the other *The Litanies of Jesus, & of the B[lesse]d Virgin Mary & of the holy Angels with the short office of the Angels* printed in 1720[65] this will be no bulk & is for one who has paid me the money for it here so please to put it to the accounts of

Honoured Sir / your most obliged humble servant / [Cecily Tunstall]

If the *think well on't* be not sent please to let her bring that the best wishes of a most happy Easter attend your self & Lady from our Honoured Lady & all friends.

---

[64]   Untraced.

[65]   *The litanies of Jesus, of the B. Virgin Mary, and of the holy angels. With the short office of the angels* ([London?], 1720). A copy of this popular work can be found in the library at Mapledurham.

**74.** *CT to MS at Lincoln's Inn. 5 May 1737 (NS) (answered 12 May 1737 OS).* Blount MSS, C 64/142

Louvain May 5 1737

Honoured Sir

This owns the favour of yours April 8 o:s. I did not design to trouble you till you let me know whether I should send Lady Catherine's Certificate as it is or not but am pressed to send this inclosed it being to a Lady who has her Daughter at hammersmith & waits for an occasion to send her here to us which I fear will be too late to come with Mr H: Haydocke if so please to put her in mind of Mr Hansby who designes for these parts soon as they tell us also Mrs Knight of Kingerby near Market Rasen in Lincolnshire has writ to me to desire me to let her know when I hear of any one that is to come out of England to bring over any young ladys for us now I think it will be in vain for me to undertake it for before I can know of it & give her notice it will be too late so that I must beg you'll let her know when you hear or know of any good opertunity to send one here or for what she does not plainly say she designs to send her daughter yet. Our Lady &c desires if nothing is to be done with Mrs Throckmorton & the Heir of Lady Lithcotts[66] with out Law that you may use your discretion if any aparent reason to hope it may be gain'd with much Less cost than the charges of the Law Suit will come to if we lose it. Mrs Johnson will write to Mr Fell to see if he who has

---

[66]   Robert Brent Lytcott.

been wholy to blame for putting our money out so can't at Least bring them to some reason or assist you in bringing such proofs as may help to gain our right please to do what you can to get money of Mrs Hyde before Mr Hansby comes over for when he's once out of her way she'll do nothing my Lady Catherine with her humble service bids me tell you again the same I had the honour so often to tell you that you'r master to satisfy your self for the trouble you've had & will have about her affairs & we thought to find if when we have your accounts that you promised so long pray do your self justice & if I could have em once a year it would be much better for I must make every year a reckoning before our chief Superiour & therefore the expences would be more equal if I had yours in every year since Mr Dillon the merchant will not own he has Miss's mony I must beg you'll desire Mr Day to get it of him that paid him for the 2 boys at Dowey[67] for as there are 2 marchants it may be that he who has it for her will not pay it but to Mr Day this with the best wishes & service of our Honoured Lady & all friends concludes me

Honoured Sir / your most humble & obedient servant / Cecily Tunstall

---

[67]  The English College, Douai.

**75.** *CT to Mrs Mary Strickland at Queen Square, London, with copy of Mrs Strickland's answer, in her hand. 19 May 1737 (NS).* Blount MSS, C *64/143*

Lovain May 19 1737

Madam

I beg you'll allow of this liberty suposing Mr Strickland out of town or so busy that I can't have the favour of an answer to that wherin I desired his advice about Lady Cath's Certificate of Life I must even send it by Mr. H. Haydock if I can't have a word or two about it as also to forward the inclosed & send this little bit of Paper to Mr Day that he may get Miss Dillon's money of the marchand Dillon this with all our best wishes & service to your self & spouse is all from

Madam / your most humble servant / Cecily Tunstall

*[Then in hand of Mary Strickland]*

I receved your Letr & should have answerd it sooner had not Mr Strickland writ him self to you the Post before yours came to me & he told me he had writ to you about three weeks before he has not been out of town if he had nothing would have been neglected in your affairs for he is a Person of such strict Justice & Honour that I am sure no body ever sufferd through his fault, and I believe Madam very few to be found if any that duse as he has often dun to do Honour to your Bills paying

Money out of his one [own] Pocket when you have drawn before he has receved the Sumes you have drawn for Peoppel often send you word the[y] have paid Mr Strick[land] when those payments are in Bills & not be receved some times in thurty days after & then with a great deal of trouble this I know becaus I have after Mr Strick[land] has been out of town severall times Payed your bills before I have had Monny such care he has allways taken not to disopint you I wish our Payments would be payd when due but mony in some Peopels hands is hard to be got out I must do Mr Strick[land] this justis as to say his Character was before I was Married just as I see & those that know him have always found the advantage of being in his hands & the diferance of his usage from others. I have been 17 years his Wife & his Merits dayly increase my admiration & respect for him & tho he dont writ Madame so often as you would have him I am sure I may say he writts as often as he can do you any service.

**76.** *CT to MS at Lincoln's Inn. 28 May 1737 (NS) (answered 10 June 1737 OS).* Blount MSS, C *64/144*

Lovain May 28 1737

Honoured Sir

Since I can't have the favour of an answer to what I writ the begining of April to know whether I should sent Lady Catherine's Certificate as it was or venture to get Mr Daniel to change it I've after long expectation sent it & got it alterd & now send it you he did it by chance he says. I've received almost £200 of Mrs Neesum here which Lord Rivers left her so that when you have a good sum in your hand I must get you to return it down into the Country to her but there is time enough for that when I hear she's safe at York if my Br Tunstall has not yet paid the £20 & Br Constable the £41 they owe here I could write to 'em to pay it to her at York it would be near'r home & I would pay the persons concern'd out of her money I have here please to Let Mr Burgis know with my service that I've had all the parcels he's sent: but yet not the *Siners guide* nor the *Pocket manuel* nor the *Littanys & prayers* that used to be joined to my Cousin Crathorn's Little Book of *morning & night prayers*[68] which if he would get & take all that is due for the spectacles & Books I've had & these he may send em the same way or by Mrs Perry, I'm sorry she did not know of good Mr Hansby who has brought Grace Lathouse very soon & safe & is very gratfull to you & your Lady for the care you had to send one to the wagon for her I beg what ever cost you was at

---

[68] Probably Anon., *A practical catechism upon the Sundays, feasts and fasts of the whole year* (n.p., 1711).

[that] you'll please to deduct it of &c please to find here our Honoured Lady's & all our gratfull acknowledgments for all favours & believe me Honoured Sir / your most obliged humble servant / Cecily Tunstall

---

The *think well on't* I writ for last please to get Mr Burgis to send with the rest not to put you to the trouble 'tis the new one of Mr Chals[69]

---

[69]   Richard Challoner.

**77.** *CT to MS at Lincoln's Inn. 15 June 1737 (NS) (answered 18 June 1737 OS).* Blount MSS, C *64/145*

Louvain June 15 1737

Honoured Sir

Though I can't have the favour of an answer to so many Letters yet I find my [*sic*] Mr Day's to me the reason why you have not yet had Miss Dillon's money is because you don't know what sum to demand I thought Mrs Dillon had given orders when she sent the money now since we've staid so very Long Miss Dillon says she's writ again to her mother to have the half year due since may last so that we must have in all £37 10s 0d twenty two & ten shillings for the pension for a year & half & 15 for her use as her Father promised her she says £20 a year & 5 for the half year in all as sd £37 10s 0d . This I hope will be soon demanded & got I'm afraid Mrs Parry has never met with you Sir or not got the Letter I inclosed for her at Easter for if she had she'd have come Long or this as we supose I beg you'll let Mr Burgis know what I writ in my last that he may sent em & that I've got the 2 parcells he sent before & believe me ever

Honoured Sir / Your most humble servant / Cecily Tunstall

Our Honoured Lady's best wishes attend your self & Lady & also your & our friends

**78.** *CT to Mrs Mary Strickland at Queen Square, London. 9 July 1737 (NS).* Blount MSS, C *64/146*

Lovain July 9 1737

Madam

I would not lose one post day that you may lose no time if you design to send any one to the same place where Miss Eyre[70] is 'tis Berlaijmont's[71]

---

[70]   Pensioner? The Eyre family had numerous daughters.
[71]   Fondation de Lalaing et de Berlaijmont.

at Bruxells where they have better Education as we think than any other house Miss Eyre might have learned French here if she pleased for we keep an old Lady very well boarn for that purpose but young people will not aply them selves when they can help it but there they can hear no English so must learn. She nor any other of our pensioners ever stais there in winter because they use only stoves which does not agree with the English Constitutions. 'Tis mutch Dearer there than here for the pension alone is £20 & they must pay for all they use & washing & if sick all particulars in fine they give nothing but meat & drink & lodging the person must have knife fork & spoon table linning but that may be counted included in the £20 because those that live in the Town & find sheets table linning &c pay less. Our pension is but £15 when they find themselves in cloathes but we take care of all other Conveniences for 'em so that sick or well they only find 'em selves wearing cloaths & dancing master's &c the name of the Lady who now govern's the House is Madame de Alsase or alsace & is called the Prevote this is all I can tell of it if I'm capable of serving you in any thing else please to command your humble Servant / Cecily Tunstall

———•·•———

My neeces are much yours.

**79.** *CT to MS at Lincoln's Inn. 19 July 1737 (NS) (answered 15 July 1737 OS).* Blount MSS, C *64/147*

Louvain July 19 1737

Honoured Sir

I must beg you'll send to Mr Wyke to get this Bill payd for Mrs Eliz Smith who arived her[e] the 17 instant she tells us that Mrs Wybourn[72] is at London & very ill our Honoured Lady writ to her some time ago to put her in mind of an old debt of £36.11s.6d. wch is owing to our house on account of her daughter Charity who was here pensioner with me 36 years ago Mrs Smith says you are imployd about her afairs so I hope you will get us this money & please to let us hear from you which will much oblige

Honoured Sir / your very humble servant / Cecily Tunstall

---

[72] Lettis Wybarne.

**80.** *CT in Louvain to MS at Lincoln's Inn. 19 August 1737 (NS) (answered 18 August 1737 OS).* Blount MSS, C *64/148*

Louvain Aug: 19 1737

Honoured Sir

I hope by this you have enough to pay what I owe Mrs Mary Neesum I received of her here the sum of 2564 8s 0d florins exchanged money 8 of our stuyvs wch makes £25 8s 8d in English money but she must lose the exchange which is a shilling per pound sterling my Br Constable has paid her £21 0s 0d of this sum the rest you may return her by my Cousen Bryan Tunstall to whom I've writ to desire he will take her aquitance as fast as he pays her if I knew he had money in his hands for Dowey College he might pay her that & you give the like sum to Mr Day which would be a shorter way pray in your next let me know whether my Lord Montgomery had the Letter which was writ & inclosed to you for him & whether we may expect the favour of an Answer from his Lordship I both fear & hope that you will have all Mr Piget's[73] practice which though I heartily wish you the benefit of; yet fear you'll have so much more business that you'll have no time for things of less importance. I should be very glad to know whether you've had the rest of Miss Dillon's money you only having had £20 & she demands £11 10s 0d more to make [£]37 10s 0d which she was orderd to demand & told she might have for asking & I've paid her the like sum on that assurance I must beg you'll pay Mr Collingwood what he has layd out for us which I can't just[l]y tell you but let him have what he demands as also Mr Burgis who I fear you've not seen since mine I hope your Lady had mine wherin I gave her an account of the Ladys at Berllemonts at Bruxells to chuse her sister there for her Guardian she being minor herself in hopes to have her share of her uncle Eyre's will pray let us have your oppinion of this matter whether there's any likelyhood of gaining or whether the will is valid in favour of the widow you may if you please get a coppy of the will & send it us. Also I hope you'll deal with Mr Fell to get the interest of the money he owes if nothing else can be done to sue Mrs Throckmorton for her part of it if nothing else will do services & all good wishes attends your self & Lady from our Honoured Lady & all other friends here please to let me know what you pay Mrs Neesum & what you have re[ceive]d since yours of July 15 o:s: which will much oblige
Honoured Sir / your most obliged humble servant / Cecily Tunstall

—————•◦•—————

Please to pay my Cousen Peggy Cholmeley what she is desired to lay out for us for Books &c.

---

[73] Nathaniel Pigott, barrister.

**81.** *CT in Louvain to MS at Lincoln's Inn. 6 September 1737 (NS).*
Blount MSS, C *64/149*

Louvain Sep: 6 1737

Honoured Sir

I received the honour of yours of Aug 19 and I latly gave Mr Melling
a little Bill of eight pound which you'll please to pay Mr John Shepperd
on sight I find Mrs Neesum is not in any great hast of her money so that
I may draw one hundred Pound to satisfy those who I owe it to & by
that time that Lady Catherine's is payd she may have what is her due she
has had £21 of my Br Constable & I will write to my Cousen Bryan[74]
at York about it. The same day I had yours I heard your Daughter was
safe at the Berllemonds. I could have wished she had come first here
for some time for 'tis a very melancholy thing to go to a french house
before one understands something of french. We should have made her
doubly welcome & 'twould not have cost you a farthing but since 'tis
done & miss Peggy[75] is with her I hope she'll like very well if any thing
lies in our powers to serve her we shall be very ambitious of it this our
Honoured Lady with her best wishes & service to your Lady & self bids
me tell you the same services attends you both by all that have the honour
of your aquaintance here Mr President Witham[76] has been latly here &
still always gives the highest praises of your Son[77] in all kinds that can
be expressed my nephew is now at the same College to my great joy.
As I said I'll draw if you please a Bill of one hundred pound on you as
usual this Post & remain

Honoured Sir / your most humble servant / Cecily Tunstall

———•◦•———

Lady Catherine hopes you'll get her money soon.

———————

[74]  Bryan Tunstall.
[75]  Margaret Eyre.
[76]  President of the English College, Douai.
[77]  John Strickland.

**82.** *CT to MS at Lincoln's Inn. 7 October 1737 (NS) (answered 21
October [1737]).* Blount MSS, C *64/150*

Louvain Ocr: 7 1737

Honoured Sir

Mrs Dillon has been here & has payd me all dues so that if you've
received any more from the marchand Dillon since the £26 11s 0d you
must please to give it back. If you've had any thing for Lady Catherin

yet, please to let us know. Mrs Neesum has writ latly that she desired her money from you so if she has no more from my Br Constable she must have just the sum of £222 sterling 14 shillings. This I've let her know & given her a direction to you but if my Br has paid her any more since the £21 she owns from him she'll let you know I suppose she'll take it of the Ariares [arrears] or in fine you'll please to pay it to her orders. Miss Eyre is to come home soon & I fear your Daughter will want her much that is if she had no French before she came over our Honoured Lady desires here humble service to your Lady & self please to accept the same from

Honoured Sir / Your most humble servant / Cecily Tunstall.

I must put you in mind of your promise to let me know what would be acceptable to your self & Lady I've expected the whole sumer & now 'tis almost winter yet I have not the satisfaction to hear. I must beg Mr Burgis or my Cousen Pegge Chol[meley]: may send 2 of Mr Gother's Books for the sick[78] &c with the *Sinners guide* & *Pocket manuel* & the addition of Cousen Will Crathorn's *Morning & night prayers*[79] that is all the rest [*illeg.*] named [*illeg.*] be had before & please to pay him.

---

[78] John Gother, *Instructions and devotions for the afflicted and sick* ([London?], 1697).
[79] Not identified.

**83.** *CT in Louvain to MS at Lincoln's Inn. 5 November 1737 (NS).*
Blount MSS, C *64/151*

Louvain no: 5. 1737

Honoured Sir

I hope before this you've received Lady Catherine's Anuity. She enquires every post if I've not yet heard of it & as I'm yearly obliged to give in my accounts of all received & layd out & what ever is due to us or what we owe so I beg you'll not take it amiss that I beg to know what is done or adoing about the £300 Mr Fell lost us for the persons friends who is to be taken on that said £300 has writ latly that they hear it may yet be recover'd also please to let us know whether you've done any thing to Mrs Hyde to oblige her to pay her Debt & Mrs Throckmorton who as I've before writ & empowerd you to sue or use as you thought fit. Please also to let us know when we may hope to receive what Lord Petre has promis'd to pay of Coll: Rads:[80] & when we shall have Mrs

---

[80] Colonel Thomas Radclyffe.

Wybourne's Debt: also I beg leave to claim your promise of your accounts & about the money you put out 2 years ago which we hope you've paid your self out of for Sallery & Letters & what Lady Catherine desired you'd take for what you've done in her afaires, also whether you've paid Mrs Neesum the £222 & odd or whether she will take any or stay till Cousen Bryan[81] or my Br[82] pay's her for I gave her your direction & choise, in all these particulars I hope you'll be so good as to satisfy me as soon as time will alow. Mr Jesup when here promised me to pay you £15 more when he arrived so pray put him in mind of it & if you see Mr Burgis desire he'll send the Books & please to pay him & Mr Shepperd if not already done which will much oblige

Honoured Sir / your most humble servant / Cecily Tunstall

Our Honoured Lady my sisters & all friends desire your Lady & self may find here their most kind service. If you see Mr Brinkhurst or his sisters please to put em in mind that they owe for a year & halfs pension for the 2 last that was here £45 & more but I dont think we shall ever get it yet if not clamed they may pretend they knew nothing of it.

---

[81]   Bryan Tunstall.
[82]   Cuthbert Constable.

**84.** *CT in Louvain to MS at Lincoln's Inn. 11 November 1737 (NS) (answered 18 November 1737 OS).* Blount MSS, C 64/152

Louvaine novem 11 1737

Honoured Sir

Yours of oc: 21 o:s: I received with great Joy for that Lady Catherine desired me to write agane about it which I did last post I'm sorry we did not know sooner of the Lace you desire for Mr Jesup got safe with his & I think it a great hazard in a Letter or at least one can send but a part of it or each row for the Ruffles & the same of the Mob: & so by piecemale. We must have it from the Lace marchands at Bruxelles for we here do none I must draw a Bill on you for £100 this Post because Mrs Smith[83] & Sir William Gerard &c want their mony but for Mrs Bentley she has drawn a Bill as they tell me on you for her £10 10s 0d for she's at Bruxelles. I hope we shall have the pleasure at least next sumer to see your Daughter when our Honoured Lady keeps her Jubily & at the clothing of miss Pegy Eyre which we hope you nor your Lady

---

[83]   Sr Elizabeth Mary Winefrid Smith.

will not refuse in case they Live so Long Mrs Neesum as we supose will stay for all or part of her money till my Br or Cousen Bryan will pay part so that I only draw part of what you have now. Please to find here Lady Catherines & our Honoured Ladys service & accept the same from

Honoured Sir / your most humble servant / Cecily Tunstall

---

I hope you'll see my Br[84] & sister who talk'd of going to the bath at Michelmass if you do pray let him know his 2 daughters are well & give all our Loves to him & mind him of what I writ to him about last also please to confer a Little with him about Lord Petre's debt to our House because the Anuitys runs up & several are for maintenances.

---

84  Cuthbert Constable.

**85.** *CT to MS at Lincoln's Inn. 6 December 1737 (NS) (answered 12 December 1737 OS).* Blount MSS, C *64/153*

Louvain Decem 6: 1737

Honoured Sir

The three hundred pounds debt we charge Mr Fell with comes from his having lost so much of our money which Mr Willm Wollascott paid him for his sister here & he instead of paying my Bill for the sayd sum which I drew on him refused it & it was protested & then pretended he'd writ for our consent to put out to interest the said sum upon as good security as any in England but 'twas [mani]fest by the bond on Mrs Throckmorton that he took that way to apease us & sent us a bond [on] Lady Litcote for the said sum. Mrs Jonson has inclosed a Letter to him to see if any thing can be done Mr Day can inform you the best way on account of the said Loss we had by Mr Fell did our business for us till Mr Haydocke took it & after told us no one could so well help us to recover the said sum as your self please to supply the address to him for we do not know it. If you should know where Mr Hansby lives please to let him know that our Honoured Lady who is to be named as the Executor and administrator of Mrs Mary Worthington & who impowers you to act & offers to give or let you make a Letter of Atturney if need be but we desire nothing to be done till Mr Hansby's advice be asked who may be admitted to see her perhaps I had some time ago a Letter from your Lady for which I beg she may find here all my best thanks & will not trouble here with a letter apart till I can get an occasion Miss Eyre & all her other acquaintance are well & remember 'em most kindly to her please to let me know if a Letter to my Br Constable can forward the affair of Coll: Radclyffe but he asured me 2 years ago that he had entirely given up all that part of Lady marys it having been left to the family the yearly pensions should certainly be payd especially Cousen Barbara Crathornes which was Left her for a maintenance for her Life & was paid till 1730 as you may see by my former letter this was left her by my Aunt Anne Radclyffe long before the rest was given by Coll: Rad:[85] to severall persons in our house & I fancy if Lord Petre was apprised of it he would pay that at Least for the Longer it runs on the greater debt will be contracted I should be very glad to have it now for we've had great Expences & Law Suites this year & shall have in all Likelyhood still greater the next & if it be not payd soon I shall maybe not have the satisfaction to pay debts which the House has contracted for want of it for our rents are so ill paid here that we have not nigh enough to pay the expences of the year without suplys from England & this was one of the best next to Lady Catherine Rad: I beg your speedy advice how to act on these points & believe me ever

Honoured Sir / your obliged humble servant / Cecily Tunstall

---

Our Honoured Lady & all friends here begs you will accept their best wishes & service to your self & Lady.

---

[85]  Colonel Thomas Radclyffe.

**86.** *CT to Mrs M[ary] Strickland at her house in Queen Square, Ormond Street. 16 December 1737 (NS).* Blount MSS, C *64/154*

Lovain Decem. 16 1737

Madam

I'm infinitly obliged to you for your good advice & more for giving it in so obliging a maner & ofering to help to execute it. But I not having the honour to be aquainted wth Mr White: think that Mr Day who is perfectly well apprised of that afair if he pleased to act on it may do it more effectualy so beg you'll please to send him the inclosed & put both to our accounts as I hope Mr Strickland will do all I've the honour to write to s[*illeg.*] [f]or him self I've got a piece of Cambrick for you such as I judged best for a deep mourning & have sent it to our marchand woman Mademoiselle Broeta to send of as soon as possible unless you will please to let me know very speedily a Better way & when I know to which of her Correspondances she's sent it will let you know for to pay the Custom which I beg you'll put to our accounts & accept this small present & if you like it may comand more which occasion I embrace with pleasure & wish it lay in my power to oblige either Mr Strickland or your self. I must beg you'll make our Honoured Lady's best wishes acceptable to Mr Strick[land] with mine & all that have the honour of his aquaintance Miss Eyre my neeces begs you'll accept the same as well as Madam / Your most obliged humble servant / Cecily T[unstall]

**87.** *CT to MS at Lincoln's Inn. 29 December 1737 (NS) (answered 30 December 1737 OS).* Blount MSS, C *64/155*

Lovaine 29 De: 1737

Honoured Sir

I've received with pleasure your accounts & have compar'd 'em with our Book & find all very exact only could have wished you'd have been pleas'd to have taken what you judged fit for Lady Catherine's afairs that you've adjusted, so pray be as good as your word & send it the next Letter I find you've not yet had the 2nd £20 of Lady Gerard but she writing to Mr Melling that she'd orderd the like sum to be paid to you I hope I may venture to draw it with the £83 15 11½d which you own to be due to us & a Bill less than £100 does not yeald so good exchange so that I beg if you have not sent to Mr Wyke that you will & I this post will draw a Bill of 100 on you the £3 &c remains till more come to it my Br[86] writes he has money in London & will soon order us & his 2 children but how much he does not say tho' I've given him my accounts some months ago. I long to have a Line from your Lady about the Cambrick I've sent to Antwerp in order to ship of unless she speedily send me word what better way she has if not I hope she'll get it soon if 'tis not gone yet & I orderd the Custom to be paid for it & that it may be put to our accounts by you if they come for it. I being advised not to venture any other way. I beg your Lady & self will accept our Ladys & mine & all our familys best wishes of a happy new year & all the blessings that attend the most prosperous both spiritual & temporal as much as they may further the first I've had a Letter from Mr President[87] who always praises your Son to the highest degree but not above his merits my neeces & sisters & Miss Eyre join in all best wishes &c I should be glad to know whether it would farther the affair of Lady Petre if I writ to my Br Constable about it as I desird in my last a word of advice would oblige

Honoured Sir / your most obliged humble servant / Cecily Tunstall

---

[86] Cuthbert Constable.
[87] Dr Robert Witham.

**88.** *CT to MS at Lincoln's Inn. 25 February 1738 (NS) (answered 10 March 1737/8 OS).* Blount MSS, C *64/156*

Louvain Feb: 25 1738

Honoured Sir

This comes to let you know that I've given Mr Melling a Bill of Eight £ which Mr Shepperd must receive of you I hope before this you've had some money from my Br Constable which he said he had at London out of which this & also what Cousen Pegge Cholmeley knows I owe her for I can't tell yet so that you'll please to let her take what she thinks fit for Twist & Books also if you have enough in your hands you'll please to Let her have £5 for Miss Irelands which they've desir'd her to lay out for them & e'er long Mrs Tuffden will pay you some money for 'em. Mademoiselle Broeta never told me till this last post to whom she sent the Cambrick for your Lady but now she says she has sent it to Mr Samuel Grymes in the Citty & that he'll deliver it to your Lady or if he forgets that you'll please to send to him for it I have no direction to him but I believe he comes for the payment of her Bills some time so that you may know him if any thing be to be paid for the Custom &c pray put it to our accounts I'm very sorry she had it not long e'er this for now it will do no service I fear I sent it almost 4 months ago but no ships went then pray with my service let your Lady know this & also whether she had a Letter from me with one inclosed to Mr Day from whom I've never had any answer about Mr Fell's mony if you see Mr Burgis or else Cousen Peggy Cholmeley may get the *Pocket manuel* which I writ to him for long ago please to let us know as soon as conveniently you can whether my Br Constable has paid the money I menetion'd for till I hear I can't give my sisters their part of it. Our Honoured Lady & all others friends &c begs you & your Lady may find here all that is kind &c the same from

Honoured Sir / your most humble servant / Cecily Tunstall

Please to give Cousen Peggy Cholmeley orders if Mr Burgis has not done so himself to get Mr R: C: *Think well ont*[88] which I desired him long ago to get 1 or 2 of also the *Bona mors* but not the little Book but one made by a Jesuit which is as big as a Manuel but not so thick. I think it is called *A pious association for the obtaining a happy death.*[89] Price 1s 0d. Cousen Peggy sent Mr Gothers *practical Cat[echism]s* in place of Cousen W: Crathornes which she was desired to send last time if his is to be had we should be glad of it she may get it of him at Hamersmith

---

[88]  Richard Challoner, *Think well on't* (1728).
[89]  Anon., *A pious association of the devout servants of Jesus Christ crucify'd, and of his condoling mother the blessed Virgin Mary; for the obtaining a happy death* (London, 1738).

for 'tis not at the Bookselars if any Bookselars have the *spiritual Combate*[90] one in our House desires it but I can't find it in the Catalogue if you see Mr Burgis or Cousen Pegs pleas[e de]sire 'em to see for these Books & please [pay] 'em money for 'em.

---

[90]  Lorenzo Scupoli, *The spiritual combat*. First published in Italian 1589.

**89.** *CT to MS at Lincoln's Inn. 27 March 1738 (NS).* Blount MSS, C *64/157*

Louvaine March 27: 1738

Honoured Sir

This is to wish you & your Lady a most happy Easter & to let your Lady know I've had the honour & favour of hers & have imediatly sent & writ to Mademoiselle Broeta to know by whom she sent the Cambricke & what ship for there it must be found out as I suppose. Mrs Rodbourne is in great pain about her Father so that she begs you'll do her the favour to enquire after him & let us know as soon as possibly you can or procure some of his family to write to her 'tis 6 or 7 months she's heard nothing of him. Mrs Crathorn had a promise of her Aunt Cockaine to sent her a parcel of old cambrickes to make flowers of she begs you'll sent em as soon as you receive 'em to cousen Peggy Cholmeley to be sent with the Childrens Box for our House please to let me know if you have any money for us of my Br Constable who said he had orderd some at Xmass & if you have let Cousen Pegge Cholmeley pay her self out of it what she layd out for us if Mr Burgis comes to London let him pay him self if you please what he has layd out or will lay out for us as he promised to do this with the best wishes & prayers of our Honoured Lady & all our family for your Self & Lady & all your family with my 2 neeces service & all acquaintance is the best I can conclude my self

Honoured Sir / your most humble servant / Cecilia Tunstall

**91.** *CT to MS at Lincoln's Inn. 4 April 1738.* Blount MSS, C *64/158*

Louvaine April 4 1738

Honoured Sir

I had this day the honour of your Ladys which she favourd me with & find by it that there is £10 for this house so that I draw this day a Bill of £100 on you as usual because Mrs Smith[91] will want her money &

---

[91]  Sr Elizabeth Mary Winefrid Smith.

besides my Cousen Betty Willoughby's £20 will be due on our Easter day which is your Lady day so I count you'll have something left besides what you'll please to pay to Cousen Peggy Chol: &c I've had an account from Mademoiselle Broeta that Mr Grimes has now found the Cambrick for your Lady: if any custome is due for it I beg youll pay him & put it to our accounts. I fear it comes too late to do any service it being just such as Lady Manson[92] had for deep mourning. At least I hope your Lady will accept the good will, & our Honoured Lady's & my best wishes of a most happy & joyfull Easter the like my 2 neeces & all friends begs she & you will accept from

Honoured Sir / your most humble servant / Cecilia Tunstall

---

[92]  Monson?

**92.** *CT to MS at Lincoln's Inn. 18 April 1738 (NS) (answered 21 April 1738 OS).* Blount MSS, C *64/159*

Louvaine April 18 1738

Honoured Sir

I send you here inclosed Lady Catherine's certificate where you'll find Mr Daniel has made a little mistake seting 9 of March o:s. for 29 of March o:s. which seems to correct it self by seting the 9 April n:s. If this be of any consiquence we will get it alterd by him but as I'm advised to let it pass I leave it to your judgement. I hope your Lady has at last had the Cambrick: better late than never as they say but I fear too late to be serviceable it being only proper for deep mourning Mr Grimes sais he only had it 2 days after your Lady sent for it but I sent it the 3 decem n:s. in hopes to have had the pleasure to hear it came in time for the design'd use so I hope your Lady will accept the will for the deed. My Lady Petre writ lately to Lady Catherine that she hoped now things would soon be settled so that Lady Cath: &c would be payd: now my Br Constable also writes that Lord Petre & he have referd themselves wholly to you Sir about the accounts not yet setld between his Lordship & my Br &c. so that he says you may help us to get payment at least of Cousen Barbara Crathorne's Annuity which has been unpaid since 1729 due for 1730 &c which can not be disputeable because my Aunt Anne Radclyffe left or rather gave it her in her life time & both the Coll:[93] & his Brother Frank: were bound for the payment of it this you may see by the Copy I sent 2 year ago. Please to let us know if you've had the £60 my Br says he's paid & also Cousen Willoughby's £20 & if you've

---

[93]  Colonel Thomas Radclyffe.

done any thing yet to force Mrs Hide to pay us & what can be done to Mr Fell &c which will much oblige

Honoured Sir / your most obliged humble servant / Cecily Tunstall

---

My Honoured Lady's best wishes attends your self & Lady & also all ours if not too late of a most happy & many of 'em Easters our Honoured Lady hopes you will not deny to let us have your daughter's good Company at her Jubily it will be kept this sumer but when I can't yet tell because our Church is not repaird & how long it will be before 'tis dry we can't just tell.

**93.** *CT to MS at Lincoln's Inn. 29 April 1738 (NS).* Blount MSS, C *64/160*

Louvain April 29 1738

Honoured Sir

I've drawn an other Bill of £100 on you this day because Lady Gerard has write twice that she paid you £40 for her son here & my Br Constable has paid £60 before as he writ 6 weeks ago & said he would pay £20 more as soon as he came to London but if he does not the £60 [& S]r Williams £40 will pay the Bill & besides Cousin [*illeg.*]nore has paid a small sum & Mr Barkley & my Br Constable & Tunstall will soon sent each 30 more. I should not have been so hasty but that Sir William Gerard is orderd by my Lady his mother to remove to Liege & can't stay for his money so tho' I've had no notice from you yet I hope you will not take it amiss being sure 'tis pd. I long to hear your Lady has had the Cambrick at long run & that you & she will not deny our Honoured Lady's petition to have the pleasure of your daughters Company at her Jubeley but yet the time is not fixt, for we've been forced to make reparations which will retard it some months perhaps I can't yet tell her Lad[yship] will not be denied so we beg your consents & that you both may find her the best wishes & services of all friends & particularly

Honoured Sir / your most humble Servant / Cecily Tunstall

**94.** *CT to MS at Lincoln's Inn. 13 May 1738 (NS).* Blount MSS, C *64/161*

Louvain May 13 1738

Honoured Sir

We beg you'll be so good as to let us know if wht we've done already is not sufficient to impower you to act against Mrs Hyde If you mean that your daughter must be in the inclosier[94] while she's here our Lady will procure a Licence from his Em[inen]ce[95] for without that we can't but for young Lady's he makes no great difficulty, her Ladyship begins the 15 of June n:s. so that there is a month now full to it. As soon as I had your Lady's Letter I writ to Mademoiselle Broeta who said that the widow had told her that she was very well left & should keep up trade & do in all things as in her husbands life I desired she would positively order em to send Mrs Strickland her Cambricke without any more delay so with my humble service pray let her know that I'm truly mortified she should hav had so much trouble & all for nothing. Mrs Crathorn says that her Aunt Cockain promis'd to send her a bundle of fine old Cambrick to make flowers of if you have had it or when it comes to your hand please to send it by the first safe occasion she thinks Mr Jones was to be the first he's long spoke of coming over & if he does will willingly take it she's sure. As soon as you give your daughter leave to come we'll take all the care you require & any else in our power's that she may be easy when here wishing any better occasion to shew how much I am

Honoured Sir / your most obliged humble servant / Cecily Tunstall

---

94   Enclosure.
95   The Archbishop of Mechelen.

**95.** *CT to MS at Lincoln's Inn. 28 May 1738 (NS)*. Blount MSS, C 64/162

Louvain May 28 1738

Honoured Sir

This is to let you know that this day I've drawn a Bill on you for £160 the which you may receive of Mr Wyke as soon as ever you please suposing you've had my last with the said Bill which Mrs Smith[96] would have him pay as soon as you can he having her money ready [when] you demand it. I beg also that if one Mr John Martin or any other whosoever in his name shall come to demand £5 as a debt he pretends Mrs Magrath must pay, for her Br as Mr Martin pretends but she will not pay it nor can he prove it so that if he comes she desires you'll refuse payment. she not being liable to pay any more than she has paid nor did she ever hear of it till now. & tis 6 years almost that he's been dead. Pray if my Br[97] designes to make us a visit let me know for perhaps he'd surprise us but I beg you'll let us know that we may get some good Lodging i[n the]

---

96   Sr Elizabeth Mary Winefrid Smith.
97   Cuthbert Constable.

Town for we have none proper here at present for Mr & Mrs Wollascott has the 3 best rooms. Mrs Wollascott desires all that's kind to your Lady, so does all friends here we've leave for your daughter to come in to our House if we may have the favour of her Company which is the desire of / Honoured Sir /your most humble servant / Cecily Tunstall

**96.** *CT to MS at Lincoln's Inn. 20 June 1738 (NS) (answered 19 June 1738 OS).* Blount MSS, C *64/163*

Louvain 20 of June 1738

Honoured Sir

Your long silence puts me in some concern for your health as also refusing us the favour of your Deserving Daughters company the Jubily week after having granted us that favour which refusal was made by your Cosen Mannock she promising you would satisfy us as to that point. I must put you in mind of Mrs Winefred Hyde who they tell me lives at a village close to the Bath the name I've forgot which they tell me 'tis Weston not so very near as I said to Bath. Please upon payment of £450 to deliver to Con[sello]r: Webb these papers. I hope you'll remember Mrs Wybournes debt to our House now the year is out or thereabouts since her death. I hope you'll confer with my Br[98] about Lady Petre's debts on account of my Aunt Anne Radclyffe & Coll: Radclyffe. Please to make our compliments acceptable to your lady & if my Br is yet in town to let him know his dear Girls are well they & Miss Eyre present their most kind service to your Lady & self accept the same from her who is Honoured Sir your most humble Servant / Cecily Tunstall

---

[98] Cuthbert Constable.

**97.** *CT in Louvain to MS at Lincoln's Inn. 4 July 1738 (NS) (answered 30 June 1730 OS).* Blount MSS, C *64/164*

Louvain July 4. 1738

Honoured Sir

I this day had the honour of yours dated June 19:O.S. & tho' you have but a very small sum in your hands now yet I must draw a Bill this post on you of £60 [£]35 of which is [*illeg.*] is Mrs Bently's who is in great hast of it before she goes for England so presuming you have it already or equivalent my Br Tunstall having long ago paid £20 & some what more for us & Mr Monington & several others as Mr Shelldon of Winchester & Mr Rodburn so that at least I hope before they come for payment we shall have in your hands the said sum. I've this day together with my

Bill of £60 writ to Mademoiselle Broeta to let her know that your Lady has not had the Cambrick yet & that I suspect they sold it when the mourning was first in voge this will make em in honour make it good at least if they have done so. Pray my respects & service to your Lady & accept the same from our Honoured Lady & all other friends from
    Honoured Sir / your most humble servant / Cecily Tunstall

**98.** *CT in Louvain to MS at Lincoln's Inn. 7 July 1738 (NS) (answered 28 July 1738 OS).* Blount MSS, C *64/165*

Louvain July 7 1738

Honoured Sir

    I've had a letter this day from Mademoiselle Broeta, who says the exchange is now at the highest & will not be so for any time; so that I beg you'll see to get Mrs Stapleton's £450 &c as soon as possible, & Lady Catherine's but if you receive the other first as you may when you please to deliver the papers to Mr Webb: who has had the money in his hands some time let me know pray without staying for Lady Catherins for if I don't hear soon the return will fall very likly. Mademoiselle Broeta also says she's writ a very sharp letter to Mr Gryme's clerk: who had the Cambrick & at the same time she sent a whole cargo of the same for them to sell so that they could not pretend to want it for mourning this with my humble service please to tell your Lady. Mr Hasby [Hansbie?] has been here one moment, who tells me Mrs Hyde is in London & never has been from thence, tho' Mrs Blundell told me she lived near Bath as I told you in my last pray let us know what is to be done to impower you to act for us. Our Honoured Lady with her service to your self & Lady desires you to act against the said Mrs Hyde either in her name or yours for she's you know the only heir of Mrs Worthington she leaves it wholly in your hands. Please also to let us know if you've had £3 from Lord Langdale which his Lordship desired me to lay down for his man Bourgeoise's father here some months ago. Also what you think of what Mr Day says of Mrs Throckmorton & Lady Litcotts Heirs which I told you of in my former letters. Pray please to take what you said you would let Lady Catherine know of for your pains out of the £100 when you get it. My Lord Petre's & Br I hope will soon settle affairs, it being as my Br[99] says wholy in your hands who I hope will as soon as y[ou] can get it or at least part which will much oblige
    Honoured Sir / your most humble Servant / Cecily Tunstall

---

[99]   Cuthbert Constable.

**99.** *CT to MS at Lincoln's Inn. 17 July 1738 (NS).* Blount MSS, C 64/166

Louvaine July 17: 1738

Honoured Sir

I've drawn bills on you this post for £450.00s.0d. of Mrs Stapleton's but Mr Stapleton writes that he had given orders to Mr Webb to pay her pension &c so that you'll please as soon as possible to get it for as soon as all is paid he requires a general acquittance from us or you may if you please ask Mr Webb if yours in our [name] is not sufficient. Lady Shrewsbury writes that she [sent] you 50 shillings for her niece here before she left London. I believe you've forgot to let us know of it, or else her Ladyship has orderd it & it has not been perform'd. Please to let me know. I find by yours that you've only had £30 for Mrs Bentley in place of £35 10s 0d which she writ to you about so that I leting her know it she sends the bill here inclosed for the rest I drew & paid her. The Cambrick must have been snip'd of for I took it for a whole piece & the person that sold it said it only wanted about 2 or 3 inches which was cut for a priest's bands; & I could find no other of that sort whole which I then feared might tempt em seeing it cut to cut still more unsuspected. This with my humble service please to tell your Lady tho' I won't pretend to know who was the thief it having pasd many hands before it came to Mr Grimes's servants. Please to let me know when you have Lady Catherines £100 & please to pay your self out of it before you give me notice I fear it will be the last we shall have for her for she decays fast & has lived a fair time. We shall have a very great loss of her for money put out here is at very small interest & that ill paid & with great trouble to those that are to collect it if I may use that term for 'tis as hard to get our own money as to raise a tax. I hope we shall have Cousin Crathorn's yearly annuity which I've never had since I've been in this place & if Lady Catherins fails I shall not be able to pay the expences of the House without new suply's. The constant rains have quite spoild our wheat god give us patience. I hope that will be the first money that Lord Petre pays it being the best secured demand we have on his Lordship I beg in your next I may have some news of it, & pray let me know whether Lord D[erwentwate]r has got his pardon as our news here says or rather English news papers that have been sent us.[100]

---

[100] This letter appears to go on to another page, which may have been lost.

**100.** *CT to MS at Lincoln's Inn. 22 August 1738 (NS) (answered 1 September 1738 OS).* Blount MSS, C *64/167*

Louvain Aug: 22 1738

Honoured Sir

Yours of July 28 O.S. which I receiv'd & shall follow your direction as to the drawing Bills or any thing else that may be to your satisfaction if I know how I always do draw em at 2 days sight but now I've drawn one on you for Mrs Smiths[101] £100 & one £30 more to it of ours I hope my giving you 8 days will be sufficient if you have not yet receiv'd it of Mr Wyke I could always give as many days but think the Bills may not sell so well if I allow so many days for they desire always speedy payment for example Mr Wollascott gave me a Bill to send on 20 days sight & it is now a month since it was presented & no payment so that 'tis in danger to be protested. 'Tis now above a year since Mrs Wybourne dyed I hope you'll remember the debt due to our House on account of her daughter's pension here 'tis £36.11s.6d. pray be as good as your word in letting us know what you'll please to demand for your trouble in Lady Cath: Rad: afairs & whether you've had the £100 yet. Due last Lady day. Also what our Honoured Lady must do to empower you to act in the affair of Mrs Hide for we're sure she can not appear in person there & whether she can't give a Lettre of Atturney or what else is necessary if it should be a woman that is to represent Mrs Mary Worthington when you have settled the accounts between Lord Petre & my Br[102] please to remember that there is one concerned that I did not state right for I now & not before find that the poor woman calld Mrs Swinny did not dye till the year 1721 5 May so that something more is due to her than I stated it that is to her Heirs. Please with our Honoured Ladys & my best respects & service to your Lady & self so believe me ever

Honoured Sir / your most obliged humble servant / Cecily Tunstall

---

[101]  Sr Elizabeth Mary Winefrid Smith.
[102]  Cuthbert Constable.

**101.** *CT to MS at Lincoln's Inn. 25 September 1738 (NS).* Blount MSS, C *64/168*

Louvain Sep: 25 1738

Honoured Sir

This comes to desire you if possibly you can to pay Mr Cuthbert Haydocke a Bill which in 10 or 15 days he'll send you for 'tis a sum that I've long owed him & now he is in sum hast for it but I doubt not but that before it comes to your hands you'll either have had Lady Cath:

Rad: Annuity or a sum sufficient to pay that small Bill of £25 15s 3d but if it should happen so I hope you be so good as to advance that sum for us. Pray do what ever you can to hasten Lord Petre's our payment of at least part of the debt. The Annuity for Cousen Barbara Crathorn can't be refused that is setled on her by my Aunt Anne Radclyffe & both her nephews Frances & Coll: Radclyffe were bound for the payment of £20 a year or £400 payd down which is most extreamly wanted & never was denyed till I had the misfortune to be in this post which is a great trouble to me corn is now excessive dear & without some supply I can't provide for our great family therfore most humbly beg you'll use all possible means to get us some part of this or some other old debt I've long ago given you an account of the arrears of these debts so need only renew the memory of them we're very sensible you've a very great weight of business on your hands but still in the place I'm in I can't dispence with my self from tezing you which I hope your goodness will pardon as well knowing it is my duty to endeavour to get what I can to satisfy just expences our Honoured Lady & all friends joyns in our offer of service to your Lady & self which concludes me

Honoured Sir / your obliged humble servant / Cecily Tunstall

**102.** *CT to MS at Lincoln's Inn. 14 October 1738 (NS).* Blount MSS, C *64/169*

Louvaine Oc: 14 1738

Honoured Sir

I hope by this time you've come up to town again, so I've drawn a Bill of £100 at 15 days' sight on you, to the order of Mademoiselle Broeta as usual, so that will be sufficient time I hope if you are not ready sooner. I hope also to hear in your next about Mrs Wybourne's Debt, she having been now dead long above a year. If you have forgot the sum 'tis just £36 11s 6d, also what you've done to Mrs Throckmorton & Lady Litcot's Heirs. I've spoke to Mr Hansby as he passd by here about Mrs Hyde he says either man or woman may pass for Mrs Worthington's representative, so that since you were so kind as to offer us to let us use your name, why may't you act in your own name; or let us know what we must do to empower you or any other. I hope we shall hear soon of a conclusion of Lord Petre's & my Brother's accounts that we may have our due, as both his Lordship & my Lady has graciously promised us. I send you here a Bill for £10 which I lent Mr Sheldon of Winchester when he & his family were here. Please to accept the best wishes & service of our Honoured Lady, to your self & Lady, the same from us 3 & my 2 nieces for alas since I writ last I've lost the best of sisters, who as she was the eldest has always been a mother to us all & to me in particular;

pray if you see any one from Hammersmith, let my Cousen Crathorne there know this for he's the nighest relation we have, whose prayers we most esteem, which will much oblige

Honoured Sir / your most humble servant / Cecily Tunstall

I beg in your next you'll let me know whether you deliverd up to Lawyer Webb[103] Miss Stapletons writing I hope not for she's not yet received what her father promised her besides her £450 which is all we've had & he said he'd given orders for pension &c besides which must be enquired into I beg to know for tho' before I let you know thus much yet I never had an answer.

---

[103]  Edward Webb.

**103.** *CT to MS at Lincoln's Inn. 7 November 1738 (NS) (answered 6 November 1738 OS).* Blount MSS, C *64/170*

Lovain No: 7: 1738

Honoured Sir

'Tis so long since I'd the Honour to hear from you that I must needs beg that favour as soon as possible for tho' I staid according to your desire till after your October was begun before I drew Lady Cath: £100 yet now that no:[104] is nigh with you & will be begun before this comes to your hand. I hope you'll no longer defere that also pray if you have time look if in May or June my Br Constable paid a £20 which he promised with the 10 which you own'd in June 19 but no: £20 I believe he forgot for he writ (the first time I see Mr Strickland I'll pay him £20 together with the 10 I promised my daughters to make up the £60 I paid last £80.) This £20 I've never heard of so that either the Letter was lost that it was in or he forgot to pay it, which is more likely. For you had the £10 but no £20 that I know of unless since your last which he would have told us of, if paid after he went down to Burton Constable. Mrs Hacon desires to know if her Br Bartley has not paid her her little pension pray let me hear soon if you have any Considerable Summ for we want money very much at present towards building, or rather repairing our Church I hope at least Mrs Wybourne's Debt will be paid my 2 Brothers said they'd paid one £30 the other £10 so that with some little addisions I may draw soon for now the returns are good & I hope the £10 Bill I sent came before you went down into the Country of Mr Sheldons is paid you by Mr Wright for us pray let us hear if any hopes to come handed of Lord Petre's business & Mrs Hydes Mrs Throckmortons &c as in my last I

---

[104]  November.

mensiond. Our Honoured Lady & all friends as if named are much your & gives their Service to your Lady

the same from / Honoured Sir / your very humble Servant / Cecily Tunstall

If Miss Blevin comes to you for money for some things we desired her to buy & send by Mrs Bentley pray pay her & put it to my account. Tell Mr Gifford of Chillington that Miss Green is desperate for her pension; he owes two years together with money for clothes.

**104.** *CT to MS at Lincoln's Inn. 24 November 1738 (NS)*. Blount MSS, C *64/171*

Novem 24: 1738 Louvain

Honoured Sir

You'r in the right as to the 3 first sums they were own'd in yours of Sepr: 1ˢᵗ only the £3 3s 0d from Miss Langdale was only £3 0s 0d so that we did not know who it was for till my Cousen Bryan Tunstall writ me word the other day that he wonderd we had not heard of the £3 3s 0d. from Mrs Hutson for her Cousen here for that h[e had or]derd Mr Day to pay it the 2d of August last [My] Brothers £20 I believe he never payd it although he said when he writ in May that he would pay it with the £10 which you had & owned long since. I've writ to him about it for I'm sure we never had it. Our Honoured Lady with her kind service bids me tell you that she hopes at least you'll have the debt of Mrs Wybourn now soon for she's been long above a year dead & you assured us you would procure us that sum now we are in very great want for we have begun a work in our Church which requires ready money & we must not spend our Principal so that we have no other means but to get all arrears as soon as we can pray in your next let us know how long you think it will be before Lord Petre's afaires will be settled & we paid at least the yearly pensions if not yet arrears for it will amount still higher & higher if defer'd & consequently harder to pay all at a clap: for we hear his Lordship is dip'd in vast Buildings &c so that we fear we shall be the last payd we beg you'll use your best Interest to get us a speedy payment at least of the anuitys which no Justice can refuse as that of Cousen Crathorn's 20 a year which is above 8 years behind hand pray let us know how Mrs Hyde & the 2 Ladys that Mr Fell engaged that £300 to goes to work for patience tho a great virtue yet in those afaires as I always find only renders such persons much more unwilling to pay at last than at first for the longer they are permitted to keep other peoples money the harder it is to get it [out of] their hands I shall draw a Bill of £150 on you at 10 days sight this post: because Cousen Bryan writes me word he's orderd Mr Day to pay you £23 18s 0d from Mr Trapes & my

Br Tunstall so that will make the sum & you have [£]1 18s 2d in your hands if no more comes, tho' cous: Willoughby expects £20 from her Cousen Eliz: Willoughby very soon if not paid: this with all due respects & service to your Lady &c from all friends & acquaintance is all from

Honoured Sir / your most obedient & humble Servant / Cecily Tunstall

If you see Mr Gifford of Chilington tell him if you please that Miss Green is in great want of her pension as well as we for he owes for 2 years the 7 of last August & for clothes that she was to find her self in she's very uneasy to want & he promised to make all even after last Easter & yet we heard nothing.

**105.** *CT to MS at Lincoln's Inn. 9 December 1738 (NS).* Blount MSS, C *64/172*

Louvaine Decem: 9 1738

Honoured Sir

I doubt not but that you'll see Mrs Bentley before she sets out for our parts if so pray desire her to take the Books that Mrs Hacon orderd Miss Betty Bleven to buy for us & I hope she's been with you for money & left em with you to sent if I did not forget to desire you to pay her what she layd out for the Books at least if I did I desire you'll do it now if she has got the Le[tter that M]rs Hacon writ about em by Mr Hasbey [Hansbie] if you [see] Mrs Bety Blevin or Mrs Bentley pray desire one of them to get, if out of the press a *Christian Directory or Persons Resolutions*[105] which it seems is printed by subscription this present year if not to late to subscribe yet, pray do it for us, & also the *Life of Bishop Fisher*;[106] also subscribed for this year. & if possible to sent these 2 at least for us & if not out of the press or yet unprinted lay down the money according to the order of the subscribers or get Mrs Bleven to do it but please to give her money for it & place it to our account. I hope you'll have had Cousen Willoughby's money before this for she's had notice from London that it is paid: we hope to hear of more debts paid. I'm heartily sorry to hear Lady Petre's has an other girl & no heir yet to that noble family. Our hon'd Lady & all friends are much yours & desire you'll accept with your Lady all our best wishes & am

Honoured Sir / your most obedient & humble Servant / Cecilia Tunstall

---

[105]  Robert Parsons, *Parsons his Christian directory, being a treatise of holy resolution ... Put into modern English* (London, 1709).

[106]  Presumably the biography of 1655 issued under the name of Thomas Bayly but in fact a re-issue of an earlier work translated into Latin by Richard Hall.

**106.** *CT to MS at Lincoln's Inn. 9 January 1738 (NS).* Blount MSS, C 64/173

Lovain Janu: 4 1738/9

Honoured Sir

Mrs Ledger has writ to her sister here that she had returnd £35 to be paid you by the Dutchess of Cleveland's Banker & that she expected that very day she writ an account of your having had it now Sir 'tis about 15 days ago that she's had the Letter & is much in pain till she hears that you've had it it being on an urgent occasion I hope if you have not already writ that you will & please to let me know what more you've in your hands for at this present the exchange runs very high but will very soon alter so must again iterate the petition to hear from you instantly our Honoured Lady & all acquaintance joyns in our well & best wishes of a happy new year to you & Lady & all your family & many more which is the prayers & wishes of

Honoured Sir / your very humble servant / Cecily Tunstall

**107.** *CT to MS at Lincoln's Inn. January 1739 (NS) (answered 16 January 1738/9 OS).* Blount MSS, C 64/174

Louvaine January 1739 n:s.

Honoured Sir

I'm in daily hopes of a letter from you but as yet have had none since the 6: novem: old stile Mr Stapleton writ a week ago that he would or had orderd Mr Webbe to pay £14 more upon condition that you should deliver him our Honoured Ladys acquitance that now we had no further demands upon him for his daughter so pray please to demand that sum of Mr Webbe as soon as possible which with several other sums which I beg to know in particular what they are since your last that I may draw a Bill before the fall of the exchange which I fear if I don't hear soon will certainly as usual at this time a year [fall] to our great loss. Mrs Johnson desires to know whether her letter to Lord montgomery was re[ceive]d by his Lordship & again I beg to know if the money for Mrs Walker &c be paid the Books I writ about last time I've desired Mr Collingwood to be so good as to send for me to Mrs Broeta so if you have 'em or if too much trouble to get 'em only pay him & Miss Bleven for what they got & he will send 'em all to Mrs Broeta together with those that Mr Burgis orderd Mr Moggen[107] to deliver to you when called for. this with our best respects to your Lady from our Lady & [*illeg.*] & all friends concludes

Honoured Sir / Your most humble servant / Cecily Tunstall

---

[107] Thomas Meighan?

**108.** *CT to MS at Lincoln's Inn. 27 January 1739 (NS).* Blount MSS, C *64/175*

Lovain Janu: 27 1739

Honoured Sir

This comes to beg the favour of you to forward the 2 Inclosed[108] & to let either of 'em have what money they ask for on our account & to get one of 'em to procure those Books I've at several times writ for & desired you'll please to get Mr Burges to send me but he having been long out of town I've never had any of 'em I won't desire Mrs Bentley to bring any thing of that nature for it may inconvenience her but she may deliver 'em to Mr John Collingwood or if he's not in Town to his Br Thomas to send to Broeta I've never had the honour to hear from you since the end of November that is the 22 n.s. when I had yours of the 6 o.s. I now only beg since you are so taken up wth affairs of greater weight that you will order your clerk or some one you can trust to let us know what different sums & from & for whom in our house you may have received especially that of Mrs Walker who said she paid £35 to the Banker of the Dutchess of Cleveland long ago & we must iterate again the intreating you to let us know either by your self or any whom you please but also 'tis now too late for the great advantage of the exchange which has fallen considerably lower than 'tis been several months our Honoured Lady begs this favour of you & that your Lady & self may find all best wishes & services from all other friends besides I am

Honoured Sir / your most humble & obedient servant / Cecilia Tunstall

I've thrust Mrs Blevins's Letter into Mrs Bentley's but you'll easily take it out to send each one their's as soon as you can.

---

108   To Mrs Betty Blevin and to Mrs Bentley.

**109.** *CT to MS at Lincoln's Inn. 31 January 1739 (NS).* Blount MSS, C *64/176*

Lovain 31 January 1739

Honoured Sir

I was overjoyed to see your hand but sorry to find you'd been so ill. I had a very particular occasion to have money here on a Bill of exchange which I've drawn on you this day to the orders of Mademoiselle Broeta as usual but I hope this time you'll not be angry I've been obliged to give it only 3 days sight but it will be long enough before it be presented for 'tis but sent this very day so I hope t'will be no inconvenience having always previous advice of it. I hope next Letter you'll get at least Mrs

Wybourns money which is £36 11s 6d my Lady Catherine Rad: had a Letter from her niece Lady Petre who says she'd been long flatterd wth the hopes & promises that very soon things would be quite settled that we might receive our dues but still defer'd she sais you'll let us know when we shall have the money you'll please to mind my Lord that many of the rents are Life rents that the interest runs up very high if not paid yearly &c When you're able I hope you'll please to remember your promise to Let Lady Catherine know what she owes you & what is done to Mrs Hyde & Lady Lithcott & Mrs Throckmorton &c our Honoured Lady & all friends presents their Service to your self & Lady the same from
Honoured Sir / your most humble Servant / Cecily Tunstall

**110.** *CT to MS at Lincoln's Inn. 6 March 1739 (NS) (answered 9 March 1738/9 OS).* Blount MSS, C *64/177*

Louvain March 6 1739

Honoured Sir

Our Reverend Mother with her best wishes & service bids me put you in mind of the Debt left by Mrs Wybourn which nothing but death could have hinderd her from paying her self as she asured her Ladyship a very little time before her death & we are informed from the same family that you had a considerable sum left in your hands in order to satisfy all debts & they often write to Mrs Smith[109] that they very much wonder we are not yet payd this Reverend Mother orders me to tell you & that we shall not expect nor consent to be left to the mercy of the young Esqr: but must require this of you as having power to raise it if you have no more of that said money in your hands now: as I've often writ before but could never have any positive answer about this makes me now more pressing as not only now wanting it very much having begun a great piece of work in our church which without that & other suplys we can't finish but also finding we shall be the last paid though the Debt be the eldest perhaps of any our Honoured Lady begs a speedy & satisfactory answer to this if being in your power as we know & has been long in which you'll much oblige
Honoured Sir / your very humble servant. / Cecily Tunstall
My sisters & nieces begs their most humble service to your Lady.

---

[109]  Sr Elizabeth Mary Winefrid Smith.

**111.** *CT to MS at Lincoln's Inn. 20 March 1739 (NS).* Blount MSS, C 64/178

Lovain march 20 1739

Honoured Sir

Mrs Crathorn has orders from Dunkerque to draw a Little Bill upon you for money she layd out for the use of Master Paston when here & for his journey when he went from hence this was Eight pound six shillings & 3 pence which she desires you'll please to pay wth our money when you have sufficient sum for our House she having borrowed the said sum but not thinking it worth drawing a Bill apart for that unless you desire it as you seem to do in yours to Mrs Paston if you have the money that is owing for Mrs Wybourn ready & any more for us please to let us know & we'll draw this wth it. Mrs Johnson with her thanks & service desires you'll please to send the inclosed as directed it being an answer to that my Lord[110] was so gratious as to favour her with she begs you'll be so good as to do to her 2 former in sending empty your own clerk this being the last she will Honour you with. I believe our Honoured Lady & all friends desire their kind service to your Lady & best wishes of a happy Easter attends you both from
Honoured Sir / your most humble servant / Cecily Tunstall

Pray let us have the pleasure to hear of your health in your next for we fear sometimes when we hear nothing a great while & has had but a bad account of it from dunkerk & tho my niece writ to your daughter at Bruxells to know how you did she's had yet no answer tho at other times she's so obliging as to correspond with us.

---

[110]   Lord Derwentwater.

**113.** *CT to MS at Lincoln's Inn, 26 March 1739 (NS).* Blount MSS, C 64/179

Louvain March 26 1739

Honoured Sir

This comes with our best wishes of a happy Easter though I fear you're not so nigh it as we who want but 3 days & to let you know I draw a Bill of £60 on you this post for with the money that you order me to draw for Mr Paston it will I hope not leave you quite bare. I hope you'll not take it ill of us for we only writ what we had from the family of Mrs Wyborne & being in want of the money otherways should not have writ so but was advised by no means to rely on the young gentleman for payment I hope since we can't have this that something will be done in order to get Mrs Hydes debt & the Lady Lithcote &c for I see no thing can be got for by continual duning & pressing pray at least when you can let us know when any hopes of an agreement between the Executors &c & Lord Petre for else we can't tell what to do having relied so many years on the payment & get nothing but hopes given us for any of these as soon as Lady Day is past with you we shall get the Certificate for Lady Catherine's Life rent renew'd our Lady & all friends &c begs your Lady & self may find here her best wishes & service from

Honoured Sir / Your most humble servant / Cecily Tunstall.

**114.** *CT to MS at Lincoln's Inn. 14 April 1739 (NS).* Blount MSS, C *64/180*

Louvain April 14 1739

Honoured Sir

This is to forward the Certificate of Lady Cat: Radclyffe's Life. I beg in your next to know whether it should be renew'd at the half years end for in my Lord's time it was always paid at penticost & martlemiss so that if it pleases God she lives a half year longer it may not be lost. We beg to know what is doing or done to Mrs Hyde for if she dies I fear we shall lose the money also Mrs Johnson is very solicitous about Lady Lithcot's & Mrs Throckmortons Debt: pray if Mr Megghen[111] has not brought you 3 sets of *Church Annals* send to him for 'em for they are paid for long ago & Mr Collingwood would send 'em. Mrs Hacon has never heard from Poor Mrs Betty Blevin makes her fear her letter was not deliver'd she was desired to procure some Books & that you'd pay her & place it to our account as also Mrs Bentley: because long ago I desired you'd please to get Mr Burgis to procure 'em but he has I believe never been in Town since so that one of these Lady's would be so good I believe as to get 'em for us. This I believe will come before your Easter I hear it falls very low this year our Honoured Lady my sisters & nieces all join in their hearty wishes of a most happy Easter to your self & Lady

Honoured Sir / your most humble servant / Cecily Tunstall

---

[111] One possible identification is the bookseller Thomas Meighan.

**115.** *CT to MS at Lincoln's Inn. 2 June 1739 (NS) (answered 12 June 1739 OS).* Blount MSS, C *64/181*

Louvain June 2 1739

Honoured Sir

'Tis so long since I've had the honour of a Line or 2 from you that I fear your ill health has been the cause we hear of several small sums being paid as Cous: Willoughby's £20 S[iste]r Hacon £8 S[iste]r Carew 2 or 3 guineas besides many others which I beg to hear of as soon as possible 6 guineas paid you by Mr Shepperd for my 2 nieces I hope you've had Lady Catherines Certificate long before this but have heard nothing yet of it Mr Jesup has paid also £15 as Miss writes which was owing to our House on her account: pray let us know if any thing is done about Mrs Hyde Lady Lithcot Mrs Throckmorton & when we may hope to get the debt of Lord Petre &c Mrs Wybourn for we are at present in great want of money for our Church which we would fain get soon into again being very much straitned for Room where we now are & without a good suply of money the work will not advance which makes us press so much & which if Lord Petre knew perhaps he might be prevaild on to pay at least those that ought to be so yearly we beg you'll hasten all these as soon as possibly you can which will much oblige our Honoured Lady & all our House as well as

Honoured Sir / your ever obedient humble servant / Cecily Tunstall

**116.** *CT to MS at Lincoln's Inn. 23 June 1739 (NS) (answered n.d.).* Blount MSS, C *64/182*

Louvain June 23 1739

Honoured Sir

I can't but think some Letters have been lost for 'tis now 3 months since I'd the favour of your last & am pressd every day to put you in mind of the several sums paid by different persons I think I did not name £12 from Mr Bartlet. For the future if you would be so good as to give a little note to the persons that pay's you money for our House which they send to us to give us notice that you've had such & such sums then we should not need to stay so long before we draw the money or if you are so taken up that you can't do this if you have a clerk that you can trust he might write in your place which I beg again as soon as possibly you will please to order or write by the post & not by any opportunity for that is the longer way they talk of opening letters so that some times I think yours have been lost but yet others hears very frequently out of England. I hear your Daughter is gone from Bruxells but we never have had the favour to see her tho we had your promise for it. Our Honoured

Lady & all friends desires you & your Lady will accept their kind service my poor Little niece Winefried has been very dangerously ill of a fevour which lay so in her head that she yet remains stone deaf which is a sad thing for a child of 9 year old to be but we're advised not to do any thing to her ears so must have patience as long as God pleases so conclude as ever

Honoured Sir / your most humble servant / Cecily Tunstall

**117.** *CT to MS at Lincoln's Inn. 1 July 1739 (NS) (answered 24 August 1739 OS).* Blount MSS, C *64/183*

Lovaine July 1: 1739

Honoured Sir

This day I've drawn a Bill on you for £90 tho you say but £85 but I find above 90 in the receipt tho I think 2 guineas of it is for some one in another House viz for Mrs Betty Engelfield but as you've put 2 guineas also for Mrs Magrath from Mrs Carew I think there is some mistake for Mrs Magrath says Mrs Andrews[112] promised a small sum for her it may be only the names wrong placed for we knew that Mrs Carew has had 2 guineas promised her & not Mrs Magrath unless that of Mrs Englefield be for her please to explain this in your next you said in yours of March 9th that you was promis'd a years Interest due for Mr Milbourn we hope 'tis now paid so that if you have not otherways sufficient to answer the Bill that or some other will surely come & we have so seldome news from you that people can't stay for their money till I can get it so please to excuse me for not giveing you more than on 3 days sight to pay the Bill for it will be time enough before they come for the payment on't please to find here the Reverend Mother & all services from friends as named the same from

Honoured Sir / your most obedient humble servant / Cecily Tunstall

---

[112] A possible identification is Prudence Andrew of Pudding Norton, Norfolk.

**118.** *CT to MS at Lincoln's Inn. 11 September 1739 (NS).* Blount MSS, C *64/184*

Lovain Sep 11 1739

Honoured Sir

Yours of Aug 24 was truly welcome as all are from you & would have been doubley so had we heard of any good sum of money paid to you either by Lord Petre or that debt of the Late Mrs Wybourn's or any part of Lady Lithcotts or Mrs Throckmortons she being now dead I hope her heirs are able to do some thing. Some time ago you put us in hopes to have the yearly rent of Mr Milborn which I hope you've got e'er now for tho' we want money extreemly now to finish our work in the Church yet I must pay Mr Haydocke his yearly rent which he has not had this great while paid & being now in Town he wants it extreemly but I can't give him a Bill for it till I hear you have in your hands a sum that will answer it. As for Lady Catherine Rad: she leaves it wholly to you to pay what must be payd & only desires to have it soon. We understand by Mr Hyde that he has delivered a Bundle of Papers to be forwarded to us if still in your hands please to give 'em to Mrs Hills who has her orders about 'em we also here [hear] you have the Bond or deed of trust for Mrs Smiths[113] Portion or Settlement which being drawn in your name must be deposited in some other hands as the custom is. Our Honoured Lady has this post writ to Mr Thomas Worthington to do as you propose for his Sister. In the mean time we humbly beg if you can do any thing or tell us how to hasten the payments of Lord Petre's debt for some way or other we must have money or else we can't go forward with the Church which occasion when lost can't be recovered without imense cost. so that trusting to your care our Honoured Lady hopes to hear soon of some thing considerable I'll write to my Br[114] if a word or 2 from him may not hasten the payment of Lord Petre. I remain

Honoured Sir / your most humble servant / Cecily Tunstall

The service & good wishes of all friends attends your self & Lady & dau[ghte]r in hast.

---

[113]   Sr Elizabeth Mary Winefrid Smith.
[114]   Cuthbert Constable.

**119.** *CT to MS at Lincoln's Inn. 12 October 1739 (NS) (answered 15 October 1739 OS).* Blount MSS, C *64/185*

Louvain octo: 12 1739

Honoured Sir

We had notice by Mr Eyre that he had pay'd you £525 & that you had Received the said sum wherefore on mature consideration we all thought I might safely draw upon you for the said sum the Exchange being now very good & a prospect of its falling very low If I'd stayd longer I've given you 12 10 & 20 days & only sent one Bill at three days' sight so I hope you'll please to honour 'em all without fail I staid some days still hoping you'd have favour me wth a notice of it but was force'd for the above said reasons to draw. I beg you'll please to put me out of pain about this point at first sight & also whether it were not proper now to have a new Certificate of Lady Cat: Rad: life for the half year that this day is due in case she dyes before the whole year be so. it used to be paid by half years by my Lord her Father so that your advice is desired on these 2 points & what else you have if the Annuity for Lady Day for the same she asks me every day if 'tis paid please to forward the inclosed as soon as possible & accept all services &c from our Honoured Lady &c to yours I am

Honoured Sir / your ever humble servant / Cecily Tunstall

**120.** *CT to MS at Lincoln's Inn. 3 November 1739 (NS) (answered 2 November 1739 OS).* Blount MSS, C *64/186*

Lovaine No: 3. 1739

Honoured Sir

Tho' the Honour of yours of Oc: 15. gave me great satisfaction putting us out of pain for the Bills being protested, yet there are several afairs yet undesided which were expected long for the final desigeon [decision] of hearing by yours to Mrs Eliz: Smith that you've been at Ingerstone[115] we didn't doubt but the affair so long hanging would be finished to our satisfaction, & are not a little surprised that not one word of that matter is mensioned also what is done in Mrs Throckmortons &c Mrs Wybarnes debt we know others are payd that have not so long wanted their money therefore by orders of our Honoured Lady &c I must be very pressing for a speedy payment. The same day I had yours our Honoured Lady had also a Letter from Mr Thomas Worthington who offers his service very kindly but at the same time says he's not so proper a person in his judgment as his nephew who for reasons known to us we don't care to employ & we having a neece of the Lady Mrs Worthington in our house why can't the Letters be taken out in her name, or as is thought in our House Mrs More is intitled the best to it before this I supose you've had Cousen Willoughbys £20 & tho' you don't name the £20 Bill from my Br Tunstall being returned that wanted Endorcing yet I doubt not but you've had it before now Lady Catherin with her service begs you please to get her money as speedily as possible Mr Haydon [Haydocke] he seemed in hast of his money so that I wonder he's not yet sent for't we shall consider & let you know whether 'tis necessary for Lady Catherine to make an other will having made one some years ago which we have by us whereby she constituted a very worthy Gentleman in England her Heir & executor please to favour me wth a speedy answer as to all these particulars & you'll much oblige

Honoured Sir / your most obedient humble servant / [Cecily Tunstall]
All our best wishes & service attends your Lady & daughter.

---

115 Ingatestone Hall, Essex, the principal seat of Lord Petre.

**121.** *CT to MS at Lincoln's Inn. 17 November 1739 (NS) (answered 26 November 1739 OS).* Blount MSS, C *64/187*

Louvaine Novem 17: 1739

Honoured Sir

I had the honour of yours of novem: 2d this day & have drawn Bills for £100 on you at 10 days sight & have left you sufficient to answer Mr Haydocks demands I hope you'll soon get Lady Cath: money for she is not pleased to have it so long a doing we paid more for the return out of the Country for 2 years ago than that half Guinea comes to tho' we'd rather have it without if possible as to Mr Worthington if he must need to be imploy'd we must get the Consent of his masters on this side the Sea, but will not have to do wth his nephew. As I told you in my last & you may tell him as much if you please, if you've none of Mrs Wyborns money in your hands you'll please to deal with the young man about it as for your self for since you have given him money that should have paid old debts you'll best get it of him for we shall not apply to him but to you as being Exec[uto]r to his mother & we have your promise that you would take care we should be paid & we know as I had the honour to tell you before that since you've paid others that were after us you can't deny to see the same justice done to us this our Honoured Lady with her respects bids me tell you may your Lady & all your family find here as due from our Honoured Lady my sisters & nieces the same from

Honoured Sir / Your most humble servant / Cecily Tunstall

**122.** *CT to MS at Lincoln's Inn. 30 December 1739 [NS] (answered 7 January 1739/40 OS).* Blount MSS, C *64/188*

Louvaine 30 December 1739

Honoured Sir

This comes to wish your Lady & self a most happy new year & also to let you know that this Day I've drawn a Bill for £170 on you not doubting but you've had Lady Catherines money before now or at least I know you may have it for asking the rest I know you have & Cousen Cholmeley wants hers in fine I could stay no longer for at the new year the Exchange falls & so we lose much at least I've given you time enough at 20 [days] sight I've drawn my Bill so that I'm sure you may have more long before they come for payment. I hope before it be long you'll receive some more money from my Br Constable, & pray let us hear what is to be had from Lord Petre for the arrears runs on for that money & especially for my Cousen Crathorn who ought to have it yearly & no body can hinder her of it tho it had been in the Go[vernme]nts hands much less should Lord Petre be so long behind hand. for at

Last he must be to pay a Larger sum, we are in great want of it at present Corn & all things are here excessive dear. Now Sir you'll give me Leave to remind you of an old Promise which I find in yours of July 15 1737 which I'll give you in your own words which are as follows as I said July 15 1737 Mr[s] Wyburne is dead but has provided for the payment of her Husbands Debts, so that yours of £36 11s 6d is very safe & will be payd in a short time[.] she has appointed me one of the Executors of her will this is Sir word for word yours as said & I hoped then we should not have needed putting you so often in mind on't but I've found since that I did it too late for as I've often writ you've paid others that had not wanted it so long as we I hope you've had the Interest of Mr Milbourns money for I shall want a sum in your hands soon in looking over letters I find in yours of 1738 June 30 where I find these words I have been suing Mrs Throckmorton for her debt & I think we now have good bail for the payment of it so that I expect both Principal & Interest next Mich[ael]mass term. You've so much other business that I hope you will not take it ill that I put you in mind of ours for when I did not want it I was very patient but I hate debts & so both by Dutty & inclination must do what I can to get payment that I may pay what I owe which without these helps I can't do I must also add these words out of yours of July 28 1738 as follows. I am now endeavouring to settle the Accounts between Lord Petre & Mr Constable in the taking of which particular Care shall be taken of your demands I shall expect the payment of Mrs Throckmortons money next term, & Mr Lythcott promises payment of his Mothers Debt as soon as part of the Estate is sold. & this with the best wishes of our Lady is what she orders me to mind you of & that you'll please to remember you have Copys of all our demands on Lord Petre for Lady mary rather the Coll:s[116] debts & particularly that Annuity mentiond so often by me of £20 per annum for Cousin Crathorn left or given rather by my Aunt Anne Radclyffe for which both her nephews Francis & Thomas were bound & their heirs &c as you may see by the said Copy so conclude

Honoured Sir / Your most humble servant / Cecily Tunstall

---

116   Lady Mary Radclyffe and Colonel Thomas Radclyffe.

**123.** *CT to MS at Lincoln's Inn. January 1740 (NS).* Blount MSS, C *64/189*

Lovain January 1740

Honoured Sir

I should have writ last week to desire you to take the money Mr Power would have paid you & give him if you please your note in our names but realy I thought it not necessary but we find he would not pay you without our orders to you to receive it which as yet we never needed to do & you if you please may always give a note as is required without our orders which pray please now to do & let me know if yet Lady Catherins money is paid for I've drawn it & received it as I had the honour to let you know please to send to Mr Porter as soon as you can for he's not pleased that we had not told you to give such a note I'm sorry you did not receive it when offerd but its done our Honoured Lady & all the rest of your friends desires you may find here their best wishes of a new year & the same is the wishes of

Honoured Sir / your very humble servant / Cecily Tunstall

I hope your Lady will accept the same wishes &c

The sum you're desired to give a Note for is £18 odd but I can't just remember how much more.

**124.** *CT to MS at Lincoln's Inn. 27 January 1740 (NS).* Blount MSS, C *64/190*

Louvaine Jan: 27: 1740

Honoured Sir

Yours of Jann 7th O:S: gave me both a great satisfaction & concern. I was glad Lady Catherines money was paid & I'm sorry you should think, we've any design to put our affairs in other hands: all our house has a great esteem & value for you & 'tis our opinion that our business can't be safer but at the same time they often blame me for not putting you in mind oftener of your promise Concerning Mrs Wybourne's debt & because they know you've such a multiplicity of business on your hands that unless each concerned solicites for dispatch first come first served so that I was obliged to look over old letters which I cited in my late Letter being persuaded that if you'd rememberd our debt to have been the oldest you'd not have payd other's that were behind us. Nor would you have given it out of your power to pay us now when you had it so easy before as to Mr Wybourne we [have] no sort of reason to expect he'll pay us nor can we come again upon him for it but if you pleased you can let him know that we press you much for the performance of your promise in your former letters in 1737 which I cited to you in mine.

Our Honoured Lady heard from Mr Thomas Worthington Br to our Lady & he wonderd he heard no more of that affair if you remember he was in the north I'm not sure whether I told you this before or no but for sureness repeat it here. I've asked advise as to the 2 persons concerned in the £300 & all say that we must look to our selves & get payment & that they can't say we've not given them sufficient time & never yet seen penny of Interest which as well as principal we demand for 'tis the only maintenance of a person in our house & as to Lord Petre's money 'tis above 3 years since my Br[117] said that we were to demand payment of his Lordship & that since Lady Anne's marriage he'd no more to do in it but that both parties had put it into your hands who was then busy in settling matters & accounts & yet still we find our selves as far off as ever & less hopes to see an end this at present is a great concern to us who has so far depended of this & Mrs Wybournes that we have run in debt considerably for our Church on this score which otherwise we should never do for we're strickly forbiden to spend any principall & for our yearly revenues they scarce will pay daily expences. So that we're now greatly at a loss pray let us have your advice what to do in this case whether any means can be used to raise a Sum out of those debts sufficient to pay the wood at least we bought one £200 we had but want more than £200 more for that we were forced to pay the poor workmen with the £100 that was given us by a good friend. I've writ to my Br but he says he can do nothing more now. We have such excessive cold weather[118] that it freezes at the fire side the ink & my fingers so that I can scarce scrat only to subscribe my self

Honoured Sir / your very humble Servant / Cecily Tunstall

I don't know whether you've heard of the death of your cousin Doctor Thomas Strickland, Bishop of Namur, who dyed the 14 of this month in Louvain, where he came to get advice.

---

[117]  Cuthbert Constable.

[118]  The winter of 1739/40 was one of the coldest on record, leading to major crop deficiencies (see Brian Fagan, *The Little Ice Age: How Climate Made History, 1300–1850* (New York: Basic Books, 2000), p. 157; Paul Langford, *A Polite and Commercial People: England 1727–1783* (Oxford: Oxford University Press, 1989), p. 442).

**125.** *CT to MS at Lincoln's Inn. February 1740 (NS) (answered 22 February 1739/40 OS).* Blount MSS, C *64/191*

Lovain Feb: 17: 1740

Honoured Sir

This is to give you notice that 2 days ago I gave one John Lee a Bill upon you for his Wife called Frances Lee for 6 Guineas which I had here of him & I supos'd that you'd have by this £10 of Mr Bartlet for his sisters here so that when the said woman sends you the Bill I hope you'll please to pay it for the poor man knew no other way to get money to his wife I believe she get some one at London that does the affairs of Lord Tenam[119] for he says that family is the nighest to them that's all I can say to't if you have any considerable sum please to let us know for we want money very much & you'll oblige

Honoured Sir / your most obedient humble servant / Cecily Tunstall
All our services attend your Lady & Daughter.

---

[119]   Lord Teynham.

**126.** *CT to MS at Lincoln's Inn. 3 March 1740 (NS).* Blount MSS, C *64/192*

Louvaine March 3 1740

Honoured Sir

Least my last might be lost I'm desired by one Mr Lee to get 6 Guineas to his Wife in Kent to whom I gave a Bill on you for so much he says he's writ to the Gentleman that is in Lord Tenhams family to send to you for it so pray please to pay it on sight of the Bill for the poor woman writes again in great want on't please to let me know whether you've receivd any money for our house for we're in great want all things excessive dear especialy lent dyet & all people here so poor that they can't pay their rents. Our Honoured Lady & all friends desires their best wishes of a happy Lent &c the same from

Honoured Sir / your most obedient humble servant / Cecily Tunstall
My respects &c to your Lady & daughter my nieces are their humble servants.

**127.** *CT to MS at Lincoln's Inn. 29 March 1740 (NS).* Blount MSS, C 64/193

Louvain March 29 1740

Honoured Sir

This is to give you notice that I've drawn a Bill on you for £60 & also given a small Bill for Mr Peter Brown of four Guineas & fourteen shillings I was in hopes of more coming to make a Bill of £100 but hearing no news of any I'm forced to draw this the owners wanting it I shall in a few posts send you a new certificate of Lady Catherine's Life if it please god to give her Life till then I believe I did not explain right what I meant by asking if the said Certificate should not be renewed every half year t'was only in case of death that we might at least demand a half year if no more falls due when God pleases to call her & whether they would pay the Arrears if nothing could prove her to have been alive at the end of the half year: this was what I meant; & not that we expected the commissioners to pay it every half year as your answer seemed to me that you took it in that sence our Honoured Lady & all friends & relations here are much yours, & your Ladys, to whom pray my most humble Service as also my neeces I'm much obliged to you Sir for your concern for my neece Winny: she is not in danger of death but of being Deaf caused by a malignant feavour that she had in Summer which has left her very ill remains I wish here in her native air where it might perhaps be better remedied & I've told my Br[120] as much & remain as ever

Honoured Sir / Your most obliged humble servant / Cecily Tunstall

---

[120] Cuthbert Constable.

**128.** *CT in Louvain to MS at Lincoln's Inn. 5 April 1740 (NS) (answered 7 April 1740 OS).* Blount MSS, C 64/194

Lovain April 5 1740

Honoured Sir

I have by orders of my Br Constable drawn a Bill of Exchange on you this day at 10 days sight not doubting but you'll have had that sum as he says he's sent you £50 & bids me draw it as soon as I will the exchange falls so that I would stay no longer & if the Bill is not paid you Mr Shepperd or my Cousen Cholmeley can I belive give it but I don't doubt but it will be paid before they come for it please to let me know if you have any other considerable sum for us for I'm in great want: corn & all other necessarys are twice as Dear as they've been this 10 years that I've had to do with 'em, & yet money scarcer far than it has ever been, all Rents behind hand. Next Letter if please God I'll send

Lady Catherines Certificate it not being yet past Lady Day your old stile I can't have it done now, for I suppose it must be a year & a day. Our Honoured Lady & all friends & acquaintance beg you'll make their & my service acceptable to your Lady & Daughter & accept the same from
Honoured Sir / your very humble servant / Cecily Tunstal

**129.** *CT to MS at Lincoln's Inn. 19 April 1740 (NS) (answered 14 April 1740 OS).* Blount MSS, C *64/195*

Louvain April 19 1740

Honoured Sir

This comes to wish you your Lady & all your worthy family a happy Easter & with all to let you know that a Lady in our family who is a relation of the late Mr Wybourne had an account the other day that there is no none to look after his affaires & that if we don't procure payment of our debt his wife will take Letters of administration he dying intestate if you'd been pleas'd to have paid us while you had the sum design'd for that end in your hands we should not have needed either to have applyed to the Heirs or anyone else our Honoured Lady had a Letter from the late Mrs Wybourn with a promise to pay that debt the very first money she touched which only death hinder'd her from performing pray Sir let no more delays be made but see that we are satisfied soon or else we shall loose it this is all at present for Lady Catherines Certificate is not yet come back from Brusselles so conclude in hast
Honoured Sir / your most humble servant / Cecily Tunstall

**130.** *CT to MS at Lincoln's Inn. 22 April 1740 (NS).* Blount MSS, C *64/196*

Louvain April 22 1740

Honoured Sir

I send you here the Certificate of Lady Catherines Life & she with her service desires you please to get it as soon as possibly & not give 'em so long a time as they've had this 3 or 4 years past, our Honoured Lady & all friends & acquaintance desires you'll please to accept their best wishes & services the same pray to your Lady & daughter from my nieces &c I belive my 2 nieces will have the honour to see you this summer we having hopes that change of Air may help poor Winny's Deafnes & make the other grow who is very little of her Age I beg if you have any considerable Summs for us to let me speedily know I am, with all respect Sir
Honoured Sir / your most obedient humble servant / Cecily Tunstall

**131.** *CT to MS at Lincoln's Inn. 3 May 1740 (NS) (answered 16 May 1740 OS).* Blount MSS, C 64/197

Louvain 3 May 1740

Honoured Sir

I send you here the original Bond as you require. Some time ago we heard by Mr Bernard Hyde her Br[other] that she lived at Hammersmith but our Honoured Lady writ to her & sent it to my Cousen Crathorn some time before his death but he suddenly took weak & ill to Look for her but one of those good Ladys writ to my niece Constable that no such person was to be found there so that I can't tell where youll find her but if Mr Hansby be in London I beg you'll get him to inform her that we shall sue her if she does not prevent it very speedily. As I'm writing this & all yesterday & the night past there has fallen so great a snow that none in our House tho' several past 70 has ever seen so much fall in so short a time. we've had now 8 months of winter it begining in September & ever since we've had snow & frost so that we are in great danger of loosing the fruits of the Earth god give us patience. the 1 of this month I received the favour of your 2d Letter [of] April 14. what I ment was only that you'd please to let the widow of the Late Mr Wybarne know of our pretention that she might not have reason after to say we had not made our claim to the sum so often named & promised to be soon paid this I was orderd to do & not my own inclination but by an indispensable obligation incumbent on my [me] so I hope youll please to believe me as ever

Honoured Sir / your very humble servant / Cecily Tunstall

My service waits on your Lady & daughter &c as well as all your friends here.

**132.** *CT to MS at Lincoln's Inn. 3 June 1740 (NS).* Blount MSS, C 64/198

Louvain June 3: 1740

Honoured Sir

This owns the favour of yours of may 16: o:s. & I've drawn a Bill on you at 20 days' sight for £150 which if you've not yet quite enough to answer I doubt not but you'll have more than enough before the Bill is presented. we expecting from several hands our Honoured Lady & all acquaintance are much yours & desires their Service may attend your Lady & Daughter the same at the request of

Honoured Sir / your most obedient humble servant / Cecily Tunstall.

**133.** *CT to MS at Lincoln's Inn. 5 August 1740 (NS) (answered 1 August 1740 OS).* Blount MSS, C *64/199*

Lovain Aug 5 1740

Honoured Sir

I should have writ 3 weeks ago to desire you'd let Mr Stafford have what money he will want or has layd out for us but for his Journey back I hope he'll receive of my Cousen Cholmeley or else where my Br[121] has money for I have not enough for that in my hands of my Brs. Mrs Moningtons desires to know if you've had their money from Mr Kerend for they'd notice long ago that it was paid please to let me know if you've any other money & that you'll let Miss Bleven have a guinea which good Mrs Hacon promised her before her death & our Honoured Lady has given it me so that you'll pay her if you please when you see her. I've been so concerned for the loss of her & having such a press of business on my hands by her death that I had not time to write since my neece set out for England I should be glad to hear she was safe at London having only heard that they landed safe at Dover as we suppose for the Letter came dated out of England & only paid from Ostend if you see Mr Stafford or my neece be so good as to let us know for Cousen Cholmeley nor she are not quick at their Pens my service attends your Lady I am

Honoured Sir / your most obedient humble servant / Cecily Tunstall

---

[121] Cuthbert Constable.

**134.** *CT to MS at Lincoln's Inn. 17 August 1740 (NS) (answered 15 August 1740 OS).* Blount MSS, C *64/200*

Louvain August 17. 1740

Honoured Sir

This day I had the honour of yours & have drawn a Bill of £50 on you at 10 days' sight Miss Ogle desires to know whether you've not forgot her money which Mr Day sayd he'd payd long ago as to Mr Stafford he's come back here above 10 days ago having conducted my little neece safe to London but I much fear to little purpose by what my Cousen Nutty Chomley writes who also went with her. She's at her sister Peggy's now. Our Honoured Lady gives her most humble service to your self & Lady so does all your other friends & acquaintance here please to accept the same from

Honoured Sir / Your most humble servant / Cecily Tunstall

**135.** *CT to MS at Lincoln's Inn. 26 August 1740 (NS).* Blount MSS, C *64/201*

Louvain Aug 26 1740

Honoured Sir

This ownes the favour of yours of the 8 Aug which we consulted on & resolve to leave it to your care still if you can apply it again on good Land security let us know who & where, & let the bond be in the same hands as before & also the deed of trust of Mrs Eliz: Smith also. I belive you had forgot that she desired that favour of you by me before in case of death it being thought necessary least your Heirs might supose it your own as being drawn in your name I also writ about it to Mr Day who will keep it when you deliver it to him Mrs Smith thinks the £10 you own in your last is the same that Mr Hill paid you before but you name in one Mr Hille & in the last but one Mr Wyke so she desires to know whether or no 'tis the same Mrs Ogle expected £20 this considerable time. Please to let Mr Day know that we expect my Cousen Bryan Tunstall will pay him £13. 7 shillings & that we desire he'll send 3 of St Austins *Confessions* & please to deduct it out of the said money from Mr Trapps paid by Mr Tunstall please to let me know what money you have for us besides the £54 which is the Interest of the said £400 which we should be glad to draw as soon as we can all services attend your Lady & self from

Honoured Sir / your most humble servant / Cecily Tunstall

**136.** *CT to MS at Lincoln's Inn. 2 September 1740 (NS) (answered 29 August 1740 OS).* Blount MSS, C *64/202*

Louvain 2 Sep: 1740

Honoured Sir

Miss Ogle being in a French House & in very great want of her money I've drawn this day a Bill upon you at 3 days' sight only because I can have better exchange when 'tis not on many days' sight I've drawn £70 the £50 you had for us of Mr Milbourne I hope you've had of Mr Gifford & Porter also before now but not being yet sure I can't draw for that our Honoured Ladys compliments attends your Lady & self the same from all other friends & from

Honoured Sir / Your most obedient humble servant / Cecily Tunstall

**137.** *CT to MS at Lincoln's Inn. 16 September 1740 (NS).* Blount MSS, C *64/203*

Lovain Sepr: the 16 1740

Honoured Sir

I received the favour of yours of the 29 Aug: & must draw on you a £20 as you'll find by Mr Haydockes Bill I must beg you'll remember the £70 Bill I drew last was the 54 of Mr Milbournes Interest & Miss Ogle's £20 that was forgot before so that you need not pay it out of Miss Greens nor Mrs Cholmeleys for you'll find when you've added that £20 that you'll have yet in your hands above £20 when Mr Haydocks Bill is paid. I hope Mr Porter will pay his Daughters pensions the year is above out so pray please to take it when he offers for if you remember he writ he had offerd & you had no orders to receive it also if Mr Stapleton offers to pay £5 for his Daughters use please to give him an acquitance in our Honoured Ladys name for he requires it or else will not pay it I supose Mr Day will pay the £13 &c when Cousen Brian receives it of Mr Trapps which he must have done long eer this if Letters have not miscarry'd. Please to make all our Services acceptable to your Lady & Daughter & accept the same from

Honoured Sir / Your most humble servant / Cecily Tunstall

**138.** *CT to MS at Lincoln's Inn. 30 September 1740 (NS) (answered 10 October 1740 OS).* Blount MSS, C *64/204*

Louvain Sep: 30 1740

Honoured Sir

This is to inquire after an affair which I'm affraid is now out of your memory: above 5 years ago you sent me an Act of Renunciation to be executed by Lady Catherine which was done according to orders & sent May the 21 1735 without which (according to your Letter of May 2d 1735) an administration cannot be taken out here to Mr Arthur Radclyffe the reason of this Administration is to impower Mrs Dacres & Lady Mary Petre to Receive of the late Ld Darwentwaters Executors £2000 due to Mr Arthur Radclyffe of which one fifth that is to say, 400 will belong to Lady Catherine thus far your said Letter & again without which Sir John Webb is advised he cannot safely pay the money. Now what we would know is what that renounciation imports for as we are informed & was so several years ago is that there is yet in Sir John Swinburns hands more money of the said Mr Arthur Rad[clyffe] to be devided for Lady Catherine never designed by that act to quit any other divident or share but only to satisfy the said persons that she had received her part of the £2000 then to be divided & of which she received by you soon after £389 13s 5d which with £10 6s 7d is the £400 now in your hands to be put out again at Interest Sir John Swinburn & his Lady were here the other day & said that they understand a part of the £300 which they have in their hands belongs to us & the rest to Sir Marmaduke Constable £200 they think is for us & that they paid interest for it to others for their share My Cousen Haggerstone many years ago told us of this remainder to be divided so that we hope not to be excluded by that renunciation & desire your speedy answer for we have forgot the contents of it having taken no copy so have only your letter which I've just now cited, if Sir John says any thing about it you need not speak of the said renunciation unless it cutts of Lady Catherine from any further claim which we don't understand it did for she nor we did never consent to relinquish her just due share to her Brs Effects she had 2 Shares before of 2 different Dividents without any such act signed or any thing but an acquitance given by our Agent for the receit of the same so that we would not have it put into their heads unless I say the said act imports so much I beg also the favour of you Sir if you can tell me without any further inquiery what the £10 was layd out in what Cous: Cholmeley had of you for tho' we've received several things she bought for persons in our House yet I can't be sure whether 3 guineas which she gave Mr. Stafford to pay his Journey back hither was included which sum if it was I must pay to my Br Constable's account but unless you can tell me without further enquiry of Cos: Cholmeley's I beg you'll not do it for they are apt to take things ill of me so that I must use some other means to know unless they gave you their Bill for the same at large our Honoured Lady & all acquaintance desires your Lady & self may find here their most kind services the same from

Honoured Sir / your most obliged humble Servant / Cecily Tunstall

***

I beg you'll please to forward the inclosed to Cousen Cholmeley as soon as you can.

**139.** *CT to MS at Lincoln's Inn. 11 October 1740 (NS)*. Blount MSS, C 64/205

Lovaine Octo: 11: 1740

Honoured Sir

My Br[122] has writ to me twice that he had paid a Bill of £40 to my Cousen Peggy Cholmeley which is due to our House now my Cousen Chol: writes that the Bill of £40 is for Mrs Anne Tunstall it seems my

---

[122] Cuthbert Constable.

Brs House keeper or steward has made the mistake however I beg you'll send to her for it & that you've orders from us to receive it & if you have any thing more I hope you'll let us know that I may draw it, I beg you'll please to do what you can to get us some of our long unpaid debts, especially Lord Petre's for realy we are in great want of money all things are so excessively dear & the people here all so poor that if I had not supplys out of England we could not live on our Rents here as they are paid I at least beg the favour of you Sir to let us know the reason why so long delays are still put to the payment or agreement between Lord Petre & Lady Mary Radclyff's' Ex[ecuto]rs that I may satisfy those that has demands upon it also when we may hope to have Mrs Wybourn's money & Mrs Hydes Lady Lithcots & Mrs Throckmortons especially the first which is most considerable in which you'll much oblige

Honoured Sir / your most humble & most obedient servant / Cecily Tunstall

**140.** *CT to MS at Lincoln's Inn. 25 October 1740 (NS).*

Lovain October 25. 1740

Honoured Sir

I had this day the favour of yours of Oct: 10, o:s. & am desired to beg the favour of you Sir to give us an account of Mr Rodbourn whether Dead or alive & if dead whether he made a will or no for we have heard that he's dead without any further account of it this as soon as possible you can also please to demand payment of Lady Cath: Rad:s Annuity for 'tis now 8 months since her Certificate of life was sent I've drawn a Bill of £70 on you this Day at 10 days' sight which as I count can want but 7 shillings of what you yet have in your hands that I know of & hope far more will be before the Bills are payable if not I hope for this time you'll exuse me for I'm in great want of money & am dun'd on all sides & know not what way to turn me to get supplys corn Butter flesh & all things are so excessively dear that if we have not ready money we can't live on credit which makes me press so estreamly. I don't hear the like scarceity from any Letter out of England except my 2 Cousen Willowbeys who of all others I fancy have the least reason to complain who are single women & have good fortunes & I only look on it as an excuse for their not having paid their Cousen's pension in time but this to your self if you please & only beg that you'll do what you can to get us some of our dues. we promised Mr Chorley sometime ago if he had occasion for money, on account of expences done by him that you'd supply him that is when more comes into your hands either from Mr Hill or my Br Constable who both must pay us good sums already due I can't tell whether Mr Hill or Mr Wyke will pay the £40 due the 21 of this instant but I dare say Mr Hill will take care on't so don't say any thing

to him for Mrs Smith[123] has writ [to him] about it please to make all our services accep[table t]o your Lady & Daughter & accept the same from
Honoured Sir / Your very humble servant / Cecily Tunstall

---

[123]  Sr Elizabeth Mary Winefrid Smith.

**141.** *CT to MS at Lincoln's Inn. 8 November 1740 (NS) (answered 17 November 1740 OS).* Blount MSS, C *64/207*

Lovain no: 8 1740

Honoured Sir

I hope by this time you're come to Town again, & that you'll please to send to my Cousen Cholmeley who is ready to pay you £40 which my Br Constable has twice writ to me about the first Letter was in Sep: where he says after a very few days' advice my Cousen Margaret Cholmeley has my orders to pay for your House the sum of £40 it seems when he writ to her he by mistake [he] said for my Sister Anne but 'tis neither for my Sister Anne nor me but owing to the house & what we want extremely they have also £20 for my Cousen Willoughby when youve received it please to let me know Mrs Elizabeth Smith's Annuity is due & you are to receive it from the respective Law[y]ers of Mr Sheldon & Mrs Wells's I suppose they'll pay it first to Mr Hill & he to you there's a Bill of £5 from Mrs Isabella Smith please also to put within the Inclosed five & twenty shillings & send it by a secure hand addressed to Mr Peter Plowden to be left at Adlam's Coffee House near Turn Stile in Lincolns Inn Fields: & put it to my Account, & let me know if it is deliver'd. I beg you'll not fail to send to my Cousen Cholmelys & let them know that as yet we've neither heard of Box nor stays in either Box if they could find Cap: Moody who was the person charged with them it would perhaps be found out my neece Constable is in the greatest want of them possible our Services attend your Lady & self & am as ever
Honoured Sir / Your ever obedient & humble servant / Cecily Tunstall

**142.** *CT to MS at Lincoln's Inn. 2 December 1740 (NS) (answered 22 December 1740 OS).* Blount MSS, C *64/208*

Louvain Decem: 2d 1740

Honoured Sir

I just now had the honour of yours of no: 17 which was very satisfactory & I've drawn upon you for £190 at 10 days' sight before they come for payment you'll have some more in your hands as my Br Tunstall promises so that you'll please to pay Mr Thomas Collingwood if he demands it for Books &c which has been long due to him but as we can't heare from him I can't tell you the sum which he paid to Mr Lewis unless you see him or either of 'em can tell what was paid if you do see Mr Lewis please to ask him & bid him give you the *Gospels & Epistles, Lessons, Collects,& Graduals, for all Sundays & feasts in the whole year, in English:*[124] divided into two tomes P: 65 please to tell him 'tis not the *instructions of the Epistles & Gospels* that we would have but as above & pay him & then we'll see to get 'em over with Mrs Johnsons parcel I've only time at present to subscribe my self

Honoured Sir / your most humble servant / Cecily Tunstall

---

[124] By Richard Challoner.

**143.** *CT to MS at Lincoln's Inn. 9 January 1741 (NS) (answered 19 January 1740/1 OS).* Blount MSS, C *64/209*

Lovain January 9 1741

Honoured Sir

This owns the Favour of yours of Decr 22 I think you've forgot the [£]7.2s.0d. which Mr Wilson sent up long ago for my sister Ann: when he sent a letter inclosed in yours al[*illeg.*] my Cousen Grace Palmes says she'd advice from my Steward of Paborn[125] [?] that he'd paid £3 to you I must beg also that you'll please to look over your Accounts for the £70 I drew Sep: 1 was not out of the £215 which you acknowledged in yours of no: 17 but what you had before in your hands therfore of the 215 there remains yet 25 before I had this last which was [£]57 8s 0d which without counting the [£]7 2s 0d for my sister which I doubt not but you've had before now at least I'll venture to draw £80 on you this day on 10 days' notice not doubting but you'll find sufficient in your hands before 'tis drawn at least. I must beg you'll forward the inclosed & please in your next to let us know the Day that our £400 was again put out. Mrs Smith with her service bids me tell you she thought you'd drawn out of the writings what belonged to our House & they being drawn in your name you should have given a Deed of trust to a 3d Person who we have chosen, which was Mr Day. the settlements being but one writting you can't have that but might have had an abstract of what belonged to us. this she thought was done long ago but since 'tis not she will write to Mr Hide about it. Our best wishes of a happy new year attends your Lady & self from

Honoured Sir / Your most humble servant / Cecily Tunstall

---

[125] Paderborn?

**144.** *CT to MS at Lincoln's Inn. 17 February 1741 (NS) (answered 13 April 1741 OS).* Blount MSS, C *64/210*

Louvaine Feb: 17: 1741

Honoured Sir

Mrs: Smith had a Letter yesterday from Mr Hyde who asures her he left a Copy of the Settlement for our House in your hands last year before he left London by wch you might see how to make yr deed of trust. So I hope youll find it & if 'tis lost let us know that we may procure you another copy the Deed must not be made for or in the name of Mrs Elizth: Smith but to our house or our present Lady and her heirs &c this with her service Mrs Smith desired me to let you know or else after her death we could not claim it this you know Sir I doubt not better than we but sometimes one does not reflect of things our best wishes attends your Lady & daughter I am

Sir / your humble & obedient servant / Cecily Tunstall

Please to let me know in your next if ever Mrs Knight paid a guinea which she owes us since last March: if not I'll put her in mind on't.

**145.** *CT to MS at Lincoln's Inn. 18 April 1741 (NS).* Blount MSS, C *64/211*

Lovaine April 18: 1741

Honoured Sir

I staid till I could send you the inclosed Certificate of Lady Catherine's Life I hope they will not be so very slow in paying her as of late years: this with her service she bids me tell you. Miss Ogle has had notice of £40 being paid for her long [ago] & she is in great hast for it, therefore begs to know whether you have re[ceive]d it for she must return into England I fear before I can draw her Bill for it. Therefore begs you'll let us know as soon as possibly you can. Several others has also heard of money paid to you which I can't think of now, but you'll know what you have, pray let us know whether there's no hopes of Mrs Wibourn's debt being paid &c our Honoured Lady with her best wishes to all your family desires to know whether a kind Letter to Mrs Hyde would be of any service Mr Ha[n]sby seems to think it would but she has tryed once or twice & the letters came back one to Hammersmith by advice of her rambling Br who told us she lived there, but no such person could be found there. I'm sorry you've lost the Paper that contained our part of the Settlement of Mrs Elizabeth Smith's effects for we should have had a year & half paid before now by right & not one farthing yet received which is strange. The inclosed is directed according to Mr Hansby's advice but if you Sir know any more sure our Honoured Lady begs the favour of you to change it we beg your Lady & self may find here our humble service & remain as ever

Honoured Sir / your most obedient & humble servant / Cecily Tunstall

Sir pray be so kind as to let us know if there be any hopes of Lord Petre's money due to our House being paid for these 2 years all things are vastly dear & all rents here very ill paid so that I must reiterate the same request as to all other debts due to us.

**146.** *CT to MS at Lincoln's Inn. 28 April 1741 (NS).* Blount MSS, C *64/212*

Lovain 28 April 1741

Honoured Sir

I had the Honour of yours of April: 13 & have drawn a Bill of £70 at 3 days' sight on you for it. I hope you've got Lady Catherine's Certificate before this. Our chief Ladys are all persuaded by the 2 Mrs Smiths themselves to authorise you to demand the whole £1000 of Mr Sheldons & Mrs Well[s]'s Stewards for we are convinced that we shall not be paid regularly or even at all perhaps since the very first time there is nothing to be had this Mrs Smith will let each concernd know & then you'll please to let us know whether it will be necessary to send you a Letter of Atturney or what else you may think fit & if this takes place there will be no need of any other deed of trust as for Mr Lytcott please to let him know we're resolved to go to law for our money which he has owned to be a just debt as I have it in yours so that perhaps when he knows our final resolution he may be glad to spare the cost if not proceed by the athority of our Lady &c. I hope you've send [sent] the Letter to Mrs Hyde before now. Our Lady & all 3 sisters &c desire you & your Lady may find here our best wishes & service my neece joyns wth us in the same to your Daughter I am

Sir / Your most obedient humble servant / Cecily Tunstall.

**147.** *CT to MS at Lincoln's Inn. 16 May 1741 (NS).* Blount MSS, C *64/213*

Lovain May 16 1741

Honoured Sir

I was forced to send a Bill today for Miss Green at 10 days' sight for that she had not money for her Journey & she shew'd me a Letter wherin Mr Gifford said he'd payd you £28 16s 8d which she had great need of & signed her Bill her self as you'll find. Mrs Elisabeth Smith desires you'll write to Mr Bellasse & to Mr Lancelot Kerby Attarney who had orders one from Mr Shelldon of Winchester & the other from Mrs Wells to pay 3 half years of her Annuity their Directions are as follows To Rowland Bellasse Esqr in St Peters street in Winchester Hampshire the other as named above at his house in Winchester you'll please to let 'em both know that we've given you full power to proceed against 'em in case of non payment for she desires us to secure the principal that she may have no more trouble about it[.] they seemd at first rather to wish we'd take it all in but we thought it in safe hands but now we find there is no hopes of payment since the first fails only please to warn 'em of it that they may not be surprised if a Letter of Atturney be needful we can send you one please to let us know what money is paid since the last which will much oblige

Honoured Sir / your very humble servant / Cecily Tunstall

**148.** *CT to MS at Lincoln's Inn. 19 May 1741 (NS).* Blount MSS, C *64/214*

Louvaine May 19 1741

Honoured Sir

This comes to desire you'll please to send to Mr Day to know whether he has received £21 19s 0d for Mrs Johnson she having notice of its being paid by her sister Ledger who says she had sent it to Mr President at Dowey.[126] So she hopes 'tis not too late to hinder its being sent thither if Mr Day makes difficulty to keep it back at least let it be stoped till Mr President or Mr Petre sends orders to whom we'll write about it Mr [Mrs?] Johnson has something in your hands which she begs you'll send the first Person that comes over 'tis salve or something of that nature our Service attends your Lady & selve from

Honoured Sir /your very humble servant / Cecily Tunstall

---

126  Dr William Thornburgh.

**149.** *CT to MS at Lincoln's Inn. 6 June 1741 (NS) (answered 12 June 1741 OS).* Blount MSS, C *64/215*

Louvain June 6 1741

Honoured Sir

This is to beg the favour of you to forward the inclosed we having yet no direction to your Cousen & not doubting but that you'll know whether they be arrived or no at least send to know of my Cousen Cholmeley where they said they'd go & please to pay Mrs Strickland what she'll lay out for my neece for a pair of stayes we hear my Br Tunstall has sent up £16 1s 0d also £5 for Mrs Isabella Smith Cousen Willoughby £20 & more which we should be glad to hear that you have received for sometimes they write I've paid such a sum to Mr Strickland when perhaps 'tis only a Bill not payable on sight Mr Day has a sum of 21 more or less & 19s as I take it for Mrs Johnson we're in great want of money things being yet vastly dear & should be much obliged to you could we get Lord Petre's debt paid or any other due to us pray let me know when we may hope to have Mrs Wybourn's money & whether any hopes of geting any thing from Mr Brinckhurst for his 2 sisters which he often promised to pay if you ever see him or whether he dare shew his head for debt & whether you ever sent our Honoured Lady's letter to Mrs Hyde & if any thing is done to Mr Litcot this with our Honoured Lady's humble service she desires to know I've forgot whether I ever desired you from Mrs Johnson to forward to us a pot of ointment or some such thing all our services attend your lady & self from

Honoured Sir / your most obedient & humble servant / Cecily Tunstall

**150.** *CT to MS at Lincoln's Inn. 29 June 1741 (NS).* Blount MSS, C *64/216*

Lovaine 29 June 1741

Honoured Sir

I've drawn a Bill of £50 on you the day I had the favour of yours of the 13 June os & hope that before now you've sent to Mr Day for perhaps Mr President[127] has forgot to desire him to pay it to you for he certainly has it & has had it some considerable time but yet I've not drawn it as you'll see there are several others that should pay you money so that I hope e'er long I may draw a more large sum: if you are not in great hurrys I should be very glad you'd please to sent me your accounts for 'tis so long since that I can't tell how to make mine with out it & shall give up my place soon I believe: this is not to hinder your more pressing afairs but only to beg that you'll at least be ready if I do give up my office in a month or 2. I believe Mrs Strickland did not need money for my neeces' stayes because she writ that they were made before she had time to give orders about 'em I've not heard that Mr Bellacis[128] &c have paid the arrears of Mrs Smiths annuity yet, so that it will be necessary for you to write to 'em for we can't be any longer without our money & if

---

[127]  Dr William Thornburgh, President of the English College, Douai, 1738–50.
[128]  Bellasis.

they refuse to pay the Interest we must Sell the land that is ingaged for it, this Mrs Elizabeth Smith much desires her self, else I had not writ it before, she said what could she expect hereafter if the very first 2 years they refused payment. So pray press it hard upon them for Mr Sheldon writ he'd given orders long ago to Mr Bellase. Only send the parcel for Mrs Johnson to Mr Shepperd & he'll get it to us by a young woman that is coming here. Since I writ this we have notice that there is £50 paid to you by orders of Mr Sheldon & Mrs Wells so that if you've not yet writ please to stay till the 2d year is out & let me know whether you have the money for she writes that 'tis actualy in your hands we have at present a very good occasion to put out money so that our Honoured Lady with her service desires you'll be so good as to let us know whether we may expect the payment of Lord Petre's debt soon & Lady Catherin's share in the dividend Sir John Swinburn's spoke of here some months ago for if there is we would rather let it be in your hands till the Person calls for it if not we must find some other way for as yet I can't tell whether 'tis to be paid down in England or at Paris. I am

Honoured Sir / your most humble servant / Cecily Tunstall

**151.** *CT to MS at Lincoln's Inn. 17 July 1741 (NS) (answered 17 July 1741 OS).* Blount MSS, C *64/217*

Lovain July 17 1741

Honoured Sir

I received a Letter the last week from Mrs Knight where she sends me a Copy of an acquitance signd by your Lady July 2d 1740 for [£]11s 0d which Mr William Hare paid her for 'twas what I layd out for her in 1739 & could never hear it was paid I suppose 'twas quite forgot you being out of town. Mrs Eyre desires you'll send the watch as soon as any occasion serve or rather please to send it to Mr Shepperd & he'll find I hope an occasion if he does not Mr Collingwood can I believe. Mrs Johnson with her service desires you'll send to Mr Day about the £21 9s 0d which he had some time in May & she writ to Doway not to have it sent thither but paid to you you'll please to forward the inclosed to him if Mr Stapleton offers to pay £5 for his daughter please to give him an acquitance for it it will be due the 15 Aug: n:s. & he requires an acquitance so please to give it in our names our Honoured Lady presents you her most humble service please to accept the same from

Honoured Sir /your most humble servant to command / Cecily Tunstall

Our services attends your Lady & Daughter

**152.** *CT to MS at Lincoln's Inn. 22 July 1741 (NS) (answered 17 July 1741 OS).* Blount MSS, C *64/218*

Louvain July the 22 1741

Honoured Sir

This day Miss Porters had notice that their F[athe]r has paid you £33 13s 0d & odd so that I've given Mr Melling a Little Bill for £10 which he's paid me here for them they having use for it here & he having occasion for it at London so that if Mrs Bentley comes for it you'll please to pay it on sight Mrs Johnson having stayd so long for an occasion desires you'll send her Pot of ointment as the little Bill directs please to find here all due to your self & Lady for our Honoured Lady my sisters & neece to your daughter also please to accept the same from
Honoured Sir / your most humble & obedient servant / Cicely Tunstall

**153.** *CT to MS at Lincoln's Inn. 4 August 1741 (NS) (answered 7 August 1741 OS).* Blount MSS, C *64/219*

Aug: 4: 1741 Louvain

Honoured Sir

I was honor'd with yours of July 17 the other day & have drawn a Bill on you this day for £70 which I know you have in your hands after paying my 2 small Bills one to Mr Haydocke & the other to Mrs Bentley Mrs Smith with her humble service bids me tell you that she had a letter from her sister Wells dated June the 14 where she says that she stayd till she could certainly tell her she had paid into your hands £50 40 for our house & 10 for her & that she had paid considerably for getting the money returned up to London this seems very positive & yet you seem to speak only of £25 which Mr Wright told you he had an order to pay pray demand the £50 if you have it not already for 'tis strangely odd. I hope you'll have Lady Catherin's soon she asked me about it long ago shall we never hear of Mrs Wybourne's debt &c I long to make all accounts even & am as ever
Honoured Sir / your most humble servant /Cecily Tunstall

Please to forward the inclosed as soon as conveniently you can & accept all our services.

**154.** *CT to Mrs [Mary] Strickland at her house in Queen Square. 5 September 1741 (NS).* Blount MSS, C *64/220*

Lovain Sep: 5 1741

Honoured Madam

I must needs beg the favour to you in your spouse's absence to alow me to adress my Neece Constable to you who sets out from us the 8: of this month she'll make only a very short stay in London but desires much the honour of your Company or your Daughter's while she stays. We are so fraid of the small Pox for her that we would not have her go into any publick place either for divotion or diversion if posible we relying upon your civility & obliging temper presume thus far to trespass upon your goodness which will not only oblige my Br Constable but also
    Madam / Your most humble & most obedient servant / Cecily Tunstall
    My neece & sisters are much yours.

**155.** *CT to Mrs [Mary] Strickland at her house in Queen Square. September 1741 (NS).* Blount MSS, C *64/221*

Lovain Sep: 22 1741

Madam

I must once more trespass upon your goodness to recommend my neece Constable to your care the little time she stays at London that you'll be so good as to procure her the best Taylor to take mesure of her for a pair of stays & what ellse she wants for she has no cloths fit to appear in but I would not have her stay in London they may be send down into the Country when made I must also beg you'll also inquire if Lady Clifford be in Town for unless she be & will take my neece down with her I must also beg you'll be so good as to procure one to conduct my neece home to Burton this in case my Br has not already provided for that for in no case he will not have my Cousen Cholmeleys have the Government of her but this to your self Madam if you please. The servant may go down with her but she must have some woman that can be trusted & will dress her &c this Madam I should not have the assurance to beg of you but that I hope my Br will take as the greatest honour & favour & on account of the old friendship between him & your spouse which will eternaly oblige as well him as
    Honoured Madam / your most obliged & most humble servant / Cecily Tunstall

Permit me dear Madam to inclose one herein to my neece in case she's not yet arrived which I long to hear of & would add to all other favours if by one word of answer you'll please to give us notice of

**156.** *CT to MS at Lincoln's Inn. 6 October 1741 (NS) (answered 13 November 1741 OS).* Blount MSS, C *64/222*

Louvain octo: 6 1741

Honoured Sir

I hope this will find you well & safe return'd from Bath where I hear you have been which I did not hear till last week I took the freedom to recommend my neece Constable to your Lady's care in your absence but fear she had not the honour to meet with your Lady which I am doubly sorry for because I writ to her inclosed to your Lady to tell her her Papa's orders for her taking a Coach to herself & company to go down to Burton in & that he would send over to meet her at Barton which is some distance from Burton. This I fear will come too late now if she has not met with your Lady before pray put letters &c to my account which was writ either to your Lady or any other expences about my neece. If you have not received £15 from Mr Crathorn please to go or send to Mr Wright for he has it & has had it for his sister her[e] some time Mrs Heneage also says she'll pay or has pd £21 if not please to see about it also let us know if we mayn't draw Lady Catherin's Annuity now & what more you had since your return pray be so good as to let us know whether Nicolas our Servant who went over with my neece is gone into the Country with her & if he is not coming over again for if he has time before he comes over be so good as to instruct him where he may find the following Books & if he has not money enough with him you will please to let him have what is wanting either for his return or expences please to make my service acceptable to your Lady & daughter & if my neece be with you please to let her know we've had the satisfaction to have received her Letter which was long expected we'd been in vast pain for her not knowing what was become of her pray tell Nicolas to write to us all particulars concerning 'em & that he get us these Books &c

*A short View of the History of England* 2d edition by Bevil Higgons Esqr; price 5s

*The Garden of the Confraternity of our Bd Lady of Mount Carmel* price 3s: *The 30 days prayer to our Blessed Lady*

*The scripture penitents written originally in French* by Mr Godeau *& translated into English embellished wth 22 copper plates* price 5s. *An introduction to the celebrated Devotion of the most holy Rosary* price 1 shilling half a dozen of these

Mr Haydocke desires that Nicolas will bring Collyflower seed for a crown or 2 or any other curious seed he can get or plants or grafts. I am / Honoured Sir / your most humble servant / Cecily Tunstall.

Mrs Johnson desires to know whether you've not had a packet for Mrs Ledger.

**157.** *CT to MS at Lincoln's Inn. 13 October 1741 (NS) (answered 9 October 1741 OS).* Blount MSS, C *64/223*

Lovain Octor: 13 1741

Honoured Sir

Tho' I writ last post but one I must again trouble you being in great want of money & by a Letter I had the honour to receive this day from your Lady, I find you'll not come to town till November o:s: which will be too long to stay for a Bill I gave you on account last time that Mr Wright has money for Mrs Crathorn £1 .& what I want most is Lady Catherine's Annuity therefore I beg you'll order the said sums or more if any received to be paid to Mr Day on whom I may draw for 'em I beg a speedy answer that I may draw a Bill. I beg a thousand pardons for the freedome I've taken to recomend my neece to your Lady & when I did so never knew that your Lady was in the Country otherwise would never have had the face to desire such a favour tho' realy I was in great straits she having a great dislike to be with my Cousen Cholmeleys & for a young creature to be in common lodgings would not have been proper, else I would not have beg'd this favour, as to the Charges I'll be sure to have all paid to the last farding but can never I fear return the kindness & civilitys confer'd on my neece tho's I hope she will not be wanting to make the best acknowledgments in her power tho's she's of a very few words yet she's very sensible of kindness which she's been used always to meet with from your relations in a very singular maner I mean your Cousen Gery Strickland[129] who's Lady I'm in great pain for expecting as she guesed this Michaelmass to be brought to bed we never fail to pray for her which is almost the only return we can make for all favours & which we never fail to do for your self & family as a duty incombent on

Sir / Your most humble & obedient servant / Cecily Tunstall

---

[129]  Jarrard Strickland of Sizergh.

**158.** *CT to Mrs [Mary] Strickland at her house in Queen Square. 13 October 1741 (NS).* Blount MSS, C *64/224*

Lovain Octo: 13: 1741

Madam

I'm in the utmost confusion to think what trouble I've given you which I never design'd: for had I known you'd been out of Town I should never have desired so great a favour which I'm infinitely obliged to you Dear

Madam for & shall let my Br[130] know. I hope my neece is gone down before now if not pray Madam be so good as to procure some careful person & a servant to conduct her according to her Papa's orders which I fear miscared if so it was that she should make no stay at London but take a Coach to her self & company & that he would send over to meet her at Barton which is 7 miles of Hull as they say I can imagine that she never writ to let her Papa know when she arived at London which we could not do as not knowing when it was. I'm truly sorry both for the trouble she's given you madam & the danger of getting the small pox in London if she's yet with you I beg madam you'll hasten her down & that she may't go in the Stage Coach which will add more to the favours already confer'd on us by your self & spouse to which I beg my most kind acknowledgments & am

Madam / your most obliged & humble servant to command / Cecily Tunstall

---

[130]  Cuthbert Constable.

**159.**  *CT to MS at Lincoln's Inn. 26 October 1741 (NS) (answered 13 November 1741 OS).* Blount MSS, C *64/225*

Louvain Octo: 26 1741

Honoured Sir

I've drawn a Bill on you this day for £130 at 6 days sight as you desired. When I made the Bills I'd forgot the £25 you had so long ago of Mrs Wells's for her sister Mrs Smith but hope you'll have the other £25 very soon & Miss Heneage's pension cousin Willoughby's Annuity &c I lookd as you bid me in your Lady's Letter & I find there (My family is fixt in the Country till November in which month I shall come to Town). I've had a Letter this day from my Br Constable who owes the obligation he owes your Lady & self for all favours confer'd on his Daughter & I hope he will return the kindness it being in his Power not in mine my neece arrived safe the 6.os. as he says he chides me for giving you & your Lady so great a trouble indeed if I'd known your Lady had been in the Country I should never have taken that Liberty but as I said in my last I had no other way she not careing to be with my Cousen Cholmeleys so I hope she pardon this too great freedom & accept my most grateful acknowledgments. I beg Sir you'll remember your promise of sending your accounts soon & believe me ever

Honoured Sir / Your most humble servant / Cecilia Tunstall

Our servant[131] arrived safe the 17 of this Instant with his charge & Mrs Eyre thanks you for her Watch he gave me an account of the 4 guineas so that I'll place it to my Br's account & you'll please to put it in yours to me or our House if my neece took any money of you you'll be so good as let either me or my Br know & you shall be repaid with [our] thanks if Mr Skelton has [*illeg.*] paid all charges I beg Sir [*illeg.*] the trouble was more then enough [*illeg.*] without [*illeg.*]

---

[131] Nicolas.

**160.** *CT to MS at Lincoln's Inn. 7 November 1741 (NS) (answered, n.d.).* Blount MSS, C *64/226*

Lovain Novr: 7. 1741

Honoured Sir

Tho' I writ latly & drew a Bill on you for £130 yet I'm desired to let you know that Miss Heneage's pension is ready & has been some months. I think it is one Mr George Petre that has it if you have not yet had it please to inquire before I finish this I'm ask'd where he lives but I believe he paid it to Mr Day in your absence Mrs Talbot desires youll look among your receits if Lady Shrewsbury has not paid a sum for her within 3 months of this. Mrs Johnson begs if you have received a Packet of sheets directed to Mrs Ledger that you'll please to forward it down to her it was sent by Brudges. I forgot also to desire you'll pay Mr Williams for drugs & Gumbs he sent. Also for Indigo to Mr Collingwood I'll desire he will come to you for it I can't just tell the sums but they know & will ask no more than due to them. I've asked where Mr George Petre's lives but can't get any intelligence about him but that he had orders to pay her pension please to let me know if you've had it if not I know what to do. My service attends your Lady I've let my Br[132] know what trouble & charges she was at on my neeces' account I hope he'll acknowledge 'em in a better manner than I can who am hers &

Honoured Sir / Your most obliged & humble servant / Cecily Tunstall

---

[132] Cuthbert Constable.

**161.** *CT to MS at Lincoln's Inn. Undated [November 1741] (answered 27 November 1741 OS).* Blount MSS, C *64/227*

Honoured Sir

I beg you'll do me the favour to send to Mr Wright & let me know as soon as you've had the money & whether yet Miss Heneages pen[sion]

&c is paid I can't tell whether in my last I desired to know whether you've receiv'd a parcel of sheets to be forwarded to Mrs Ledger & that you'll please to see whether you've not had some money for Mrs Talbot within some 3 or 4 months we heard by a Letter from Gant to one in our House that my Lady Petre was brought to bed of a fine Son. I beg know whether it is true or no, for 'tis some weeks ago & we hear no more on't we should be overjoid if 'tis true & beg you'll please to congratulate with the Lady from us all. We must again put you in mind of Mrs Wybourn's Debt & who we shall address our selves to for payment of my Cousen Barbara Crathorn's Annuity which was left her by my Aunt Anne Radclyffe & is an indisputable debt to our family whoever has the Land or money tied for the payment of it & has now run up ii years' arriers are due this Martlemiss & I should be very sorry to be forced to deliver up my post with such a considerable debt unpaid perhaps for want of duly soliciting the payment. If you hear any thing of Mrs Hyde or what can be done either to her or to recover the rest of Mr Fell's debt which you seem'd some time ago to have good hopes of please to try which will much oblige our Honoured Lady who desires you'll accept her best wishes & prayers which is also the heart's desire of

Honoured Sir / your most humble Servant / Cecily Tunstall

———•◦•———

The Lady & Daughter I hope [*blot*] my Br Constable has returnd due thanks for [the] favours to his daughter.

**162.** *CT to MS at Lincoln's Inn. 30 November 1741 (NS).* Blount MSS, C *64/228*

Louvain Novr: 30 1741

Honoured Sir

I've had the Honour of yours of the 13 of this month & will stay some days in hopes to hear that you've re[ceive]d the £25 which Mrs Eli[zabe]th Smith sent you a Bill for on Mr Wyke or Mr Wright for I've forgot which of 'em but I hope you have the Bill. We have had the good news confirm'd of Lady Petre's son so won't give you any further trouble on that head. Miss Swinburne desires you'll get this to her Papa, I wish you could see him for when he was here he promised he would see us paid the Interest that has run up of Lady Catherine's share of the last divident of her Br Arthurs. I beg you'll look if Lady Shrewsbury has not paid a sum for Mrs Ann Talbot within 2 or 3 months. Also if my Cousen Willoughby's £20 be paid to you yet pleas to make our compliments to your Lady & accept of the same from

Honoured Sir / Your most obedient humble servant / Cecily Tunstall

———•◦•———

If I don't hear from you I hope you will allow me to draw for £100 in 8 days I mean.

**163.** *CT to MS at Lincoln's Inn. 13 December 1741 (NS).* Blount MSS, C *64/229*

Louvain December 30 1741

Honoured Sir

I had the honour of yours of Nov the 27 this day & have drawn a Bill on you for £100 on 6 days' sight. I'm very glad to know who to apply to for our arrears of several Annuities & therefore must beg you'll send the Copys down to Burton which I sent you of all the Deeds given us by my Aunt Ann Radclyffe & the Colonel[133] I'll let my Br[134] know this day that I've desired you to send him the said Copys & I'll first let him know what is behind hand for my Cousen Barbara Crathorn's Annuity if you have 'em not by you I must get 'em new copy'd but I sent 'em all to you 6 or 7 years ago if you have 'em please to write on the back what is due for each adding the years since I stayted 'em Cousen Crathorns is 11 years now full fallen last Martinmiss just past £220 at £20 per annum the rest is to be as I said adding only so many years more. My compliments to your Lady & Daughter please to accept the best wishes of

Honoured Sir / Your very humble servant / Cecily Tunstall

---

133   Colonel Thomas Radclyffe.
134   Cuthbert Constable.

**164.** *CT to MS at Lincoln's Inn. 8 January 1742 (NS) (answered 8 January 1741/2 OS).* Blount MSS, C *64/230*

Louvain January 8 1742

Honoured Sir

I'm desired by several in our House to get you to pay for some Books which they've sent for to Mr Francis Nedom[135] he must bring you a Bill when he has sent of the Books I can't tell whether I told you in my last that the 2 Mrs Bartlets has notice that their Br has paid you £27 for them to be imployed as he orders which they ought to do as speedily as they can but till you please to let us know whether or no you've had the money they can't have it if my Cousen Willoughby's money is paid or any other Lady Shrewsbury it seems had paid you that sum that we asked about & now more I hope you'll at last find time to send

---

135   Francis Needham.

the accounts that we may make all even before I take leave of you. I'm realy in the utmost confusion to find by your Lady's letter which she latly favour'd me with that my Br Constable has not yet in any manner of way made any acknowledgement for all the extraordinary Kindness & civilitys received by my neece when at London by your Lady could I have forseen that I should never have had the confidence to have recommended her to her tho' perhaps 'tis the greatest advantage to her that ever she'll meet with in her life yet I'm truly sorry to have procured it for her without having it in my own power to make any return at least tho' I can't possibly requite the Kindness yet I beg you'll let me know all expences that she has put your good family to which I'll promise to get my Br to pay to the last farthing I suppose he's been so busy about Lady Mary Radclyffe's affairs that he has deferred all others till that is finished for he has never writ nor yet paid us what our House had layd out for my neece's Journey &c but all this will not nor can I excuse his neglect I've this post writ to my neece about it very pressingly tho' indeed she long ago writ us word with great sence of gratitude of all that goodness your Lady had for her & how happy she was in her Company. I must conclude with all our best wishes of a happy new year to your Self & Family & am with much sincerity

Honoured Sir / Your most humble servant / Cecily Tunstall

**165.** *CT to MS at Lincoln's Inn. 24 January 1742 (NS).* Blount MSS, C *64/231*

Louvaine January 24 1742

Honoured Sir

I received the honour of yours of the 8 of this instant & I've drawn a Bill of £60 on you at 6 days' sight: Mrs Cholmeley here desires you'll pay £5 to her neece Marget Cholmeley she'll know why also please to pay Mr Williams & his partner if not already done for drugs we've had by our man Nicolas. I fear I forgot then to desire it. I supose the £10 you own for Mr Green is the same [as] that in your last but Sir you said was for Mrs Ann Collingwood & you'd only the Bill then for't & which I paid her as being due for several things Mrs Green when here bought at shops in town please in your next to tell me for I take it to be the same & not for Mr Green who is in our Town & would have told me if it was for him & besides he's not related at all to the Capt I hear Mrs Hide has a sister at the Spelicans at Bruxells & we design to ask of her where her Sister lives for whether she ever got any letter we writ or no I can't tell but she's never answerd any unless t'was she or some one for her that sent a Letter directed to our Honoured Lady in French but not a Letter within that any body could find out. Some times we guess if one Language some times an other in fine we can make nothing on't you don't say whether you've the Deeds that coll Radclyffe gave here & which I send you, that is copys of 7 or 8 years ago for if they are lost we must get 'em copy'd over again to send my Br[136] but I hope either Lord Petre's or you will find 'em. I beg you'll not take it ill that I put you in mind again of Mrs Wybourn's debt so that as soon as money can be raised to pay debts we ought to come first as being the first that can claim a right to be paid for Mrs Charity Wybourn was here in 1700 1701 1702 & that money which I want was for her pension & lent for her Journey. I know certainly that the Dominicans have had what was due to them tho' 7 or 8 years behind us. In my next I hope to give you some information of Mrs Hyde in the mean time I am wth all sincerity

Honoured Sir / Your obliged humble servt / Cecily Tunstall

My best wishes & service to your Lady & Daughter.

---

[136]  Cuthbert Constable.

**166.** *CT to MS at Lincoln's Inn. 13 February 1742 (NS).* Blount MSS, C *64/233*

Lovain Feb 13 1742

Honoured Sir

I aplyd myself according to your advice to my Br Constable for payment of Coll: Thomas Radclyffe's Debt to our House & this is his answer as for you or any one's expecting I should pay the Collonel's Debts to your House I must beg to be excused & have already offerd Lord Petre to make over the Collonel's Estate to him, & if he accepts of it he ought to pay all the incumbrances upon it, & no Body can expect that I must pay the Coll's debts out of my own Estate for as the debts were Coll: Radclyffe's from whence can his debts be supposed to be discharg'd then from his Estate. Thus you see Sir we are driven from pillar to post & none will own the Debt. we must seek to do our Selves right some other way if you can tell us any safe & quick for delays are only chicans as they say in french for if 'tis our undisputed due why not better soon payd than to let the Arriers run up to such a great sum that it will be very hard to pay it all at once I shall enquire what method my Cousen Hanford used to get what my Aunt Ann Radclyffe left him & his Br & Sister for they've been payd this 12 years ago whether he put it up in Chancery or now. I also writ to my neece to let her know how shamefull it was that my Br nor she had never writ nor return'd your Lady their gratful acknowledgments for all favours shewn her by your

Lady which my Br assured me he did over & over 9 times so that I fear letters miscarried: he's very angry at me for thinking him capable of so great an ingratitude as that would be. Pray with my humble service to let her know that for my part I'm incapable to render due thanks & can only give my poor mite of prayers & thanks & gratful acknowledgments which I shall never forget as long as I am

Honoured Sir / Your most obliged humble servant / Cicely Tunstall

**167.** *CT to MS at Lincoln's Inn. 9 March 1742 (NS) (answered 2 April 1742 OS).* Blount MSS, C *64/233a*

Lovain March 9 1742

Honoured Sir

This is to desire you'll pay when call'd for £5 to Mrs Marget Cholmeley which her Aunt returns her back it being so much more than she should have had the last time or in fine she knows why also our Honoured Lady has had a Letter from my Br Constable wherin he promises to do his best to get us payment of what debts is due to us from Lady Mary & the Late Coll: Radclyffe so that if you have our Copys of the Bonds that I sent you in 1736 or can get 'em back from Lord Petre's you'll please to send 'em to my Br Constable I find in a Copy of a Letter which I then wrote to you that I told you Lady Mary Rad: in 1718 had redeem'd her Brother's Estate for £11000 this I was informd of by Lady Catherine who said she was sure of it if so it certainly belongs to her Ex[ecuto]rs: & may be proved by writings sure if true I hope to have your accounts soon for I must make all even very soon so beg if possible you'll let me have that satisfaction before we take leave which will much oblige her who shall ever remain

Honoured Sir / Your obliged humble servant / Cecily Tunstall

**168.** *CT to MS at Lincoln's Inn. 11 May 1742 (NS) (answered 14 May 1742 OS).* Blount MSS, C *64/234*

Lovain May 11 1742

Honoured Sir

This is to forward the Certificate of Lady Catherine's Life which till this day we could not get Mr Daniel to Legalize I can't imagine why Mr Neny [?] jnr has solicited it this month & at last with much threatening he has antedated to make up. I fancy he suspects she's dead but on what account we can't guess for she's now better than she's been this many years. When the family paid it it was payable every half year so that all here think she should sign a like Certificate at the half year's end or else they will not pay what may be due when she dies this I write about some years ago but you did not then answer I beg you'll do it now for why should we lose it for a little trouble. Please to let us have what you have receiv'd since your last or before Mrs Knight says he [*sic*] had notice of £1 2s 0d but you have not named it besides some other small sums. I long to have your accounts which you promised me long please to find here our Lady's & all friends' service's which attend likewise your Lady & Daughter. I am

Honoured Sir / your most obedient humble Servant / Cecily Tunstall

**169.** *CT to MS at Lincoln's Inn. 22 May 1742 (NS).* Blount MSS, C 64/235

Louvaine May 22 1742

Honoured Sir

I've drawn upon you Bills for £100 at 10 days' sight being in great want of money for Miss Porter's &c we having notice that Mr Porter has paid £37 1s 3d for their use Mrs Rodburne has notice also of fifty shillings for which you gave [a] Bill Mrs Knight long ago had notice of £1 2s 0d Mrs Johnson £5 1s 6d paid to you by Mr George Thornburgh also if not yet paid at least before this is payable. My Br Tunstall will pay £15 for us. I hope you'll receive other sums for us & that I shall have your accounts very soon which will much oblige

Honoured Sir / your very humble servant / Cecily Tunstall

Please to make my service acceptable to your Lady & Daughter.

**170.** *CT to MS at Lincoln's Inn. 1 June 1742 (NS).* Blount MSS, C 64/236

Lovain 1 June 1742

Honoured: Sir

I received the favour of yours & have drawn a little Bill on you for £50 at 10 days' sight tho' I had drawn before for 100 yet not to lose the exchange which falls daily I must draw as fast as I can I must beg to know whether or no you mistook in the sum of £30 from Mr Sheldon for Mr Hill writ the same post & owned only 25 so pray let us know if [the] sum of Mrs Knight was paid in January as she had notice of £1 2s 0d my compliments pray to your Lady if you know whether my neece Winny by gone down pray let us know we hear she's had the measles & got well over 'em. I believe you'll see Mr Worthington so pray if you do discourse him what may be done about Mrs Hyde's affaire & if any thing be paid for our mony out at rent with you let us know &c Lady Litcots Mrs Wybourn's debts &c the accounts you've promised which will much oblige

Honoured Sir / your obedient & humble servant / Cecily Tunstall

**171.** *CT to MS at Lincoln's Inn. 19 June 1742 (NS) (answered 23 June 1742 OS).* Blount MSS, C *64/237*

Lovain June 19 1742

Honoured Sir

This is to beg you'll forward the inclosed as soon as possible because else it will be too late to send the things which Mr Kirwood has in his hands for Mrs Daniel which she desires to have by Miss Parry & the other young Lady that is for us very soon. I expect dayly your accounts which you were pleased to promise me so long ago & till I have 'em I can't possibly regulate my own. I must earnestly beg you'll do me this favour which will highly oblige

Honoured Sir / your most obedient humble servant / Cecily Tunstall

**172.** *CT to MS at Lincoln's Inn. 7 August 1742 (NS).* Blount MSS, C *64/238*

Louvain August 7 1742

Honoured Sir

This owns the favour of yours of July 23d & I've drawn only a Bill of £50 on you because I've given Mr Haydocke a Bill of £18 10s 0d due to him last May. Please to pay also a little Bill of £1 0s 0d to Mr Williams if he comes for it Mrs Johnson desires if you see Mr Maire[137] on what account the £6 is for she's had no notice of it. Please to send the inclosed aquitance to Mr Thomas Stapleton who on sight on't will pay £5 for his Sister's use this her Br requires from us he lodges at No: 16 in Glocester Street. Please to forward the inclosed. We're very sensible of your loss of Lord Petre[138] & are also more in pain for your Poor Lady who we have the most tender concern for not hearing whether her Ladyship has also had the same fatal disease being left with child as we heard but since we can't tell how it goes for God sake if you hear let us know. I do[n]'t know whether in my last I desired you'd pay Mr Needam[139] if he demanded a sum for Books & if he brings 'em to you please to send 'em to Mrs Bently who designs for us or if any comes before her pray let us have 'em by the first. We hear my neece Winny is better since she parted with Cousen Nutty that is as we suppose the air of her own

---

[137] John Maire, London lawyer.
[138] Robert James Petre, 8th Baron Petre died of smallpox. One of Strickland's two main patrons, Petre was married to Anna Maria, daughter of the executed Jacobite Earl of Derwentwater.
[139] Needham.

Country has done her good. My most humble service to your Lady, my Sisters join in all grateful thanks to her for her care of my neece & am
Honoured Sir / your most humble servant / Cecily Tunstall

**173.** *CT to MS at Lincoln's Inn. 21 September 1742 (NS) (answered 14 October 1742 OS).* Blount MSS, C *64/239*

Louvain Sep: 21 1742

Honoured Sir

I've long expected the accounts you promised me which tho' late yet better than not at all tho' I can't hope to have the satisfaction to even all at parting as all others have done that have preceded me yet my successor will have it at the very first I hope yet. I'm no more in the same post but only because Mrs Towneley is much indisposed & can't apply her self to the business required. Otherways she'd some weeks ago have had the honour to write to you. I must beg leave to wish your Daughter Blount much joy which I did long ago but then premature as it seems now 'tis sure I think having had it from several hands. I can scarce hope to have Lady Catherine Rad: Annuity before the close of my affairs tho' in your last you put us in hopes to have it sooner than the last year & 'tis 6 or 7 months after date: so pray if possible let me have this satisfaction. Mrs: Daniel desires you'll let Mr Wm Kirwood have 16 shillings or more if he calls for it being value received by me for what he layd out for her at London. I hope you & your Lady will accept some small tokens I'll send by Mrs Bentley if I can as a mark of gratitude for all favours tho' I can't pretend to requite as your merits deserve only to shew my good will if power was not wanted our Honoured Lady & all friends & acquaintance joyn in all that is kind to your Lady & self the same from
Honoured Sir / Your most obliged humble Servant / Cecilia Tunstall

**174.** *CT to MS. 1 February 1743 (NS).* Blount MSS, C *64/240*

Lovain Feb: 1 1743

Honoured Sir

If paper could blush this would to have been so long before I send you the so long promised present but till now I have not met wth a favourable occasion the Box I believe by this is sent of by one Cap: Collice or Callice from Bridges[140] the 2 chain & watch strings I hope you'll accept. The same favour I beg of your Lady to accept the two Bouques & 2 pair of shoes which tho' not by far fit for her use yet I beg she'll accept for

---

[140] Bruges.

some one of her little Daughters I wish I could have had any embroidered on sattin or velvet but I could not get any better so hope she'll accept the widow's mite in good part it not being in my power to return all her favours conferd on my neece. I hope she'll believe twas no fault of mine but only want of power our Procuratrix begs you'll remember your promise to send her your accounts which will both oblige her &

Honoured Sir / Your most obedient & humble Servant / Cecily Tunstall

Please to put this Letter to the account of our House.

**175.** *Christina Towneley to MS at Lincoln's Inn. 1 July 1743 (NS).*
Blount MSS, C *64/241*

July the 1st 1743

Sir

Since I was favour'd with yours of the 10th of last month I have drawn a bill for £100 payable to Mademoiselle Broeta and as I expect several small bills shall leave the rest till I receive them. I am glad to hear your Lady is better with the Hott weather which we have had a good deal of, Mr Mead's letters came safe under your Cover and I am

Sir / your most obedient humble servant to command / Christina Towneley

**176.** *Christina Towneley to MS at Lincoln's Inn. 23 July 1743 (NS).*
Blount MSS, C *64/242*

Sir

'Tis with pleasure I congratulate with you on the birth of your grandson,[141] who I hope God will preserve for your comfort, and his future Glory, I have not failed to put Madam More in mind to recomend both the Mother, and son, to the prayers of our family, whose sincere good wishes attend them, and you, the day before I was favour'd with yours of the 4th of this instant, I had writ and enclosed a bill which I hope you have received, and I have this day drawn 2 bills on you, one of £100 payable to Mademoiselle Broeta, and another of £18 10s 0d payable to Mr Cuthbert Haydocke or his Order, Madam More and Mrs Tunstall desire their complyments to you, and I am

Sir / Your most obedient humble servant to command / Christina Towneley

Louvain July the 23d 1743

---

[141] Michael Blount III (1743–1810).

**177.** *Christina Towneley to MS at Lincoln's Inn. 27 August 1743 (NS)*
*(answered 26 August 1743 OS).* Blount MSS, C *64/242*

Aug the 27th 1743

Sir

I have this day drawn a bill on you payable to Mr Peter Browne for
ten guineas and hope soon I shall hear from you that you have my too
last, and the interest due from Mr Spellman which you gave me hopes
of some months ago, pray what comes of Mr Lithcoate, 'tis some time
ago since Madame More bid me tell you that if faire means would not
do, she desired you would try rigour, but you have not favour'd me with
an answer to that point yet, and we should be pleased to know if any
thing is yet done in the affair, which will much oblige
Sir / your most obedient humble servant to Comand / Christina
Towneley.

**178.** *Christina Towneley to MS at Lincoln's Inn. 4 February 1744*
*(NS) (answered 23 March 1743/4 OS).* Blount MSS, C *64/242*

Sir

I am favour'd with yours of the 2d and 13th of January with your accounts,
which I find perfectly to agree with your letters, and my account, and am
well pleas'd to see my debts to you pay'd, but sorry thers no mention yet of
Mr Spellman's arriers being pay'd, which you gave me hopes of sometime
ago, Madame More and Mis Eyre have according to your Orders executed
the instrument you sent, which I return back in this, as yet wee have heard
nothing from Mr Fell, but his Corespondant will give him a second Epistle,
which if he does not think fit to answer, we must take some other measures,
since I was favour'd with yours Lady Catherine was taken ill of a Cold
which made us fear to loose her, but she is something better now, but for
fear of any accident, I beg you'll let me know if the will she made, and is
seald up by a Notery, must be realized here before it be sent to you, which
point I beg your answer to imediately, not knowing if she will ever get over
it, and then I shall be at a loss what to do, I am pleased to hear that Colonel
Radclyffs affaires are like to be finished, and I hope now it is in yours hands
[*sic*] it may come to a happy Conclusion, theres an Irish Gentleman here has
desired to have thirty pound payd to you, for which I have given him your
direction, in order to draw it over with ours, but if it is any inconveniency
to you Sir please to let me know, and I shall not accept of those Comissions
for the future, my Compliment Attend your Lady & family, and I beg the
same to Mrs Ann Mannock and am
Sir / your most Obedient humble servant to Comand / Christina
Towneley
Feb the 4th 1744. N:S:

**179.** *Christina Towneley to MS at Lincoln's Inn, directed via Holland.*
*13 March 1744 (NS) (answered 23 March 1743/4 OS).* Blount MSS, C
*64/243*

Sir

Having no letter from you since the 13th of Jan: and hearing the
French have seized too packets at Ostend, I resolved to write to you by
Holland, and beg you will do me the favour to answer me the same way,
for tho' several have given us notice of paying you money, I don't Care
to draw till I have it from your own hand to prevent mistakes, and Mis
Meads are in want of theirs, which their father writes was pay'd to you
the 17th of Jan: direct for me Chez Mr Broeta Marchand in den Gulden
Rick in de Couper Straet to Antwerpen par Hollande, Mrs Magrath orderd
some money to be payd to you on her account please to let me know if
you have it and be assured I am
Sir / your obedient servant / Christina Towneley
March the 13th 1744 N:S:

**180.** *Christina Towneley to MS at Lincoln's Inn via Helversluyce. 10*
*April 1744 (NS).* Blount MSS, C *64/244*

Sir

I was favour'd with yours of the 23d of last month, and beg you will
Continue to direct yours for me to Mr. Broeta, for at this Juncture people
are not content to have their money Lye in London; sao I have this day
drawn two bills on you Sir, one of £125 0s 0d payable to Mademoiselle
Broeta, and one of £4-0-0-0 [*sic*] to Mrs Cholmeley Milliner, I shall be
glad Mr Spellman keeps his good resolutions, and I hope Mrs Wyburne
will not forget her promis of paying the Old debt, which she assured
should be Cleard at Xmass, Mr Fell has not yet answer'd his letter, but
as wee don't yet know whither the affairs of Mr Grey be ended, wee are
not willing to trouble him with a second, as wee hear that affaire has
made much noise, I don't doubt but you can tell me if it be finnish'd
which I whall be pleas'd to know in your next, Lady Catherine seems
to have taken a new lease of her life, and I shall as soon as signd send
you her Certificate, 'tis a great satisfaction to find Mr Constable is come
to some agreement, an amicable I think is always best between good
Christians, I find you have not heard of Mrs Magrath's money, which she
expected would have been payd directly, when it is, pray don't faile to
write, for the person that is to pay it, will Come here for her acquittance,
and till wee know you have it she will not Care to give it, parhaps the
present uncertaintys may be the Cause that affair is not finished, since
the French have proclaimed Warr our Garisson encreases dayly, but none

of our Countrey folks these at Bruxells have received great Honnours from Prince Charles[142] who Came out of his Coach to Compliment the hors gards, which has a little affronted the troops of this Countrey, who he bid march on, I had forgot to ask sir if you did not receive from Mr Rookby 2 guineas for Mrs Margret Knight last midsummer which is not acknowledged either in your letters or last Account, my Compliments to your Lady and family and Mrs Mannock, and be assure [*sic*] of my being sir

your most Obedient humble servant to Comand / Christina Towneley

April the 10th 1744

---

[142] Prince Charles Edward Stuart, the 'Young Pretender' (1720–88).

**181.** *Christina Towneley to MS at Lincoln's Inn via Helversluyce. 21 April 1744 NS (answered 28 May 1744 OS).* Blount MSS, C 64/245

Sir

I am obliged to trouble you with a second letter to enclose Lady Catherine's Certificate, and to beg the favour of you to send this letter to Mrs Ann Mannock whose direction Mrs Daniel does not know, she desires her Compliments to you as does all our family & I am

Sir / your most Obedient humble Servant / Christina Towneley

April the 21ˢᵗ 1744

**182.** *Christina Towneley to MS at Lincoln's Inn. 29 July 1744 NS.* Blount MSS, C 64/246

Sir

Perhaps before you receive this the Lady the enclosed is directed to, may have been to enquire after it, hers to Madam More being of an Old date, in which she desired the answer might be sent to you, and that she would take Care to Call for it her self, the Contents being what she did not Care to have known to any but her self, your of the 16th of June I answerd soon after I received it, and beg'd to know if Mr Porter had not pay'd you a sum of Money for his daughter, but as some of the letters that went by the same post miscarried, I thought it best to repeat it here, some of the persons Concernd in that money being impatient to have their debts payd, which have been long promised, wee have not yet heard from Sir John[143] but I hope you have had his orders about Lady

---

[143] Sir John Webb.

Catherine's Will, wee sopose now young Mrs Wyburne is Marrid, that the affairs in that family are regulated, and that Mrs Charity[144] will think of paying the debt here she was so solicitous about, till it Came to her turn to pay it, I desired in one of myne your advice about Mr Fell who has not yet thought proper to answer his Corespondant here, and if Mr Grey's law sute be not ended I sopose will be to no purpose to trouble him again, Lady Sturton[145] past this town in her way to Leige, but I did not see her, as she Comes back wee hope for that honnour, she is the[y] tell us in good spirits, and her Lord likely to be himself again, some say the[y] are preparing a house at burham[146] to live in, my Compliments and good wishes attend all your family being

Sir / your Most humble and most obedient servant / Christina Towneley

July the 27th 1744

---

144   Mrs Charity Wybarne.
145   Lady Stourton. Presumably Catherine Walmesley (1697–1785), Lady Stourton from 1733.
146   Bornhem.

**183.** *Christina Towneley to MS at Lincoln's Inn. 6 October 1744 NS. On verso: copy of Mr Fell's account, 23 April 1733.* Blount MSS, C 64/247

Sir

I am favour'd with your account & have drawn 3 bills to Mademoiselle Broeta each £100. and am glad the Certificate came safe to you and will be of service to us, wee have had no lettre from Sir John Webb whither there is liklyhood the remaining part of the dividen of Mr Arthur Radclyffe will be payd him, wee have a Coppy of a letter Mr Arthur[147] writ to Sir John Swinburne in which he desired Lady Catherin might have her full share in it, but whither that Can be of service I do not know, no more than I do, why neither interest nor principall was pay'd her Ladyship as the rest was. You are in the right Sir that the money you Charged to Mrs Parry is what I mention'd from my Lady Stanley. As to Mr Fell's debt to us I shall give it you up in his own words in his last account to us, on the other side of my paper,[148] by which you will see his debt to us and what security for it, which bonds Mrs Tunstall telles me are in your hands, the first of which on Mrs Throckmorton[149] you Received and pay'd us the beginning of Feb: 1740/1 the principal with 13 years

---

147   Daniel Arthur, banker.
148   The verso consists of a copy of Mr. Fell's account.
149   Mrs Throckmorton.

and 25 days interest £165.6s.10d. the rest of his debt remaines as it did when he gave up his account having received neither principal nor interest of the £202.15s.5d. and as wee heard he had sufficient money left him, wee think it Just he should pay us whats our due, without our sueing Mr Lithcote for it, I hope what I have said may give you light enough into this affair to act for us, and if you think proper for me to do any thing more about it, please to favour me Sir with your instructions which shall be duly Complyed with by

Sir / your most Obedient humble servant to Comand / Christina Towneley

Oct the 6th 1744

p.s. / please to send the enclosed to Mrs Bate.

[Mr Fell's account:]

| | |
|---|---|
| Receits | £893.18s.9d. |
| Disbursts | £892.18s.10d |
| ballance | 19s.9d. [*sic*] |

Started this account Ap. 23, 1733 when there was nineteen shills and nine pence due to ballance by me C. Umfreville

| | |
|---|---|
| As to the 3 hunderd pounds | £300 |
| And one year and quarter int at 4 pr Ct | £015 |
| in all | £315 |
| Mrs Trockmorotns bond &c | £100 |
| inter from dec: 23. 1728 to Lady day | £026:5s.0d. |
| Lady Lithcotes bond and Judgment | £129 |
| inter: from Aug. 1724 to last Lady d[ay] | £055.9s.4d. |
| expences of entering the Judgment | £002.10s.0d. |
| in all | £313.4s.4d. |
| Due | £315 |
| Given | £313.4s.4d. |
| Still due | £1.15s.8d |
| add the ballance | 19s.9d. |
| due in all | £2.15s.5d. |

**183.** *Christina Towneley to MS at Lincoln's Inn. 27 October 1744 (NS) (answered 12 November 1744 OS).* Blount MSS, C *64/248*

Sir

Tho' I have not been favour'd with a letter from you since Mr Suit pay'd Mis Jesup's money, yet as he sent your Note here I hope you will not think me too hasty in drawing on you 3 bills of each £100, since I have a perticular reason for doing it, and should be sorry if prove any inconveniency to you, there is one one [*sic*] Mr Dayly[150] who has order'd a sum of money to be pay'd to you, which his Correspondant says he has pay'd you, if it be true be pleased to give me advice of it in which you will oblige

Sir / your most Obedient humble servant to Comand / Chritina Towneley

Oct the 27th 1744

---

150   Mr Daly.

---

**184.** *Christina Towneley to Mrs Mary Strickland. 18 May 1745 (NS).* Blount MSS, C *64/249*

Madam

The favour of your Answer I had the pleasure to Receive a few days ago, but am very sorry you have been so much out of health in this time of affliction and trouble, and makes me regreat that my affairs obliged me to importune you at such an unreasonable a time, but as the Merchant was impatient about the bill I was oblige [*sic*] to write, Mr Maire having not yet had sufficient money to answer the bill, and the small sum he had I was obliged to draw imediately, so that I should be very much obliged to you Madam to order that £100 to be payd to Mr Maire, that wee may prevent the protest of the bill, a Charge would not be at all agreable, to either you or me, the writings that are so necessary for Mr Maire to have are Lady lythcoats bond and what belongs to that affair which Mr Strickland in his last to me told me it was time to take Care of, Mr Lythcoate being a bad manager, Mrs Smith's[151] settlement must be Changed, all which Madam Can't be done till Mr Maire has the writings which made me press that affair, not but I am very sencible you Can't serve every body at once yet where there is danger that delay may prove of ill Consequence it is excyusable to ask for the assistance necessary, I have sent a Coppy of our good and deserving friends accounts, and I am much obliged to you Madam for the particulars you will please to give

---

151   Sr Elizabeth Mary Winefrid Smith.

Mr Maire of our affairs, to whom you will pay all money belonging to us in your hands as it shall be Convenient, and his acquittance will be your discharge, and if I Can be of farther service please

Madam / to Comand your Most Obedient humble servant / Christina Towneley

May the 18th 1745

# LETTERS FROM THE SPELLIKENS (DOMINICAN CONVENT), BRUSSELS, 1728–36[1]

*Blount MSS, C 41/171193*

**1.** *MXE to MS at Gray's Inn. 4 February 1728 (NS?).* Blount MSS, C 41/171

Brussells the 4 of Feb: 1728

Sir

I had the honour of yours with Mr: Hansbies, and find by both our Bussiness hath been at Stand: and the Miscarage of letters the cause, three hath been sent about it that I now perceive never came to Mr: Hansbies hand: if you find the security good, we determin to continue the Money in the same Famely ; if Mrs Attmoors is added to the Capitall of the Bond upon a perpetual rent; we propose to joyn as much of the Arrears as will Make it up a 1000 pound, provided, as is said, you have security to your likeing; and Method taken that the Income be regularly paid up every halfe year: Mr: Hansbie statted the accounts of our House some years and thorowly understands our affairs if you pleas Sir to speak to him; he will Make it clear to you about the Arrears. I have writ to him and repeat hear again nothing hath been paid since March 1715; but 100 pound in the year 1720: and 20 pound in the year 1725. Deducting this 120; theres 14 years (at 40 a year) due next March 1728; it hath been a great damage to us to want this Rent so long ; and I do assure you as Mr: Hansbie can testifie, wee was forc'd to suply ourselves with our Capitall here in place of it. Mr: Hansbie thorowly understands the Matter; and is a better accountant then I , He will cast it up as you think fitting the Life rent separated from the other & I hope Sir this will come as soon as you expect and that with the rest from Mr: H: you will have a clear understanding of the Matter and don't doubt of a good conclusion, being in so worthy hand as yours

---

[1]  In a bundle numbered 'No. 17/ F' and marked '23 letters from Mrs. Elerker to MS 1734. I imagine she was a nun'.

I am with much respect / Sir / your / Most obliged Humble servt: / Sir: Margaret Xav: Ellerker / Pro:[curatrix]

**2.** *MXE to MS at Gray's Inn. [September or October 1728 (NS)] (answered 11 October 1728 OS).* Blount MSS, C *41/172*

Sir

Last Post gave us the Honour of yours, all return thanks for your kindnes and Car, are unanimously satisfied with the advantageous Settlement you have concluded; acknowledging our selves Infinitly indebted to your prudence and Conduct, to which it is owing, not forgeting your Charity in advancing the £5 3s 11d to Compleat the sum of 1040 that will be at 5 per: Cent in his Graces[2] hands. The second point Sir you will pleas to manage it, so that we may not fail of having the Income of it Constantly paid out every halfe year, your goodness Incourage me to petition you will take the trouble to receive for us, and setle both princible and Intrist as you judge best for our Security. You know wee are dubbly Dead to the Law: being pa[pists]: & R[eligious]: all joyn in there Respects to you and your Lady, with the addition of there Prayers. Wee expect to see Mr: Hansbie soon, hes much wanted here: I hope e'r long Sir to repay what we are indebted, being to receive 40 pound this month, for a Lady that hath put on our Livery a few days agoe being

Sir / your obedient Servant / Sister M: X: Ellerker / Pro:

---

[2]　William Herbert, 2nd Duke of Powis.

**3.** *MXE to MS. 12 June 1733 (NS).* Blount MSS, C *41/173*

Brussels the 12 June 1733

Sir

I find the D[3] do's not pay, nor keep his word as to money matters, Lady Lucy[4] his Graces Sister Attackd him three months a goe for payment of our Intrist and ashur'd us wee wood soon find the good Effect of her endeavors in having our Money paid, but nothing appears yet I am satisfied we should soon hear from you if it came to your hand: this disapointment, with several others here of Rents being delayd paying makes us so out of Money. I desire you wood send a bill for the little you have Received from Mr: Paston. When you get that from the D: I will draw upon you for it; a more advantageus way. then you can send

---

[3]　Duke of Powis.
[4]　Lady Lucy Herbert.

it us; Mr: Hansbie came here from B[5]: last night left my little Gallant in perfect health ; I grombled he did not bring him, he said wee must have patience till the vacance then he hath promist we shall have the little Gentelman. In the Intrim my Respects to Mama. I shall be sure to write how Matters stand when I have seen my Little Rooge I am with due Respect

Sir / your Most humble servant / Sister Margaret Xaveria Ellerker Pro: Madam Broeta returns her kind Service to you & your Lady

---

[5]  Bornhem.

**4.** *MXE to MS, 7 November 1733 (NS).* Blount MSS, C *41/174*

Brussels the 7th of Nov: 1733

Sir

I hope his Graces Stuard will keep his word and pay the Intrist due now, a late Letter from Lady Lucy the D[uke']s: Sister assures us, she will still use her Intrist with his Grace that we be for the future regularly payd, ad's she do's not doubt but to prevaile: Mrs: Brown having ended her Charges Mrs: Chilton (who's brother and famely I believe you may know) succeeds gives you her Respects, and me the honour, by her orders of Corresponding with you still: makes me address me selfe to you, for finishing an Affair out of our Speer; a deserving young gentelwoman that's engaged wth us in the Novit: (hath the mismortune [*sic*] to hear of her Fathers Death) Mr. Short of Berry[6] her fortune 300, was Left her by her Gran Mother Short, Conditionally, if she live to be of Age, if not, 'twas to fall among her brothers and sisters; and the Intrist 15 a year, to be paid her, till she posess the Capital; upon this Condition wee received her with the promiss of our having Sufficient Security, before her Prof: which now draws neer. If you please Sir to discover this Affair with Mr. Bostock Merser that maryed her Aunt, and procure such Security as you judge proper, with which all here will be well Satisfied, if the said Security is not Setled in six weeks, she will be forced to defer her wedding day, which she's very worthy off, and it will be a great mortification to the ferverous young Lady to have it put off. And if Mr. Bostock tender you any Money for her pention, be pleasd to receive it, I hope Mr. Paston hath paid the years Intrist, I shood be glad to find you have it, that I might draw upon you to lay in a good Stock of Corne and provision, which they begin to by up in order to supply the Armies thus early. I beg my Respects to your Lady; I was glad not

---

[6]  Bury St Edmunds.

long agoe to assure her, your Charming Son, my Little Galant is as well as you and she can Wish, Learns well, Labours at his book and loves it, [*illeg.*]both manly and wellbehaved, beloved both by Maisters and Studients for his egenuity and good humore. I am with much respect

Sir / Your most humble servant / Sister Margaret Xav: Ellerker /Pro:

**5.** *MXE to MS at Gray's Inn. 30 June 1734 (NS).* Blount MSS, C *41/175*

Sir

I have orders from our Governes, to enquire what Money hath been paid to your hand for Mrs Segrave use (who's Grandmother Lady O'Neal I believe you might know) Mr. Mening last post writ to the young Lady saying he had paid a sum of money to you for her, but never mentioned what it was; our agreement for Mis's fortune was 350 pound sterling and 25 for her weding close [clothes] exchange and if you've reced: it shall be glad to draw a bill for the 25. the 350 we all desire you will endeavour to place at Intrist if you have prospect off doing it soon if not wee are advised to draw it over the Change going well; we have not heard from Mr: Hansbie since the 27 of May he then told us you and Mr: Bostock was agreed about the £300 for Mis Short we understood you have dominion off. We have a third, in order to setle here a Lady of your Acquantance Mrs Andrews in part provides for; which money she may pay you for us you'l pleas to Receive; I believe she will pay 50 pound for Si[ste]r Yate before the Midle of August, another 100 she's to give; that will I think be paid yearly till 'tis out. I have not had the honour of a Line since I desired you [to] pay ten pound to Mr: Penson for Mrs: Bennet to be placed to our account Mr: Bostock payd with the 300; payd for another of the Mrs: Shorts thats here, I beg my service to your Lady, the little gentelman is well, studies assiduously, be pleased to favour with a seepdy [*sic*] answer

Sir / your / most humble servant / Sister Margaret Xav: Ellerker

The last of June 1734

**6.** *MXE to MS at Lincoln's Inn. 24 August 1734 (NS).* Blount MSS, C *41/175*

Augt. the 24 1734

Sir

I was favour with yours of the 25 p[en]ult and the 6th instanter with the Copy of the Agreement with Mr. Bostock which seems very Consciencious and clear both as to him and us: we are much oblig'd to you for it, and also for placeing Mrs Segraves fortune so quickly and at so high intrest which indeed is a great service to us; Mr Hansbie thinks it best to be Declared in Trust for Mrs: Ann Chilton Residing at Bruxelles in the Par[ish] of St: Gudelay: we have had lately paid us about 6 or 700 pound sterling and am much at a loss how to get it put out: Intrist is Reduced so low here, if you Charitably can find an occation of putting it out there tho' wee shou'd loose by the return: it would in my opinion be better, then to let it ly dead sum time perhaps, and after all that can here be hopd for, is three and a halfe per ct. or four current which is as we call it 6 pence exchange pd us for 7d. I fear you have little hopes of the Dukes performance notwithstanding his Graces promises to Mr: Hansbie and Lady Lucy to spur him on; Mr: Hansbie is gon to his adue to Louvain and Burhy:[7] Intends for London very soon Reverend Mother returns you her kind Service and thanks, the first Money wee recei[v]ed wee shall think of making some satisfaction to you, tho' wee can never repay your care and kindness; wee shall ever have a rediness and will for it; I beg my respects to your Lady, I shall soon see my Little Gallant and am

Sir / your most obliged servant / Sir Margerite Xav: Ellerker / Pro

Many thanks for rectifying my Mistake as to your address I shall observe it & beg pardon for the past.

---

[7] Bornhem.

7. *MXE to MS. 20 November 1734 (NS)*. Blount MSS, C *41/177*

Sir

I was favour with yours of the 1st Instant 'twas most agreeable news to Mrs: Chilton and all the rest that you'l have so soon a good occation of putting out the Money which is a very great Kindness to us: you may be sure of 600 pound before Chrismas this is to advertize you, when you please, you may Receive 380 pounds of Mr: Samuel Grimes Banker in London: it must be demanded in the name of Mr: John Baptist Vannuffle Merchant of Lace in Brussels he having given his order this post to Mr: Grimes to pay the said Summ to you, or your order ; when you have acqua[in]ted me with the Receit of it I shall pay the equivalant to Mr: Vannuffle here.

Wee have a Capitall that was paid inn at Bridges[8] in the hand of Lady Lucy Herbert of 220 pounds which I have writ this post to desire her Ladyship it might be returnd to you as soon as posible these 2 Som's [I]

---

[8] Bruges.

mention makes up six hundred. and if Mrs: Andrews pays you 50 you may add that to the six hundred. if you shoud prevail with the Duke for all the Arrears (which is more then to be hoped for) wee might add 50 more and make it up 700.

There is one from Bur:[9] left your little Gentleman yesterday very well : Im very glad Mr: Hansbie is entirely recoverd: I think he told me he advised Sir with you about a life Rent of 10 pound a year that hath three years in arrears Left by Mr: Coalman to his Daughter that Setled here;[10] and gave us some hopes of your geting the Money for us; makes me take the liberty to mention abt it; wee must ever acknowledge our obligations for all your care and kindness, Mrs: Chilton joyns with the rest of our Famely in there due Respects, they and I being

　　Sir / your / most obliged humble Servt / Sister Margarit Xav: Ellerker

November the 20 1734

---

[9]　Bornhem.
[10]　Anne Ursula Coleman.

**8.** *MXE in Brussels to MS. 27 November 1734 (NS).* Blount MSS, C *41/178*

　　　　　　　　　　　　　　　　　　　　Brussells the 27 Nor 1734

Sir

　　A Letter from Lady Lucy Herbert last post forces me [to] give you this trouble; her Ladyship desires you wood draw upon her for the 220 pound, she will answer at Sight, desireing to have a letter of advice the same Post; fearing she shall not find an occation to Return soon enough. Her Lship adds in this letter that she hath writ to His Grace her Brother as effecatiously as she could to have our Rent paid, and did not doubt but we shoud have all that was due imediatly, perhaps your endeavors to second hers may prevail, if it shoud be paid in time it woud be best for you to keep it, that you might have the less to draw from Bridges,[11] the change goes high above seven pound in the hundred. I believe you will have Mrs: Andrews go before Chrismas; pray Sir if you see Mr: Hansbie with our dutyfull Respects pleas to tell him wee desire he wood see paid to you the 10 pound wee are to have from Mrs: Hide, I hope you will be secure of 600 or 650, My letter of 8 day agoe (I sopose with you er this) to advertize you to take 380 pound of Mr: Samuel Grimes Bankquear in London in the name of Mr: John Baptist Vannuffle Lace Merchant in Brussels. I beg my Respects to your Lady being

　　Sir / your most obliged humble Servant / Sister Margaret Xav: Ellerker

---

[11]　Bruges.

**9.** *MXE to MS. 23 December 1734 (NS).* Blount MSS, C *41/179*

Sir

    I have the favour of yours of the 3d: instant. Mr: Vannuffle seem's
as much Concernd and Surprizd as I, that Mr. Grimes did not pay the
380 pound upon your demand. He hath repeated his orders to him this
post warmly, not to fail the payment of the said sum to you. Am sory for
the trouble it gives you: a letter ten days agoe from Mr: Hansbie gave
account he had pd you £20: and said he had 25 more (that he prevaild to
have for our Sister Catherin Hide) at our appointment I answerd without
loosing a post, desird he wood burn all the Plat Rivers to Run into your
Hand; he had then writ to Mrs Andrews for £30 she shood a paid long
agoe, least that shood not do: R[everend] M[other] writ to her this post
& desird without delay the 30 p might be paid to you or Mr: Hansbie I
believe it won't fail nor the 10 from Mrs: Hide, if so, with the £10 you
had from Mr: Paston as I take it makes 195 p: added to the 380 come
to 575. If Mr: Hansbie hath any to return perhaps you may have of him
25p: to make up the £600. I shall answer it here, to Burh:[12] as the cha[n]
ge goes; to avoide your trouble for drawing upon Lady Lucy, where you
will certainly be answerd with payment at sight for what you may want.
God in Heaven Reward your [service] and Charity for Mr. Daly. I am
prodigiously assured she will get the Arrears you mentiond, shee hath
sufferd much with great patience Humillity and Christian Currage. If
you have her money in your hand, I could give her what you will want
to make up the 600; or which wood be best of all, if you shoud be so
fortunate as get the 30 p arrears due to us from her Sister Coalman: I
beg you'l forgive this trouble and pardon all my blunders here I am not
very well to day; R[everend] Mother desires you shood find her kind
cordial wishes of a good Chrismass and happy new year & the same to
your Lady; Gratitude obliges us all to have in continual Remembrance
the trouble you take; and Service you do us I am
    Sir / your most obliged servant / S Margaret Xav: Ellerker
December the 23 1734

---

[12] Bornhem.

**10.** *MXE to MS. 28 [February? December?] 1734 (NS).*[13] Blount MSS, C *41/180*

Feb: the 28 1734

Sir

The ten pound you Receivd from Mr: Paston be pleasd to pay to Mr: Penson Loyer,[14] for Mrs: Bennet at Mrs Noruse[15] at Norwige in Norfolk. Mr. Hansbie writ last post to Mr: Bostock to press him to give satisfaction to you as to Mis Shorts £300 and Intrist : that she may not have the Mortification of Staying longer for her Pro[fession] having so just pretentions to the Money left her by her Grand Mo: with Plate lining &c besides I wish the Du[ke] may pay before the Change fall 'tis now full eight per cent Mr: Hansbie gives to you and your Lady his Respect to whom I desire mine your little gentleman is very well, Learns Admirable as they tell me, R[everend] M[other] asshures you of her due Respect, to whom I joyn mine being

Sir / your / most humble servant / Sister M: Xav: Ellerker Pro:

---

[13] Addressed to Gray's Inn (and so probably sent in February). Endorsed with a December date by another hand, but the smudged date on the letter looks more like 'Feb' (only the first letter is unclear).
[14] Lawyer.
[15] Norris?

**11.** *MXE to MS. 29 December 1734 (NS).* Blount MSS, C *41/181*

Sir

I send this at the request of Mrs: Daily with her due Respects and most gratefull thanks, she petitions when the money is redy, you will pleas to draw the Bill for me, or advertize me to draw upon you; if the bill shood be drawn in her name it wood certainly be seased: secondly Mrs: Daily desires you to keep 40 pound of the Money which she is obliged to pay to Mrs: Ann Ritchards who will be advertizd when tis redy to Receive it: thirdly ardently begs you will find some means to secure her Annuity may be Regularly paid her for the future.

I hope you've mine in Answer to the last you favour me with. Mr Vannuffle asshure me you will not fail of having the 380 of Mr: Grimes. The change hether is so high I give 311 – 11 Gul exchange money for the returning the 300 / I tryd Mr: Decleve and other Bankers, they aske more.

As I said before what you'l want to make up the 600 be pleasd to draw from Lady Lucy; I must repeat my wishes of many happy new years to you and your Lady. Shall be glad to hear from you being always

Sir / your most obliged humble Servant / Sister M: X: Ellerker

Decemb: the 29 1734

Mr: Hansbie hath Mrs: Dalys account concerning the Arrears.

**12.** *MXE to MS. 26 January 1735 (NS).* Blount MSS, C *41/183*

Jan: the 26 1735

Sir

Last night I was favour'd with yours of the 31 past, heartily Mortified at the trouble you had in twice demanding the Money of Grimes and the Confusion to you and my self in the disapointment of puting it out: I never had had such a blunder in all the time we had done business; Mr: Vannuffle is the person above this 20 years wee always have recourse to in all our Affairs for Assistance or advise, but I always thought there was in this some sort of shouffleing, and wondered why he did not according to the Common way of exchange he gave me a Bill to send to you. I askd him since the new year if he had a letter that the money was paid, no he wonders he had not, I told him our money layd redy counted out for him as soon as I heard from you you had received the other: the Change is now so high the Banqueers here Mr: Decleve, and likewise Mr: Nettine I've try'd em both now demand for the returning £380 thirty five pounds 12 shills 10d which is so prodigious a loss up on that sum, as wood take two years income of the said sum to make good. Madam Chilton and the rest think it more prudent to let it ly to wait for a more favourable return.

Mr: Hansbies letter before I writ last to you sais he had procured out of the division 125 ff for Sister Catherin Hyde, in his hand, at our appointment I answer'd him 'twas desird he wood pay it to you, and never doubted of your haveing it and 10 pounds wee lent Mrs: Wine Hide: expect both to be given to you or this. Wee have an unexpected expence come upon us by the late great Tempest wee have an incloster wall bloun down to the ground, and another Incloser walle a great breach in it few escaped some damage, many have much greater than wee, thank God tho' it fell in the Street no body was hurt wee got it made up with deal and Post, till the season to Build.

I sent to dear Mrs: Daily that part of yours: that concern'd her; 'tis a great Comfort to her to find you so cordial a friend, with due respect she and wee shall be glad to have the Letter of Atturney, and to do as you Instruct as she repeats her petition that for the future, when Arrears are paid in it may be in your power to see it paid her as it falls due. Our Sister Ann Coalman dyed the 7 of February 1733. her Father left her ten pounds a year for her Life of which three years was owing us, when she died besides from Michaelmass till the 7 of Feb: but Mr: Hansbie told me in England they don't pay life rents if they die before the rent day, it's not so here, they pay to the last day they live; wee had a rent upon her Life at Bridges.[16] Mr: Arthur was the person that paid this Annuity and hath her Acquitances, which she was three years behind, I hope you will get it at least wee shall be much obligd to you for endeavouring to procure it. Madam Chilton with all our Famelly presents there Respects with due sence of your Charity and goodness and the many Obligations wee have, keep you in memory among us. I am

Sir / your most obliged humble Servant / Sister Margaret Xav: Ellerker

---

[16]  Bruges.

**13.** *MXE to MS. 16 February 1735 (NS).* Blount MSS, C *41/183*

Feb: the 16. 1735

Sir

A letter from Mr: Hansbie last Post tells your in Pain about the money Van[n]uffle should have returnd; e'r this I believe you have mine to let you know the money is still safe in our hand and if the occation is not past of putting it out as you Charitably desingd for us, it will be a kindness to take it; the Change this last 14 days being considerably falln, [I] durst not send a Bill today least it should be to late, if not, the Change here to London is 56 Sk [?] for a pound sterling; if you think fitt, or find it more expeditious to draw upon Mrs: Chilton at sight it lies redy Counted out or if you approve better of our sending it by Mr: Nettien Banker by a Bill at sight to you: Mr: Hansbie says he's put the little sums into your hand which as I take it make just £204 10s 0d. if it will supply what your occation Requires, Mrs: Chilton had rather send but just 300 (least the expences of the walls falling should cost more then she expects, but if you have Engaged your word for six hundred as we mentiond to you it is just and reasonable that you shood have it. I beg a line, without loosing a Post, and R[everend] M[other] with due respect desires you'l please to give by her order 2 Gineys to Hd: Dear Mr: Hansbie. I fogote [forgot] the Intrist of Mrs Shorts india Bonds and Mis Segraves upon Mrs: Shevereux[17] is payable every halfe year. Wee writ to D: P:[18] very very pressingly upon the fall of our walls, & Ld [Lady] Lucy [Herbert] the same, and I'm shure your endeavours, & Mr: Hansbies will be added, if all this will not prevail for payment wee must have Patience. I am with perfect Respects

Sir / your most obliged humble Servant / Sister Margaret Xav: Ellerker

---

[17]  Elizabeth Devereux?
[18]  The Duke of Powis.

**14.** *MXE to MS. 9 March 1735 (NS).* Blount MSS, *C 41/184*

Sir

I write this at the request of Mrs: Daly & send the coppy of her nephews last letter to her he hath writ several before to presse her to assign over the money that she expects her arrears from to him but he allways positively refuses it and told him shee has nothing to do with the money in Irland that they can't get. She begs sir you will put a stop to her nephew Coalman takeing that money; wee expected the Letter of Atturney you mentiond and shood be glad to Signe it with her, in hopes to get our little arrears too. She sent the other piece of a Coppy of a letter she lately had, that shews theirs little to be expected from the money in Irland, that he woud have her depend on.

Pray Sir please to pay 9. pound to Mr: Penson the lawyer, for Mrs: Bennet at Mrs: Noreses[19] of Norwige in Norfolke: wee are in expectation daly to hear from you; which will be very agreeable to

Sir / your most obliged humble Servant / S: Margarit X; Ellerker

March the 9th: 1735

*John Coleman to his aunt Madam Power Daly: copy letter, 17 February 1734/5*

Dear Aunt,

I received your letter, not much to the purpose. For what I writ is true; and if you won't consent, must take some. But as I told, you shall have it out of Ireland. But that you shan't want shall have a hundred here at present, and the rest soon, if you will send me an answer if you will agree,

From your affectionate Nephew J. Coleman.

Postscript: If you don't answer to what I write, must stop all. For charity begins at home.

*A Copy of the Postscript of Mr. Edmond Flanagan's Letter, dated Carrowreague, Jan: the 13th. 1734/5.*[20]

I can assure you, Mr Greene, in the Memory of the oldest Man on Earth, Mony was not seen so scarce in this nation, as now it is. No Buying of any Thing, excepting Eatables. All Farmers are broke. All the poor People daily going a begging, God knows where to find it. Estated Men daily pressed by their Creditors. In short no Mony.

---

[19] Mrs Teresa Norris.

[20] This postscript is physically on the same sheet and in the same hand as Coleman's letter. It highlights the difficulties raising funds from families at home, themselves struggling. The situation in getting funding from Ireland (which suggests that the convents were taking in Irish women) appears to have been particularly acute.

**15.** *MXE to MS. 4 June 1735 (NS) (answered 12 September 1735 OS).* Blount MSS, C *41/185*

The 4 of June 1735

Sir

I was favour'd with yours ([in] four days from the Date) and exceeding glad to find the D:[21] had cleard all the Intrist. The great expence of Rebilding our Incloser wall, that was bloun down by the great wind last January, forces me to draw upon you for 125 pound I gave a bill in favour of Mrs: Broeta of Antwerp; Mr: Hasbie[22] told me in his last you was out of Town he wanted to give you more money for us, that he had in his hand, and had more to Receive then, wee never had such good fortune in our lives; and Atribute a great part of it to your Charitable kind care and Conduct in puting out Money for us, which other ways wood lye dead; wee are so helpless in such Affairs; wee can never sufficiently pray for you, and yours, nor express how Infinitly wee are obliged to you; and beg you will do justice to your Self for writing, postage, expences and as you take from others for business done; Mrs: Colman writ to her sister Daily 20 pound of the Money that came from France was kept, as part of the 30 that was in Arrears for the life here of our Sister Coalman; and they tell me 'tis in Mr: Arthurs hand, who always payd that rent. I wish you could, or Mr: Hansbie, get Mr: Arthur pay it, and take your Acquitance. The second Mis Short is within 7 weeks of finishing her prentisship; there is 50 pound belongs to her with the Intrist upon the same footing as her Sisters was, if the lifes still of Age; if not it goes to the other Children; if you wood manage this little affair with Mr: Bostock to have it securd 'twood be a Charity; shee will stay ells till they do give you security for it, for I do assure wee do not get things clear'd and done, before there settled with us; wee can get nothing after. Our Ma[da]me and all our Famely joyns in there Respects and best wishes to you and your Lady, to whom I desire mine being

Sir / Your most obliged humble servant / Margaret Xav: Ellerker

---

[21] Duke of Powis.
[22] Mr Hansbie.

**16.** *MXE to MS. 9 November 1735 (NS) (answered 2 January 1735/6 OS).* Blount MSS, C *41/186*

Novemb: the 9th: 1735

Sir

I was favour'd with your obliging letter at your going a broad, and hope this will find you returnd in perfect health wee all come to meet you with our due Acknowledgements hearty thanks, and Prayers for your Prosperity and happyness, your continued care kind good management hath much Augmented our Rents, which add to our obligations, you manage for us, so much better then wee do for ourselves, as is evident in what follows: last June wee Lent 500 pound to Edward Dicconson Esqr of Rightington in Lankeshire, a worthy Catholick and good Estate for four per cent exchange, wee had a writing drawn here, our security is upon a farm he boat for 12 pound, which is not in any Setelment, he's now in England and designs to be back before Chrismass in his return promised to waite upon you to have our Security drawn as you judge proper: if you have any papers or Coppyes to send over to us he's a very secure hand: about this time I believe 50 pound will be paid to you that was procurd by a kind friend for our Mis Nutle Short, and hope you will take care of Mr Bostock what security you think fiting for the 50 in his hand she hath had no Intrist for it since her Fathers Death. Wee are curious to know what Intrist her Sisters Indibonds produces; I hope as you do the D:[23] will pay the Intrist as it falls due Lady Lucy advises us allways to take it every half year to prevent it runing up by Arrears: if you have not, hope you will have soon Mr: Pastons little Rent; that wee may repay what you kindly lay down for us; and beg when you have received Money you wood please to pay to Mr: Penson for Mrs: Bennet nine pound, and place it to your account: Mr: Coulman Daily think her selfe happy to have so good a friend to trust to make both her and us hope for a good Conclusion with the young Gentelman and his Mother; but believe they will still put of payment if they can. I beg my Respects to your Lady and am with due Affection and Esteem

Your most humble Servant / Margaret Xav: Ellerker

---

[23] The Duke of Powis.

**17.** *MXE to MS. 25 January 1736 (NS) (answered 28 June 1736 OS).*
Blount MSS, C *41/187*

Jan the 25 1736

Sir

I was favour with your obliging kind letter of the 2d instant: all here joyn in their thanks, and cordial wishes of many happy new years to you and your Lady. All hear are intirely satisfied with what money you put out for us, and with what securety you think fitt to take wee all determin tis much more secure to rely upon your judgment then our own; and heartily thank God wee have such a true Friend to depend upon: but can't comprehend how you have so much money of ours as you mention to put out viz first to Mr: Kingsdon 291 the 3d of March

laste. Secondly your of the 12 of September, just before you went out of Town, Acquants us, with your puting out for us 400 (upon the same security of the 1040) at 5 p cent, the securety you mention to take date the 14 of June 1735: accordingly I Regesterd those tow in our Rentall, according to your computation then, there was due to you for balance £32 4s 2d. In your last you speak of £200 to Mr. Paston the 4 of June, and £200 to Mr. Warpole,[24] the 4 of September, and mark to your selfe only £58 16s 10d for Balance: tho' you'v Received neither of the £50: belonging to Mis Nutte Short, nor the Intrist from his Grace; nor do you mention £10 Mrs: Andrews was to pay October last; give me leave to repeat again I can't Imagin where you had so much Money of ours. Mr. Bostock is writ to this post to pleas to give you the £50, or security for it with the Intrist, this as likely to live as any I know. I've not yet seen Mr. Dicieson; but will be sure to observe your kind advice, and press for the Deeds being sent to you to draw securety according to agreement. Mrs. Daly was favourd with yours, and glad she hath this affair in your hand; I hope you will get hers, and the 50 due for Sister Coleman to us. I shall impatiently expect to hear from you being with perfect Respect
Sir / Your / Most humble servant / Margaret Xav: Ellerker

---

[24]  Perhaps Edward Walpole of Dunston, Lincs.

**18.**  *MXE to MS. 23 June 1736 (NS) (answered 28 June 1736 OS).*
Blount MSS, C *41/188*

June the 23 1736

Sir

'tis long since wee had the honour of a letter from you; I shood be glad to know if you have had from Mr. Bostock the £500 with the Intrist for Miss Nutle Short; if you have Received more for her, from Mrs Diccison that Gentelman I have not yet seen but expect him every day and then according to your kind advice will press for the writing being sent to you, that wee may have the security that was agreed upon. Pray let me know if you have 10 pound from Mrs Andrews, & the Income upon Sister Shorts Indebonds, she's now within a few months of Age, then wee shall desire to take that three 100 out of that setuation to have it at your desposing it pleas to be so good to put it out when you can find a fitt place for it I hate publick funds, so many are ruind by 'em and no Redress, even in this Catholick Cuntrey: I've a true satisfaction to hear His G[race the] D[uke of] P[owis]'s silver and Lead &c: succeeds so well wee shood be exceeding glad of our Little Rent if you can prevail to have it soon; I think my time draws near an end always; I've been this several months always ill; I have been long in this office and now in September next my time if I live so long will finish; and shood be glad before that to pay off sum Bills; and leave all things in that order as may be expected; they will find there Circomstances and Rents much better within this 15 years since I was first Procur[atrix] wee are indeed indeded to you for it; and I shall ever have a gratefull memory and endeavor to give all the Rest a dew sence of it and there great obligation to you: Madam Chilton desires you may find here her true Respects, and is solitious you have from us a return according to justice and gratitude, in your sparing your time is of great value, and business can't be done without expences Coatches, postage: it wood be a pleasure to us to do what is agreeable to you if a pice of fine Cambrick or any thing you can think off besides your expences; wood be acceptable to your Lady wee shood have a Satisfaction to send it being with much affection and Esteem her and

Sir / Your most humble Servant / Sister M: X: Ellerker

I've not seen a line from Mr. Hansbie long

**19.** *MXE to MS. 11 August 1736 (NS).* Blount MSS, C *41/189*

Brussels Augt the 11 1736

Sir

Three days agoe Mr: Dickeson past here with his Lady for Spae,[25] I attack'd him about the writing being brought to you that the Security might be drawn; He ashure me after he returns from Spae he shall soon goe for England, and then you shall have writings or the £1000 [?] paid you in, which I shood like very well; tho' I believe him a very worthy gentleman and good Christan but he's very slow in paying and wee have fifty pound a year Life Rent upon him for the young widow Short, besides the Intrist of the 500, they have a great charge, 8 heatful [?] fine Children, and his Lady young enough to have many more: the Lady assures me the 50 she procures for Mis Nutty Short shall be paid to you before November. Mrs Andrews was writ to and I hope hath paid the £10, if so that you have receivd it, or Mr Kingdons I shood be glad to draw for it with the Balance which will give a Bill for as soon as I can have the favour of a line from you by the first Convenience I can meet with. I shall have the Satisfaction to send a piece of the finest Cabrick I get in Brussels which wee beg your Lady to Accept of with a bit of our work; to which we joyn our Prayers and thanks for your care and kindnes being with much Affection and Respect

Sir / your most obliged humble servant / Margaret Xaveria Ellerker

---

25  Spa.

**20.** *MXE to MS. 5 September 1736 (NS) (answered 15 October 1736 OS).* Blount MSS, C *41/189*

Sep: the 5 1736

Sir

I gave a bill to day in favour of Mr. Nettien for the Balance 29 14s.4d. Met with a good occation to send the pice of Cabrick by Mr. Felex a gentelman belonging to Ld. Montegue. It was directed to you at your Chambers, I cold not find the address that to your house, I beg you'l make all our Complements to your Lady, wee desire her acceptance of that small present from cordial kind hearts that is as much as can be her and
Sir / your most humble servants / Margaret Xav: Ellerker

**21.** *MXE to MS. 3 November 1736 (NS) (answered 19 November 1736 OS).* Blount MSS, C *41/191*

Brussels No: the 3d 1736

Sir

I was favour with yours of the 15 past, and fear His Grace[26] will pay in the 1040 at the end of the year: and shall be much obliged to you to find a place for it. As also for demanding the Intrist of Mr. Kingdon, Mr. Paston &c where due; Mrs. Andrews hath 20 pound to pay. I'm glad you will settle the 50 with Mr. Bostock; and wish wee could get in Mis Shorts 300 half in the Inde Bonds; because we hear they have Sunk the Intrist to 3 p: cent, and now as is said, offer to pay in the Capital with Six p: cent; which wee all should be glad off if the trustees wood be so favourable as give leave to take it in that wee may not loose the occation, she not being at Age till the begining of the next month; and another advantage offers at Present of puting it out upon good Security here for 4 p: cent exchange money, and there wood be the return upon it must be more advantageous then to have it there at 3. I beg as soon as may be to have your Answer to this, because wee must Accept, or Refuse this occation of putting it out. I condole with you for the loss of the Lady your Mo[ther]:[27] besides other devotions, wee shall not faile to have the office of the Dead said for her: I'm truly sorry for our friends Mr: Daily; Lord Fingole[28] lay out the Circomstances to be deplorable enough. Is there any hopes of the 30 due to our Sister Coalman: wee heard Mr. Hansbie hath fallen of his hors and much hurt ; wee should be glad to know how he do's, and where he is, wee have not heard from

---

[26]  Duke of Powis.
[27]  Mrs Bridget Strickland.
[28]  Lord Fingall.

him this may months, which concerns us he being a person wee have a great value for. Mr: Dickeson is not yet come back from Spae. I am with entire Respect

Sir /your most obliged humble servant / Sr Margaret Xaveria Ellerker

**22.** *MXE to MS. 14 December 1736 (NS).* Blount MSS, C *41/192*

Sir

I was favour'd with yours of the 19 past, am glad you considerd better then I, And did not speak about the Ind bond that now falls, she beeing att [*illeg.*] the 15 Instant wee beg youl please to pay ten pound to Mrs: Bennet, maried to Mr. Park she desires the money may lay in your hand till calld for by Mr: Wood: your news of Mr. Hansbie Recovery was very agreeable: Mrs Letetice Barker is still liveing: wee shall draw upon you for the Rest of the Money er it be long; are much obliged for your care and kindnes in taking our Affairs so to heart, and am

Sir / Most sincerely yours / Sist, M X Ellerker

Decr the 14 1736.

**23.** *MXE to MS. 21 December [1736] (NS). In a very unsteady hand. Dated 1736 by Strickland.* Blount MSS, C *41/193*

Sir

Please to pay to Mr. Hansbie three Gynney: and at the time most proper to take out the 300 out of the Bank of England Mrs Andrews hath promisd £50. I am so ill I can't write but always

Sir / your most humble servant / Margaret Xa Ellerker

Decebr the 21

# LETTER FROM THE BENEDICTINES AT BRUSSELS (ABSTRACT)

*Blount MSS, C 117/56*

**1.** *Lady Mary Crispe to MS. 3 May 1730 (NS) (answered 3 May 1730 OS).* Blount MSS, C *117/56*

Lady Mary Crispe in Brussels to Mannock Strickland at Grays Inn, enclosing a copy of a letter from Sir Harry Englefield[1] to [a young lady in Lady Crispe's convent] (a near relation of Sir Harry) concerning an estate in Clerkenwell settled by entail on his aunt Mrs Armstrong (the young lady's grandmother), with a rental of the estate (all ground rents in Clerkenwell amounting to £190 13s 4d; tenants' names given), and asking his advice as to what the young lady may insist upon, she being 21 next July and not being willing to sell 'at an under rate.' Michael Blount I (also a relative of the young lady) will call to provide further information. With a copy of Sir Henry Englefield's letter and a rental of Mrs Armstrong's estate as delivered to him by her London agent Thomas Carnan. Englefield states that it is entailed on his aunt Armstrong (the girl's grandmother) for life, then on her mother, then on her and then on him; she cannot receive any benefit from it during her aunt's life, and her father's reputed assignment of the reversion to a London merchant is probably invalid as he had no claim to it during her mother's lifetime. Lady Crispe is concerned that if the young lady dies without heirs the estate goes to Sir Henry.

---

[1] Of Whiteknights, near Reading.

# MISCELLANEOUS LETTERS

*Blount MSS, C 123/48; BL Add. MS 28288*

**1.** *Mary Henly in London to Mrs Clark, a widow, at her house in Holywell, Flintshire. 3 August 1723.* Blount MSS, C *123/48 [Abstract]*

Mary Henly in London to Mrs Clark, a widow, at her house over against the Star Inn at Holywell, Flintshire, referring to Lady Fleetwood and a variety of religious matters.

**2.** *Lady Benedicta Fleetwood to John Caryll. 13 August 1730 (NS).* BL *MS Add. 28228, fols 408–9*

To: John Caryll of Greensteed / by Horsome [Horsham] Post / in Sussex. Aug. the 13 1730

Sir

The contents of your last letter to D[ame]: Benedicte much surpris'd me, particularly your refusing to pay what's justly due to our house, in your hands lyes the greatest part of our secure maintenance, therefore if not duly payd how can we subsist. I'm counseld to take the principall out of your hands which I'm resolv'd to doe, so be pleas'd to returne the ££ 1000 to Mr Strickland of which I'l give him advice, so soon as I here [hear] t'is in his hands I'le send you a recept of the same or the security I have in your owne hand.

This Sirr I belive will not be disagreeable to you by the expretion you made use of to D[ame] Ben[edicta], these are your words, As to any interest mony I cannot supply her yet a while, which is a sensible mortification to me & the more when I reflect how unfortunately for me the principall was made due & by what you say I'm convinc'd you have a wroung [wrong] notion concerning the principal & how you understand it was made due.

I hope Sir you will not take in ill part what I have sade for I should be very loath to disoblige a person I have allways lookd upon as a true friend to our house & am sure, every one here has a just valu & regard for your self & family, but none more than

Sr / your oblig'd humble servant / Bene Fleetwood

Next Mickelmas there will be 4 years interest due for the ££ 1000 (& three years & half from Winchelsea which together makes ££ 340. the want of this money has been boath inconvenient & a great losse to me which I hope you'l consider & see whather in contience you can proceed so.

[*Copy answer, September 1730, fol. 414, refuting her allegations – not a refusal but an acknowledgment of responsibility for debt payment. Points to willing payment of two years' interest together for repair of their wall, which caused disruption to his payment schedule, and to her refusal to take his advice not to sell Hoes Farm, 'one of the best incomes belonging to your house'. On the subject of the transfer to MS, he points out that six months' notice is normal practice, but he will make the transfer when he can although not necessarily immediately.*]

**3.** *MS to John Caryll. 17 November 1730 (OS).* BL MS Add. 28228, fols 426–7

To / John Caryll Esqr at / Ladyholt / By Midhurst Bag / Sussex
London Novr. 17th. 1730.

I have the favour of yours, and Shall take care that the thirty pounds you Send Bills for is remitted to Dunkerque According to your direction. I think you can not have a properer person for your Trustee than Mr. Tooker, whose name my brother's Mortgage was taken in.[1] He Desires an Assignment of that Mortgage, which being but Matter of common forme neither you nor Mr. Tooker Will find any difficulty in Executeing a proper Deed for that purpose. The fresh Security Shall be prepared with all Expedition, and though Mr Cotter is a Stranger to you, yet I can Assure you he is a very honest Man. I am pleasd to hear what you write me of Mr. Mackenzie, for whome I had a most Sincere friendship and esteem, nor doe I think his body can be better disposed of than to be Deposited in your Vault at Harting. The Salterns, upon which a Client of mine has a Mortgage for £.1200 and near two years Interest, are Devised to Lady Mary Caryll, in trust, as I apprehend, for Lady C[arington]. I Shall be proud of being Serviceable to Lady Mary in her Executorship, on [or?] any thing else She shall please to lay her Commands upon me in. I hear of Nothing that has been done lately towards the purchase of Sir Wm Gage's farm, which I think Ld. Petre ought by no Means to let Slip out of his hands. The last I heard of it was they Expected a Particulaar and price from you; but Mr. Walton is here, and I will talk to him about it to who am

Sir. / your most obedient humble Servt / Mannock Strickland.

---

[1] This is probably Roger Strickland, Mannock's older brother, who owned the family estate at Thornton Bridge, North Yorkshire.

# PART II

# ACCOUNTS

# ST MONICA'S, LOUVAIN: CASH DAY BOOK, 1733–44

These accounts represent an accurate transcript of Strickland's accounts, errors included (which occur mostly in the Louvain data for 1733–5).

1733
RECEIPTS

To the House at Louvain Dr.

| | | | £ | s. | d. |
|---|---|---|---|---|---|
| July. | 16 | Reced of Mr Hugh Haydocke | 346 | 12 | 11 |
| | | Reced of Do a Bill Mary Norman on Mr John Cheslin to the order of Isabella Jesup | 10 | 0 | 0 |
| | 22 | Reced of Ld Stafford for the use of Miss Eyre | 3 | 3 | 0 |
| | 27 | Reced of Mr Monington by Mr Kirwood for the use of Mr Monington's brother | 12 | 12 | 0 |
| Augt. | 23 | Reced of Mr Francis Cholmeley for the use of Mrs Elizabeth Cholmeley | 6 | 5 | 0 |
| | | Reced of Mrs Margaret Cholmeley for the use of Mrs Ursula Cholmeley | 14 | 19 | 0 |
| | 24 | Reced of Mr Rodbourn for the use of his Daughter | 2 | 10 | 0 |
| Sepr. | 7 | Reced of Mr Day | 15 | 4 | 3 |
| | 15 | Reced of Mr Berington for the use of Mrs Green | 0 | 17 | 6 |
| | 18 | Reced of Mrs Cecily Tunstall by Bill from Louvain | 20 | 0 | 0 |
| Oct. | 27 | Reced of Mr Rodbourne for 50 days Int of Lady Catherine Radclyffe's Annuity due 31. Decr. 1731 | 13 | 14 | 0 |
| | 30 | Reced of Mrs Eliz and Cass Willoughby for the use of Mrs Eliz Willoughby | 20 | 0 | 0 |
| Novr. | 3 | Reced of Thomas Markham Esqr for the use of Mrs Macgrath | 5 | 0 | 0 |

1733
PAYMENTS

| | | | £ | s. | d. |
|---|---|---|---|---|---|
| July. | 30 | Pd Mrs Cecily Tunstall's Bill to the order of the Widow of Mr Charles Broeta | 200 | 0 | 0 |
| | | | 0 | 2 | 6 |
| July. | 30 | Pd Mrs Cecily Tunstall's Bill to the order of the Widow of Mr Charles Broeta | 200 | 0 | 0 |
| Augt. | 10 | Pd Do's Bill to the order of Do | 130 | 0 | 0 |
| Sepr. | 29 | Pd. Do's Bill to the order of Mrs. Ann Savil | 5 | 0 | 0 |
| Oct. | 27 | Pd. Mr. Rodbourn his Bill for obtaining a Warrant from the Treasury for payment of Lady Catherine Radclyffe's Annuity | 42 | 7 | 10 |
| Novr. | 3 | Pd. Mr. Day money he had paid Mr. Wright in Discharge of Mr Silvertop's Bill | 5 | 8 | 0 |

| | | | | | |
|---|---|---|---|---|---|
| | 5 | Reced of Mrs Orme for the use of Mrs Cockain | 2 | 2 | 0 |
| | 13 | Reced of Mr Jeffery French for the use of Mr Christopher French | 15 | 15 | 0 |
| | 15 | Reced of Mrs Pruden | 9 | 9 | 0 |
| Decr. | 5 | Reced of Mr Day on Account of Miles Philipson Esqr deced | 5 | 0 | 0 |
| | | Reced of Do for the use of Mr Dowce | 1 | 1 | 0 |
| | 6 | Reced of Ralph Crathorn Esqr by Mr Brigham | 30 | 0 | 0 |
| | 15 | Reced of Mr Basil Bartlett for the use of his Sisters | 6 | 10 | 0 |
| | | Reced of Mrs Pierse for the use of Mrs Mary Hacon | 7 | 3 | 0 |
| | 17 | Reced of Mrs Knight for Mrs Jennings | 2 | 2 | 0 |
| | 20 | Reced of Mr Rodbourn for his Daughter | 2 | 10 | 0 |
| Janry. | 2 | Reced of Lady Montaigue | 1 | 15 | 0 |
| | 4 | Reced of Mrs Frances Smith for her Sister Isabella | 8 | 0 | 0 |
| | 9 | Reced of Mr Wollascott for Mrs Mary Wollascott | 10 | 0 | 0 |
| | 16 | Reced of Mr Palms for his Sister Grace | 1 | 10 | 0 |
| | | Reced of Mr Day for Mr Melling | 1 | 15 | 0 |
| | 22 | Reced of the Honble Philip Howard Esqr for Mrs Justina Johnson for the use of Miss Pen Stonor | 31 | 0 | 0 |
| | 31 | Reced of Mrs Betty Willoughby | 5 | 0 | 0 |
| Febry. | 19 | Reced of the Countess of Shrewsbury for Mrs Anne Talbot | 13 | 0 | 0 |
| | 26 | Reced of Mr Yate a year and half's Pension due last Christmas for Miss Sheldon | 22 | 10 | 0 |
| March. | 8 | Reced of Mrs Lavery for the use of Mrs Jones's | 4 | 4 | 0 |
| | | | 681 | 3 | 8 |
| March | 21 | Reced of Mr Standish Howard for Mrs Daniel | 5 | 5 | 0 |
| | 23 | Reced of Mr Stapleton Viz for his Daughter Charlott's board £.20: for her Dancing £.3. and for her pocket £.2:2:0 | 25 | 2 | 0 |

| | | | | | |
|---|---|---|---|---|---|
| | 14 | Pd. Mr. Edmund Burgis | 1 | 13 | 6 |
| | 20 | Pd. Mr. Haydocke one third of a Quarters Sallary | 0 | 16 | 8 |
| | 22 | Pd. Mrs Cecily Tunstall's Bill to the order of the Widow of Mr Charles Broeta | 100 | 0 | 0 |
| Janry. | 12 | Pd Do's Bill to the same order | 100 | 0 | 0 |
| | | | 585 | 8 | 6 |
| Janry. | 22 | Pd. Mr. Challoner | 1 | 1 | 0 |
| | 31 | Pd. Mr Burgis | 1 | 3 | 6 |
| | | | 587 | 13 | 0 |

1734
RECEIPTS

| | | | £ | s. | d. |
|---|---|---|---|---|---|
| March | 25 | Reced by the ballance of the above written Account | 123 | 15 | 2 |
| Apr. | 8 | Reced of Mr Berkeley for Mrs Mary Hacon | 4 | 0 | 0 |
| May. | 1 | Reced of Mr Christopher Ward for Mrs Teresa Lamb | 30 | 0 | 0 |
| | 9 | Reced of Mr Ashmall for his Sister | 0 | 10 | 6 |
| | 10 | Reced of Mrs Killingbeck for Miss Crathorne | 2 | 2 | 0 |
| | 16 | Reced of Mr Collingwood for his Sister Anne | 4 | 4 | 0 |
| | 17 | Reced of Mrs Ann Carew for Mrs Margaret Carew | 2 | 2 | 0 |
| | | Reced of Mr Watson for Lady Ca. Radcliffe | 100 | 0 | 0 |
| | 29 | Reced of Mrs Heneage for Mrs More | 5 | 0 | 0 |
| | | Reced of Mr Shepperd for Mr Melling | 1 | 3 | 0 |
| | 30 | Reced of Mr Rodbourn for his daughter | 2 | 10 | 0 |
| June | 11 | Reced of Mrs Elizabeth & Cassandra Willoughby for Mrs Bett Willoughby | 20 | 0 | 0 |
| | 17 | Reced of Mr Tunstall for his Sisters | 20 | 0 | 0 |
| July | 4 | Reced of Mr Sears for Mrs Bellasis | 2 | 2 | 0 |
| | | Reced of Mrs Pruden | 11 | 7 | 8 |
| | 5 | Reced of the Countess of Shrewsbury for Mrs Anne Talbot | 2 | 10 | 0 |
| | | | 331 | 6 | 4 |
| July | 9 | Reced of Ralph Crathorn Esqr by Mr Brigham | 10 | 0 | 0 |
| | 15 | Reced of Mrs Ryan for Mr Haydocke | 1 | 16 | 0 |
| *Error* | | Reced of Mr Tunstall for Mrs Tunstalls | 20 | 0 | 0 |
| | 19 | Reced of Mr Fra: Cholmeley for Mrs Betty Cholmeley | 2 | 10 | 0 |
| | 27 | Reced of the Honble Philip Howard Esqr for Miss Pen Stonor | 31 | 0 | 0 |
| | | Reced of Mr Day | 27 | 15 | 0 |
| | | | 424 | 7 | 4 |

1734
PAYMENTS

|  |  |  | £ | s. | d. |
|---|---|---|---|---|---|
| March. | 23 | Pd Mr. Day for books | 0 | 2 | 6 |
|  |  |  | 587 | 15 | 6 |
|  |  | March 25th 1734 Remains due to ballance | 123 | 15 | 2 |
|  |  |  | 711 | 10 | 8 |
| Apr. | 26 | Pd Mrs Cecily Tunstall's Bill to the order of the Widow of Mr Charles Broeta | 120 | 0 | 0 |
| June. | 14 | Pd her Bill to the order of Mr Turville | 130 | 0 | 0 |
|  |  | Pd Noteing the said Bill the same being directed to my Chambers and not to my house as desird | 0 | 2 | 6 |
|  |  |  | 250 | 2 | 6 |

| | | | | | |
|---|---|---|---|---|---|
| July. | 29 | Reced by the ballance of the above written Account | 174 | 4 | 10 |
| Augt. | 1 | Reced of Mr Rowland Lacon | 20 | 0 | 0 |
| Oct. | 2 | Reced of Mrs Cholmeley for Mrs Willoughby | 20 | 0 | 0 |
| | 14 | Reced of Mr Berkeley for Mrs Mary Hacon | 6 | 15 | 0 |
| | 25 | Reced of Cuthbert Constable | 25 | 0 | 0 |
| | | Reced of Do for Mrs Ann Tunstall | 25 | 0 | 0 |
| Novr. | 4 | Reced of Mrs Knight for Mrs Jennings | 2 | 2 | 0 |
| | 6 | Reced of Mrs Isabella Jessup for her daughter | 20 | 0 | 0 |
| | 8 | Reced of Mr Jones for his Sisters | 2 | 2 | 0 |
| | 18 | Reced of Mr Burgis for Mrs Justina Johnson | 5 | 0 | 0 |
| Decr. | 1 | Reced of Mr Thos Collingwood for Mrs Ann Collingwood | 6 | 6 | 0 |
| | 3 | Reced of Mr Crathorn | 30 | 0 | 0 |
| | 9 | Reced of Mr. Watson by Mr. Hutton for Lady Catherine Radclyffe | 100 | 0 | 0 |
| | 16 | Reced of Lady Montaigue by Mr Ashmall | 1 | 15 | 0 |
| | 20 | Reced of Mrs Bartlett for her daughters | 9 | 0 | 0 |
| | | Carried over | 447 | 4 | 10 |
| Decr. | 23 | Reced of Mr Wollascott for Mrs Mary Wollascott | 10 | 0 | 0 |
| | 27 | Reced of Mr Collingwood for Mrs Ann Collingwood | 2 | 2 | 0 |
| Janry. | 14 | Reced of Mr Rodbourne for his daughter | 2 | 10 | 0 |
| Febry. | 11 | Reced of Lady Shrewsbury for Mrs Ann Talbot | 2 | 10 | 0 |
| | 14 | Reced of Mr Maire £5 for Mrs Ursula Towneley and 2 Guineas for Mrs Ann Collingwood in all | 7 | 2 | 0 |
| | 17 | Reced of Mr Knight for Mrs Knight | 2 | 2 | 0 |
| March. | 3 | Reced of Mr Constable for Mrs Tunstalls | 15 | 0 | 0 |
| | | Reced of Mrs Margaret More for Mrs Cecily More | 3 | 3 | 0 |
| | 4 | Reced of Mr Hardcastle on Acct of Mr Robinsons Sickness | 20 | 7 | 0 |
| | 13 | Reced of Mr William Sheldon of Winchester for Miss Isabella Smith | 20 | 0 | 0 |

|  |  |  |  |  |  |
|---|---|---|---|---|---|
|  |  | 29 July 1734 Due to ballance | 174 | 4 | 10 |
|  |  |  | 424 | 7 | 4 |
| July. | 29 | Pd. myself as over charge in my last Acct. I having twice charged myself with £.20. Reced of Mr Tunstall, of whome I had but one £.20 | 20 | 0 | 0 |
| Augt. | 26 | Pd Mrs Cecily Tunstall's Bill to the order of the Widow of Mr Charles Broeta | 170 | 0 | 0 |
| Novr. | 18 | Pd. Mr Burgis | 2 | 11 | 6 |
| Decr. | 10 | Pd her Bill to the same order | 130 | 0 | 0 |
|  |  | Carried over | 322 | 11 | 6 |
| Febry. | 13 | Pd. her Bill to the order of the Widow of Charles Broeta | 120 | 0 | 0 |

| | | | £ | s. | d. |
|---|---|---|---|---|---|
| | 21 | Reced of John Belson Esqr for his Sisters Maintenance | 42 | 0 | 0 |
| | | Reced of Mr Rowland Lacon | 41 | 0 | 0 |

1735
RECEIPTS

| | | | £ | s. | d. |
|---|---|---|---|---|---|
| [March] | 31 | Reced of Mr Berkeley for Mrs Mary Hacon | 6 | 15 | 0 |
| | | Reced of Mr Trapps | 7 | 16 | 9 |
| Apr. | 29 | Reced of Mrs Willoughbys for Mrs Eliz. Willoughby | 20 | 0 | 0 |
| May. | 23 | Reced of the Honble Philip Howard for Miss Penelope Stonor | 34 | 7 | 6 |
| June. | 9 | Reced of Mrs E Smith for Mrs Isabella Smith | 6 | 0 | 0 |
| | 19 | Reced of Mr Arthur Radclyffe's Administratrices Lady Catherine's fifth share of £.2000 (after deducting her share of £51 12s 11d for Charges) paid then by Sr John Webb | 389 | 13 | 5 |
| | 20 | Reced of Mr Rodbourne for his Daughter | 2 | 10 | 0 |
| | | | 1082 | 3 | 6 |
| June. | 20 | Reced of Mr Stapylton for his daughter | 25 | 0 | 0 |
| | 23 | Reced of Mr Christopher Ward for Mrs Teresa Lamb | 94 | 0 | 0 |
| July. | 11 | Reced of Cuthbert Constable Esqr. | 20 | 0 | 0 |
| | 28 | Reced of Mr Robert Witham by Mr Day | 6 | 0 | 0 |
| | | Reced of Mr Stapleton by Do for Miss Stapleton | 12 | 11 | 0 |
| | 29 | Reced of Mrs Winifred Hyde by Mr Hansbie on Acct of Interest | 10 | 10 | 0 |
| | | Reced of Mr Kirwood for Mrs Moningtons | 14 | 0 | 0 |
| | 31 | Reced of Lady Shrewsbury for Mrs Ann Talbot | 2 | 10 | 0 |
| Augt. | 1 | Reced of Mrs Lavery for Mrs Jones | 2 | 2 | 0 |
| | 28 | Reced of Mr Robert Witham by Mr Day | 6 | 0 | 0 |
| | | | 1268 | 16 | 6 |
| Augt. | 11 | Reced by the ballance of the above Acct. | 481 | 1 | 8 |
| | 22 | Reced of Mr Rodbourne for his daughter | 6 | 0 | 0 |

1735
PAYMENTS

|  |  |  | £ | s. | d. |
|---|---|---|---|---|---|
| Mar. | 29 | Pd her Bill to the same order | 50 | 0 | 0 |
| Apr. | 3 | Pd. Mrs Winifred Ireland | 16 | 15 | 0 |
| May. | 23 | Pd. Mr Shepperd for two books | 0 | 12 | 0 |
| June. | 20 | Pd. Mr Rodbourn on Lady Catherine Radclyffe's Account | 0 | 7 | 6 |
|  |  |  | 510 | 6 | 0 |

| July. | 17 | Pd. Mrs Cecily Tunstall's Bill to the order of Mr Hobbs | 4 | 2 | 4 |
|---|---|---|---|---|---|
|  |  | Pd. her Bill to the order of Mr Cuthbt Haydocke | 30 | 0 | 0 |
|  | 28 | Pd Mr Day for books | 0 | 10 | 0 |
|  |  | Pd. her Bill to the order of the widow of C. Broeta | 120 | 0 | 0 |
|  |  | Pd her Bill to the same order | 100 | 0 | 0 |
|  | 20 | Pd myself two years Salary due this day | 20 | 0 | 0 |
|  |  | Pd for writeing out the three Accounts | 0 | 5 | 0 |
|  |  | Pd in Postage of Letters from the 16th of July 1733 to the 11th of Augt. 1735 | 2 | 11 | 6 |
| Augt. | 11 | Remains in Mr Strickland's hands to ballance | 481 | 1 | 8 |
|  |  |  | 1268 | 16 | 6 |

| | | | | | |
|---|---|---|---|---|---|
| | 28 | Reced of Mr Collingwood for his Sister | 2 | 2 | 0 |
| Sepr. | 5 | Reced of Mr Witham by Mr Day | 5 | 0 | 0 |
| | | Reced of Mr Day for Mr Melling | 3 | 18 | 6 |
| | 22 | Reced of Mrs More | 3 | 3 | 0 |
| Oct. | 6 | Reced of Mrs Smith | 26 | 0 | 0 |
| | | Reced of Mr Berkeley | 6 | 15 | 0 |
| | 13 | Reced of Mr Wollascott | 10 | 0 | 0 |
| | | Reced of Mrs Jesup | 21 | 0 | 0 |
| | | Reced of Ralph Crathorne Esqr | 30 | 0 | 0 |
| | 25 | Reced of Lord Langdale | 1 | 18 | 6 |
| | 31 | Reced of Mr Stapylton a Legacy | 5 | 0 | 0 |
| Novr. | 3 | Reced of Mrs Willoughbys for Mrs Elizabeth Willoughby | 20 | 0 | 0 |
| | | Reced of Mrs Cholmeley for Mrs Ursula Cholmeley | 14 | 0 | 0 |
| Novr. | 13 | Reced of Mrs More and Mrs Cary for Miss Bostocks | 13 | 1 | 0 |
| | 19 | Reced of Mrs Dillon | 26 | 11 | 0 |
| Decr. | 9 | Reced of Mr Sheldon of Winchester | 15 | 0 | 0 |
| | 10 | Reced of Mrs Cecily Tunstall by Mr. Hinde's Bill on Mr Day | 9 | 7 | 3 |
| | 19 | Reced of Mr Hugh Haydocke for his Br[other] | 4 | 15 | 0 |
| | 23 | Reced of Lady Shrewsbury for Mrs Ann Talbot | 2 | 10 | 0 |
| | | Reced of Lady Petre for Mr Gilbt Haydocke | 16 | 7 | 7 |
| | 30 | Reced of Mr Bartlett for his Sisters | 12 | 10 | 0 |
| Janry. | 3 | Reced of Mr Crathorne | 92 | 13 | 3 |
| | 8 | Reced of Mr Jones for Mrs Jane Jones | 5 | 0 | 0 |
| | 21 | Reced of Lady Montague | 1 | 15 | 0 |
| | 24 | Reced of Mr Watson in full of Lady Catherine Radclyffe's Annuity due the 25th day of March 1735 | 122 | 14 | 8½ |
| | 26 | Reced of Cuthbert Constable Esqr | 70 | 0 | 0 |
| | | Reced of Mr Francis Cholmeley for Mrs Elizabeth Cholmeley | 2 | 10 | 0 |
| Febry. | 9 | Reced of Mr Wollascott for his Sister | 15 | 0 | 0 |
| | 19 | Reced of Mr Rodbourn for his daughter | 2 | 10 | 0 |

| | | | | | |
|---|---|---|---|---|---|
| Sepr. | 6 | Pd. Mrs. Cecily Tunstall's Bill to the order of the Widow of Charles Broeta | 100 | 0 | 0 |
| Novr. | 28 | Pd her Bill to the same order | 150 | 0 | 0 |
| | | | 250 | 0 | 0 |
| | | Pd. Mr Clayton Milborne on a Mortgage of his estate in Kent which is to Carry Interest at 5 p Cent from the first day of Novr last | 300 | 0 | 0 |
| Janry. | 13 | Pd him more upon the same Security | 100 | 0 | 0 |
| | 26 | Pd. Mrs Cecily Tunstall's bill to the Widow of Mr Charles Broeta | 150 | 0 | 0 |
| | | Pd Mr Watson for the Return of Lady Catherine Radclyffes Annuity | 1 | 0 | 0 |
| Febry. | 18 | Pd Mr Burgis | 2 | 12 | 6 |

| | | | £ | s. | d. |
|---|---|---|---|---|---|
| | 23 | Reced of Mr Cantrill for Mrs Margt Cary | 2 | 2 | 0 |
| March. | 16 | Reced of Mrs Peggy Cholmeley for Mrs Cecily Tunstall | 6 | 16 | 0 |
| | 22 | Reced of Mrs Betty and Cassandra Willoughby for Mrs Elizabeth Willoughby | 20 | 0 | 0 |
| Apr. | 3 | Reced of Mr Richd Caryll for Mrs Wollascott | 5 | 5 | 0 |
| | 12 | Reced of Mr Berkeley for Mrs Mary Hacon | 3 | 15 | 0 |
| | | | 1086 | 1 | 5½ |

## 1736
## RECEIPTS

| | | | £ | s. | d. |
|---|---|---|---|---|---|
| Apr. | 14 | Reced of Mr Burgis for Mrs Kath: Walker | 5 | 0 | 0 |
| | 19 | Reced of Lawrence Tunstall Esqr £3 for his Sister Pulcheria and £20 for his 4 Sisters | 23 | 0 | 0 |
| | | Reced of Mr Day for Mr Melling | 3 | 10 | 0 |
| May. | 4 | Reced of Mrs More and Mrs Cary by Mr Cantrill | 17 | 17 | 0 |
| | 14 | Reced of Lady Shrewsbury for Mrs Ann Talbot | 2 | 10 | 0 |
| | 15 | Reced of Mrs Smith for Mrs Isabella Smith | 8 | 0 | 0 |
| | 21 | Reced of Mr Day for Mr Robt Witham | 20 | 0 | 0 |
| | | Reced of Mr Hyde for Mrs Wollascott a legacy | 1 | 1 | 0 |
| | 27 | Reced of Mrs More | 3 | 3 | 0 |
| June. | 2 | Reced of Mr Monington for his Sisters | 14 | 0 | 0 |
| | 4 | Reced of Mrs Greene for Miss Magdalen Greene | 10 | 10 | 0 |
| July. | 1 | Reced of Mr Rodbourn for his daughter | 2 | 10 | 0 |
| | 2 | Reced of Mrs Lucy Knight | 50 | 0 | 0 |
| | 10 | Reced of Mr Day for Mrs Palmes | 3 | 0 | 0 |
| | 12 | Reced of Mr Wollascott for his Sister | 5 | 0 | 0 |
| | 15 | Reced of Messrs Walton and Boag a year's Annuity due to Lady Catherine Radclyffe at Lady day 1736 | 100 | 0 | 0 |
| | 22 | Reced of Mrs Tufton for Miss Irelands | 22 | 0 | 0 |
| Augt. | 20 | Reced of Mr Stapleton for his daughter | 25 | 0 | 0 |

| Mar. | 16 | Pd. Mrs Cecily Tunstall's bill to the order of the Widow of Mr Charles Broeta | 140 | 0 | 0 |
| | | Pd her Bill to the same order | 100 | 0 | 0 |
| | | Pd. Mr Clayton Milborne on a Mortgage of his estate in Kent which is to Carry Interest at 5 p Cent from the first day of Novr last | 300 | 0 | 0 |

## 1736
## PAYMENTS

| | | | £ | s. | d. |
| --- | --- | --- | --- | --- | --- |
| Apr. | 14 | Pd Mr Burgis on Mrs Mary Hacon's Account | 2 | 14 | 0 |
| May. | 13 | Pd. Mrs Tunstall's Bill to the order of Mrs Mary Talbot | 5 | 0 | 0 |
| | 25 | Pd her Bill to the order of the Widow of Charles Broeta | 60 | 0 | 0 |
| July. | 9 | Pd her bill to the order of Mr Cuthbt Haydocke | 20 | 0 | 0 |
| | 10 | Pd her Bill to the order of the Widow of Charles Broeta | 40 | 0 | 0 |
| | 15 | Pd Messrs Walton and Boag for the Return of Lady Catherine Radclyffe's Annuity | 1 | 0 | 0 |
| Augt. | 28 | Pd Mrs Tunstall's Bill to the order of the Widow of Charles Broeta | 150 | 0 | 0 |

| | | | | | |
|---|---|---|---|---|---|
| | 26 | Receded of Cuthbert Constable Esqr | 20 | 0 | 0 |
| Sepr. | 9 | Receded of Mrs Tufton pocket money for her daughters | 2 | 2 | 0 |
| | 21 | Receded of Mrs Elizabeth & Cassandra Willoughby | 20 | 11 | 0 |
| | 23 | Receded of Mrs Helen Petre | 3 | 1 | 0 |
| Oct. | 15 | Receded of Mrs E. Smith for her Sister | 5 | 0 | 0 |
| | 20 | Receded of Lord Langdale | 1 | 18 | 0 |
| | | Receded of Mr Berkeley for Mrs Hacon | 3 | 15 | 0 |
| Novr. | 4 | Receded of Mr Molyneux for Mrs Bentley | 5 | 0 | 0 |
| | 8 | Receded of Mr Jesup £30 for the house and £10 for Mrs Eliza Daniel in all | 40 | 0 | 0 |
| | 11 | Receded of Mrs Orme for Mrs Cockain | 2 | 2 | 0 |
| | 22 | Receded of Lady Shrewsbury for Miss Talbot | 5 | 5 | 0 |
| | | | 1510 | 16 | 5½ |
| Novr. | 22 | Receded of Cuthbert Constable Esqr | 20 | 0 | 0 |
| | | Receded of Mrs Fisher for Mrs Cockain | 0 | 10 | 6 |
| | 26 | Receded of Mrs Moore and Mrs Cary | 15 | 3 | 0 |
| | 29 | Receded of Mr Brian Tunstall | 10 | 5 | 6 |
| | | Receded of Mr Brian Palms for his daughter | 1 | 10 | 0 |
| Decr. | 11 | Receded of Mr Day for Mr Melling | 2 | 17 | 2 |
| | 18 | Receded of Mr Wm Stanford for Mr Charles Stanford | 10 | 0 | 0 |
| | | Receded of Mr Collingwood for his Sister | 2 | 2 | 0 |
| | 23 | Receded of Lady Montague | 1 | 15 | 0 |
| Jan. | 8 | Receded of Mr Rodbourn for his daughter | 2 | 10 | 0 |
| | 11 | Receded of Mr Constable for his daughters | 30 | 0 | 0 |
| | | Receded of Mr Franc[i]s Cholmeley for Mrs Elizabeth Cholmeley | 5 | 0 | 0 |
| | 13 | Receded of Mrs Heneage for Mrs More | 5 | 5 | 0 |
| | 31 | Receded of Mr Bartlet for his Sisters | 15 | 10 | 0 |
| Febr. | 7 | Receded of Mrs Peggy Cholmeley for Mrs Ursula Cholmeley | 12 | 0 | 0 |
| | 9 | Receded of Mrs Bartlet for her daughters | 2 | 2 | 0 |
| | 14 | Receded of Mr Tufton for the Miss Irelands | 26 | 1 | 0 |
| | | Receded of Mr Row: Lacon for Mrs Magdalen Green | 30 | 0 | 0 |
| | 25 | Receded of Mrs Andrews for Mrs Bentley | 10 | 0 | 0 |

| | | | | | |
|---|---|---|---|---|---|
| Oct. | 4 | Pd her Bill to the order of the Widow of Cha: Broeta | 100 | 0 | 0 |
| Novr. | 18 | Pd Mrs Betty Blevin on Mrs Mary Hacon's Acct. | 3 | 15 | 0 |
| Decr. | 4 | Pd Mrs Gage on Mrs Macgrath's Account | 2 | 2 | 0 |
| | | | 1428 | 3 | 6 |
| Decr. | 13 | Pd Mrs Tunstall's Bill to the order of the Widow of Charles Broeta | 70 | 0 | 0 |
| Febr. | 4 | Pd her Bill to Mr Shepperd | 4 | 17 | 0 |
| | 12 | Pd Mr Chorley on Mrs Macgrath's Acct | 8 | 2 | 5 |
| | 15 | Pd her Bill to the order of Mrs Broeta | 100 | 0 | 0 |

|  |  |  | £ | s. | d. |
|---|---|---|---:|---:|---:|
|  | 28 | Reced of Mrs More for Mrs More | 3 | 3 | 0 |
| March. | 9 | Reced of Mr Wm Sheldon of Winchester | 50 | 0 | 0 |
|  | 14 | Reced of Mr Burgis for Mrs Walker | 25 | 0 | 0 |
|  | 28 | Reced of Mr Berkeley for Mrs Hacon | 6 | 15 | 0 |

## 1737
### RECEIPTS

|  |  |  | £ | s. | d. |
|---|---|---|---:|---:|---:|
| Apr. | 6 | Reced of Mrs Elizabeth and Cassandra Willoughby for Mrs Betty Willoughby | 20 | 0 | 0 |
|  | 7 | Reced of Mr Rooksby's Bill upon his brother | 10 | 0 | 0 |
| Apr. | 26 | Reced of Mrs Eliz. Smith for Mrs Isabella Smith | 5 | 0 | 0 |
| May. | 6 | Reced of Mrs Moore and Mrs Cary | 20 | 0 | 0 |
|  | 13 | Reced of Mrs Dillon | 26 | 11 | 0 |
|  | 23 | Reced of Mrs Parry for Mrs Ursula Towneley | 10 | 10 | 0 |
|  | 28 | Reced of Mr Day for Mr Witham | 20 | 0 | 0 |
| June. | 9 | Reced of Mr Monington for his Sisters | 14 | 0 | 0 |
|  |  | Reced of Mrs Tunstal of Wycliff by bill | 20 | 0 | 0 |
|  | 10 | Reced of Mrs Carew | 10 | 10 | 0 |
|  | 17 | Reced of Mr Wm Stanford for Mr Charles Stanford | 12 | 0 | 0 |
|  | 23 | Reced of Mr Rodbourn for his daughter | 2 | 10 | 0 |
|  | 25 | Reced of Lady Shrewsbury for Miss Ann Talbot | 2 | 10 | 0 |
| July. | 8 | Reced of Mr Shepperd for Mrs Mary Bentley | 10 | 0 | 0 |
|  | 13 | Reced by Mrs Smith's bill upon Mr Wyke | 40 | 0 | 0 |
|  | 20 | Reced of Mrs Carew | 11 | 0 | 0 |
| Augt. | 4 | Reced of Mrs Tufton for her daughters | 26 | 1 | 0 |
|  | 12 | Reced of Mr Francis Cholmeley for Mrs Elizabeth Cholmeley | 2 | 10 | 0 |
|  | 16 | Reced of Mr Sheldon for Mrs Isabella Smith | 15 | 0 | 0 |
|  |  | Reced of Mr Staplylton for Madame More | 42 | 0 | 0 |
|  |  | Reced of Mr Palms for his Sister Grace | 4 | 0 | 0 |
| Sepr. | 17 | Reced of Mr Sheldon for Mrs Isabella Smith | 5 | 0 | 0 |
|  | 23 | Reced of Messrs Walton and Boag a years annuity due to Lady Catherine Radclyffe at Lady Day 1737 | 100 | 0 | 0 |
|  | 24 | Reced of Mr Jessup | 30 | 0 | 0 |

| Mar. | 1 | Pd Mr Burgis | | 2 | 2 | 0 |

---

|   | 1737 PAYMENTS | | | | |
|---|---|---|---|---|---|
|   |   | £ | s. | d. |
| [Mar.] | 26 | Pd her Bill to the same order | 100 | 0 | 0 |
|   |   |   | 1713 | 4 | 11 |

| May | 7 | Pd Mrs Tunstal's Bill to the order of the Widow of Charles Broeta | 100 | 0 | 0 |

| Sepr. | 23 | Pd Messrs Walton and Boag for the return of Lady Catherine's Annuity | 1 | 0 | 0 |
|   | 29 | Pd her Bill to the order of Widow of C Broeta | 100 | 0 | 0 |

| | | | | | |
|---|---|---|---|---|---|
| Oct. | 7 | Reced by Mrs Smith's bill upon Mr Wyke | 30 | 0 | 0 |
| | 11 | ~~Reced of Mr Molyneux for Mrs Bentley~~ | ~~10~~ | ~~10~~ | ~~0~~ |
| | 12 | Reced of Lady Gerard for Mr Melling | 20 | 0 | 0 |
| | 14 | Reced of Mrs Elizabeth and Cassandra Willoughby for Mrs Betty Willoughby | 20 | 0 | 0 |
| Novr. | 7 | Reced of Mr Wm Stanford for Mr Cha: Stanford | 18 | 0 | 0 |
| | | | 2345 | 7 | 7½ |
| Novr. | 12 | Reced of Mr Berkeley for Mrs Hacon | 6 | 15 | 0 |
| | 15 | Reced of Mr Cantrill for Mrs Carew | 1 | 1 | 0 |
| Decr. | 1 | Reced of Mr Constable for his daughters | 4 | 0 | 0 |
| | 8 | Reced of Mrs Florence Jones for Mrs Jones | 5 | 15 | 6 |
| | | | 2362 | 19 | 1½ |
| Decr. | 12 | Reced by the balance of the above Account | 83 | 15 | 11½ |
| | 21 | Reced of Mr Franc[i]s Cholmeley for Mrs Elizabeth Cholmeley | 2 | 10 | 0 |
| | 22 | Reced of the Countess of Shrewsbury for Miss Ann Talbot | 2 | 10 | 0 |
| | 26 | Reced of Mr Sheldon of Winchester for Mrs Isabella Smith | 10 | 0 | 0 |
| | 30 | Reced of Lady Gerard for Mr Melling, wch was omitted in my last Acct, the money having been paid into my hands the 18th of Novr last | 20 | 0 | 0 |
| Jan. | 4 | Reced of Lady Montaigu | 1 | 15 | 0 |
| | 17 | Reced of Mr Rodbourne for his daughter | 2 | 10 | 0 |
| | 25 | Reced of Mr Constable for his Sisters and Mrs Crathorne | 12 | 0 | 0 |
| | | | 135 | 0 | 11½ |
| Febr. | 7 | Reced of Mrs Tufton for her daughters | 26 | 1 | 0 |
| | 17 | Reced of Mr Bartlett for his Sisters | 11 | 10 | 0 |
| Mar. | 4 | Reced of Mr Milbourne two years Int of £300 due the first day of Novr. 1737 and two years Int of £100 due the 13th day of Jan. 1737 in all | 40 | 0 | 0 |
| | 6 | Reced of Mrs Stafford for Mrs Moon | 1 | 1 | 0 |
| | 16 | Reced of Lady Gerrard for Mr Melling | 40 | 0 | 0 |
| | 17 | Reced of Mr Sheldon of Winchester | 10 | 0 | 0 |
| | 20 | Reced of Mrs Rodham for Mrs Walker | 6 | 1 | 0 |
| | 23 | Reced of Mr Constable for his daughters | 60 | 0 | 0 |

| | | | | | |
|---|---|---|---|---|---|
| Oct. | 15 | Pd her Bill to Mr Thomas Day | 10 | 0 | 0 |
| | | | 1924 | 4 | 11 |
| Novr. | 19 | Pd Mrs Tunstal's Bill to the order of the Widow Broeta | 100 | 0 | 0 |
| | 24 | Pd her Bill to Mr John Shepperd | 8 | 0 | 0 |
| Decr. | 3 | Pd Mr Day Mrs Neesum's Draft upon me by Mrs Tunstal's order | 222 | 14 | 0 |
| | | Pd myself two years Salary due the 20th of July last | 20 | 0 | 0 |
| | | Pd for writing out this Account | 0 | 5 | 0 |
| | | Pd in Postage of Letters from the 11th of Augt 1735 to the 12th of Decr. 1737 | 3 | 19 | 3 |
| | 12 | Remains in Mr Strickland's hands to balance | 83 | 15 | 11½ |
| | | | 2362 | 19 | 1½ |
| Jan. | 6 | Pd her Bill to the order of the Widow Broeta | 100 | 0 | 0 |
| | 26 | Pd Mr John Hill by her order | 10 | 0 | 0 |
| Febr. | 17 | Pd her Bill to Mr John Shepperd | 8 | 0 | 0 |
| | | | 118 | 0 | 0 |

### 1738
### RECEIPTS

| | | | £ | s. | d. |
|---|---|---|---|---|---|
| Apr. | 5 | Reced of Mrs More | 6 | 16 | 6 |
| | 17 | Reced of Mr Berkeley for Mrs Mary Hacon | 7 | 13 | 0 |
| | 18 | Reced of Wm Stanford Esqr for Mr Charles Stanford | 20 | 0 | 0 |
| | 21 | Reced of Mr Sheldon of Winchester for Miss Smith | 15 | 0 | 0 |
| | | Reced of Mrs Ann Carew for Mrs Margaret Carew | 2 | 2 | 0 |
| | 22 | Reced of Mr Day for Mr Melling | 3 | 0 | 0 |
| May. | 16 | Reced of Mr Cantrill for Mrs Margt Carew | 2 | 2 | 0 |
| | 19 | Reced of Mrs Tunstall by Mrs Eliz Smith's Bill upon Mr Wyke payable to me | 100 | 0 | 0 |
| June. | 12 | Reced of Lady Gerard for Mr. Melling | 10 | 10 | 0 |
| | | Reced of Mr Constable for his Daughters | 10 | 10 | 0 |
| | 22 | Reced of Mr Monington | 14 | 0 | 0 |
| | 23 | Reced of Mr Stapleton for Mrs More | 400 | 0 | 0 |
| | | Reced of Do for his Sister Charlot | 50 | 0 | 0 |
| | | Reced of Mr Tunstall by Bill pd this day | 24 | 0 | 0 |
| | 26 | Reced of Mrs Bentley by Bill from Mrs Ormonby | 30 | 0 | 0 |
| | | | 1024 | 17 | 5½ |
| June. | 30 | Reced of Mr Rodbourne for his daughter | 2 | 10 | 0 |
| July. | 1 | Reced of Lord Langdale | 3 | 0 | 0 |
| | | Reced of the Countess of Shrewsbury for Mrs Ann Talbot which I forgot to place to Account when paid | 2 | 10 | 0 |
| | 13 | Reced of Mrs Bentley by her Bill upon me to Mrs Tunstall's order | 5 | 10 | 0 |
| | 25 | Reced of Mrs Tufton for her daughters | 26 | 1 | 0 |
| Augt. | 2 | Reced of Miss Langdale | 3 | 3 | 0 |
| | 9 | Reced by Mrs Smith's Bill upon Mr Wyke | 100 | 0 | 0 |
| | | Reced of Messrs Walton and Boag a year's Annuity due to Lady Catherine Radclyffe at Lady Day 1738 | 100 | 0 | 0 |

1738
PAYMENTS

| | | | £ | s. | d. |
|---|---|---|---|---|---|
| Apr. | 17 | Pd Mrs Tunstal's bill to the order of the Widow of Mr Charles Broeta | 100 | 0 | 0 |
| May | 2 | Pd her Bill to the same order | 100 | 0 | 0 |
| June. | 1 | Pd her Bill to the same order | 160 | 0 | 0 |
| | | | 478 | 0 | 0 |
| July. | 4 | Pd her Bill to the order of the Widow of Mr Charles Broeta | 60 | 0 | 0 |
| Augt. | 4 | Pd Mr Burgis | 1 | 4 | 6 |
| | 12 | Pd her Bill to the order of the Widow of Mr Charles Broeta | 250 | 0 | 0 |
| | | Pd her Bill to the same order | 200 | 0 | 0 |
| | 30 | Pd her Bill to the same order | 130 | 0 | 0 |

| | | | | | |
|---|---|---|---|---|---|
| Oct. | 10 | Reced of Mr Constable for his Daughters | 30 | 0 | 0 |
| | | Reced by Mr Sheldon's Bill on Mr Wright | 10 | 0 | 0 |
| | | Reced of Mr Alexander Knight for Mrs Marga-ret Knight | 1 | 1 | 0 |
| | 20 | Reced of Mr Robert Stanford for Mr Charles Stanford | 40 | 0 | 0 |
| Novr. | 3 | Reced of Mr Berkeley for Mrs Hacon | 8 | 6 | 6 |
| | 13 | Reced of Mr Brian Tunstal | 23 | 18 | 0 |
| | 20 | Reced of Mr Giffard for Mrs Magdalen Grene | 40 | 0 | 0 |
| | 21 | Reced of Capt Francis Green by Mr John Green | 10 | 0 | 0 |
| Decr. | 1 | Reced of Mrs Betty & Cassandra Willoughby for Mrs Elizabeth Willoughby | 30 | 0 | 0 |
| | | Reced of Mrs Barbara Cholmeley for Miss Ogle | 7 | 2 | 0 |
| | | Reced of Mr Franc[i]s Cholmeley for Mrs Eliza Cholmeley | 2 | 10 | 0 |
| | | Reced of Mrs Peggy Cholmelely for Mrs Ursu-la Cholmeley | 5 | 5 | 0 |
| | | | 1465 | 13 | 11½ |
| Decr. | 22 | Reced of Lady Shrewsbury for Miss Talbot | 2 | 10 | 0 |
| | | Reced of Mr Widdrington for Mrs Mary Wool-lascott | 1 | 11 | 6 |
| Jan. | 1 | Reced of Nicholas Stapleton Esqr. | 14 | 0 | 0 |
| | 14 | Reced of Mrs Dorothy Legard for Mrs Cather-ine Walker | 30 | 0 | 0 |
| | | Reced of Do for Mrs Catherine Johnson | 5 | 0 | 0 |
| | 16 | Reced of Mr Rookby for Mrs Margt Knight | 3 | 3 | 0 |
| | 20 | Reced of Mr Rodbourn for his daughter | 2 | 10 | 0 |
| | 30 | Reced of Mr Stonor a Debt due from his Sister Pen | 0 | 17 | 6 |
| Febr. | 7 | Reced of Mr Francis Cholmeley for Mrs Eliza-beth Cholmeley | 2 | 10 | 0 |
| | 17 | Reced of Mr Tufton for Miss Irelands | 26 | 1 | 0 |
| March. | 9 | Reced of Mr Robert Stanford for Mr Charles Stanford | 20 | 0 | 0 |
| | 16 | Reced of Mrs Jesup | 15 | 0 | 0 |

|  |  |  |  |  |  |
|---|---|---|---|---|---|
|  |  | Pd myself a years Salary due the 20th of July last | 10 | 0 | 0 |
| Oct. | 28 | Pd Mr Hawkins a Bill for books | 0 | 4 | 3 |
| Novr. | 6 | Pd her Bill to the same order | 100 | 0 | 0 |
| Decr. | 4 | Pd her Bill to the same order | 150 | 0 | 0 |
|  |  |  | 1379 | 8 | 9 |
| Febr. | 5 | Pd her Bill to the order of the Widow of Mr Charles Broeta | 140 | 0 | 0 |

1739
RECEIPTS

| | | | £ | s. | d. |
|---|---|---|---|---|---|
| Apr. | 3 | Reced of Mrs Constable for Miss Constable | 6 | 6 | 0 |
| | 13 | Reced of Mr Berkeley for Mrs Hacon | 8 | 6 | 6 |
| | 17 | Reced of Mrs Eliz & Cassandra Willoughby for Mrs Betty Willoughby | 20 | 0 | 0 |
| | 25 | Reced of Mrs Petre for Mrs Moore | 2 | 6 | 10½ |
| *Error* | 30 | ~~Reced of Mr Englefield for his Sister Betty~~ | ~~2~~ | ~~2~~ | ~~0~~ |
| May. | 3 | Reced of Mr Alexr Knight for Mrs Margt Knight | 10 | 10 | 0 |
| | 14 | Reced of Basil Bartlett Esqr for his Sisters | 10 | 0 | 0 |
| | 16 | Reced of Mrs Carew for Mrs Macgrath | 2 | 2 | 0 |
| June. | 8 | Reced of Mr Monington for his Sisters | 14 | 0 | 0 |
| | | | 1662 | 8 | 4 |
| June. | 29 | Reced of Mrs Knight for Mr Haydocke | 1 | 1 | 0 |
| July. | 2 | Reced of Mr Brian Tunstall for Miss Ogle £7 10s 0d her pension £5 for expences in all | 12 | 10 | 0 |
| | | Reced of Mr Day for Mr Melling | 3 | 0 | 0 |
| | 9 | Reced of Mr Rodbourne for his daughter | 2 | 10 | 0 |
| | | Reced of Lady Shrewsbury for Miss Talbot | 2 | 10 | 0 |
| Augt. | 20 | Reced of Mr Tunstall by Bill | 10 | 0 | 0 |
| Sepr. | 17 | Reced of Thomas Eyre Esqr | 525 | 0 | 0 |
| Oct. | 15 | Reced of Lady Shrewsbury for Mrs Ann Talbot | 7 | 0 | 0 |
| | 16 | Reced of Mrs Hills a yrs Annuity due to Mrs Isabella Smith at Mich last | 10 | 0 | 0 |
| | 17 | Reced of Mrs Tufton for her daughters | 27 | 0 | 0 |
| | 19 | Reced of Mr Constable | 60 | 0 | 0 |
| | | Reced of Mr Francis Cholmeley for Mrs Elizabeth Cholmeley | 2 | 10 | 0 |
| Novr. | 1 | Reced of Mrs Betty and Cassandra Willoughby for Mrs Elizabeth Willoughby | 20 | 0 | 0 |
| | 7 | Reced of Mr Berkeley for Mrs Hacon | 8 | 6 | 6 |
| | 23 | Reced of Nicholas Stapylton Esqr for Miss Charlott Stapylton | 5 | 0 | 0 |
| | 26 | Reced of Mrs Mary Cholmeley for Mrs Ursula Cholmeley | 54 | 0 | 0 |
| Decr. | 1 | Reced of Mr Edwd Bartlet for Mr[s] Ann Bartlet | 0 | 3 | 0 |
| | 21 | Reced of Mr Rodbourne for his daughter | 2 | 10 | 0 |

1739
PAYMENTS

| | | | £ | s. | d. |
|---|---|---|---|---|---|
| Apr. | 5 | Pd her Bill to the same order | 60 | 0 | 0 |
| | | | 1579 | 8 | 9 |

| | | | £ | s. | d. |
|---|---|---|---|---|---|
| July. | 3 | Pd Mrs Tunstal's bill to the order of the Widow of Mr Charles Broeta | 90 | 0 | 0 |
| | | Pd Mrs Betty Blevin | 0 | 6 | 0 |
| Oct. | 19 | Pd her Bill to the same order | 100 | 0 | 0 |
| | 22 | Pd her Bill to the same order | 125 | 0 | 0 |
| | 24 | Pd her Bill to the same order | 100 | 0 | 0 |
| Novr. | 3 | Pd her Bill to the same order | 200 | 0 | 0 |
| | 20 | Pd her Bill to the order of Mr Cuthbert Haydocke | 22 | 15 | 3½ |
| | 28 | Pd her Bill to the order of the Widow of Mr Charles Broeta | 100 | 0 | 0 |
| | | | 2317 | 10 | 0½ |

| | | | £ | s. | d. |
|---|---|---|---|---|---|
| | 22 | Reced of Lady Shrewsbury for Mrs Ann Talbot | 2 | 10 | 0 |
| | | | 2417 | 18 | 10 |
| Decr. | 26 | Reced of Messrs Walton and Boag a year's Annuity due to Lady Catherine Radclyffe at Lady Day 1739 | 100 | 0 | 0 |
| Jan. | 16 | Reced of Mr Bartlett for his Sisters | 10 | 0 | 0 |
| Feb. | 14 | Reced of Mr Dale for Miss Ogle | 12 | 10 | 0 |
| | 20 | Reced of Mrs Tufton for her daughters | 27 | 6 | 0 |
| Mar. | 22 | Reced of Cuthbert Constable Esqr | 50 | 0 | 0 |
| | 31 | Reced of Mr Berkeley for Mrs Hacon | 8 | 6 | 6 |

1740
RECEIPTS

| | | | £ | s. | d. |
|---|---|---|---|---|---|
| May. | 2 | Reced of Mrs Cockaine for Mrs Crathorne | 20 | 0 | 0 |
| | 5 | Reced of Mr Hills for Mrs Elizabeth and Isabella Smith | 10 | 0 | 0 |
| | 10 | Reced of Mr Challoner for Mr Haydocke | 92 | 6 | 0 |
| | 12 | Reced of Mr Tunstall by bill for his sisters | 15 | 0 | 0 |
| | 16 | Reced of Mrs Carew for her Daughters | 2 | 2 | 0 |
| | 23 | Reced of Mr Dail for Miss Ogle | 20 | 0 | 0 |
| June. | 2 | Reced of Mrs Stubbs for Mrs Cholmeley | 5 | 0 | 0 |
| | 4 | Reced of Mr Wyke for Mrs Eliz Smith | 10 | 0 | 0 |
| | 6 | Reced of Mr Monington for his Sisters | 14 | 0 | 0 |
| July. | 1 | Reced of Mr Rodbourne for his daughter | 2 | 10 | 0 |
| | 15 | Reced of Lady Shrewsbury for Mrs Ann Talbot | 2 | 10 | 0 |
| | 18 | Reced of Mr Challoner for Mr Haydocke | 10 | 0 | 0 |
| | | Reced of Mrs Willoughby of Nottingham for Mrs Betty Willoughby | 7 | 18 | 0 |
| Augt. | 1 | Reced of Mrs Ann Carew for Mrs Margaret Carew | 2 | 0 | 0 |
| | 2 | Reced the principal and Interest secured by Clayton Milborne Esqr. | 454 | 0 | 0 |
| | 28 | Reced of Mr Franc[i]s Cholmeley for Mrs Eliz Cholmeley | 5 | 0 | 0 |
| | | | 3298 | 7 | 4 |

| | | | £ | s. | d. |
|---|---|---|---|---|---|
| Decr. | 26 | Pd Messrs Walton and Boag for the Return of two years Annuity due to Lady Catherine Radclyffe | 2 | 0 | 0 |
| Jan. | 28 | Pd her Bill to the order of the Widow of Charles Broeta | 170 | 0 | 0 |
| ffeb. | 20 | Pd her Bill to the order of Mrs Frances Lee | 6 | 6 | 0 |
| Mar. | 28 | Pd her Bill to the order of Mr Peter Brown | 4 | 18 | 0 |

### 1740
### PAYMENTS

| | | | £ | s. | d. |
|---|---|---|---|---|---|
| Apr. | 12 | Pd her Bill to the order of the Widow of Charles Broeta | 60 | 0 | 0 |
| | 19 | Pd her Bill to the same order | 50 | 0 | 0 |
| June. | 9 | Pd her Bill to the same order | 150 | 0 | 0 |
| July. | 23 | Pd Mrs Blevin by the order of Mrs Justina Johnson | 1 | 1 | 0 |
| Augt. | 28 | Pd Mrs Margt Cholmeley her Bill of things bought by her | 10 | 16 | 10 |
| | | Pd her Bill to the order of the Widow of Mr Charles Broeta | 50 | 0 | 0 |
| | | | 2822 | 11 | 10½ |

| | | | | | |
|---|---|---|---|---|---|
| Augt. | 28 | Reced of Mr Walter Lacon for Mrs Magdalen Grene | 42 | 0 | 0 |
| Sepr. | 3 | Reced of Mrs Tufton for her Daughters | 44 | 5 | 0 |
| | 6 | Reced of Mrs Ann Carew for her Daughter | 0 | 10 | 6 |
| Oct. | 20 | Reced of Marmaduke Tunstall Esqr | 7 | 2 | 0 |
| Novr. | 10 | Reced of Cuthbert Constable Esqr. | 40 | 0 | 0 |
| | | Reced of Mrs Eliz & Cassandra Willoughby for Mrs Betty Willoughby | 20 | 0 | 0 |
| | 14 | | | | |
| | 13 | Reced of Mrs Smith by her Draft on Mrs Hill | 5 | 0 | 0 |
| | 14 | Reced of Messrs Walton and Boag a years Annuity due to Lady Catherine Radclyffe at Lady Day 1740 | 100 | 0 | 0 |
| | 15 | Reced of Mr Porter for his Daughters | 50 | 0 | 0 |
| | 26 | Reced of Mr Wm Wollascott for the use of Mrs Mary Wollascott | 10 | 0 | 0 |
| Decr. | 8 | Reced of Mr Berkeley for Mrs Hacon | 5 | 11 | 0 |
| | | Reced of Mr Bartlett for his Sisters | 11 | 0 | 0 |
| | 13 | Reced of Mr Stapleton Errington for his Daughter Charlot | 5 | 0 | 0 |
| | 18 | Reced of Mr Brian Tunstall | 13 | 7 | 0 |
| | 22 | Reced of the Countess of Shrewsbury for Mrs Ann Talbot | 12 | 10 | 0 |
| Jan. | 8 | Reced of Mr Cantrill for Mrs Margt Carew | 3 | 1 | 0 |

| | | | | | |
|---|---|---|---|---|---|
| | | Pd myself two years Salary due the 20th of July last | 20 | 0 | 0 |
| Sepr. | 3 | Pd Mr. Milward a Bill on Mr Haydock's Account | 1 | 5 | 6 |
| | 9 | Pd Mr Gyles a Bill for the administracon to Mrs Mary Worthington | 3 | 5 | 0 |
| | 11 | Pd her Bill to the order of the Widow of Charles Broeta | 70 | 0 | 0 |
| Oct. | 10 | Pd her Bill to the order of Mr Cuthbert Haydocke | 20 | 0 | 0 |
| Novr. | 1 | Pd her Bill to the order of the Widow of Charles Broeta | 70 | 0 | 0 |
| | | Pd Mrssrs Walton and Boag for Return of the years Annuity reced p Contra for Lady Catherine Radclyffe | 1 | 0 | 0 |
| | | Pd Mr Anthony Wright for the use of Lady Crispe in part of £600 principal Money Secured upon the estate of Edwd Spelman Esqr in Norfolk wch £400 carries Interest at 5 p Cent from the 19th day of Sepr last | 400 | 0 | 0 |
| | 17 | Pd Mr Peter Plowden by Mrs Tunstall's direction | 1 | 5 | 0 |
| Decr. | 22 | Pd her Bill to the order of the Widow of Charles Broeta | 190 | 0 | 0 |

| | 19 | Reced of Mr Edward Webb £100 Prin. and £65:6:10 for 13 years and 25 days Interest thereof at 5 p Cent due 17th Inst in Discharge of the late Mrs Throckmorton's bond | 165 | 6 | 10 |
|---|---|---|---|---|---|
| | | Reced of George Palmes Esqr. For Mrs Grace Palmes | 3 | 0 | 0 |
| | 23 | Reced of Mrs Heneage | 13 | 12 | 0 |
| | | Reced of Mr Haydocke for his Daughter | 2 | 2 | 0 |
| | | | 3851 | 14 | 8 |

| ffeb. | 11 | Reced of Mr Daile for Miss Ogle | 20 | 0 | 0 |
|---|---|---|---|---|---|
| Mar. | 21 | Reced of Do for Do | 20 | 0 | 0 |
| Mar. | 24 | Reced of Mrs Hatch for Mrs Laitus | 30 | 0 | 0 |

## 1741
## RECEIPTS

| | | | £ | s. | d. |
|---|---|---|---|---|---|
| Apr. | 7 | Reced of Mrs Weld for Mrs Jane Jones | 3 | 5 | 0 |
| | 17 | Reced of Peter Giffard Esqr for Miss Magdalen Green | 28 | 16 | 8 |
| May. | 2 | Reced of Sr Henry Tichborne for Mrs Isabella Smith | 5 | 0 | 0 |
| | 8 | Reced of Mrs Betty and Cass: Willoughby for Mrs Eliz. Willoughby | 20 | 0 | 0 |
| | 11 | Reced of Mr Tunstall for his Sisters | 16 | 1 | 0 |
| June. | 10 | Reced of Mrs Ann Carew for Mrs Margaret Carew | 2 | 0 | 0 |
| | 12 | Reced of Mrs Monington for the two Mrs Moningtons | 14 | 0 | 0 |
| | 18 | Reced of Rowld Bellasise Esqr for Mrs Smith | 25 | 0 | 0 |
| | 20 | Reced of Mr Wollascott for his Sister | 10 | 0 | 0 |
| | 25 | Reced of Mr Franc[i]s Petre for Mrs Justina Johnson | 21 | 19 | 0 |
| July. | 11 | Reced of Mr Cholmeley for his Aunt | 5 | 0 | 0 |
| | 15 | Reced of Mr House for Miss Rodbourne | 5 | 0 | 0 |
| | | Reced of Mrs Knight, which was paid to my Wife by Mr. Wm Hore July 2d 1740, but omitted to be charged by me | 1 | 1 | 0 |
| | 17 | Reced of Mr Porter for his Daughters | 33 | 13 | 6 |

| | | | £ | s. | d. |
|---|---|---|---|---|---|
| Jan. | 19 | Pd her Bill to the same order | 80 | 0 | 0 |
| Feb. | 17 | Pd Messrs Kempson and Williams for Drugs | 13 | 10 | 0 |
| | 18 | Pd her Bill to the order of the Widow of Charles Broeta | 160 | 0 | 0 |
| | | | 3852 | 17 | 4½ |

### 1741
### PAYMENTS

| | | | £ | s. | d. |
|---|---|---|---|---|---|
| May | 2 | Pd Mrs Tunstall's bill to the order of the Widow of Charles Broeta | 70 | 0 | 0 |
| June. | 1 | Pd Mrs Magdalen Green's bill to the same order | 28 | 16 | 8 |
| July. | 1 | Pd her Bill to the order of the Widow of Charles Broeta | 50 | 0 | 0 |

| | | | | | |
|---|---|---|---|---|---|
| Augt. | 4 | Reced of Messrs Walton & Boag a yrs Annuity due to Lady Catherine Radclyffe at Lady Day 1741 | 100 | 0 | 0 |
| | 23 | Reced of Miss Ogle for Mrs Jones | 14 | 19 | 0 |
| | | Reced of Mr Nicholas Stapleton | 5 | 0 | 0 |
| | | | 4247 | 9 | 10 |
| Oct. | 16 | Reced of Mrs Catherine Heneage | 21 | 0 | 0 |
| | 23 | Reced of Ld Langdale for Mrs Christina Towneley | 9 | 12 | 0 |
| | 30 | Reced of Mrs Clayton for Mrs Isabella Jessup | 10 | 10 | 0 |
| Novr. | 9 | Reced of Mrs Magdalen Green by Bill for Mrs Ann Collingwood | 10 | 0 | 0 |
| | 11 | Reced of Mr Thomas Mead for his Daughters | 32 | 0 | 0 |
| | 20 | Reced of Mrs Tunstall by Mrs Eliz Smith's Bill upon Mr Anthony Wright | 25 | 0 | 0 |
| | 23 | Reced of Mr Geo: Reynoldson for Mrs Grace Palmes | 3 | 0 | 0 |
| | 30 | Reced of Mr Basil Bartlett for his Sister | 27 | 0 | 0 |
| Decr. | 1 | Reced of Lady Shrewsbury last sumer £2:10:0 and now £2:10:0 for Mrs Ann Talbot | 5 | 0 | 0 |
| | 14 | Reced of Capt Grene for Mrs Grene | 10 | 0 | 0 |
| | 17 | Reced of Mrs Betty and Cassandra Willoughby for Mrs Elizabeth Willoughby | 20 | 0 | 0 |
| ffeb. | 16 | Reced of Mr Crathorne | 10 | 0 | 0 |
| Mar. | 15 | Reced of Mrs Ogle | 7 | 10 | 0 |

| Augt. | 4 | Pd Messrs Walton and Boag for return of the years Annuity reced p Contra for Lady Catherine Radclyffe | 1 | 0 | 0 |
|---|---|---|---|---|---|

| Sepr. | 25 | Pd Mr. Kempson for Drugs | 3 | 4 | 0 |
|---|---|---|---|---|---|
|  | 26 | Pd Mr Nicholas Sentron | 4 | 4 | 0 |
|  |  |  | 4010 | 2 | 0½ |
| Augt. | 8 | Pd her Ladyship's bill to the order of the Widow of Charles Broeta | 70 | 0 | 0 |
|  | 12 | Pd her Bill to the order of Mr John Mellling | 10 | 0 | 0 |
|  |  |  | 4090 | 2 | 0½ |

| Novr. | 3 | Pd her Bill to the order of the Widow of Mr Charles Broeta | 130 | 0 | 0 |
|---|---|---|---|---|---|
|  | 24 | Pd her Bill to the same order | 100 | 0 | 0 |

| Decr. | 25 | Pd her Bill to the order of Mr Cuthbert Haydocke | 18 | 10 | 0 |
|---|---|---|---|---|---|
| Febr. | 4 | Pd her Bill to the order of the Widow of Mr Charles Broeta | 60 | 0 | 0 |
| Mar. | 1 | Pd Mr Needham the Bookseller a bill | 4 | 19 | 0 |
|  | 15 | Pd Mrs Peggy Cholmeley | 5 | 0 | 0 |
|  |  |  | 4408 | 11 | 0½ |

1742
RECEIPTS

| | | | £ | s. | d. |
|---|---|---|---|---|---|
| [Mar.] | 26 | Reced of the Earl of Shrewsbury for Mrs Anne Talbot | 6 | 6 | 0 |
| Apr. | 2 | Reced of Mrs Heneage Widow | 13 | 10 | 0 |
| | | Reced of Mr Wm Wollascott for Mrs Mary Wollascott | 5 | 0 | 0 |
| | 12 | Reced of Mr House for Mrs Isabella Rodbourne | 2 | 10 | 0 |
| | | | 4465 | 7 | 10 |
| May. | 7 | Reced of Mrs Porter | 87 | 1 | 3 |
| | 8 | Reced of Mrs Legard | 5 | 1 | 6 |
| | 12 | Reced of Mr Wm Sheldon £25 for Mrs More and £5 for Mrs Smith in all | 30 | 0 | 0 |
| | | Reced of Sr Hen: Tichborne for Mrs Is. Smith | 5 | 0 | 0 |
| | 15 | Reced of Mr Maire for Mrs Johnson | 6 | 0 | 0 |
| June. | 1 | Reced of Mrs Eliz. & Cassandra Willoughby for Mrs Betty Willoughby | 20 | 0 | 0 |
| | 4 | Reced of Edwd Weld Esqr for Mrs Jones's | 5 | 0 | 0 |
| | 21 | Reced of Lady Shrewsbury for Mrs Ann Talbot | 2 | 10 | 0 |
| July. | 3 | Reced of Mr Tunstall for his Sisters | 16 | 1 | 0 |
| | 6 | Reced of Mrs Monington £14 for Mrs Monington and £5 for Madame More | 19 | 0 | 0 |
| | 9 | Reced of Mrs Frances Wells for her Sisters | 30 | 0 | 0 |
| | 20 | Reced of Mr Trapps | 12 | 7 | 3 |
| | 21 | Reced of Mr Hinde | 1 | 2 | 0 |
| Augt. | 3 | Reced of Mr Thomas Stapleton | 5 | 0 | 0 |
| | 4 | Reced of Mrs Heneage | 12 | 1 | 0 |
| | 13 | Reced of Mr Mead for his Daughters | 32 | 0 | 0 |
| | 17 | Reced of Mr Berrington for the use of his Brother | 12 | 0 | 0 |
| | | Reced of Mrs Bostock for Mrs Carew | 1 | 1 | 0 |
| Oct. | 27 | Reced of Mr Palmes for Mrs Grace Palmes | 3 | 0 | 0 |
| | | Reced of Mrs Knight for Do. | 0 | 6 | 0 |

1742
PAYMENTS

|  |  |  | £ | s. | d. |
|---|---|---|---|---|---|
| June. | 2 | Pd Mrs Tunstall's bill to the order of the Widow of Mr Charles Broeta | 100 | 0 | 0 |
|  | 23 | Pd her Bill to the same order | 50 | 0 | 0 |
| July. | 22 | Pd Mr Needham a Bill on Mr Haydock's Account | 1 | 7 | 0 |
|  | 23 | Pd Myself two years Salary due the 20th of this month | 20 | 0 | 0 |
|  | 24 | Pd Mr Kirwood Mrs Tunstalls bill for | 1 | 0 | 0 |
|  | 26 | Pd her Bill to the order of Mr Cuthbert Haydocke | 18 | 10 | 0 |
| Augt. | 18 | Pd her Bill to the order of the Widow of Mr Charles Broeta | 50 | 0 | 0 |
| Sepr. | 23 | Pd Mr Kirwood | 0 | 16 | 0 |
|  | 25 | Pd Mr. Needham a Bill on Mr Haydock's Account | 0 | 9 | 3 |

| | | | £ | s. | d. |
|---|---|---|---|---|---|
| | 28 | Reced of Mr Wollascott half a year's Annuity due Mich last to his Sister | 5 | 0 | 0 |
| | 29 | Reced of Miss Ogle by Bill for Mrs Alicia Jones | 12 | 0 | 0 |
| | | | 4737 | 3 | 10 |
| Novr. | 18 | Reced of Mrs Margaret Cholmeley for Mrs Elizabeth Cholmeley | 5 | 0 | 0 |
| | 22 | Reced of Mr House for Mrs Rodbourne | 5 | 0 | 0 |
| | 24 | Reced of Mr Mead for his daughters | 2 | 2 | 0 |
| | 25 | Reced of Messrs Walton and Boag a year's Annuity due to Lady Katherine Radclyffe at Lady Day 1742 | 100 | 0 | 0 |
| | | Reced of Basil Bartlet Esqr | 10 | 0 | 0 |
| | | | 4859 | 5 | 10 |
| Decr. | 3 | Reced by the ballance of the above Acct. | 145 | 10 | 6½ |
| | 22 | Reced of Mr Bostock for Mrs Carew | 1 | 1 | 0 |
| | 23 | Reced of Thos Berrington Esqr for the use of Mr Joseph Berrington | 14 | 0 | 0 |
| Jan. | 4 | Reced of Lady Shrewsbury for Mrs Ann Talbot | 2 | 10 | 0 |
| | 5 | Reced of Mrs Betty and Cassandra Willoughby for Mrs Elizabeth Willoughby | 20 | 0 | 0 |
| Feb. | 9 | Reced of Mrs Helen Petre | 1 | 1 | 0 |
| | 21 | Reced of the Widow Heneage for her Daughter Miss Betty Heneage | 12 | 1 | 0 |
| | 25 | Reced of Lord Langdale | 5 | 0 | 0 |
| Mar. | 15 | Reced of Mr Rooksby for Mrs Margt Knight | 1 | 1 | 0 |
| | 16 | Reced of Mrs Legard for Mrs Johnson | 2 | 0 | 0 |
| | 24 | Reced of Mr Thos Berrington for Mr Joseph Berrington | 8 | 0 | 0 |

## 1743
## RECEIPTS

| | | | £ | s. | d. |
|---|---|---|---|---|---|
| Apr. | 14 | Reced of Mrs Mary Hill for Mrs Isabella Smith | 8 | 17 | 10 |
| | | | 221 | 2 | 4½ |
| | 22 | Reced of Mr Jesup for his daughter a Bill payable at 25 Days | | | |
| Sight | 50 | 0 | 0 | | |
| Sepr | 10 | Reced of Mr Yearsley for Mr Towneley | 20 | 0 | 0 |

| | | | £ | s. | d. |
|---|---|---|---|---|---|
| Novr. | 20 | Pd Mrs Towneley's Bill to the order of the Widow of Charles Broeta | 62 | 2 | 0 |
| | 25 | Pd Messrs Walton and Boag for return of the years Annuity reced p Contra for Lady Katherine Radclyffe | 1 | 0 | 0 |
| | | | 4713 | 15 | 3½ |
| Decr. | 3 | Remains in Mr Strickland's hands to ballance | 145 | 10 | 6½ |
| | | | 4859 | 5 | 10 |
| Jan. | 5 | Pd Mrs Towneley's bill to the order of the Widow of Charles Broeta | 100 | 0 | 0 |
| | 24 | Pd her bill to the order of Mr Broeta | 60 | 0 | 0 |
| Febr. | 21 | Pd her Bill to Mrs Mary Cholmley | 6 | 10 | 0 |

1743
PAYMENTS

| | £ | s. | d. |
|---|---|---|---|

| | | | | | |
|---|---|---|---|---|---|
| Oct. | 11 | Reced of Thomas Berrington Esqr for Mr Joseph Berrington | 5 | 0 | 0 |
| | | Reced of Mrs Helen Petre wch was paid me by Mr Ashmall 11th May 1742 but then forgot to be charged | 1 | 2 | 0 |
| | 15 | Reced of Mr Reynoldson for Mrs Grace Palmes | 3 | 0 | 0 |
| Novr. | 1 | Reced of Mrs Bostock for Mrs Carew | 1 | 1 | 0 |
| | | Reced Oct. 27th of Wm Wollascott Esqr for his Sister | 5 | 0 | 0 |
| | 11 | Reced of Messrs Walton & Boag a years Annuity due to Lady Catherine Radclyffe at Lady Day 1743 | 100 | 0 | 0 |
| | | Reced of Thomas Berington Esqr for Mr Joseph Berington | 13 | 0 | 0 |
| | 17 | Reced of Mr House for Mrs Rodbourne | 5 | 0 | 0 |
| | 22 | Reced of Lady Tichborne for Mrs Isabella Smith | 5 | 0 | 0 |
| | 28 | Reced of Mr. Williams of Helliwell for Mrs Monington | 1 | 11 | 0 |
| Decr. | 17 | Reced of Mr Franci[i]s Cholmeley for Mrs Eliza Cholmeley | 2 | 10 | 0 |
| | | Reced of Lady Shrewsbury for Mrs Ann Talbot | 2 | 10 | 0 |
| | 30 | Reced of Mrs Elizabeth & Cassandra Willoughby for Mrs Betty Willoughby | 20 | 0 | 0 |
| | | | 750 | 13 | 0½ |
| Jan. | 6 | Reced of Ld Langdale for Mrs Christina Towneley | 3 | 0 | 0 |
| | 17 | Reced of Mr Mead for Mrs Magrath | 37 | 19 | 0 |
| | 31 | Reced of Mrs Cath: Heneage for her Daughter | 12 | 1 | 0 |
| Feb. | 1 | Reced of Basil Bartlett Esqr for his Sister | 10 | 0 | 0 |
| | 10 | Reced of Mr Berington for his Brother | 12 | 0 | 0 |
| | 22 | Reced of Sr John Swinburne for his Daughter | 30 | 0 | 0 |
| | 28 | Reced of Mr Reily by Bill for Mr Edmd Reily | 5 | 11 | 1 |

| | | | | | |
|---|---|---|---|---|---|
| Oct. | 15 | Pd Mrs Towneley's Bill to the order of Mr Charles Broeta's Widow | 41 | 0 | 0 |
| Novr. | 11 | Pd Messrs Walton and Boag for return of the years Annuity reced p Contra for Lady Catherine Radclyffe | 1 | 0 | 0 |
| | 16 | Pd her Bill to the order of Mr Peter Brown | 5 | 16 | 0 |
| | 26 | Pd her Bill to the order of Mr Thos Stapleton | 2 | 2 | 0 |
| | 30 | Pd myself by Mrs Towneley's order for reassuring and Remitting £1500 of Lady Catherine Radclyffe's money at the rate of two Guineas for every hundred pounds | 31 | 10 | 0 |
| Decr. | 9 | Pd her bill to the order of the Widow of Mr Charles Broeta | 63 | 0 | 0 |
| | 21 | Pd her bill to the same order | 81 | 10 | 0 |
| | | Pd myself a years Salary due the 20th of last July | 10 | 0 | 0 |
| | | Pd Postage of Letters from the 12th of Decr. 1737 to the 12th of Decr. 1743 | 6 | 11 | 6 |
| | | | 730 | 13 | 4 |
| Jan. | 5 | Remains in Mr Stricklands hands to ballance | 19 | 19 | 8½ |
| | | | 750 | 13 | 0½ |

1744
RECEIPTS

|  |  |  | £ | s. | d. |
|---|---|---|---|---|---|
| Apr. | 4 | Reced of Mrs Bostock for Mrs Carew | 1 | 1 | 0 |
|  | 12 | Reced of Wm Wollascott Esqr for his Sister | 5 | 0 | 0 |
|  | 14 | Reced of Mrs Wollascott for her Sister | 1 | 1 | 0 |
| May. | 2 | Reced of Mr Yearsley | 40 | 0 | 0 |
|  | 4 | Reced of Mr Berington for his brother | 20 | 0 | 0 |
|  | 11 | Reced of Sr John Swinburne for his Daughter | 20 | 0 | 0 |
|  |  | Reced of Mrs Wells for Mrs Smith | 41 | 1 | 0 |
|  | 21 | Reced of Mar: Tunstall Esqr for his Sister | 15 | 0 | 0 |
| June. | 14 | Reced of Lady Shrewsbury for Miss ffitzpatricks | 18 | 8 | 6 |
|  |  | Reced of Do for Mrs Ann Talbot | 2 | 10 | 0 |
|  | 18 | Reced of Mrs Winifred Heneage for Mrs More | 5 | 0 | 0 |
|  | 21 | Reced of Mr Porter | 72 | 11 | 1¼ |
|  | 29 | Reced of Mrs Monington | 7 | 0 | 0 |
|  |  | Reced of Mr Rookby (as he saies) for the use of Mrs Margaret Knight, being money I forgot to charge myself with | 2 | 2 | 0 |
| July. | 18 | Reced of Mr Tuite for Mrs Isabella Jessup | 20 | 0 | 0 |
|  | 23 | Reced of Mrs Betty and Cassandra Willoughby for Mrs Eliz. Willoughby | 20 | 0 | 0 |
|  |  | Reced of Mr Francis Cholmeley for Mrs Elizabeth Cholmeley | 2 | 10 | 0 |
|  | 27 | Reced of Mrs Winifred Heneage for her Daughter | 12 | 1 | 0 |
|  |  |  | 415 | 16 | 8¼ |
| Augt. | 21 | Reced of Mrs Parry | 60 | 9 | 6 |
|  | 22 | Reced of Mrs Legard for Mrs Johnson | 2 | 0 | 0 |
|  | 24 | Reced of Mr Mead for Mrs Macgrath | 21 | 0 | 0 |
|  | 30 | Reced of Messrs Walton and Boag a year's Annuity due to the late Lady Catherine Radclyffe at Lady Day 1744 | 100 | 0 | 0 |

1744
PAYMENTS

| | | | £ | s. | d. |
|---|---|---|---|---|---|
| March. | 31 | Pd her bill to the order of Mr Bradley | 3 | 17 | 0 |
| Apr. | 20 | Pd her bill to the order of the Widow of Mr Charles Broeta | 125 | 0 | 0 |
| May. | 4 | Pd her bill to Mrs Margaret Cholmeley | 4 | 0 | 0 |
| July. | 4 | Pd her bill to the order of the Widow of Mr Charles Broeta | 44 | 13 | 0 |
| | 6 | Pd her bill to the same order | 100 | 0 | 0 |
| | | | 277 | 10 | 0 |
| Augt. | 29 | Pd her Bill to Mrs Mary Parry | 4 | 0 | 0 |
| | | ~~Pd Cousin Bodenham's bill to the order of Mr Henry Bostock~~ | ~~10~~ | ~~10~~ | ~~0~~ |
| | 30 | Pd Messrs Walton and Boag for return of the year's Annuity reced p Contra for Lady Catherine Radclyffe's Executor | 1 | 0 | 0 |

| | | | | | |
|---|---|---|---|---|---|
| | 31 | Reced of Mr Thos Berrington for Mr Joseph Berrington | 10 | 0 | 0 |
| Sepr. | 12 | Reced of Cuthbert Constable Esqr for Mrs Moore | 130 | 0 | 0 |
| | 26 | Reced of Mr Tuite for Mrs Isabella Jessup | 300 | 0 | 0 |
| | | Reced of Geo Palmes Esqr for Mrs Grace Palmes | 3 | 0 | 0 |
| | 28 | Reced of Sr John Swinburne for his Daughter | 5 | 0 | 0 |
| Oct. | 10 | Reced of Mr Nicholas Stapleton for his daughter | 5 | 0 | 0 |
| | 26 | Reced of Cuth Constable Esqr for Mrs Tunstalls | 25 | 0 | 0 |
| | | Reced of Mrs Bostock for Mrs Carew | 1 | 1 | 0 |
| | 30 | Reced of Ralph Crathorne Esqr | 12 | 0 | 0 |

[*No more transactions – Mannock Strickland died 19 November 1744*]

| | | | | | |
|---|---|---|---|---|---|
| Sepr. | 15 | Pd her bill to the order of the Widow of Mr Charles Broeta | 120 | 0 | 0 |
| Oct. | 10 | Pd her bill to the same order | 100 | 0 | 0 |
| | 13 | Pd her bill to the same order | 100 | 0 | 0 |
| | | Pd another of her bills to the same order | 100 | 0 | 0 |
| Novr. | 7 | Pd her bill to the same order | 100 | 0 | 0 |

# SPELLIKENS (DOMINICAN CONVENT), BRUSSELS: CASH DAY BOOK, 1728–44

|  |  | 1728 RECEIPTS | £ | s. | d. |
|---|---|---|---|---|---|
|  |  | Reced of B. Stonor by Mr. Shepherd | 100 | 0 | 0 |
| Oct. | 21 | Reced of his Grace of Powis half a years Annuity due to Mrs. Atmore at Mich. 1728 | 7 | 10 | 0 |

|  |  | 1729 RECEIPTS | £ | s. | d. |
|---|---|---|---|---|---|
| Novr. | 22 | Reced of Do. Half a years Interest of £1040. Secured to Lady Howard and due the 26th of December 1728 | 26 | 0 | 0 |
|  |  | Reced of Do. Half a years Annuity due to Mrs Atmore at Lady day 1729 | 7 | 10 | 0 |
|  |  |  | 141 | 0 | 0 |
|  |  | Reced by the balance of the above Acct | 34 | 5 | 1 |
| Febr. | 13 | Reced half a years Interest of the above £1040. due the 26th. of June 1729 | 26 | 0 | 0 |
|  |  | Reced by the balance of the above Acct | 34 | 5 | 1 |

## 1728 PAYMENTS

| | | | £ | s. | d. |
|---|---|---|---|---|---|
| Oct. | 21 | Pd. his Grace of Powis the balance of an Account | 105 | 3 | 11 |

## 1729 PAYMENTS

| | | | £ | s. | d. |
|---|---|---|---|---|---|
| July. | 3 | Pd. myself for drawing duty and Ingrosing of Lady Howard's Declaracon of Trust to Mrs. Parker | 1 | 1 | 0 |
| | | Pd. my Clerk for writing fair copies of the Bond Indenture & Declaracon of trust | 0 | 10 | 0 |
| | | | 106 | 14 | 11 |
| | | Remains due from me to ballance | 34 | 5 | 1 |
| | | | 141 | 0 | 0 |
| Dec. | 19 | Pd. by Mr. Cantillon's Bill on Mr. De Cleves for 309 Florins payable to Mrs. Barker's Order | 30 | 0 | 0 |
| | | Pd. myself by Mrs. Ellecker's order | 4 | 4 | 0 |
| Febr. | 17 | Pd. by Mr. Cantillon's Bill on Mr. De Cleves for 265 Florins payable to Mrs. Barker's Order | 26 | 0 | 0 |
| | | | 60 | 4 | 0 |
| | | Remains due from me to Ballance | 70 | 2 | 9 |
| | | | 130 | 6 | 9 |

## 1730 RECEIPTS

|        |    |                                                                                                                                                                                                        | £   | s. | d. |
|--------|----|--------------------------------------------------------------------------------------------------------------------------------------------------------------------------------------------------------|-----|----|----|
| Jan.   | 7  | Reced a years Interest of the said £1040 due the 26. of June 1730                                                                                                                                       | 52  | 0  | 0  |
|        |    | Reced a years Annuity due to Mrs Atmore at Lady day 1730                                                                                                                                                | 15  | 0  | 0  |
|        |    | Reced of Mr. Richd. Coffyn Interest for £80 lent the 1st. Of July last and £50. lent the 7th. of Augt. Last the sd £80. and £50. being part of £200. paid me the 26th of May last by Mr. Morgan Hansbie | 3   | 1  | 8  |
|        |    |                                                                                                                                                                                                        | 130 | 6  | 9  |

|  |  |  |  |  |  |
|--|--|--|--|--|--|
|  |  | Reced by ballance of my last Account | 70 | 2 | 9 |

## 1731 RECEIPTS

|        |    |                                                                                                                                        | £  | s.  | d. |
|--------|----|----------------------------------------------------------------------------------------------------------------------------------------|----|-----|----|
| June.  | 12 | Reced half a yrs Interest of the £1040. due the 26th of December 1730                                                                   | 26 | 0   | 0  |
|        |    | Reced a years Annuity due to Mrs. Atmore at Lady day 1731                                                                               | 15 | 0   | 0  |
| Febr.  | 2  | Reced of Mr. Paston half a years Interest of £200. Secured upon his Estate in the Name of Mr. Henry Cranmer and due the 15th. day of Sept last | 5  | 0   | 0  |
| March. | 1  | Reced by Mrs. Julia Browne's Bill on Mr. Standish Howard for 336. Gilders payable at ten days Sight to my order                         | 31 | 10  | 0  |

## 1732 RECEIPTS

|  |  |  | £ | s. | d. |
|--|--|--|---|----|----|
|  |  |  |   |    |    |

## 1730 PAYMENTS

|  |  |  | £ | s. | d. |
|---|---|---|---|---|---|
| Febr. | 9 | Pd. by Mr. Cantillon's Bill on Mr. De Cleves for 725 Florins payable to Madame Browne's Order | 70 | 2 | 9 |

## 1731 PAYMENTS

|  |  |  | £ | s. | d. |
|---|---|---|---|---|---|
| June. | 22 | Pd. by Do's Bill on Do. for 425 Florins payable to the same order | 41 | 0 | 0 |

## 1732 PAYMENTS

|  |  |  | £ | s. | d. |
|---|---|---|---|---|---|
| May. | 31 | Pd. by Do's Bill on Do. for 385 Florins payable to the same order | 36 | 10 | 0 |
|  |  | Pd. Mr. Cranmer upon his Executing the Declaracon of Trust to Mrs. Barker | 0 | 10 | 6 |
|  |  | Pd. myself for drawing Duty & writing the Declaracon of Trust | 1 | 1 | 0 |
|  |  | Pd. for Postage of Letters | 1 | 11 | 9 |
|  |  |  | 150 | 16 | 0 |
|  |  | Remains due from me to ballance | 58 | 16 | 9 |
|  |  |  | 209 | 12 | 9 |

## 1733 RECEIPTS

|  |  |  | £ | s. | d. |
|---|---|---|---|---|---|
| May. | 23 | Reced of his Grace of Powis a years Interest of the said £200. due the 15th. day of Sept 1732 | 52 | 0 | 0 |
|  |  | Reced of Mr. Paston a years Interest of the said £200. due the 15th. Day of Sept 1732 | 10 | 0 | 0 |
|  |  |  | 209 | 12 | 9 |
|  |  | Reced of Mr. Paston a years Interest of the said £200. due the 15th. Day of Sept 1732 | 10 | 0 | 0 |
|  |  |  | 209 | 12 | 9 |
| June. | 22 | Reced by ballance of my last Account | 58 | 16 | 9 |
| Novr. | 3 | Reced of Mr Paston a years Interest of £200 due the 15th day of Sepr last | 10 | 0 | 0 |

## 1734 RECEIPTS

|  |  |  | £ | s. | d. |
|---|---|---|---|---|---|
| July | 6 | Reced of Mr Segrave for the use of Miss Fanny Segrave | 375 | 0 | 0 |
| Novr. | 21 | Reced of Mr Hansbie for Mrs Yates | 20 | 0 | 0 |
| Jan. | 8 | Reced of Mrs Winifred Hyde by Mr Hansbie for Mrs Catherine Hyde | 120 | 0 | 0 |
|  | 18 | Reced of Do by Do for Do | 10 | 0 | 0 |
|  |  | Reced of Miss Andrew for Mrs Yates | 30 | 0 | 0 |
| March. | 9 | Reced of his Grace the Duke of Norfolk | 21 | 0 | 0 |
|  | 13 | Reced back the principal money put out upon Mrs Devereux's estate and Six months and 57 days Interes | 361 | 9 | 7 |

## 1733 PAYMENTS

| | | | £ | s. | d. |
|---|---|---|---|---|---|
| | | June 22d. 1733. Sent Mrs. Browne a Copy of this Account | | | |
| July. | 20 | Pd. Mrs Ellerker's Bill to the order of Mr. Charles Broeta's Widow | 58 | 0 | 0 |
| | | Pd myself by her order fo[r] Co[ach] hi[re] &c: | 0 | 16 | 9 |

## 1734 PAYMENTS

| | | | £ | s. | d. |
|---|---|---|---|---|---|
| June | 26 | Pd. Mr Penson for the use of Mrs Bennet | 10 | 0 | 0 |
| July. | 15 | Put out on a Security of Mrs Devereux's Estate at 5 p Cent Int | 350 | 0 | 0 |
| | 26 | Pd her Bill to the order of the Widow of Charles Broeta | 25 | 0 | 0 |
| Sepr. | 19 | Pd. Mr Richard Moreton for his trouble in attending to execute a Declaracon of trust to Mrs Chilton for the £350 | 0 | 10 | 6 |

## 1735 RECEIPTS

|          |    |                                                                                    | £    | s. | d. |
|----------|----|------------------------------------------------------------------------------------|------|----|----|
| May.     | 10 | Reced of his Grace of Powis 3 years Int of £1040 due the 26 of Decr 1734           | 156  | 0  | 0  |
|          | 14 | Reced of Mr Hansbie                                                                 | 16   | 1  | 0  |
| June.    | 3  | Reced of Do                                                                        | 23   | 19 | 0  |
| July.    | 4  | Reced of Do                                                                        | 15   | 6  | 9  |
| Oct.     | 27 | Reced of Mr Paston two years Interest of £200 due 26 June 1735                     | 20   | 0  | 0  |
| Jan.     | 8  | Reced of his Grace of Powis half a years Int of £1040 due 26 June 1735            | 26   | 0  | 0  |
|          | 15 | Reced of Mr Arthur for Mrs Howard together with a Seal                             | 3    | 3  | 0  |

## 1736 RECEIPTS

|          |    |                                                                                    | £    | s. | d. |
|----------|----|------------------------------------------------------------------------------------|------|----|----|
| May.     | 4  | Reced of Mr Wright two years Int of the three India Bonds in his hands             | 21   | 0  | 0  |
|          |    | Reced of his Grace of Powis half a yers Int of £1040 due 26 Decr 1735             | 26   | 0  | 0  |
|          |    |                                                                                    | 1313 | 16 | 1  |
|          |    | Reced by the balance of my last Account                                            | 27   | 11 | 4  |
| Oct.     | 23 | Reced of Mr Wright a years Int of £300 India bonds in his hands                    | 10   | 10 | 0  |

## 1735 PAYMENTS

| | | | £ | s. | d. |
|---|---|---|---|---|---|
| Mar | 31 | Pd. Mrs Mary Dod money lent on a Mortgage of Mr Kingdon's Estate in Somersetshire dat 25th of March | 291 | 0 | 0 |
| June | 12 | Pd Mrs Ellerker's Bill to the order of the Widow of Mr Charles Broeta | 125 | 0 | 0 |
| Augt. | 30 | Pd. Mr Penson for the use of Mrs Bennet | 9 | 10 | 0 |
| Decr. | 23 | Pd Do for the use of Do | 9 | 0 | 0 |
| Jan. | 15 | Pd Mr Arthur for Postage of Letters | 0 | 2 | 6 |
| | | Pd. Mr Daniel Axtell upon an Assignmt of a Security on Mr Paston's estate in Norfolk which bears date the 4th of June 1735 and carries Interest from that Day | 200 | 0 | 0 |
| | | Pd. Mr Edward Walpole upon Security of his Bond and Judgement the bond bearing date the 9th of Sepr 1735 from which day the same Carries Interest | 200 | 0 | 0 |
| | | Pd myself a Bill for business | 6 | 7 | 6 |
| | | Pd postage of Letters &c | 0 | 17 | 6 |
| | | Remains due from me to Ballance | 27 | 11 | 4 |
| | | | 1313 | 16 | 1 |

## 1736 PAYMENTS

| | | | £ | s. | d. |
|---|---|---|---|---|---|
| Sepr. | 10 | Pd Mrs Elleckers Bill to the order of Mr Nettien | 27 | 11 | 4 |

| | | | £ | s. | d. |
|---|---|---|---|---|---|
| Novr. | 13 | Reced by half a years Int of £291 Securd by Mr Kingdon's Mortgage and due at Mich 1735 | 6 | 11 | 0 |
| | 15 | Reced of his Grace of Powis Nine months and 50 days Int of £1040 due this day | 46 | 2 | 2 |
| Decr. | 22 | Reced of Mr Shuttleworth for Mrs Young | 1 | 0 | 0 |
| Febr. | 14 | Reced of his Grace the Duke of Norfolk money secur'd upon his Grace the Duke of Powis's estate | 1040 | 0 | 0 |
| | | Reced of Mr Paston a years Interest of £200 due the 15th of Sepr 1736 | 10 | 0 | 0 |
| | | Reced of Mr Paston a years Int of other £200 due the 4th of June 1736 | 10 | 0 | 0 |

## 1737 RECEIPTS

| | | | £ | s. | d. |
|---|---|---|---|---|---|
| Apr. | 27 | Reced of Mrs Dicconson by bill from Mr John Chadwick for Miss Ursula Short | 50 | 0 | 0 |
| | | | 1201 | 14 | 6 |

| | | | £ | s. | d. |
|---|---|---|---|---|---|
| Jan. | 22 | Pd Mr Wood for the use of Mr Park | 9 | 10 | 0 |
| | | Pd Mr Hansbie by Mrs Elleckers order | 3 | 3 | 0 |
| | 31 | Pd Mrs Chilton's bill to the order of Mr Nettien | 40 | 0 | 0 |
| March | 19 | Pd the Rt Honble the Ld Petre upon a bond taken in my Name, which carries Interest from this day at 4 p Cent | 1000 | 0 | 0 |
| Jan. | 22 | Pd Mr Wood for the use of Mr Park | 9 | 10 | 0 |

### 1737 PAYMENTS

| | | | £ | s. | d. |
|---|---|---|---|---|---|
| May. | 5 | Pd Mr Hansbie by Mrs Chilton's order | 1 | 0 | 0 |
| | | | 1081 | 4 | 4 |
| | | Remains due from me to ballance | 120 | 10 | 2 |
| | | | 1201 | 14 | 6 |

Sepr 2d. Sent Mrs Chilton a Copy of this Account

| | | | £ | s. | d. |
|---|---|---|---|---|---|
| Sepr. | 2 | Reced by the balance of the above Acct | 120 | 10 | 2 |
| | | Reced of Mr Anthony Wright by the Sale of three India Bonds put into his hands by Mr Henry Bostock, which money was paid me by Mr Wright the 25th ffebr 1736 | 318 | 3 | 4 |
| | | Reced of Mr Watkinson which was pd me the 13th of June last | 20 | 0 | 0 |
| | 9 | Reced of Mr Edwd Walpole the Principal and two years Int due this day upon his Bond and Judgement | 220 | 0 | 0 |
| Jan. | 16 | Reced of Lord Petre half a years Int of £10000 due the 19 day of Sepr last | 20 | 0 | 0 |
| | | | 698 | 13 | 6 |
| Jan. | 20 | Reced by the ballance of the last Account | 395 | 1 | 10 |
| Feb. | 16 | Reced of Mr Morris | 20 | 0 | 0 |

### 1738 RECEIPTS

| | | | £ | s. | d. |
|---|---|---|---|---|---|
| Apr. | 22 | Reced of Mr Watkinson | 0 | 10 | 6 |

| | | | £ | s. | d. |
|---|---|---|---|---|---|
| Feb. | 25 | Pd Cousin Jerry Strickland principal money Secured to him upon Mr Paston's Estate in the name of Mr. Henry Cranmer which Cousin Jerry Assigned to me and Carries Int at 5 p Cent from the 25th Febr 1736 | 300 | 0 | 0 |
| Mar. | 16 | Pd Mr Gyles for the Adminsitracon taken out by the Duke of Norfolk to the Lady Howard his Mother | 3 | 11 | 8 |
| | | | 303 | 11 | 8 |
| Jan. | 20 | Remains due from Mr Strickland to balance | 395 | 1 | 10 |
| | | | 698 | 13 | 6 |
| | | Sent Mrs Winifred Hyde a Copy of this Account | | | |
| Sepr. | 28 | Pd Madame Chilton's Bill to the order of Mr Nettien by Mr Wright | 50 | 10 | 0 |
| Febr. | 9 | Pd Mrs Hyde's Bill to the order of Mr Nettine | 30 | 0 | 0 |
| | 10 | Pd Mr Bostock money overpaid by him when he Delivered the 3 India bonds into Mr Wright's hands | 8 | 18 | 10 |

### 1738 PAYMENTS

| | | | £ | s. | d. |
|---|---|---|---|---|---|
| Apr. | 10 | Pd Mr Wood for the use of Mr Park | 10 | 10 | 0 |
| | 17 | Pd Mrs Chilton's Bill to the order of Mr Nettien | 100 | 0 | 0 |
| | 25 | Pd Lady Jernegan principal money Secured to her in the Name of Mr Moreton on Lady Carington's estate wch Lady Jernegan Assigned to me and carries Int at 4 p Cent from this day | 200 | 0 | 0 |

| | | | | | |
|---|---|---|---|---|---|
| July. | 14 | Reced of Do. | 110 | 0 | 0 |
| | | Reced of Lord Petre half a years Int of £10000 due the 19th day of March last | 20 | 0 | 0 |
| Novr. | 4 | Reced of Do the same due 19th day of Sepr. last | 20 | 0 | 0 |
| | 8 | Reced of Mr Watkinson for his Daughter | 5 | 5 | 0 |
| Decr. | 1 | Reced from the late Mr Paston's estate a yrs Int of £200 due 4th June 1737 | 10 | 0 | 0 |
| | | Reced from Do. a year's Int of £200 due 15th Sepr 1737 | 10 | 0 | 0 |
| | | | 590 | 17 | 4 |
| Decr. | 1 | Reced by the ballance of the above Acct | 145 | 5 | 0 |
| | | Reced from the late Mr Paston's estate Int of £300 from the 25th of Febr 1736 to the 15th Sepr 1737, being 6 Months and 20 days | 8 | 6 | 6 |
| | 29 | Reced of Mr Morris | 150 | 0 | 0 |
| | | Reced of Do for Mrs Fuller | 3 | 3 | 0 |
| Jan. | 18 | Reced of Mr Watkinson | 0 | 10 | 6 |

## 1739 RECEIPTS

| | | | £ | s. | d. |
|---|---|---|---|---|---|
| May. | 25 | Reced the ballance of the precedent Account | 257 | 5 | 0 |
| Augt. | 9 | Reced of Ld Petre principal money lent him on Bond and Mortgage | 1000 | 0 | 0 |
| | | Reced of his Lordship the Interest thereof at 4 p Cent from the 19th day of Sepr 1738 to the 9th day of Augt 1739, being Nine Months and 51 days | 35 | 11 | 9 |
| Sepr. | 6 | Reced of Mr Watkinson for his daughter | 0 | 10 | 6 |
| Decr. | 21 | Reced of Lady Carington a years and half's Interest of £200 due the 25th day of October last | 12 | 0 | 0 |

| | | | £ | s. | d. |
|---|---|---|---|---|---|
| Augt. | 4 | Pd Madame Chilton's Bill to the order of Mr Nettine | 45 | 13 | 6 |
| | | | 445 | 12 | 4 |
| Decr. | 1 | Remains due from me to ballance | 145 | 5 | 0 |
| | | | 590 | 17 | 4 |
| Decr. | 29 | Pd Mr Cantillon for a Bill upon Mr De Cleves at Brussels for 525 Florins | 50 | 0 | 0 |

### 1739 PAYMENTS

| | | | £ | s. | d. |
|---|---|---|---|---|---|
| May | 25 | Remains due from me to ballance | 257 | 5 | 0 |
| | | | 307 | 5 | 0 |
| June. | 7 | Pd Mrs Chilton's Bill to the order of Mr Nettine | 257 | 5 | 0 |
| Novr. | 6 | Pd Mr John Park's bill to the order of Mr Wm Wood | 10 | 0 | 0 |
| Sepr. | 29 | Pd Lord Arundell upon a Security taken in my Name, which Carries Interest at 4 p Cent from this Day | 1000 | 0 | 0 |

| Feb. | 9 | Reced of Mr Watkinson for his daughter | 0 | 10 | 6 |
| Mar. | 20 | Reced of Mr Kingdon by Mr Hoar on Account of Interest | 16 | 19 | 2½ |
| | | Reced of Mrs Hyde by Mr Edward Diccon-son's Bill upon Mr Wm Newton | 50 | 0 | 0 |

## 1740 RECEIPTS

| | | | £ | s. | d. |
|---|---|---|---|---|---|
| Apr. | 9 | Reced of the Duke of Norfolk for Mr Bernard Howards three Daughters | 3 | 3 | 0 |
| Sepr. | 12 | Reced of Mr Watkinson for his daughter | 1 | 4 | 0 |
| Decr. | 5 | Reced of Ld Arundell a year's Int of £1000 due 29th Sepr last | 40 | 0 | 0 |
| | 27 | Reced of Mr Kingdon in full for Int at 4½ p Cent of £291 to the 25th of March 1740 | 41 | 19 | 3½ |
| Febr. | 2 | Reced of Mr Watkinson for his daughter | 1 | 14 | 6 |

## 1741 RECEIPTS

| | | | £ | s. | d. |
|---|---|---|---|---|---|
| Oct. | 8 | Reced of Lady Carington a years and half's Interest of £200 due the 25th day of April 1741 | 12 | 0 | 0 |
| | | | 1472 | 17 | 9 |
| Oct. | 8 | Reced from the late Mr Paston's estate four years Interest of £200 part of £208 due 4th of June 1741 | 40 | 0 | 0 |
| | | Reced from the same estate four years Interest of £500 due 15 Sepr 1741 | 100 | 0 | 0 |
| | | | 1612 | 17 | 9 |
| | 23 | Reced by the ballance of the above Acct. | 23 | 3 | 1½ |
| Jan. | 9 | Reced of Miss Andrew | 25 | 0 | 0 |

| | | | £ | s. | d. |
|---|---|---|---|---|---|
| Jan. | 31 | Pd Mrs Sarsfield's Bill to the order of Mr Nettine | 38 | 2 | 3 |

### 1740 PAYMENTS

| | | | £ | s. | d. |
|---|---|---|---|---|---|
| Apr. | 23 | Pd Mrs Young's Bill to the same order | 67 | 9 | 8½ |
| July. | 22 | Pd Messrs Fitzgerald and Co by the order of Mrs Mary Rosa Howard | 3 | 3 | 0 |
| Oct. | 23 | Pd Mrs Young's Bill to the order of Mr Nettine | 50 | 0 | 0 |
| Jan. | 17 | Pd her bill to the same order | 50 | 0 | 0 |
| Mar. | 16 | Pd Mr Wood for the use of Mr John Parks | 10 | 0 | 0 |

### 1741 PAYMENTS

| | | | £ | s. | d. |
|---|---|---|---|---|---|
| Oct. | 8 | Pd her Bill to the order of Mr Nettine | 100 | 0 | 0 |
| | | Pd for Protest of sd Bill, Rechange, Commission and Postage | 2 | 3 | 0 |
| | | | 1588 | 2 | 11½ |
| | | Pd Postage of Letters from the beginning of the year 1736 to the 8th of October 1741 | 1 | 11 | 8 |
| | | | 2589 | 14 | 7½ |
| | | Remains due from Mr Strickland to ballance | 23 | 3 | 1½ |
| | | | 1612 | 17 | 9 |
| | | Oct 23d. 1741. Sent Mrs Hyde a copy of this Account. M.S. | | | |
| Decr. | 1 | Pd Mr John Parks by Mr. Wm Wood | 10 | 0 | 0 |

## 1742 RECEIPTS

|  |  |  | £ | s. | d. |
|---|---|---|---|---|---|
| Mar. | 27 | Reced of Do | 10 | 0 | 0 |
|  |  | Reced of Mr Kingdon two years Int of £291 due 25th Mar 1742 | 26 | 3 | 9½ |
| June. | 1 | Reced of Lord Arundell a yrs Int of £200 due 29th Sepr. 1741 | 40 | 0 | 0 |
| July. | 30 | Reced of Lady Carington a year's Int of £200 due 25th Apr. 1742 | 8 | 0 | 0 |
|  |  | Reced from the late Mr Paston's estate a years Int of £200 pt of £208 due 4th of June 1742 | 8 | 0 | 0 |
| Novr. | 18 | Reced of Mr Edward Dicconson for Mrs Ann Short | 70 | 0 | 0 |
| Decr. | 22 | Reced of Miss Andrew | 5 | 5 | 0 |

## 1743 RECEIPTS

|  |  |  | £ | s. | d. |
|---|---|---|---|---|---|
| July. | 23 | Reced of Cath Lady Petre | 10 | 0 | 0 |
|  |  |  | 225 | 11 | 11 |
| Oct. | 27 | Reced of Ld Arundel a year & four Months, wanting four Days, Interest of £1000 due 25th Jan. 1742, from which time the Interest will be paid by his Grace of Powis | 52 | 17 | 10 |
|  |  | Reced of Lady Carington a years Int of £200 due 25th Apr. 1743 | 8 | 0 | 0 |
|  |  | Reced from late Mr Paston's estate two years Int of £500 due 15th Sepr 1743 | 40 | 0 | 0 |
|  |  | Reced from the same estate a yrs Interest of £200 pt of £208 due 4th June 1743 | 8 | 0 | 0 |
|  |  |  | 334 | 9 | 9 |
| Oct. | 27 | Reced of Ld Arundel a year & four Months, wanting four Days, Interest of £1000 due 25th Jan. 1742, from which time the Interest will be paid by his Grace of Powis | 52 | 17 | 10 |
|  |  | Reced of Lady Carington a years Int of £200 due 25th Apr. 1743 | 8 | 0 | 0 |

## 1742 PAYMENTS

|  |  |  | £ | s. | d. |
|---|---|---|---|---|---|
| May. | 3 | Pd Mrs Young's Bill to the order of Mr Nettine | 50 | 0 | 0 |
|  | 28 | Pd Mr Lovett by Mrs Young's order | 5 | 5 | 0 |
| Oct. | 7 | Pd Mrs Winifred Hyde's bill to the order of Mr Nettine | 75 | 1 | 11 |
| Jan. | 21 | Pd Mrs Young's bill to the same order | 65 | 6 | 0 |
| Feb. | 9 | Pd Mr John Park by Mr. Wm Wood | 10 | 0 | 0 |

## 1743 PAYMENTS

|  |  |  | £ | s. | d. |
|---|---|---|---|---|---|
| Oct. | 26 | Pd Mrs Margaret Compton's Bill to the order of Mr Nettine | 100 | 0 | 0 |
|  |  |  | 315 | 11 | 11 |

| | | | £ | s. | d. |
|---|---|---|---|---|---|
| ffeb. | 3 | Reced by the ballance of the last Account | 18 | 4 | 10 |
| | 15 | Reced of his Grace of Powis half a years Interest of £1000 due 25th July 1743 | 20 | 0 | 0 |

## 1744 RECEIPTS

| | | | £ | s. | d. |
|---|---|---|---|---|---|
| May | 30 | Reced of Do half a years Int of the same £1000 due 25th Jan. 1743 | 20 | 0 | 0 |
| Sepr | 27 | Reced of Mr Shuttleworth for Mrs Young | 1 | 1 | 0 |

*[No more transactions: Mannock Strickland died 19 November 1744]*

|  |  |  | £ | s. | d. |
|---|---|---|---|---|---|
|  |  | Pd Postage of Letters from the 8th of October 1741. to the 3d of ffebr. 1743 | 0 | 18 | 0 |
|  |  |  | 316 | 4 | 11 |
| ffebr. | 3 | Remains due from Mr Strickland to ballance | 18 | 4 | 10 |
|  |  |  | 334 | 9 | 9 |
|  |  | ffebr. 3d 1743. Sent Mrs. Compton a Copy of this Account M.S. |  |  |  |
| March | 12 | Pd her bill to the order of Mr Nettine | 18 | 4 | 10 |
|  |  | Pd Postage of Letters from the 8th of October 1741. to the 3d of ffebr. 1743 | 0 | 18 | 0 |
|  |  |  | 316 | 4 | 11 |

### 1744 PAYMENTS

|  |  |  | £ | s. | d. |
|---|---|---|---|---|---|
| June | 9 | Pd Mrs Margaret Compton's bill to the order of Mr Nettin | 20 | 0 | 0 |
| July. | 5 | Pd Mr John Park by Mr Wm Wood | 10 | 0 | 0 |

# BENEDICTINES, DUNKIRK: CASH DAY BOOK, 1727–44

To the Lady Fletewood

### 1727 RECEIPTS

|  |  |  | £ | s. | d. |
|---|---|---|---|---|---|
|  |  | Reced of Mr Berkeley p Bill on Mr Wright | 60 | 0 | 0 |
| March. | 6 | Reced of Mr. Culcheth | 3 | 13 | 6 |

### 1728 RECEIPTS

|  |  |  | £ | s. | d. |
|---|---|---|---|---|---|
| [March] | 28 | Reced p Lady Fletewood's Bill on Mr. Wright | 25 | 0 | 0 |
|  |  | Reced p Mrs Pulton's Bill on Do. | 2 | 10 | 0 |
|  | 30 | Reced of Mrs Sanders half a years Annuity due to Mrs Eliz. Pulton at Lady day 1728 | 5 | 6 | 0 |
| Apr. | 4 | Reced of Mr Culcheth | 5 | 0 | 0 |
| May. | 28 | Reced of Talbot Stonor Esqr p Mr. Shepherd Mrs. Ann Vincent's Legacy | 20 | 0 | 0 |
|  |  | Reced of Mr. Sheldon for Miss Fermors | 45 | 0 | 0 |
| July. | 17 | Reced of Mr. Henry Sheldon for Mr. Simon Scroop | 20 | 0 | 0 |
|  | 20 | Reced of Mr Culcheth p Bill Bate on Newark to the order of John Hesketh | 40 | 0 | 0 |
|  | 25 | Reced of Mr. Stewart | 10 | 0 | 0 |
|  | 27 | Reced of Mr. Caryll | 20 | 0 | 0 |
|  | 29 | Reced of the Dutchess of Northumberland for Mrs. Cecilia Fitzroy | 5 | 0 | 0 |
| Augt. | 12 | Reced of Br. Strickland a years pention for my Mother | 30 | 0 | 0 |
|  | 28 | Reced of Mr. Berkeley p Bill on Mr. Wright | 40 | 0 | 0 |
|  |  |  | 341 | 9 | 6 |

## 1727 PAYMENTS

| | | | £ | s. | d. |
|---|---|---|---|---|---|

## 1728 PAYMENTS

| | | | £ | s. | d. |
|---|---|---|---|---|---|
| Apr. | 2 | Paid Mrs. Hyde her Bill to the order of Mr. Mathieu Fournie for | 60 | 0 | 0 |
| | | Paid her Bill to the order of Mr. Fitzgerald | 50 | 0 | 0 |
| June | 4 | Pd. her Bill to the order of Capt. Smith | 20 | 0 | 0 |
| Augt. | 26 | Pd. her Bill to the order of Mr. Malliard Du-fumier | 45 | 0 | 0 |
| | 30 | Pd. her Bill to the same order | 100 | 0 | 0 |

| | | | £ | s. | d. |
|---|---|---|---|---|---|
| Sept. | 2 | Reced of Mr. Caryll | 50 | 0 | 0 |
| Oct. | 5 | Reced of Mr. Caryll | 33 | 9 | 9 |
| | 19 | Reced of Mrs. Saunders half a years Annuity due to Mrs. Eliz. Pulton at Mich. 1728 | 6 | 12 | 6 |
| | 21 | Reced by money paid my Sister Catherine by my order | 2 | 2 | 0 |
| Novr. | 14 | Reced of Mr Caryll for Dame Mary Benedict | 5 | 0 | 0 |
| Decr. | 14 | Reced of Mr Caryll for Dame Benedict | 1 | 1 | 0 |
| | | Received of Mrs. Catherine Pearse | 20 | 0 | 0 |
| | | Received of Mr. Berkeley | 12 | 2 | 0 |
| Janry | 20 | Received of Mr. Maire for Mrs. Winny Fermor | 1 | 1 | 0 |
| | 22 | Reced by Mrs. Mary Southcott's Bill on Mr. Culcheth | 8 | 0 | 0 |
| | 28 | Reced by her Ladyship's Bill on Mrs. Wright | 28 | 0 | 0 |
| | | Reced by Mrs. Pulton's Bill on Do. | 2 | 0 | 0 |
| | 29 | Reced of Mr. Berkeley by Bill on Mr. Wright | 20 | 0 | 0 |
| | 30 | Reced of Mr. Culcheth 40s. for his sister and 40s. for Mrs. Holliwell in all | 4 | 0 | 0 |
| Febry. | 7 | Reced of Mr Caryll | 20 | 0 | 0 |
| March. | 17 | Reced of Mr. Sheldon by Mr. Vaux for Mistress Fermors | 45 | 0 | 0 |

## 1729 RECEIPTS

| | | | £ | s. | d. |
|---|---|---|---|---|---|
| Apr. | | Reced of her Ladyship a Bill on Mrs. Wright | 28 | 0 | 0 |
| | | Reced by Mrs. Pulton's Bill on Do. | 2 | 0 | 0 |
| | | | 629 | 17 | 9 |
| May. | 14 | Reced of Mr. Naylor by Bill for the use of Mrs. Alice Gregson | 10 | 0 | 0 |
| | 23 | Reced of Mrs. Saunders half a years Annuity due to Mrs. Eliz. Pulton at Lady Day 1729 | 6 | 12 | 6 |
| June. | 30 | Reced of Mr. Hardcastle for Mrs. Alice Gregson | 1 | 1 | 0 |
| July. | 2 | Reced by Mr. Wyke's promisory Note to Lady Dowager Petre | 20 | 0 | 0 |
| | 5 | Reced of Mr. Caryll by Bill on Mr. Odearn | 20 | 0 | 0 |
| | 14 | Reced by Mrs. Catherine O'Brien's Bill on Mr. Andrew Crotty | 50 | 0 | 0 |
| | 16 | Reced of Mr. Berkeley by Bill on Mr. Wright | 25 | 0 | 0 |

| Sept. | 26 | Pd. her Bill to the order of Mr. William Uré for | 49 | 0 | 0 |
| Oct. | 8 | Pd. Mr. Simon Scroop's Bill to the order of Capt. John Smith | 20 | 0 | 0 |
| | 26 | Pd. her Bill to the order of Do. | 40 | 0 | 0 |
| Novr. | 19 | Pd. her Bill to the order of Mr. Fournie | 40 | 0 | 0 |
| Janry. | 27 | Pd. her Bill to the order of the Widow Talle-ment | 40 | 0 | 0 |
| Febry. | 5 | Pd. her Bill to the same order | 33 | 0 | 0 |
| March. | 7 | Pd. her Bill to the order of Mr. Fournie | 44 | 0 | 0 |

### 1729 PAYMENTS

| | | | £ | s. | d. |
|---|---|---|---|---|---|
| Apr. | 29 | Pd. her Bill to the order of Mr. Dufumier | 75 | 0 | 0 |
| July. | 15 | Pd. her Bill to the order of Capt. John Smith | 30 | 0 | 0 |

| | | | £ | s | d |
|---|---|---|---|---|---|
| | 28 | Reced by another Bill of Mrs. Catherine O'Brien's on Mr. Andrew Crotty | 50 | 0 | 0 |
| Sept 13th 1739 | | Deduct the money menconed here to be Reced for Mr Simon Scroop | 20 | 0 | 0 |
| | | Sept. 13th 1729 Sent Mrs Sheldon a Copy of this Account | | | |
| Sept. | 3 | Reced of Mr. Berkeley by Bill on Mr. Wright | 40 | 0 | 0 |
| | | | 852 | 11 | 3 |
| | | Deduct the money menconed here to be Reced for Mr. Simon Scroop | 20 | 0 | 0 |
| | | | 832 | 11 | 3 |
| | | Sept. 15th. 1729. Sent Mrs. Sheldon a Copy of this Account. | | | |
| Sept. | 15 | Reced by the ballance of my last Acct. | 160 | 6 | 5 |
| | 25 | Reced of Mr Stewart money paid him by Mr. Berkeley's order | 21 | 1 | 0 |
| Novr. | 4 | Reced of Mrs. Saunders half a years Annuity due to Mrs. Pulton at Mich. 1729 | 6 | 12 | 6 |
| | 6 | Reced of Lady Fletewood by Bill on Mrs. Wright | 28 | 0 | 0 |
| | | Reced by Mrs. Pulton's Bill on Do. | 2 | 0 | 0 |
| | 8 | Reced of Mr Caryll by Bill on Mr. Thomas Odiarne £50 for Lady Fletewood £5 for Mrs. Romana Caryll and £5 for Mrs. Arabella Caryll In all | 60 | 0 | 0 |
| | 24 | Reced of Mr. Berkeley by Bill on Mr. Wright | 18 | 0 | 0 |
| Decr. | 30 | Reced of Mr. Culcheth | 5 | 3 | 6 |
| Janry. | 2 | Reced of the Duke of Norfolk by Mr. Lawson | 10 | 0 | 0 |
| | 19 | Reced of Mr. Sheldon by Bill on Mr. Wright | 40 | 0 | 0 |
| | 26 | Reced of Mr. Stewart | 100 | 0 | 0 |

| | | | | | |
|---|---|---|---|---|---|
| Augt. | 6 | Pd. her Bill to the order of Mr. Fournie | 33 | 0 | 0 |
| | | Pd. her Bill to the order of Mr. Keeting | 12 | 0 | 0 |
| | | Pd. in Postage of Letters Messengers and other petty Expences | 1 | 4 | 10 |
| | | Deduct the money menconed here to be paid to Mr. Simon Scroop's order | 20 | 0 | 0 |
| | | | 692 | 4 | 10 |
| | | Remains due to Ballance | 160 | 6 | 5 |
| | | | 832 | 11 | 3 |
| Sept. | 27 | Pd. her Ladyship's Bill to the order of Mr. Mathieu Fournie | 40 | 0 | 0 |
| Oct. | 25 | Pd. her Bill to the order of Mr. Mat. Fournie | 70 | 0 | 0 |
| | 30 | Pd. her Bill to the order of Mr. Mat. Fournie | 100 | 0 | 0 |
| Decr. | 3 | Pd. her Bill to the order of Capt. Maples | 10 | 0 | 0 |
| | 18 | Pd. her Bill to the order of Mr. Wm. Uré | 50 | 0 | 0 |
| Janry. | 23 | Pd. her Bill to the order of Capt. Mayple | 30 | 0 | 0 |

|         |    |                                                                                          | £   | s. | d. |
|---------|----|------------------------------------------------------------------------------------------|-----|----|----|
|         |    | Reced by money paid my Sister Catherine by my order                                      | 2   | 2  | 0  |
| Febry.  | 9  | Reced of Mr. Berkeley by Bill on Mr. Wright                                               | 48  | 18 | 0  |
| March.  | 2  | Reced of Mr Edwd. Caryll for his Sisters                                                  | 2   | 2  | 0  |
|         | 3  | Reced of Mr. Sheldon by Mr. Gage for Miss Fermour                                         | 20  | 0  | 0  |
|         |    |                                                                                          | 524 | 5  | 5  |
|         |    | March 16. 1729. Sent Mrs. Sheldon a copy of this Account                                  |     |    |    |
| March.  | 16 | Reced by the ballance of my last Account.                                                 | 84  | 9  | 7  |

## 1730 RECEIPTS

|         |    |                                                                                          | £  | s. | d. |
|---------|----|------------------------------------------------------------------------------------------|----|----|----|
| Apr.    | 10 | Reced by Mrs. Saunders half a years Annuity due to Mrs. Pulton at Lady day 1730          | 6  | 12 | 6  |
| May.    | 9  | Reced of Mr Sheldon by Mr. Mander for the use of Mrs. Catherine Sheldon                  | 12 | 10 | 0  |
| Augt.   | 7  | Reced of Mrs Englefield by Mr. Webbe for the use of Miss Betty Englefield                | 22 | 0  | 0  |
| Sep.    | 14 | Reced of Mr. Sheldon by Bill on Mr. Wright                                                | 20 | 0  | 0  |
|         | 16 | Reced of Mr. Tho: Berkeley by Mr. R. Sheldon                                              | 23 | 0  | 0  |
| Oct.    | 23 | Reced of Mr. Sheldon by Mr. Vaux for Mrs. Mary Fermor                                     | 27 | 0  | 0  |
|         |    | Reced of her Ladyship a Bill on Mr. Wright                                                | 26 | 0  | 0  |
|         |    | Reced by Mrs. Pulton's Bill on Do.                                                        | 2  | 0  | 0  |
| Novr.   | 3  | Reced of the Dutchess of Northumberland for Mrs. Cecilia Fitzroy                          | 5  | 0  | 0  |
|         | 16 | Reced of Mr. Caryll by Bill on Mr. Wright for the use of Mrs. Mary and Ms. Arabella Caryll | 10 | 0  | 0  |
|         |    | Reced of Do. by Bill on Mr. Odiarne for the use of Lady Fletewood                        | 20 | 0  | 0  |
| Decr.   | 21 | Reced of Mr. Sheldon by young Mr. Mander                                                  | 12 | 10 | 0  |
| Janry.  | 11 | Reced of Mr. Berkeley by Bill on Mr. Wright                                               | 17 | 6  | 6  |

| | | | £ | s. | d. |
|---|---|---|---|---|---|
| Feb. | 5 | Pd. her Bill to the order of the Widow Tallement | 48 | 0 | 0 |
| | | Pd. her Bill to the Order of Richd. Jackson | 60 | 0 | 0 |
| | | Pd. her Bill to the order of the Widow Marcade | 31 | 15 | 10 |
| | | | 439 | 15 | 10 |
| | | Remains due to Ballance | 84 | 9 | 7 |
| | | | 524 | 5 | 5 |

---

### 1730 PAYMENTS

| | | | £ | s. | d. |
|---|---|---|---|---|---|
| March. | 30 | Pd. her Ladyship's Bill to the order of the widow Marcade | 48 | 4 | 2 |
| Sept. | 28 | Pd. her Bill to the order of [¦¦i¦blank¦i¦¦] | 58 | 0 | 0 |
| Oct. | 31 | Pd. her Bill to the order of Wm. Keeting | 50 | 0 | 0 |
| Decemr | 10 | Pd. her Bill to the order of Mr. Nicolas Francis Doncquers | 72 | 0 | 0 |

| Febry. | 3 | Reced of Mr. Roger Meynel by Mr. Ralph Sheldon | 20 | 0 | 0 |
|---|---|---|---|---|---|
| | 24 | Reced of Lady Jernegan by Mr Phillips for Mrs. Margaret Paston | 1 | 1 | 0 |
| March. | 5 | Reced of Mr. Hardcastle for Mrs. Catterall | 0 | 10 | 6 |
| | | | 310 | 0 | 1 |

## 1731 RECEIPTS

| | | | £ | s. | d. |
|---|---|---|---|---|---|
| March. | 29 | Reced of Mr. Culcheth for his Sister Anne | 3 | 0 | 0 |
| | | Reced by money paid Sister Catherine by my order the 28th of January last | 2 | 2 | 0 |
| Apr. | 10 | Reced by her Ladyship's Bill on Mrs. Wright | 26 | 0 | 0 |
| | | Reced by money paid by Mr. Caryll into Mr. Wright's hands | 1000 | 0 | 0 |
| May. | 29 | Reced of Mrs. Fermor | 28 | 0 | 0 |
| June. | 19 | Reced of Mr. Caryll | 225 | 0 | 0 |
| July. | 5 | Reced of Mr. Tone, by Crabtree the Carrier | 50 | 0 | 0 |
| | 12 | Reced of Mr. Petre a Legacy left by his Uncle | 20 | 0 | 0 |
| Augt. | 24 | Reced of Mrs. Scroop by Mr. Ralph Sheldon | 1 | 2 | 0 |
| | | Reced of Br. Wright | 3 | 0 | 0 |
| Sept. | 2 | Reced of Mr. Wm Sheldon for his Niece Mary | 1 | 1 | 0 |
| | 16 | Reced of Mr. Short for Miss Fermors | 40 | 0 | 0 |
| Oct. | 29 | Reced of Mr. Roger Meynell by Mr. Ralph Sheldon | 23 | 0 | 0 |
| Novr. | 3 | Reced of Mr. Wm. Sheldon for his Sister Catherine | 12 | 14 | 6 |
| | 13 | Reced of Mr. Caryll for the use of his two Daughters | 10 | 0 | 0 |
| Decr. | 6 | Reced by money paid Sister Catherine by my order | 2 | 2 | 0 |
| | 15 | Reced of Mr. John Stourton for Mrs Catherine Sheldon | 40 | 0 | 0 |

| Febry. | | Pd. her Bill to the order of Mr. William Uré | 45 | 0 | 0 |
|---|---|---|---|---|---|

## 1731 PAYMENTS

| | | | £ | s. | d. |
|---|---|---|---|---|---|
| Apr. | 24 | Pd. her Bill to the same order | 35 | 0 | 0 |
| May. | 5 | Pd. Lord Montgomery in part of £.1200. Secured by Mortgage on Mr. Thornton's Estate | 700 | 0 | 0 |
| | 8 | Pd. her Bill to the order of Mr. Tho: Pulton | 100 | 0 | 0 |
| | 12 | Pd. her Bill to the order of Mr. William Uré | 32 | 17 | 11 |
| June. | 26 | Pd. her Bill to the order of Capt. John Smith | 100 | 0 | 0 |
| July. | 3 | Pd. her Bill to the order of Mr. William Uré | 50 | 0 | 0 |
| | 14 | Pd. her Bill to the order of Mr. Jean Baptiste de Segent | 22 | 0 | 0 |
| | 30 | Pd. her Bill to the order of Mr. Jacobus de Bonté | 50 | 0 | 0 |
| Augt. | 24 | Pd. her Bill to the order of Mr. Mathew Fournie | 100 | 0 | 0 |
| Oct. | 13 | Pd. her Bill to the order of Richd. Jackson | 69 | 14 | 0 |
| | | Pd. her Bill to the order of Messrs Greame and Co. | 30 | 0 | 0 |
| | 27 | Pd. her Bill to the order of Mr. G. Talbot | 6 | 13 | 6 |
| Decr. | 10 | Pd. her Bill to the order of Mr. J. Brussell | 100 | 0 | 0 |

| | | | £ | s. | d. |
|---|---|---|---|---|---|
| | 24 | Reced of Mrs. Fermor for Mrs Winifred Fermor | 20 | 0 | 0 |
| Janry. | 13 | Reced of Mrs. Englefield | 21 | 0 | 0 |
| | 17 | Reced of Edwd Sheldon Esqr | 20 | 0 | 0 |
| | | Reced of Mr. Thornton half a years Interest of £.700. due the 29th day of Novr last | 15 | 15 | 0 |
| Febry. | 14 | Reced of the Dutchess of Northumberland for Mrs. Cecilia Fitzroy | 5 | 0 | 0 |

## 1732 RECEIPTS

| | | | £ | s. | d. |
|---|---|---|---|---|---|
| Mar. | 31 | Reced of Mr. Short for Miss Fermors | 43 | 0 | 0 |
| Apr. | 7 | Reced of Mr Culcheth for his Sister | 2 | 0 | 0 |
| | | Reced of Do. for Mrs. Cecily Worthington | 0 | 10 | 6 |
| | 12 | Reced of Mr. Thomas Berkeley by Mr Ralph Sheldon for Mrs. Frances Fermor | 1 | 1 | 0 |
| | 21 | Reced of Mrs. Pearce by Mr. Bolt for Mrs. Mary Pearce | 6 | 6 | 0 |
| | 27 | Reced of Edward Sheldon Esqr | 27 | 10 | 0 |
| May. | 6 | Reced of Mrs. Scroop by Mr. Ralph Sheldon for Mrs. Catherine Sheldon | 4 | 4 | 0 |
| | | Reced of Mrs. Fermor by Mr. Maire | 35 | 0 | 0 |
| | 9 | Reced of Sr. Francis Mannock £20 0s 0d for his daughter's pension and £2 0s 0d for her pocket in all | 22 | 0 | 0 |
| | 19 | Reced of Mrs. Lavery | 21 | 0 | 0 |
| June. | 23 | Reced of Mrs. Alice Harvy for Mrs. Jane Harvy | 2 | 2 | 0 |
| July. | 17 | Reced of Mr. Harry Fermor for Mrs Placida Fermor | 9 | 8 | 0 |
| Aug. | 2 | Reced of Mr. Chorley for Mrs. Holywell | 2 | 2 | 0 |
| | | | 2055 | 0 | 1 |
| Aug. | 31 | Reced of Mr. Atwood by Mr. Ross | 40 | 0 | 0 |
| Sept. | 3 | Reced of Edward Sheldon Esqr | 25 | 0 | 0 |
| Oct. | 28 | Reced of Mr. Caryll by Bill for his daughters | 10 | 0 | 0 |
| | | Reced of Do. Bill for Lady Fletewood | 20 | 0 | 0 |
| Novr. | 6 | Reced of Mr Webbe for Miss Englefield | 20 | 0 | 0 |

| | | | £ | s. | d. |
|---|---|---|---|---|---|
| Janry. | 11 | Pd. Mr. Greenwell the Upholsterer a Bill | 10 | 15 | 0 |
| | | | 1680 | 4 | 7 |
| Febry. | 3 | Pd. her Bill to the order of Mr. Wm Uré | 50 | 0 | 0 |

### 1732 PAYMENTS

| | | | £ | s. | d. |
|---|---|---|---|---|---|
| Mar. | 29 | Pd. her Bill to the order of Mr. Mathew Fournier | 80 | 0 | 0 |
| | | | 1810 | 4 | 7 |
| June | 21 | Pd. her Ladyship's Bill to the order of Mr. Mathew Fournie | 141 | 0 | 0 |
| | | | 1951 | 4 | 7 |
| Sept. | 19 | Pd. her Bill to the order of Mr. Fournier £80. and for Noteing the same for Nonacceptance 2s.6d. in all | 80 | 2 | 6 |

| | | | £ | s. | d. |
|---|---|---|---|---|---|
| | | Reced of Mr. Day half a Guinea for Mrs. Anne Cattara and half a Guinea for Mrs. Frances Grigson | 1 | 0 | 0 |
| | | Reced of Do. for Mrs. Mary Johnson | 3 | 2 | 6 |
| | 8 | Reced of Mr. Culcheth | 5 | 0 | 0 |
| | 15 | Reced of Mr. Thornton half a years Interest of £.700. due the 29th day of May last | 15 | 15 | 0 |
| | | Reced of Edward Sheldon Esqr | 20 | 0 | 0 |
| Decr. | 5 | Reced of Roger Meynel Esqr. By Mr. Robert Daile | 25 | 0 | 0 |
| | 11 | Reced of Mr. Caryll for his Daughter Romana | 5 | 5 | 0 |
| | 15 | Reced of the Honble. John Stourton | 30 | 0 | 0 |
| Jany | 19 | Reced of Edward Sheldon Esqr by Mr. Short | 30 | 0 | 0 |
| | 27 | Reced of Mr. Culcheth for his Sister | 2 | 10 | 0 |
| Feb. | 13 | Reced of Mr. Barnaby for Mrs Mary Pearse | 5 | 5 | 0 |
| | 20 | Reced of Mr. Greenwell in part of Mr. Stewart's Note | 3 | 3 | 0 |
| | 22 | Reced of Dr Atwood by Mr. James Ross | 30 | 0 | 0 |
| | | | 2346 | 1 | 7 |
| Febr. | 23 | Reced of Edward Sheldon Esqr. | 27 | 0 | 0 |
| March. | 1 | Reced of Mr. Thornton half a years Int. of £700 due the 29th day of Novr last | 15 | 15 | 0 |

## 1733 RECEIPTS

| | | | £ | s. | d. |
|---|---|---|---|---|---|
| May. | 4 | Reced of Sr Francis Mannock by Bill | 22 | 0 | 0 |
| | | Reced by money paid Sister Catherine last Christmas by my order | 2 | 2 | 0 |
| | | | 2412 | 18 | 7 |
| May | 10 | Reced by the balance of my last Acct | 146 | 13 | 0 |
| | 11 | Reced of Mr Culcheth for Mrs Cecily Gerard | 2 | 2 | 0 |

| | | | £ | s. | d. |
|---|---|---|---|---|---|
| Decr. | 2 | Pd. her bill to the order of Nicholas du Champ | 40 | 0 | 0 |
| Janry. | 8 | Pd. her Bill to the order of Mr. Mathew Fournier | 60 | 0 | 0 |
| Febry. | 10 | Pd her Bill to the order of Mr. Wm Uré | 30 | 0 | 0 |
| | | | 2161 | 7 | 1 |
| March. | 10 | Pd her Ladyship's Bill to the order of Mr Jean Jacque Benezet | 50 | 0 | 0 |
| | 31 | Pd. her Bill to the order of Mr Mathew Fournier | 50 | 0 | 0 |
| | | Pd. myself a Bill | 3 | 5 | 6 |
| | | Pd in postage of Letters Porters and other petty expences | 1 | 13 | 0 |
| | | | 2266 | 5 | 7 |

## 1733 PAYMENTS

| | | | £ | s. | d. |
|---|---|---|---|---|---|
| | | May 10th Remains due to balance | 146 | 13 | 0 |
| | | | 2412 | 18 | 7 |
| May. | 13 | Pd. Mr Ralph Sheldon on Mr Cornwall's Acct | 1 | 18 | 0 |
| June. | 13 | Pd. Her Ladyship's Bill to the order of Mr Jacobus de Bonté | 100 | 0 | 0 |
| | 22 | Pd. her Bill to the order of Mr Wm Uré | 30 | 0 | 0 |

| | | | £ | s. | d. |
|---|---|---|---|---|---|
| Augt. | 10 | Reced of Mrs Edward Webbe | 32 | 0 | 0 |
| | 11 | Reced of John Caryll Esqr | 20 | 0 | 0 |
| Sepr. | 12 | Reced of Edward Sheldon Esqr | 50 | 0 | 0 |
| | 20 | Reced of Mr Markham for Miss Fermors | 40 | 0 | 0 |
| | | Reced of Sr Francis Mannock | 11 | 0 | 0 |
| Oct. | 5 | Reced of Mrs Meynell | 38 | 0 | 0 |
| | 18 | Reced of John Caryll Esqr | 32 | 2 | 0 |
| | 22 | Reced of the Dutchess of Northumberland for Mrs Cecilia Fitzroy | 5 | 0 | 0 |
| Decr. | 3 | Reced of Mr Scroop | 5 | 0 | 0 |
| Jany. | 2 | Reced of Edward Sheldon Esqr | 73 | 0 | 0 |
| | 10 | Reced of Mr Chorley for Mrs Helliwell | 2 | 0 | 0 |
| | 17 | Reced by money paid Sister Catherine by my order | 2 | 2 | 0 |
| | 21 | Reced of John Caryll Esqr | 20 | 0 | 0 |
| | | Reced of Do.for his daughter Bell | 3 | 3 | 0 |
| Febr. | 19 | Reced of Do a years Int on bond for £200 | 9 | 0 | 0 |
| | 26 | Reced of Mr Thornton a year's Int of £700 due the 29th day of Novr. Last | 31 | 10 | 0 |
| | 28 | Reced of Mr Chorley for Mrs Culcheth | 3 | 3 | 0 |
| March. | 6 | Reced of Dr Atwood by Mr. Ross | 40 | 0 | 0 |
| | 29 | Reced of Mr. Wm Sheldon for Mrs Catherine and Mrs Mary Sheldon | 2 | 2 | 0 |
| | | | 567 | 17 | 0 |
| | 12 | Reced of Mr James Porter for the Use of Miss Bab Acton | 500 | 0 | 0 |
| | | | 1067 | 17 | 0 |

### 1734 RECEIPTS

| | | | £ | s. | d. |
|---|---|---|---|---|---|
| Apr. | 6 | Reced of Mr Berkeley for Mrs Mary Pearse | 6 | 6 | 0 |
| May | 28 | Reced of Mr Edward Webbe | 20 | 0 | 0 |
| June. | 20 | Reced of Mr Edwd Southcott for Miss Dives | 20 | 0 | 0 |
| July. | 24 | Reced of Mr and Mrs Wyburne by Mr Belson for the use of Miss Bab Acton | 235 | 0 | 0 |
| | | | 1349 | 3 | 0 |
| July | 29 | Reced by the balance of the Acct above | 283 | 8 | 0 |

| | | | £ | s. | d. |
|---|---|---|---|---|---|
| Sepr. | 27 | Pd her Bill to the order of Capt John Smith | 55 | 0 | 0 |
| Oct. | 17 | Pd. her Bill to the order of Mr Wm Uré | 18 | 0 | 0 |
| | | Pd. her Bill to the order of Mr. Wm Keeting | 40 | 0 | 0 |
| | | Pd. her Bill to the same order | 40 | 0 | 0 |
| Novr. | 22 | Pd her Bill to the order of Mr Mathew Fournier | 100 | 0 | 0 |
| Janry. | 29 | Pd. her Bill to the order of Mr John Brussel | 73 | 0 | 0 |

## 1734 PAYMENTS

| | | | £ | s. | d. |
|---|---|---|---|---|---|
| Apr. | 9 | Pd. her Bill to the order of Mr Robt Hewer | 107 | 17 | 0 |
| | | | 565 | 15 | 0 |
| Apr. | 5 | Put out on a Security of Mrs Devereux's Estate | 500 | 0 | 0 |
| | | | 1065 | 15 | 0 |
| | | 29 July 1734 Due to Balance | 283 | 8 | 0 |
| | | | 1349 | 3 | 0 |

| | | | £ | s. | d. |
|---|---|---|---|---|---|
| Augt. | 30 | Reced of Mr Markham for Miss Fermors | 20 | 0 | 0 |
| Sepr. | 17 | Reced of Mr Meynell | 50 | 0 | 0 |
| | 21 | ~~Reced of Mr Hardcastle One Guinea for Mrs Catterall and One Guinea for Mrs Gregson~~ | ~~2~~ | ~~2~~ | ~~0~~ |
| Oct. | 9 | Reced of Mr Caryll for his Daughters | 10 | 0 | 0 |
| | 25 | Reced of Mr Chorley for Mrs Halliwell | 2 | 2 | 0 |
| Novr. | 4 | Reced of Mr Caryll from Winchelsea | 20 | 0 | 0 |
| Jan. | 30 | Reced of Edward Sheldon Esqr | 50 | 0 | 0 |
| Febr. | 10 | Reced of Do by Mr Hunt | 29 | 10 | 0 |
| | 13 | Reced of Mr Chorley for Mrs Culcheth | 5 | 0 | 0 |
| | 14 | Reced of Mr Maire £5 for Mrs Catherine Sheldon and £5 apiece for Mrs Winifred and Mary Fermor in all | 15 | 0 | 0 |
| | 15 | Reced of Mr Thornton a year's Int of £700 due the 29th day of Novr. Last | 31 | 10 | 0 |
| | 27 | Reced of Mrs Alice Harvey for Mrs Jane Harvey | 1 | 1 | 0 |
| March. | 13 | Reced back the principal money put out upon Mrs Devereux's estate and One year's wanting 23 days, Int | 523 | 8 | 6 |
| | | | 1043 | 1 | 6 |
| March | 19 | Reced of Dr Atwood | 60 | 0 | 0 |
| | 21 | Reced of Francis Maire Esqr. | 5 | 0 | 0 |

## 1735 RECEIPTS

| | | | £ | s. | d. |
|---|---|---|---|---|---|
| Apr. | 3 | Reced of Dr Atwood | 100 | 0 | 0 |
| | | Reced of Mr Ralph Johnson | 21 | 10 | 0 |
| | 26 | Reced of Mr Thomas Pippen for Mrs Martha Waters | 10 | 0 | 0 |
| | | Reced of Dr Atwood | 40 | 0 | 0 |
| | 28 | Reced of Mrs Pearce for Mrs Mary Pearce | 6 | 6 | 0 |
| | | Reced of Mr Edwd Webb for Miss Englefield | 510 | 0 | 0 |
| June | 5 | Reced of Niece Stafford | 6 | 6 | 0 |
| | 12 | Reced of Mr. Chorley | 2 | 2 | 0 |

| | | | £ | s. | d. |
|---|---|---|---|---|---|
| Augt. | 27 | Pd her Bill to the order of Messrs Henry and John Sperling | 200 | 0 | 0 |
| Sepr. | 16 | Pd. her Bill to the order of Mr Wm Uré | 75 | 0 | 0 |
| | 24 | Pd. Mr Berlekey on Miss Bab Acton's acct | 13 | 14 | 1 |
| Decr. | 19 | Pd. her Bill to the order of Mr John Brussel | 77 | 0 | 0 |
| Janry. | 31 | Pd to the order of Richd Towneley Esqr | 21 | 0 | 0 |
| | | | 386 | 14 | 1 |

## 1735 PAYMENTS

| | | | £ | s. | d. |
|---|---|---|---|---|---|
| March. | 27 | Pd her Bill to the order of Mr Jacobus de Bonté | 432 | 18 | 11 |
| Apr. | 3 | Pd. her Bill to the same order | 60 | 0 | 0 |
| May. | 2 | Pd her Bill to the order of Mr Mathew Fournier | 128 | 8 | 6 |
| | 9 | Pd her Bill to the order of Mr Jacobus de Bonté | 100 | 0 | 0 |
| | 30 | Pd. her Bill to the order of Mr. Wm Keetin | 100 | 0 | 0 |
| June. | 9 | Pd her Bill to the order of Mr Mathew Fournier | 200 | 0 | 0 |

|  |  |  |  |  |  |
|---|---|---|---|---:|---:|---:|
|  | 23 | Reced of Mr Meynel | 63 | 3 | 0 |
| July | 29 | Reced of John Caryll Esqr | 20 | 0 | 0 |
| Augt. | 12 | Reced of the Dutchess of Northumberland for Mrs Cecilia Fitzroy | 5 | 0 | 0 |
|  |  | Reced of Mr Salkeld for his Aunt | 5 | 0 | 0 |
|  | 18 | Reced of Mr Wm Sheldon for his Sister | 2 | 2 | 0 |
|  |  | Reced of Mr Roger Meynel by Mr Mayes | 220 | 0 | 0 |
| Sepr. | 5 | Reced of Do by Do | 280 | 0 | 0 |
|  | 9 | Reced of Mrs Webb | 5 | 0 | 0 |
| Oct. | 11 | Reced of Mr Caryll for his daughters | 10 | 0 | 0 |
| Novr. | 12 | Reced of Mr Chorley for Mrs Halliwell | 2 | 0 | 0 |
| Decr. | 12 | Reced of Mr Short for Miss Fermors | 20 | 0 | 0 |
|  | 23 | Reced of Edwd Sheldon Esqr | 55 | 5 | 0 |

| | | | | | |
|---|---|---|---|---:|---:|---:|
| Jan. | 21 | Reced of Mr Caryll for his daughters | 4 | 4 | 0 |
|  |  | Reced by money paid My Sister & Daughter | 5 | 5 | 0 |
|  |  |  | 2501 | 9 | 6 |
| Febr. | 12 | Reced by the balance of the last Acct | 67 | 16 | 10 |
|  | 13 | Reced of Mr Chorley for Mrs Culcheth | 6 | 0 | 0 |
|  | 23 | Reced of Mr Caryll | 20 | 0 | 0 |

### 1736 RECEIPTS

|  |  |  | £ | s. | d. |
|---|---|---|---:|---:|---:|
| Apr. | 1 | Reced of Mrs Placida Fermor by Mr Wm Sheldon's Bill on Mr Wright | 5 | 0 | 0 |
| May. | 7 | Reced of Mr Hardcastle for Mrs Anne Cattrall | 1 | 10 | 0 |
|  | 10 | Reced of Mrs Pearse by Mr Berkeley for Mrs Mary Pearse | 6 | 6 | 0 |

| | | | £ | s. | d. |
|---|---|---|---|---|---|
| July. | 3 | Pd her bill to the order of Messrs De Bonté Buijssens and De Bauque | 100 | 0 | 0 |
| Oct. | 30 | Pd her bill to the order of Mr John Brussel | 160 | 18 | 0 |
| | | Pd. her Bill to the order of Mr Wm Uré | 22 | 0 | 0 |
| Decr. | 18 | Pd her bill to the order of Sr John Jernegan | 8 | 11 | 0 |
| | | Pd Mrs Nicoll on an Assignment of a Security on his Grace the Duke of Powis's estate in North[amp]tonshire which bears date the 14th of June 1735 and carries Interest from that day | 400 | 0 | 0 |
| | | Pd Mrs Elizabeth Bird on a Mortgage of her estates in the Counties of Middx Bucks Essex and Hertford which bears date the 5th of Sepr 1735 and Carries Interest from that day | 400 | 0 | 0 |
| | 31 | Pd her bill to the order of Mr John Brussel | 115 | 5 | 0 |
| | | Pd. her Bill to the same order | 110 | 6 | 0 |
| | | Pd in postage of Letters Porters and other Small expences | 1 | 16 | 6 |
| | | Pd myself a Bill | 6 | 14 | 8 |
| | | | 2433 | 12 | 8 |
| | | 12th Febry 1735. Due to Balance | 67 | 16 | 10 |
| | | | 2501 | 9 | 6 |

### 1736 PAYMENTS

| | | | £ | s. | d. |
|---|---|---|---|---|---|
| Apr. | 8 | Pd Lady Fletwood's Bill to the order of Mr John Brussel | 72 | 16 | 0 |
| | 28 | Pd Mr John Pulton | 1 | 6 | 0 |

| | | | £ | s. | d. |
|---|---|---|---|---|---|
| | 18 | Reced of Mr Maire for Mrs Placida Fermor | 17 | 10 | 0 |
| June. | 10 | Reced of Sr Franc[is] Anderton for Mrs Ireland and Mrs Fleming | 7 | 7 | 0 |
| | 11 | Reced of Mrs Elizabeth Bird the principal Money and one years Interest wch will be due the 5th day of Sepr next upon her Mortgage | 420 | 0 | 0 |
| | | Reced of Mr Thornton a year's Int of £700 due the 29th day of Novr. 1735 | 31 | 10 | 0 |
| | 16 | Reced of Mr Chorley for Mrs Halliwell | 2 | 2 | 0 |
| | | Reced by money laid out for me at Dunkirk | 3 | 4 | 0 |
| Augt. | 12 | Reced of William Sheldon Esqr. | 145 | 2 | 0 |
| | 26 | Reced of Mr Prujean | 50 | 0 | 0 |
| Novr. | 1 | Reced of Mr Suffield for Mrs Paston | 2 | 2 | 0 |
| | 6 | Reced of his Grace of Powis a year's Int of £400 due the 14th day of June last | 20 | 0 | 0 |
| | 16 | Reced of Mr Meynell | 95 | 16 | 4 |
| Decr. | 7 | Reced by money pd my Sister by my order | 2 | 2 | 0 |
| Jan. | 27 | Reced of Mrs Culcheth for her daughter | 5 | 0 | 0 |
| March | 8 | Reced of Mr Prujean | 11 | 15 | 6 |

## 1737 RECEIPTS

| | | | £ | s. | d. |
|---|---|---|---|---|---|
| June | 9 | Reced of Mrs Cat: Sheldon by a Bill | 50 | 0 | 0 |
| July. | 18 | Reced of Mrs Pearse by Mr Berkeley for her daughter | 7 | 7 | 0 |
| | | Reced of Mr Mayes for Miss Meynels | 31 | 2 | 6 |
| | | | 1008 | 13 | 2 |
| | | Reced by two years pension due for my Daughter Eugenia | 34 | 0 | 0 |
| | | Reced by money paid to Mr Roberts | 8 | 8 | 0 |
| | | Reced by money paid on Betty Walker's Acct, and for the Carriage of my books to the Ship | 1 | 6 | 6 |

| | | | £ | s. | d. |
|---|---|---|---|---|---|
| Augt. | 13 | Pd Lord Petre money lent upon Bond and Mortgage dat 11 Instant taken in Mr Bramston's name and Declard in trust for me | 400 | 0 | 0 |
| Sepr. | 3 | Pd her Ladyship's Bill to the order of Mrs Mary Saladin | 100 | 0 | 0 |
| | 16 | Pd her Ladyship's Bill to the order of Mr Wm Whitaker | 100 | 0 | 0 |
| Oct. | 22 | Pd her Ladyship's Bill to the order of Mr John de Chosale | 120 | 0 | 0 |
| Decr. | 17 | Pd her Ladyship's Bill to the order of Mr John de Chosale | 100 | 0 | 0 |

## 1737 PAYMENTS

| | | | £ | s. | d. |
|---|---|---|---|---|---|
| July. | 25 | Pd her Bill to the order of Mr John Brussel | 100 | 0 | 0 |
| | | | 994 | 2 | 0 |

| | | | | | |
|---|---|---|---|---|---|
| Decr. | 15 | Reced by money to be paid my Sister | 2 | 2 | 0 |
| | | | 1054 | 9 | 8 |
| | | Reced by the balance of the above Acct | 7 | 5 | 8 |
| Jan. | 24 | Reced of Mrs Culcheth for her daughter | 5 | 0 | 0 |
| Mar. | 15 | Reced of Mr Caryll for Mrs Ben[edic]ᵗ. Caryll | 10 | 0 | 0 |

### 1738 RECEIPTS

| | | | £ | s. | d. |
|---|---|---|---|---|---|
| [March] | 30 | Reced of Mrs Webbe for Miss Betty Englefield | 2 | 2 | 0 |
| May. | 12 | Reced of the Dutchess of Northumberland for Mrs Cecilia Fitzroy | 5 | 0 | 0 |
| June. | 1 | Reced of Mr Edwd Caryll for his Sisters | 2 | 2 | 0 |
| | 8 | Reced of Lady Dowager Petre her share of a years Pension for Miss Paston | 7 | 10 | 0 |
| | 27 | Reced of Mr Chorley for Mrs Halliwell | 4 | 0 | 0 |
| | | Reced by my Shirts and my Wives Shifts | 29 | 6 | 0 |
| July | 3, 22 & 26 | Reced of Mrs Meynell by three Bills | 500 | 0 | 0 |

| | | | | | |
|---|---|---|---|---|---|
| Novr. | 4 | Reced of Mr Berkeley for Mrs Pearse | 6 | 6 | 0 |
| | | Reced of Lord Petre two years Int at four pr Cent of £400 due 11th of Augt last | 32 | 0 | 0 |

| | | | £ | s. | d. |
|---|---|---|---|---|---|
| Novr. | 17 | Pd Lady Fletewood's Bill to the order of Madame Marcade Widow | 50 | 0 | 0 |
| | | Pd for three yards of Duffall for Mr Cornwall | 1 | 1 | 0 |
| | | Pd Postage of Letters from the 12th of February 1735 to the 15th of Decr 1737 | 0 | 15 | 0 |
| | | Pd myself my ffee for drawing Mr Bramston's declaracon of Trust upon Ld Petre's Mortgage | 1 | 1 | 0 |
| | | Pd duty and writing | 0 | 5 | 0 |
| | | | 1047 | 4 | 0 |
| | | Remains in Mr Strickland's hands to ballance | 7 | 5 | 8 |
| | | | 1054 | 9 | 8 |

---

### 1738 PAYMENTS

| | | | £ | s. | d. |
|---|---|---|---|---|---|
| May | 17 | Pd Lady Fletewood's Bill to the order of Mr John de Chosale | 53 | 10 | 0 |
| Augt. | 19 | Pd her Bill to the order of Mr Wm Whitaker | 100 | 0 | 0 |
| | 21 | Pd her Bill to the order of Mr Thos Weston | 200 | 0 | 0 |
| Sepr. | 6 | Pd her Bill to the order of Messrs Patrk & Robt Macky | 125 | 0 | 0 |
| | | Pd her Bill to the order of Messrs Blake & Lynch | 34 | 19 | 5 |
| | | Pd her Bill to the order of Messrs George Fitzgerald and Co | 40 | 0 | 7 |
| | | | 553 | 10 | 0 |

| | | | £ | s. | d. |
|---|---|---|---|---|---|
| Decr. | 1 | Reced of Thomas Berkeley Esqr | 11 | 1 | 0 |
| | | | 621 | 12 | 8 |
| Decr. | 1 | Reced of Mr Hardcastle for Mrs Cattrall | 0 | 10 | 6 |
| Jan. | 24 | Reced of Mrs Kath: Caryll for the use of Mrs Ben: Caryll | 4 | 4 | 0 |
| Febr. | 6 | Reced of Mr Chorley for Mrs Culcheth | 5 | 0 | 0 |
| March | 9 | Reced of Sr Francis [Anderton] for Mrs Ireland | 30 | 0 | 0 |

## 1739 RECEIPTS

| | | | £ | s. | d. |
|---|---|---|---|---|---|
| Apr. | 30 | Reced of Mr Englefield for his sister Betty | 2 | 2 | 0 |
| July. | 30 | Reced of Mr Thomas Berkeley | 10 | 0 | 0 |
| Sepr. | 6 | [¦¦i¦Error¦i¦¦] Reced of Lady Dowger Petre her share of Miss Paston's Pension | 7 | 10 | 0 |
| Augt. | 29 | Reced of Mrs Meynell by Mr Mayes | 59 | 5 | 5 |
| Sepr. | 6 | [¦¦i¦Error¦i¦¦] Reced by Linnen bought for my Son and Daughter | 7 | 10 | 0 |
| May. | 17 | Reced of Lord Petre principal money lent him on Bond and Mortgage | 400 | 0 | 0 |
| | | Reced of his Lordship the Interest thereof from the 11th of Augt. 1738 to the 11th of May 1739 being Nine Months | 12 | 0 | 0 |
| | 29 | Reced of Mr Thornton three years and a half's Interest of £700 due 29th day of May 1739 | 110 | 5 | 0 |
| Novr. | 6 | Reced of Mr Chorley for Mrs Halliwell | 2 | 0 | 0 |
| | 8 | Reced of Mr Howard for Mrs Sheldon | 2 | 2 | 0 |
| Decr. | 11 | Reced of Mrs Sexton for Mrs Benedict Caryll | 2 | 2 | 0 |
| | 15 | Reced of Mr David Wells | 25 | 0 | 0 |
| | 25 | Reced by two years paid my Sister | 4 | 4 | 0 |
| | | | 1319 | 17 | 7 |
| Jan. | 18 | Reced of Mr Thomas Berkeley | 22 | 10 | 0 |

| | | | £ | s. | d. |
|---|---|---|---|---|---|
| Janry. | 27 | Pd Mr Barlow by Mrs Sheldon's order | 1 | 3 | 0 |

---

### 1739 PAYMENTS

| | | | £ | s. | d. |
|---|---|---|---|---|---|
| May | 4 | Pd her Ladyship's Bill to the order of Mr John Brussell | 100 | 0 | 0 |
| Oct. | 6 | Pd. her Bill to the order of Mr. Wm Keetin | 100 | 0 | 0 |
| Decr. | 18 | Pd. Mr Gyles for entering a Caveat upon the death of Mrs Ann Acton | 0 | 5 | 0 |
| | 27 | Pd. Her Bill to the order of Mr Francs Pool | 96 | 12 | 0 |
| | | | 851 | 10 | 0 |
| Janry. | 19 | Pd Lady Fletwood's Bill to the order of Mr John Brussel | 50 | 0 | 0 |
| | | Pd Mr Mathew Swinburne being part of £1000 lent him on Mortgage taken in Mr Bramston's name and Declared in Trust for me | 400 | 0 | 0 |
| | | | 1301 | 10 | 0 |
| | | Remains due to Lady Fleetwood to balance | 49 | 18 | 7 |
| | | | 1351 | 8 | 7 |

| | | | £ | s. | d. |
|---|---|---|---|---|---|
| Feb. | 15 | Reced of Ld Aston some time agoe £8, and now one Guinea for Mrs Lucy Smith in all | 9 | 1 | 0 |
| | | | 1351 | 8 | 7 |
| | | Reced by the balance of the above Acct | 49 | 18 | 7 |

## 1740 RECEIPTS

| | | | £ | s. | d. |
|---|---|---|---|---|---|
| Apr. | 25 | Reced of Mr Chorley for Mrs Culcheth | 5 | 0 | 0 |
| May | 19 | Reced of his Grace of Powis three years Int of £400 due 14 June 1739 | 60 | 0 | 0 |
| June | 2 | Reced of Sir Francis Anderton for Mrs Maura Fleming | 4 | 4 | 0 |
| | 6 | Reced of Mrs Harvey for her Daughter Magdalen Harvey | 1 | 1 | 0 |
| | 27 | Reced of Mrs Caryll for Mrs Benedicta Caryll | 2 | 2 | 0 |
| | 30 | Reced of Mrs Caryll for Mrs Benedicta Caryll | 7 | 7 | 0 |
| Sepr. | 6 | Reced of Mr John Howard by Bill on the late Lady ffairfax's Account | 33 | 10 | 0 |
| | | Reced of Mr Edwd Caryll for Mrs Benedicta Caryll money pd the 10th of Apr. last | 6 | 0 | 0 |
| | 18 | Reced of Lady Dowager Petre her share of a years Pension for Miss Peggy Paston | 7 | 10 | 0 |
| | | | 176 | 12 | 7 |
| Jan. | 15 | Reced of Mr Jones in part of his debt | 100 | 0 | 0 |
| | 27 | Reced of Mrs Culcheth for Miss Bab Dicconson's Pension | 12 | 0 | 0 |
| ffeb. | 26 | Reced of Mrs Culcheth for her daughter | 5 | 0 | 0 |

## 1741 RECEIPTS

| | | | £ | s. | d. |
|---|---|---|---|---|---|
| March. | 25 | Reced of Mr Thomas Berkeley | 41 | 0 | 0 |
| Apr. | 7 | Reced of Mrs Catherine Caryll for Mrs Benedict Caryll | 5 | 0 | 0 |
| June. | 20 | Reced of Mr John Howard | 5 | 5 | 0 |

| | | | £ | s. | d. |
|---|---|---|---|---|---|
| 1740 | | ffebry 21. 1739/40 Sent Mrs Sheldon a Copy of this Account. M.S. | | | |
| June | 18 | Pd her Bill to the order of Mr William Keeting | 119 | 0 | 0 |
| Octr 7 | | Pd her Ladyship's Bill for £130 of wch £80 was for a years Int of £2000 due from Mr Salkeld to Mrs Pearse. remains | 60 | 0 | 0 |
| | | | 169 | 0 | 0 |

### 1740 PAYMENTS

| | | | £ | s. | d. |
|---|---|---|---|---|---|
| March. | 10 | Pd Lady ffletewood's Bill to the order of Mr John du Chosale | 138 | 0 | 0 |
| | 12 | Pd her Bill to the order of Mr Thomas Berkeley | 20 | 0 | 0 |
| | | | 327 | 0 | 0 |
| | | Remains due to Lady Fleetwood to balance | 69 | 17 | 7 |
| | | | 396 | 17 | 7 |

### 1741 PAYMENTS

| | | | £ | s. | d. |
|---|---|---|---|---|---|

| | | | £ | s. | d. |
|---|---|---|---|---|---|
| July. | 24 | Reced of his Grace of Powis two yrs Int of £400 due 14 June 1741 | 40 | 0 | 0 |
| Sepr. | 23 | Reced of Mr Chorley for Miss Bab Dicconson | 12 | 0 | 0 |
| | | | 396 | 17 | 7 |
| | | Reced by the ballance of the above Acct | 69 | 17 | 7 |
| Oct. | 8 | Reced of Sr Henry Lawson for Miss Molly Sheldon | 17 | 5 | 6 |
| Novr. | 5 | Reced of Mrs Catherine Caryll for Mrs Romana Caryll | 2 | 2 | 0 |
| Decr. | 16 | Reced of Mr Chorley for Mrs Holliwell | 2 | 0 | 0 |
| | 17 | Reced of Mrs Henrietta ffermor | 10 | 0 | 0 |
| | 23 | Reced of Mr John Thornton | 10 | 0 | 0 |
| | 28 | Reced of Mr Edwd Webbe £8:0:6 for Mr Wm Eyston and £1:1:0 for Mrs Betty Englefield in all | 9 | 1 | 6 |
| Jan. | 21 | Reced of Mr Chorley for Mrs Culcheth | 5 | 0 | 0 |
| ffeb. | 1 | Reced of Mr Fermor for Mrs Mary Fermor | 10 | 0 | 0 |
| | 5 | Reced of Mrs Catherine Caryll for Mrs Benedicta Caryll | 2 | 2 | 0 |
| | | | 137 | 8 | 7 |
| | | Reced by Linnen as Appears by Mrs Sheldon's Account | 16 | 18 | 0 |
| | | Reced by money paid My Sister at Smass 1740 and Xmass 1741 | 4 | 4 | 0 |
| Feb. | 16 | Reced of Mr Thomas Berkeley by two Bills | 420 | 0 | 0 |

## 1742 RECEIPTS

| | | | £ | s. | d. |
|---|---|---|---|---|---|
| Apr. | 12 | Reced of Mr Chorley a Legacy left by Mrs Culcheth's Will | 10 | 0 | 0 |

Sepr. 24. 1741. Sent Mrs Sheldon a Copy of
this Account. M: S.

| | | | £ | s. | d. |
|---|---|---|---|---|---|
| Novr. | 7 | Pd her Ladyship's Bill to order of Mr John Brussel | 58 | 0 | 0 |
| | 11 | Pd her Bill to the order of Mr Nicholas du Camp | 50 | 0 | 0 |
| | | | 108 | 0 | 0 |

| | | | £ | s. | d. |
|---|---|---|---|---|---|
| | | Pd Betty Walker for some Odd things she bought | 0 | 4 | 6 |
| March | 6 | Pd her Ladyship's Bill to the order of Mrs Lemaire | 35 | 2 | 6 |
| | 23 | Pd her Ladyship's bill to the order of Mr Holden junr | 100 | 0 | 0 |

### 1742 PAYMENTS

| | | | £ | s. | d. |
|---|---|---|---|---|---|
| Apr. | | Pd her Ladyship's bill to the order of Mr Desticker | 95 | 0 | 0 |
| | | Pd her Bill to the same order | 105 | 0 | 0 |
| | 29 | Pd her Bill to the order of Mr Hovelt | 100 | 0 | 0 |

## 1743 RECEIPTS

|  |  |  | £ | s. | d. |
|---|---|---|---:|---:|---:|
| July. | 1 | Reced of Cath: Lady Petre for Lady Fleetwood | 10 | 0 | 0 |
|  | 12 | Reced of Thomas Berkeley Esqr for Do | 12 | 0 | 0 |
|  |  | Reced of Mr Thornton three years and a half's Int of £700 due 29th Novr. 1742 | 110 | 5 | 0 |
|  |  | Reced by money paid my Sister at Xmass 1742 | 2 | 2 | 0 |
|  |  | Reced by money paid for My Son Joe's Linnen and board | 19 | 3 | 0 |
|  |  |  | 742 | 0 | 7 |
| Oct. | 24 | Reced by the ballance of the above Acct | 66 | 3 | 7 |
| Novr. | 25 | Reced of Mr Berkeley for Miss Berkeley | 5 | 5 | 0 |
| Decr. | 20 | Reced of Lady Petre for Miss Peggy Paston | 10 | 4 | 6 |
|  | 26 | Reced of Mr Jones in part of Interest due to his Sister | 15 | 15 | 0 |
| ffeb. | 7 | Reced of Mr John Howard for Mrs Rigby | 1 | 6 | 0 |
|  | 9 | Reced of Mr Culcheth for Mrs Culcheth | 5 | 0 | 0 |
|  | 15 | Reced of his Grace of Powis two years Int of £400 due 14 June 1743 | 40 | 0 | 0 |

## 1744 RECEIPTS

|  |  |  | £ | s. | d. |
|---|---|---|---:|---:|---:|
| Apr. | 17 | Reced of Mr Matthew Swinburne four years Int of £400 at 4 pr Cent due 10th Decr. 1743 | 64 | 0 | 0 |
|  |  | Reced by two years Pension for my Daughter Harriet | 34 | 0 | 0 |
|  |  | Reced by money paid for her pocket | 3 | 3 | 0 |
|  |  | Reced by money paid my Sister at Xmass 1743 | 2 | 2 | 0 |
| June | 29 | Reced of Mr. Matthew Swinburne in full for principal and Int due on his mortgage | 408 | 16 | 6 |
| May. | 30 | Reced of his Grace of Powis half a year's Int of £400 due 14th Decr. 1743 | 10 | 0 | 0 |
|  |  |  | 665 | 15 | 7 |
| Sepr. | 27 | Reced by the ballance of the above Acct | 417 | 5 | 7 |
|  |  | Reced by a Doz of Cambrick Handkerchiefs | 2 | 5 | 6 |

*[No more transactions: Mannock Strickland died 19 November 1744]*

## 1743 PAYMENTS

| | | | £ | s. | d. |
|---|---|---|---|---|---|
| | | Oct. 24th. 1743. Sent Mrs Sheldon a Copy of this Account. M: S. | | | |
| Decr. | 22 | Pd Lady Fletweood's bill to the order of Mrs Constantin | 43 | 0 | 0 |
| Janry. | 26 | Pd her bill to the order of Peter Delclogue | 95 | 10 | 0 |

## 1744 PAYMENTS

| | | | £ | s. | d. |
|---|---|---|---|---|---|
| June | 15 | Pd her bill to the order of Peter Tellier | 110 | 0 | 0 |
| | | | 248 | 10 | 0 |
| | | Remains due to Lady Fletewood to ballance | 417 | 5 | 7 |
| | | | 665 | 15 | 7 |
| | | Sepr. 27th. 1744. Sent Mrs Sheldon a copy of this Account M:S. | | | |
| Oct. | 26 | Pd her Ladyship's Bill to the order of Mr. Peter Delaruelle for | 60 | 0 | 0 |

# PART III

# ABSTRACTS OF
# BILLS OF EXCHANGE
# AND OTHER DOCUMENTS

# BENEDICTINES, DUNKIRK:
# ABSTRACTS OF BILLS OF EXCHANGE

These surviving bills of exchange are included here to show the considerable extent of the northern European network which underlay the
support of the English clients; the corresponding payment requests chan-
nelled through Dame Benedicta also survive but are less informative.
A considerable range of names appears, most of them unknown and
presumably of well-disposed small traders. A few similar dockets survive
for the other convents.

**Bills of exchange issued by Dame Benedicta Fleetwood [also
Fletewood], drawn on MS, 1730–44. *Blount MSS, D* 7/44–156**

**1**. 26 March 1730 (NS). *Blount MSS, D* 7/44
£48 4s 2d to Madam Marcadé, widow, for 'value here received', drawn
on MS at Gray's Inn or if not there at Mr Wyke's, 'a goldsmith over
against Gray's Inn Gate in Holborn'. Accepted by MS 25 March (OS).
Endorsed 30 March in French with Mme Marcadé's assignment to Messrs
Bullock & Moller, whose receipt is witnessed by J.J. Helmoke.

**2**. 29 October 1730 (NS). *Blount MSS, D* 7/45
£50 to William Keetin, drawn on MS (or, failing him, Mr Wyke, goldsmith,
next to Gray's Inn Gate, Holborn). Accepted by MS 27 October 1730
(OS). Endorsed with Keetin's instruction to pay to George Lane's account.

**3**. 7 December 1730 (NS). *Blount MSS, D* 7/46
£72 to Nicolas François Doncquers, drawn on MS (or, failing him, Mr
Wyke, goldsmith, next to Gray's Inn Gate, Holborn). Accepted by MS
2 December 1730 (OS). Endorsed with Doncquers's assignment to Peter
Flower (witness: M. Martyn).

**4**. 24 May 1731 (NS). *Blount MSS, D* 7/47
£32 17s 11d to William Uré of Dunkirk, drawn on MS (or, failing him,
Mr Wyke, goldsmith, next to Gray's Inn Gate, Holborn). Accepted for MS
by Henry Trubshaw, 'clerk to M[r]. MS', 4 June 1731 (OS). Endorsed in
French with Uré's assignment of payment to Roger Marrow, who assigns
to George Green, who assigns to Wm. Hutchinson.

**5**. 4 June 1731 (NS). *Blount MSS, D* 7/44
£100 to Thomas Pulton, drawn on MS of Gray's Inn (or, failing him, Mr Wyke, goldsmith, next to Gray's Inn Gate, Holborn). Accepted by MS 31 May 1731 (OS). Payment of exchange made via John Brussell of Dunkirk and assigned to George Fitzgerald (witness: Benjamin Bretland).

**6**. 23 June 1731 (NS). *Blount MSS, D* 7/49
£100 to John Smith, drawn on MS of Gray's Inn (or, failing him, Mr Wyke, goldsmith, next to Gray's Inn Gate, Holborn). Accepted by MS 18 June 1731 (OS). Endorsed with Smith's request of 24 June 1731 (dated also from Dunkirk) for the payment to be made to his wife A. Smith and with her receipt of 26 June 1731.

**7**. 1 July 1731 (NS). *Blount MSS, D* 7/50
£50 to William [Guillaume] Uré for 'value here received', drawn on MS of Gray's Inn (or, failing him, Mr Wyke, goldsmith, next to Gray's Inn Gate, Holborn). Accepted by MS 26 June (OS). Endorsed 1 July 1731 in Flemish with Uré's assignment to John Virgoe, whose receipt in English is dated 3 July 1731.

**8**. 15 July 1731 (NS). *Blount MSS, D* 7/51
£22 to Jean Baptiste de Segent, drawn on MS of Gray's Inn (or, failing him, Mr Wyke, goldsmith, next to Gray's Inn Gate, Holborn). Accepted by MS 8 July (OS). Endorsed in French with assignment to Monsieur le Beau, 'négociant à Londres', and receipted by him 14 July (OS).

**9**. 15 July 1731 (NS). *Blount MSS, D* 7/52
£50 to Jacobus de Bonte, drawn on MS of Gray's Inn (or, failing him, Mr Wyke, goldsmith, next to Gray's Inn Gate, Holborn). Accepted for MS by H. Trubshaw 22 July 1731 (OS). Endorsed with de Bonte's instruction to make payment to Messrs De Putter & van Beeg [Beeck].

**10**. 18 August 1731 (NS). *Blount MSS, D* 7/53
£6 13s 6d to George Talbot 'for value received of him', drawn on MS of Gray's Inn (or, failing him, Mr Wyke, goldsmith, next to Gray's Inn Gate, Holborn). Acceptance by MS not noted. Signed on verso: George Trentham Talbot (witness: Edward Webbe).

**11**. 23 August 1731 (NS). *Blount MSS, D* 7/54
£100 to Matthew Fournier, drawn on MS of Gray's Inn (or, failing him, Mr Wyke, goldsmith, next to Gray's Inn Gate, Holborn). Accepted by MS 17/24 August 1731 (OS). Endorsed for payment to John Smith, who assigns payment on 21 August to his wife A. Smith, who acknowledges receipt 24 August.

**12**. 11 October 1731 (NS). *Blount MSS, D* 7/55
£69 14s 0d received from John Brussell to Richard Jackson, drawn on

MS of Gray's Inn (or, failing him, Mr Wyke, goldsmith, next to Gray's Inn Gate, Holborn). Accepted by MS 5 October 1731 (OS). Receipted by Jackson.

**13**. 11 October 1731 (NS). *Blount MSS, D* 7/56
£30 6s 0d received from John Brussell to Messrs Thomas Greame & Co., drawn on MS of Gray's Inn (or, failing him, Mr Wyke, goldsmith, next to Gray's Inn Gate, Holborn). Accepted by MS 4 October 1731 (OS). Receipted by Jacob Stallard for the Bank.

**12**. 29 November 1731 (NS). *Blount MSS, D* 7/57
£100 to John Brussell, 'for value received of him', drawn on MS of Gray's Inn (or, failing him, Mr Wyke, goldsmith, next to Gray's Inn Gate, Holborn). Accepted for MS by H. Trubshaw [n.d.]. Endorsed with assignment 29 November 1731 from Brussell in Dunkirk to Isaac Minet and 30 November 1731 from Isaac Minet to William Minet (witness: Thomas Wade for Messrs. Hankey).

**13**. 6 January 1731/2 (OS? NS?). *Blount MSS, D* 7/58
Promissory note, John Stewart of London £10 15 4d to John Greenwell at six months' notice. In settlement of attached bill from Middlemore and Greenwell dated 3 November 1731 for blankets, coverlets, 50 yards of fine green 'Kitterminster' [carpet?], 40,000 pins, canvas, and sending them by ship. Receipt dated 11 January 1731/[2] signed by John Greenwell for himself and Sarah Middlemore for settlement by Lady [Benedicte] Fleetwood via MS.

**14**. 3 February 1732 (NS). *Blount MSS, D* 7/59
£50 to William Uré 'for value received of him', drawn on MS of Gray's Inn (or, failing him, Mr Wyke, goldsmith, next to Gray's Inn Gate, Holborn). Accepted by MS 3 February 1731 (OS). Endorsed in French 3 February 1732 with assignment to Messrs Jean Estienne & Jacques Benezet (witness: A. Desmarelle).

**15**. 23 March 1732 (NS). *Blount MSS, D* 7/60
£50 to Matthew [Mathieu] Fournier 'for value received of him', drawn on MS of Gray's Inn (or, failing him, Mr Wyke, goldsmith, next to Gray's Inn Gate, Holborn). Accepted for MS by H. Trubshaw 21 March (OS). Endorsed in French with assignment to Jonathan Forward (witness: Francis Emerson).

**16**. 13 June 1732 (NS). *Blount MSS, D* 7/61
£141 to Matthew [Mathieu] Fournier 'for value received of him', drawn on MS of Gray's Inn (or, failing him, Mr Wyke, goldsmith, next to Gray's Inn Gate, Holborn). Accepted by MS 13 June (OS). Endorsed in French with assignment to Jacob Berry of Red Cross Street [London? Dunkirk?].

**17.** 6 September 1732 (NS). *Blount MSS, D* 7/62
£80 to Matthew [Mathieu] Fournier 'for value received of the same', drawn on MS of Gray's Inn (or, failing him, Mr Wyke, goldsmith, next to Gray's Inn Gate, Holborn). Accepted by MS 11 September (OS). Initialled 'J.C.' and numbered no. 21. Endorsed in French with assignment to J. Hanbury, 17 September 1732 (witness: John Rowbottom).

**18.** 27 November 1732 (NS). *Blount MSS, D* 7/63[1]
£40 to Nicolas Du Champ 'for value received of the same', drawn on MS of Lincoln's Inn Square (or, failing him, Mr Wyke, goldsmith, next to Gray's Inn Gate, Holborn). Accepted by MS 25 November (OS). Endorsed 27 November in French with assignment by Du Camp [*sic*] to Mr Je[a]n D'argent (witness: N. Silver).

**19.** 28 December 1732 (NS). *Blount MSS, D* 7/64
£60 to Matthew [Mathieu] Fournier 'for value received of the same', drawn on MS of Gray's Inn (or, failing him, Mr Wyke, goldsmith, next to Gray's Inn Gate, Holborn). Accepted by MS 28 December (OS), who then adds his new address, 'Lincoln's Inne, New Square no. 3'. Endorsed in French 1 January 1733 with assignment to Jonathan Hanbury (witness: Jonathan Clark for Messrs Morsons).

**20.** 27 January 1732/3 (NS). *Blount MSS, D* 7/65
£30 to William Uré 'for value received of the same', drawn on MS of Gray's Inn (or, failing him, Mr Wyke, goldsmith, next to Gray's Inn Gate, Holborn). Accepted by MS

**21.** 8 March 1733 (NS). *Blount MSS, D* 7/66
£50 to Jean Jacques Benezet, 'value received of the same', drawn on MS of Gray's Inn (or, failing him, Mr Wyke, goldsmith, next to Gray's Inn Gate, Holborn). Accepted by MS 2 February (OS). Endorsed in French with assignment from Uré to Antoine Cornelis Heijnderijcx, then 4 February to Jacques Le Mettre, then same date to Samuel Grimes & Co. (witness: N. Brabins for the Bank).

**22.** 18 March 1733 (NS). *Blount MSS, D* 7/67
£50 to Matthew [Mathieu] Fournier 'for value received of the same',

---

[1] Strickland moved from Gray's Inn to Lincoln's Inn in 1732; some of his correspondents were tardy in changing his address. After this date many of the transactions appear to have been dealt with at his house at 4 Queen Square (on the site now occupied by Faber & Faber, following its destruction in the Second World War). Powis House, the London home of his patron the Duke of Powis, was just off the eastern side of Queen Square in Ormond Street, on a site now occupied by Great Ormond Street Children's Hospital. The area had enjoyed a reputation since the reign of Elizabeth I as having a strong Catholic population. See Geoffrey de C. Parmiter, *Elizabethan Popish Recusancy in the Inns of Court* (London: Institute of Historical Research, 1976).

drawn on MS of Gray's Inn (or, failing him, Mr Wyke, goldsmith, next to Gray's Inn Gate, Holborn). Accepted by MS 14 March (OS) at his house in Queen Square, Ormond Street. Endorsed in French 19 March with assignment to W. Bowden (witness: Abram Atkins for Thomas Bowdler junr).

**23**. 13 May 1733 (NS). *Blount MSS, D* 7/68
Receipt, Ralph Sheldon to MS for £1 18s 0d on account of Mrs Cornwall at Dunkirck.

**24**. 7 June 1733 (NS). *Blount MSS, D* 7/69
£100 to Jacobus de Bonte 'for value received of the same', drawn on MS of Lincoln's Inn (or, failing him, Mr Wyke, goldsmith, next to Gray's Inn Gate, Holborn). Accepted by MS 5 June (OS). Endorsed 11 June with assignment to J. Ja. Benezet and 11 June to Humphrey Bell (witness: Joseph Burchell for the Bank).

**25**. 7 June 1733 (NS). *Blount MSS, D* 7/70
£30 to William Uré, drawn on MS at Gray's Inn (or, failing him, Mr Wyke, goldsmith, by Gray's Inn Gate, Holborn). Accepted by MS 9 June 1733 (OS). Endorsed with assignment of 7 June 1733 from Guilliaume Vré [*sic*] to Roger Marrow, [paid in to] Thomas Bridges (witnessed for Bridges & Dockrey [?] by John Fullilove).

**26**. 27 September 1733 (NS). *Blount MSS, D* 7/71
£55 to Captain John Smith, drawn on MS at Gray's Inn (or, failing him, Mr Wyke, goldsmith, by Gray's Inn Gate, Holborn). Accepted by MS 4 September 1733 (OS). Endorsed with assignment of 27 September 1733 to A. Smith (witness: Samuel Smith).

**27**. 15 October 1733 (NS). *Blount MSS, D* 7/72
£40 to William Keetin, drawn on MS at Gray's Inn (or, failing him, Mr Wyke, goldsmith, by Gray's Inn Gate, Holborn). Accepted by MS 10 October 1733 (OS). Endorsed with assignment of 15 October 1733 from Keetin to Messrs Foster & Greame. Receipted by Richard Foster for Foster & Greame.

**28**. 15 October 1733 (NS). *Blount MSS, D* 7/73
£40 to William Keetin, drawn on MS at Gray's Inn (or, failing him, Mr Wyke, goldsmith, by Gray's Inn Gate, Holborn). Accepted by MS 9 October 1733 (OS). Endorsed with assignment from Keetin to Messrs Whitbread & Hodgskins. Receipted by Edward Stone for Whitebread & Hodgskins.

**29**. 15 October 1733 (NS). *Blount MSS, D* 7/74
£18 to William Uré, drawn on MS at Gray's Inn (or, failing him, Mr Wyke, goldsmith, by Gray's Inn Gate, Holborn). Accepted by MS 9

October 1733 (OS). Endorsed with assignment of 15 October 1733 from Guilliaume Vré [*sic*] to Jacques Benezet. Receipted 17 October (witness: A. Desmarette).

**30**. 19 November 1733 (NS). *Blount MSS, D* 7/75
£100 to Mathew Fournier, drawn on MS at his house in Queen Square near Ormond Street. Accepted by MS 14 November (OS). Endorsed with assignment 17 November by Mathieu Fournie to Jacob Berry (witness: John Birkbeck for Messrs Morson).

**31**. 21 January 1733/4 (NS). *Blount MSS, D* 7/76
£73 to John Brussell, drawn on MS at his house in Queen Square. Accepted by Mary Strickland 22 January 1733[/4] (OS). Endorsed with assignment of 21 January 1734 from Brussell in Dunkirk to George Fitzgerald (witness: Wm Shuttleworth for Messrs Knight & Bourne).

**32**. 28 March 1734 (NS). *Blount MSS, D* 7/77
£107 17s 0d to Robert Hewer 'for value received of Mr John Brussell', drawn on MS at his house in Queen Square. No annotation of acceptance. Endorsed with assignment to John Hewer, 2 April to Messrs Bartholomew and Richard Burton (witness: J. Burchall for the Bank).

**33**. 15 August 1734 (NS). *Blount MSS, D* 7/78
£200 to Henry and John Sperling 'for value received of Mr John Brussell', drawn on MS at his house in Queen Square. Accepted by MS 8 August (OS). Endorsed with receipt (witness: Joseph Nelson for Messrs Freame & Barclay).

**34**. 19 September 1734 (NS). *Blount MSS, D* 7/79
£75 to Guillaume Uré 'for value received of the same', drawn on MS at his house in Queen Square. No acceptance noted. Endorsed in French 19 September with assignment to Jacques Benezet (witness: N. Brabins for the Bank).

**35**. 24 September 1734 (NS). *Blount MSS, D* 7/80
Receipt, Ed[ward] Goodere to MS for £13 14s 1d for the use of John Berkeley.

**36**. 12 December 1734 (NS). *Blount MSS, D* 7/81
£77 to John Brussell 'for value received of the same', drawn on MS at his house in Queen Square. Accepted by MS 6 December (OS). Endorsed 12 December with assignment to James Heywood (witness: Thomas Wade for Henry Hankey & Sons). Bill numbered: 5140.

**37**. 24 January 1735 [i.e. 1734/5] (NS). *Blount MSS, D* 7/82
Letter, Richard Towneley at Towneley (franked Manchester) to MS at Gray's Inn, referring to an order from Mrs Fleetwood at Dunkirk to MS to pay him £21. Has therefore drawn on MS for £12 to be paid to Mr

Mawood (instruction slip of same date for payment enclosed). Asks for remainder to be paid to John Maire of Gray's Inn. Endorsed with Maire's receipt of 30 January 1734[/5].

**38**. 27 March 1735 (NS). *Blount MSS*, *D* 7/83
£132 18s 11d to Jacobus de Bonte, drawn on MS at his house in Queen Square. Accepted by MS 19 March (OS). Endorsed in French 26 March 1735 with assignment from Jacobus de Bonte to Jean Duchosale (signs reassignment 28 March as 'du Chosale'), who reassigns to Jonathan Forward (witness: Oliver Topper for Richard Morson).

**39**. 3 April 1735 (NS). *Blount MSS*, *D* 7/84
£60 to Jacobus de Bonte, drawn on MS at his house in Queen Square. No note of acceptance. Endorsed 2 April in French with assignment to Jean Du Chosale, who reassigns 2 April to Jonathan Forward. Receipt witnessed 3 April by Thomas Creid.

**40**. 5 May 1735 (NS). *Blount MSS*, *D* 7/85
£128 8s 6d to Mathew Fournier, drawn on MS at his house in Queen Square. No acceptance noted. Endorsed in French 5 May by Mathieu Fournie with assignment to Micajah Perry. Perry's receipt 2 May (OS) witnessed by John Walkley.

**41**. 8 May 1735 (NS). *Blount MSS*, *D* 7/86
£100 to Jacobus de Bonte, drawn on MS at his house in Queen Square. Accepted by MS 6 May (OS). Endorsed in French 12 May with assignment from Jacobus de Bonte to Messrs Philippe and David Cantillon for value on account of Mr Harold at Dunkirk. Cantillon's receipt witnessed by Ed. Gardiner.

**42**. 19 May 1735 (NS). *Blount MSS*, *D* 7/87
£100 to William Keetin, drawn on MS at his house in Queen Square. Accepted 21 May (OS) by Mary Strickland. Endorsed 26 May with assignment by Keetin to Messrs Whitbread & Hodgskin. Receipt of 30 May witnessed by Oliver Topper for Richard Morson.

**43**. 9 June 1735 (NS). *Blount MSS*, *D* 7/88
£200 to Mathew Fournier, drawn on MS at his house in Queen Square. Accepted 3 June (OS) by Mary Strickland. Endorsed in French 9 June with assignment by Fournie to Micajah Perry. Perry's receipt of 9 June witnessed by John Walkley.

**44**. 3 July 1735 (NS). *Blount MSS*, *D* 7/89
£100 to Messrs De Bonte, Buijssens & de Bauque, drawn on MS at his house in Queen Square. Acceptance signed but undated. Endorsed 3 July (OS) in French with assignment to Thomas Thomas & Son, value on account of Wm Alexander. Receipt witnessed by E. Sandwell for the Bank.

**45**. 30 October 1735 (NS). *Blount MSS, D* 7/90
£160 18s 0d to John Brussell, drawn on MS at his house in Queen Square. Accepted 23 October by Mary Strickland. Endorsed 30 October with assignment from Brussell to Wm Whitaker. Receipt witnessed by J. Langley for the Bank.

**46**. 30 October 1735 (NS). *Blount MSS, D* 7/91
£22 to William Uré, drawn on MS at his house in Queen Square. Accepted by MS 21 October (OS). Endorsed in French 30 October with assignment from Guillaume Uré to Jacques Benezet (witness: J. Langley for the Bank).

**47**. 30 October 1735 (NS). *Blount MSS, D* 7/92
To repay a loan of £100 to Sir John Jernegan, drawn on MS at his house in Queen Square. Acceptance not noted. Endorsed with Jernegan's receipt, dated Costessy, 5 November 1735 (witness: Samuel Wilkinson (mark) 'for Mr Jernegan the goldsmith').

**48**. 31 December 1735 (NS). *Blount MSS, D* 7/93
£115 0s 0d to John Brussell, drawn on MS at his house in Queen Square. Accepted by MS, undated. Endorsed 1 January 1736 with assignment to William Whitaker, whose signature is witnessed 27 December (OS) by Robert Jones for the Bank.

**49**. 31 December 1735 (NS). *Blount MSS, D* 7/94
£110 6s 0d to John Brussell, drawn on MS at his house in Queen Square. Accepted by MS, not dated. Endorsed 1 January 1736 with assignment to William Whitaker, whose signature is witnessed 27 December (OS) by Robert Jones for the Bank.

**50**. 4 August 1736 (paid 18 December 1739). *Blount MSS, D* 7/95
Receipted bill from Thomas Gyles to MS for 5s 4d for a *caveat* entered in the goods of Mrs Ann Acton, deceased.

**51**. 2 September 1736 (NS). *Blount MSS, D* 7/96
£100 to Mrs Mary Saladin & Sister, drawn on MS at his house in Queen Square. Accepted by MS 28 August (OS), 'to be paid at Mr Wright's, goldsmith, at the Golden Cup, Henrietta Street, Covent Garden'. Endorsed assignment in French from Marie Saladin & Soeur to Messrs Thos. Greame & Co. (witness: Peter Gregory for the Bank).

**52**. 25 October 1736 (NS). *Blount MSS, D* 7/97
£120 to John Du Chosale, drawn on MS at his house in Queen Square. Accepted by Mary Strickland 14 October (OS). Endorsed with assignment in French to Messrs Haswell Broakes & Hunt (witness: E. Sandwell for the Bank).

**53**. 13 December 1736 (NS). *Blount MSS, D* 7/98
£100 to Mr Betefort Jensen, drawn on MS at his house in Queen Square.

Accepted by MS 7 December 1736. Endorsed in French with assignment to Messrs Charles Loubier & Tessier (witness: Samuel Thorne for James Martin & Co., 17 December (OS)).

**54**. 18 July 1737 (NS). *Blount MSS, D* 7/99
£100 to John Brussell, drawn on MS at his house in Queen Square. Accepted by MS 11 July (OS). Endorsed with assignment to John Armstrong, who receipts it 25 July (witness: Francis Jersey for Messrs Atkins & Co.).

**55**. 17 November 1737 (NS). *Blount MSS, D* 7/100
£50 to Madame Marcade, widow, drawn on MS at his house in Queen Square. Accepted by M[ary] Strickland 17 November (OS). Endorsed in French with assignment to Thomas Greame, merchant, in London (witness: Samuel Cooper).

**56**. 15 May 1738 (NS). *Blount MSS, D* 7/101
£ 53 0s 0d to Monsieur Jean Du Chosale, drawn on MS at his house in Queen Square. Accepted by MS, no date. Endorsed with assignment in French to Messrs Haswell Brookes & Hunt (witness: Ed Taylor for the Bank).

**57**. 17 August 1738 (NS). *Blount MSS, D* 7/102
£100 received of John Brussell to William Whitaker, drawn on MS at his house in Queen Square. Accepted by MS 9 August (OS) for payment at Mr Wright's the goldsmith. Receipted by Whitaker 11 August (OS) (witness: R. Chamberlain for Sir Joseph Hankey & Co.).

**58**. 17 August 1738 (NS). *Blount MSS, D* 7/103
£22 to William Uré, drawn on MS at his house in Queen Square. Accepted by MS 10 August (OS) for payment at Mr Wright's the goldsmith. Receipted 21 August.

**59**. 4 September 1738 (NS). *Blount MSS, D* 7/104
£125 'value received of Mr John Brussell', to Messrs Patrick & Robert Macky, drawn on MS at his house in Queen Square. Accepted by MS, no date, for payment at Mr Wright's the goldsmith's. Receipt witnessed by [*illeg.*] for Messrs Colebrooke & Co.

**60**. 4 September 1738 (NS). *Blount MSS, D* 7/105
£34 19s 5d, 'value received of Mr John Brussell', to Messrs Blake & Lynch, drawn on MS at his house in Queen Square. Accepted by MS, not dated. Endorsed receipt witnessed by J. Stallard for the Bank.

**61**. 4 September 1738 (NS). *Blount MSS, D* 7/106
£40 0s 7d, 'value received of Mr John Brussell', to Messrs George Fitzgerald & Co., drawn on MS at his house in Queen Square. Accepted by MS, no date, for payment at Mr Wyke's 'over against Grays Inn Gate

in Holborne'. Endorsed receipt witnessed by James Nowell of Messrs Knight & Shuttleworth.

**62**. 20 January 1739 (NS). *Blount MSS, D* 7/107
Note from Catherine Sheldon to MS asking him to pay to Mr Barlow what he requires for a commission which he is undertaking for them and to charge it to their account. Endorsed receipt, 27 January 1738/9 (OS?) from John Strickland to MS for 23s 0d.

**63**. 30 April 1739 (NS). *Blount MSS, D* 7/108
£100 to John Brussell, drawn on MS at his house in Queen Square. Accepted by MS, undated. Endorsed with Brussell's assignment of 30 April 1739 to George Fitzgerald & Co.; receipt of the latter witnessed by James Nowell for Messrs Knight & Shuttleworth.

**64**. 24 September 1739 (NS). *Blount MSS, D* 7/109
£100 to William Keetin of Dunkirk, drawn on MS at his house in Queen Square. Accepted for MS by Ham [?] Gyles 1 October for payment at Mr. Wright's, Covent Garden. Endorsed with Keetin's assignment of 8 October (NS) to Mr Heneage Robinson, who receipts 6 October (OS) (witness: Charles Moore for Messrs Vere & Asgill).

**65**. 2 November 1739 (NS). *Blount MSS, D* 7/110
£96 12s 0d to Francis Poole of St Omer, drawn on MS at his house in Queen Square. Accepted by MS 21 December. Endorsed 10 November with Poole's assignment to Mlle. Veuve de Sarra of St Omer and 16 December with her assignment to Jean François Delacroix and 18 December with his assignment to Messrs Williams [William?] & Thomas Fenton of Leeds, and 17 December (OS) from them to Messrs Knight & Shuttleworth, for whom James Nowell signs as witness.

**66**. 23 January 1740 (NS). *Blount MSS, D* 7/111
£50 to John Brussell, 'value received of the same', drawn on MS at his house in Queen Square. Accepted by MS 23 January (OS?). Endorsed with Brussell's assignment to Messrs George Fitzgerald & Co (witness: Thomas Burroughs for Messrs Knight & Shuttleworth).

**67**. 18 June 1740 (NS). *Blount MSS, D* 7/112
£119 to William Keetin, 'value received of the same', drawn on MS at his house in Queen Square. Accepted by MS 12 June (OS), to be paid 'at Mr Wrights the Golden Cup, Henrietta Street, Covent Garden'. Endorsed with Keetin's assignment to Mr Heneage Robinson, whose receipt is witnessed by Charles Moore for Messrs Vere & Asgill.

**68**. 28 September 1740 (NS). *Blount MSS, D* 7/113
£130 to John Mathew, 'value received of the same', drawn on MS at his house in Queen Square. Accepted by MS 29 September 1740 (OS), to be

paid 'at Mr Wrights the Golden Cup, Henrietta Street, Covent Garden'. Endorsed 6 October 1740 in French with Mathew's assignment to Monsieur Hovell and same date with Hovell's assignment to Messrs Foster & Greame. Witness: S. Mee for Messrs Colebrook & Co. Paid 7 October.

**69**. 25 February 1741 (NS). *Blount MSS, D* 7/114
£20 to Thomas Berkeley for 'value received of the same', drawn on MS at his house in Queen Square. Accepted by MS 6 March 1740/1 (OS). Endorsed in French 25 February with Berkeley's assignment to William Keetin and same date with Keetin's assignment to William Archdeacon of Bruges, and 11 March in English with Archdeacon's assignment to Robert Dillon & Co. Payment witnessed by John Roberts.

**70**. 10 March 1741 (NS). *Blount MSS, D* 7/115
£138 to John du Chosale, for 'value received of the same', drawn on MS at his house in Queen Square. Accepted by MS 3 March 1740/1 (OS). Endorsed 10 March in French with Du Chosale's assignment to John Hanbury, whose receipt is witnessed by William Dennis for the Bank.

**71**. 4 November 1741 (NS). *Blount MSS, D* 7/116
£50 to Nicolas Du Camp for 'value received of the same', drawn on MS at his house in Queen Square. Accepted by MS 3 November (OS). Endorsed in French 8 November with Du Camp's assignment to Messrs Thomas Greame & Co., whose receipt is witnessed by Stephen Mee for James Colebrook.

**72**. 9 November 1741 (NS). *Blount MSS, D* 7/117
£58 to John Brussell for 'value received of the same', drawn on MS at his house in Queen Square. Accepted by MS 2 November 741 (OS). Endorsed 9 November with Brussell's assignment to Messrs Lane Smethurst & Caswall, whose receipt is witnessed by F. Cooke.

**73**. 1 March 1741/2 (NS). *Blount MSS, D* 7/118
£35 2s 6d to Mrs Lemaire, widow [la veuve Estienne Antoine Lemaire], for 'value received of the same', drawn on MS at his house in Queen Square. Accepted by MS 26 February (OS). Endorsed 4 March in French with Lemaire's assignment to Messrs Antoine Clerambault et fils, whose receipt is witnessed for the Bank by J. Poole.

**74**. 22 March 1742 (NS). *Blount MSS, D* 7/119
£100 to Mr Holden junr [*sic*: Joseph Holding] for 'value received of the same', drawn on MS at his house in Queen Square. Accepted by MS 15 March (OS) for payment at Mr Wright's at the Golden Cup, Henrietta Street, Covent Garden. Endorsed 22 March in French with Holding's assignment to Henry Holding, whose receipt is witnessed by J. Smith for Messrs Greame & Co.

**75**. 27 March 1742 (NS). *Blount MSS, D* 7/120
£95 to Mr De Sticker for 'value received of the same', drawn on MS at his house in Queen Square. Accepted by MS 19 April (OS?) for payment at Mr Wright's at the Golden Cup, Henrietta Street, Covent Garden. Endorsed 22 April in French with De Sticker's assignment to Joseph Holding, who assigns 26 April in English to Henry Holding, whose receipt is witnessed by William Dennis for the Bank.

**76**. 27 March 1742 (NS). *Blount MSS, D* 7/121
£105 to Mr De Sticker for 'value received of the same', drawn on MS at his house in Queen Square. Accepted by MS 19 April (OS?) for payment at Mr Wright's at the Golden Cup, Henrietta Street, Covent Garden. Endorsed 22 April in French with De Sticker's assignment to Joseph Holding, who assigns 26 April in English to Henry Holding, whose receipt is witnessed by William Dennis for the Bank.

**77**. 1742 (NS). *Blount MSS, D* 7/122
£100 to Mr Hovell for 'value received of the same', drawn on MS at his house in Queen Square. Accepted by MS 21 April (OS). Endorsed 26 April in French with Hovell's assignment to Messrs Foster & Greame, whose receipt is witnessed by Stephen Mee for James Colebrook Esq., 29 April 1742.

**78**. 4 October 1742 (NS). *Blount MSS, D* 7/123
£31 17s 6d to Samuel Tonge for 'value received of William Keetin', drawn on MS at his house in Queen Square. Accepted for MS by H. Gyles, 28 September (OS). Affixed label stating that it is 'to be paid by Mr Wright in Henrietta Street'. Endorsed 4 October with Tonge's assignment to William Farnworth, whose receipt is witnessed by Henry Boldero for Sir Fr[anci]s Hankey & Co.

**79**. 4 October 1742 (NS). *Blount MSS, D* 7/124
£25 2s 6d to Peter [Pierre] Denys for 'value received of William Keetin', drawn on MS at his house in Queen Square. Accepted for MS by H. Gyles 28 September (OS). Endorsed 4 October in French with Denys' assignment to Messrs Whitbread, Hodgskin & Edwards, whose receipt is witnessed by John Mills.

**80**. 15 May 1743 (NS). *Blount MSS, D* 7/125
£75 to Mrs Lemaire, widow [la veuve Estienne Antoine Lemaire], for 'value received of the same', drawn on MS at his house in Queen Square. Accepted by MS 10 May (OS). Endorsed 16 May in French with Lemaire's assignment to Messrs Bourdieu & Desmarette, whose receipt is witnessed by R. Sargeant for Messrs Greene & Tysoe.

**81**. 9 November 1743 (NS). *Blount MSS, D* 7/126
£43 to Mrs [Aurilliez] Constantin for 'value received of the same', drawn

on MS at his house in Queen Square. Accepted by MS 14 December. Endorsed 18 December in French with Mrs Constantin's assignment to J. Hasembergue and 19 December with his to Messrs Foster Greame & Foster, whose receipt of 22 December is witnessed by Stephen Mee for James Colebrook Esq.

**82**. 23 January 1743/4 (NS). *Blount MSS, D* 7/127
£95 10s 0d to Peter [Pierre?] Delcloque for 'value received of the same', drawn on MS at his house in Queen Square. Accepted by MS 18 January (OS). Endorsed 23 January in French with Delcloque's assignment to J. Charles Desmadryl, whose receipt is witnessed by L. Thomas for James Martin Esq.

**83**. 13 June 1744 (NS). *Blount MSS, D* 7/128
£110 to Peter [Pierre] Tellier for 'value received of the same', drawn on MS at his house in Queen Square. Accepted by MS 7 June (OS). Endorsed 14 June in French with Tellier's assignment to G[uillau]me Minet, whose receipt is witnessed by John Denton for Sir James Hankey & Co.

**84**. 30 January 1747/8. *Blount MSS, D* 7/156
Copy of account entry of payment of £25 3s 0d to Lady Benedicta Fleetwood on Henrietta Strickland's account (£17 for a year's pension due 25 August 1747, £5 5s 0d for 'her charges into England', 16s 0d for her going to Calais, £1 1s 0d for pocket expenses, and £1 1s 0d to Mrs Catharine Strickland).[2]

---

[2] Fair copy entry; not in Mary Strickland's hand.

# THE SPELLIKENS (DOMINICAN CONVENT), BRUSSELS: ABSTRACTS OF MISCELLANEOUS DOCUMENTS

Like the additional Dunkirk documents, these papers from the Spellikens demonstrate the considerable extent to which the convents were integrated into the financial dealings of Flanders, drawing here on a mix of large financial businesses such as the banking operations of the Cantillon family and the firm of Geo. Waters & Co, with branches in London and Paris, working with agents such as the bankers Jean Nettine of Brussels and John Brussell.

*Bundle marked: 'XVIII century cheques signed "Margaret Ellerker"' [and others].* Blount MSS, C *129/26–64*

**1**. 17 January 1736 (NS). *Blount MSS, C* 129/26
Receipt: Morgan Hansbie to Mr Chilton of Brussels for 3 guineas via MS.

**2**. 19 April 1742 (NS). *Blount MSS, C* 129/27
Note: [Prioress] Mary Young in Brussels to MS at Queen Square to pay £50 to Mr Nettine. Accepted 24 April. Endorsed to Joseph Marquelier and then to Jacques Benezet.

**3**. 28 May 1742 (NS). *Blount MSS, C* 129/28
Receipt: Ruth Lovett to Mrs Mary Young of Brussels for 5 guineas via MS.

**4**. 11 January 1743 (NS?). *Blount MSS, C* 129/29
Note: Sister Marie Young, prioress, in Brussels to MS at Queen Square to pay £65 5s 0d to Mr Nettine. Accepted 12 January. Endorsed by Nettine for payment to the order of Messrs George FitzGerald & Cie.

**5**. 21 August 1742 (NS). *Blount MSS, C* 129/30
Note: Sister Catherine Winifride Hyde in Brussels to MS at Queen Square, London, to pay £75 1s 11d to Mr Nettine. Accepted 28 September 1742 by H. Gyles for Mrs Mary Strickland. Endorsed for payment to Mr Jean de Cleves and then to Jean Osij & fils, John James, Thomas Norton, Adam Lawry and Joseph Wear.

**6**. 14 October 1743 (NS). *Blount MSS, C* 129/31
Note: Margrit Compton to MS at Queen Square to pay £100 to Mr
Nettine. Accepted 17 October. Endorsed for payment to Alexandre F.
De Trez, then to Messrs Philip Le Francq & Abraham Baert en Cie and
Thomas Giles.

**7**. 16 March 1740[/1?] (OS). *Blount MSS, C* 129/32
Receipt: William Wood to MS for £10 by the order of and for the use
of John Park of Norwich.

**8**. 9 February 1742[/3] (OS). *Blount MSS, C* 129/33
Receipt: William Wood to MS for £10 by the order of and for the use of
John Park of Norwich. Note on verso: 'Spelicans / Jno Park'.

**9**. 23 December 1735 (OS). *Blount MSS, C* 129/34
Receipt: Thomas Penson to MXE for £9 via MS for the use of Mrs Bennett at Mr Norris's in Norwich.

**10**. 30 August 1735 (OS). *Blount MSS, C* 129/35
Receipt: Thomas Penson to MXE for £9 10s 0d via MS for the use of
Mrs Bennett at Mrs Norris's in Norwich.

**11**. 5 September 1736 (NS). *Blount MSS, C* 129/36
Note: MXE to MS at Queen Square to pay £27 11s 4d to Mr Nettine.
Accepted 3 September OS. Endorsed by Mr Nettine for payment to
Messrs George FitzGerald & Cie.

**12**. 28 May 1736 (OS). *Blount MSS, C* 129/37
MS's account note of Mr Mabbat's bill to the Spellikens for writing MS's
account with Mrs Chilton.

**13**. 17 January 1737 (NS). *Blount MSS, C* 129/38
Note: Ann Chilton in Brussels to MS at Queen Square, London, to pay
£40 to Mr Nettine. Accepted 25 January (OS). Endorsed for payment to
Mr Jean Scherenberg and then to Timothy Hollis.

**14**. 5 May 1737 (NS). *Blount MSS, C* 129/39
Receipt: Morgan Hansbie to MS: £1 by the order of Mrs Ann Chilton
at the Spellikens in Brussels.

**15**. 1 October 1737 (NS). *Blount MSS, C* 129/40
Note: Mary Ann Chilton in Brussels to MS at Queen Square, London,
to pay £50 10s 0d to Mr Nettine. Accepted 25 January (OS). Endorsed
for payment to Messrs George FitzGerald & Cie.

**16**. 8 February 1738 (NS?). *Blount MSS, C* 129/41
Note: Catherine Winifride Hyde in Brussels to MS at Queen Square,
London, to pay £30 to Mr Nettine. Endorsed for payment to Messrs
George FitzGerald & Cie.

**17**. 6 April 1738 (OS). *Blount MSS, C* 129/42
Receipt: William Wood to MS for 10 guineas by the order of and for the use of John Park of Norwich.

**18**. 23 April 1738 (OS). *Blount MSS, C* 129/43
Note: Mariane Chilton in Brussels to MS at Queen Square, London, to pay £100 to Mr Nettine. Endorsed for payment to Messrs George FitzGerald & Cie.

**19**. 29 July 1738 (NS). *Blount MSS, C* 129/44
Note: Mariane Chilton in Brussels to MS at Queen Square, London, to pay £45 13s 06d to Mr Nettine. Endorsed for payment to Charles Triponetti and then to Messrs Unwin & Lefevre.

**20**. 29 December 1738 (NS). *Blount MSS, C* 129/45
Note: Messrs P[hilip] and D[avi]d Cantillon in London to Mr Jean de Cleeves in Brussels to pay 525 florins to the order of Mrs Ann Chilton for value received of MS. [In French]

**21**. 8 June 1739 (NS). *Blount MSS, C* 129/46
Note: Mariane Chilton in Brussels to MS at Queen Square, London, to pay £257 5s 00d to Mr Nettine. Endorsed for payment to Messrs George FitzGerald & Cie.

**22**. 5 July 1739 (NS). *Blount MSS, C* 129/47
Note: John Park of Norwich to MS at Lincoln's Inn to pay £10 to William Wood.

**23**. 15 January 1740 (NS?). *Blount MSS, C* 129/48
Note: Mary Teresa Sarsfield in Brussels to MS at Queen Square, London, to pay £38 2s 3d to Mr Nettine. Endorsed for payment to Messrs George FitzGerald & Cie.

**24**. 21 April 1740 (NS). *Blount MSS, C* 129/49
Note: Mary Young in Brussels to MS at Queen Square, London, to pay £67 9s 8½d to Mr Nettine. Endorsed for payment to Messrs George FitzGerald & Cie.

**25**. 20 July 1740 (NS). *Blount MSS, C* 129/50
Instruction from Mary Rosa Howard, [Duchess?] of Norfolk, in Brussels to MS to give the 3 guineas received from the Duke of Norfolk for her account to Mr Fitzgerald to return to his correspondent Mr Nettine, banker in Brussels, from whom she has received the amount.

**26**. 19 October 1740 (NS). *Blount MSS, C* 129/51
Note: Mary Young in Brussels to MS at Queen Square, London, to pay £50 to Mr Nettine. Accepted 15 October for payment by Mr Wright at the Golden Cap in Henrietta Street. Endorsed for payment to Messrs George FitzGerald & Cie.

**27**. 12 January 1741 (NS). *Blount MSS, C* 129/52
Note: Mary Young in Brussels to MS at Queen Square, London, to pay
£50 to Mr Nettine. Endorsed for payment to Messrs George FitzGerald
& Cie.

**28**. 26 August 1741 (NS). *Blount MSS, C* 129/53
Bill of exchange: Sister Mary Young, prioress, in Brussels to MS at
Queen Square, London, to pay £100 to Mr Nettine. Endorsed in French
by M. Nettine for payment to Mr Jean Scherenberg of Amsterdam and
then to Messrs Levy Bing & fils.

**29**. 18 September 1741 (NS). *Blount MSS, C* 129/53
Printed notarial certificate from Benjamin Bonnet of London, notary, on
behalf of Messrs Levy and Ruben Salomon's of London, merchants, of
protest of the Bill of Exchange, following its presentation by Bonnet at
MS's house, where a woman to whom he spoke informed him that MS
was out of town and that she could not say anything about the bill of
exchange. On verso: 26 August 1741: Copy of the above bill of exchange
from Sister Mary Young, prioress, in Brussels to MS at Queen Square,
London, to pay £100 to Mr Nettine.

**30**. [September 1741] (NS). *Blount MSS, C* 129/53
Account of Spellerberg & Metzner for the above bill of exchange, protest,
rechange, commission and postage: £102 3s 0d.

**31**. 19 December 1729 (NS). *Blount MSS, C* 129/54
Note: Messrs Philip and D. Cantillon in London to Mr Jean de Cleves in
Brussels to pay 309 florins to the order of Mrs Letitia Barker for value
received of MS. [In French]

**32**. 26 June 1728 (OS). *Blount MSS, C* 129/55
Receipt from [unsigned] to William, Duke and Marquess of Powis, for
£195 arrears of a £15 per annum annuity.

**33**. 13 July 1733 (NS). *Blount MSS, C* 129/56
Note: MXE in Brussels to MS at Gray's Inn (redirected to 3, Lincoln's
Inn) for payment of £58 to the order of Mademoiselle de Broeta, widow
of Charles Broeta. Accepted 14 July (OS). Endorsed with assignment to
Samuel Grimes & Co. [In French]

**34**. 20 July [1734] (NS). *Blount MSS, C* 129/57
Note: MXE in Brussels to MS at Queen Square for payment of £25 to
the order of Madame de Broeta, widow of Charles Broeta. Accepted
20 July (OS). Endorsed with assignment to John Cranidge and Thomas
Giles. [In French]

**35**. 31 May 1732 (NS). *Blount MSS, C* 129/58
Note: Messrs Philip and D. Cantillon in London to Mr Jean de Cleves

in Brussels to pay 385 florins to the order of Mrs Julia Browne for value received of MS. [In French]

**36**. 6 December 1729 (NS). *Blount MSS, C* 129/59
Covering note to [MS?] from Richard Wotton of Doctors' Commons, accompanying requested copies of the wills of Anne Mohun and Henry Mohun (cost £1 and 12s 6d respectively).

**37**. 9 February 1730/1 (NS). *Blount MSS, C* 129/60
Note: Messrs Philip and D. Cantillon in London to Mr Jean de Cleves in Brussels to pay 725 florins to the order of Mrs Browne for value received of MS. [In French]

**38**. 17 February 1729/30 (NS). *Blount MSS, C* 129/61
Note: Messrs Philip and D. Cantillon in London to Mr Jean de Cleves in Brussels to pay 265 florins to the order of Mrs Letitia Barker for value received of MS. [In French]

**39**. 3 June 1735 (NS). *Blount MSS, C* 129/62
Note: MXE in Brussels to Mrs Mary Strickland at Queen Square for payment of £125 to the order of Madame de Broeta, widow of Charles Broeta. Accepted 6 June (OS). Endorsed with assignment to Samuel Grimes. [In French]

**40**. 26 June 1734 (NS). *Blount MSS, C* 129/63
Receipt: Thomas Penson to MXE for £10 via MS for the use of Mrs Bennet.

**41**. 22 June 1731 (NS). *Blount MSS, C* 129/64
Note: Messrs Philip and D. Cantillon in London to Mr Jean de Cleves in Brussels to pay 425 florins to the order of Mrs Browne for value received of MS. [In French]

# BIOGRAPHIES OF PERSONS MENTIONED IN THE TEXT

Where appropriate, the reference numbers to the *Who Were the Nuns?* database are given; readers are referred there for further information. Some information (mostly dates) comes from the Blount MSS and from Strickland's papers within them. An asterisk (*) indicates a client or associate of Strickland. Only individuals for whom further information is known are included here.

**Ailesbury, Thomas Bruce, 2nd Earl of** (1656–1741). Jacobite; member of James II's court.

**Aire, Mrs.** Presumably Mrs Eyre.

**Alsace, Mme d'**, *Prévote* of the Fondation de Lalaing et de Berlaymont (Augustinian convent in Brussels founded 1626).

***Andrews [Andrew], Bridget** (c. 1698–1783). Eldest daughter of Sir Francis Andrew (or Andrews), 4th Baronet (d. 1759) of Pudding Norton, Norfolk. Married Philip Southcote of Weybridge, Surrey, a younger son of Sir Edward Southcote of Witham, Essex, all of them Strickland clients. Sir Francis's only surviving son, William (d. 1804), being a lunatic, the estate was left to Bridget. There was a connection by marriage with the Petre family.

**Arthur, Daniel** (1620–1705), banker, of Paris and London, uncle of Mannock Strickland. Knighted by James II in 1690 but also trusted by William III. Jacobite exile in St Germain-en-Laye. His son, also called Daniel, followed his father into banking and was one of Strickland's foreign exchange sources and gained a reputation as chief banker to the Jacobites. Arthur's second wife, Anne Mannock, was the sister of Strickland's mother, Bridget. The parties to his marriage settlement in 1672 included Sir Richard Bellings, secretary to Queen Catherine of Braganza.[1]

**Ashmall, Mary (Mary Joseph) OSA** (d. 1765), WWTN LA 007. Augustinian choir nun, Louvain. Professed 1717. Daughter of Robert Ashmall,

---

[1] *Blount MSS, C* 107/3.

attorney to Lady Mary Petre and agent for the English Canonesses of the Holy Sepulchre at Liege, at which Strickland's daughter Henrietta was educated at the shared expense of her father and Lady Goring. Money for her support was supplied by Strickland via the Paris banker Richard Cantillon, paid direct to her own account once converted to French livres: £50 each in November 1735, July 1738 and September 1737. He switched this payment in 1739, using George Fitzgerald & Co. in London for transmission to the Parisian banker George Waters senior.

**Barker, Lettice [Laetitia Maria] OP** (1661–1748). WWTN BD 003. Choir nun, Spellikens, Brussels. Daughter of Robert Barker and Susana Beswick. Professed 1689. Prioress 1727–30; Sub-Prioress 1730.

**Bartlett, Catherine Perpetua OSA** (1696–1780). WWTN LA 019. Choir nun, Louvain. Daughter of Rowland Bartlett of Hill End and Castlemorton, Worcs., and Ann Tasburgh of Bodney, Norfolk. Professed 1731. The Tasburgh family were clients of Strickland.

**Bartlett, Winifred OSA** (1702–78). WWTN LA 021. Choir nun, Louvain. Sister of Catherine Bartlett.

**Bartley, Mr.** Brother of Mrs Mary Hacon.

**Berkeley [Barkley], Robert.** Strickland's only pupil, son of his client Thomas Berkeley. Three-year apprenticeship commencing 1 February 1737; fee £100.[2]

***Blount, Michael I**, of Mapledurham (1693–1739). Married Mary Agnes Tichborn of Tichborn, Hants.

***Blount, Michael II**, of Mapledurham (1719–92). Inherited Mapledurham 1739; married Mary Eugenia (1723–65), elder daughter of Mannock Strickland, in 1742.

**Bostock, Henry.** Mercer, of St Paul Covent Garden; joint lender with his wife, Peregrine, of mortgage finance for Strickland.[3] A connection with the goldsmith and broker Nathaniel Bostock of Pall Mall (active 1718–23, d. 1728) is unlikely.

**Brent, Mrs.** Sister of Lady Anne Lytcott (Margaret, Mary or Frances; the remaining sister was Elizabeth Conquest). Various members of the Brent family were implicated in the 'Popish Plot'. Their brother was the recusant lawyer Robert Brent, 'a Catholic barrister and advisor to the king ... who had helped to draft James II's 1687 Declaration of Indulgence, and established a network of Catholics and Dissenters as

---

2 *Blount MSS, E* 50/174.
3 *Blount MSS, C* 115/41, 1732.

electoral "regulators" designed to enter local public office in support of the king'.[4] The family lawyer was the Catholic barrister Nathaniel Pigott.

**Broeta, Madame.** Widow of Charles Broeta, merchant, in den Gulden Rick, Couper Straet, Antwerp.

**Brown, Julia OP** (d. 1747). Choir nun, Spellikens, Brussels. Professed 1712 as a choir nun in Galway, which she left in 1717 to found a convent in Dublin. In 1729, owing to ill health, she travelled to Brussels where she stayed with the English Dominicans. Prioress 1730–33. She returned to Dublin in 1733 to raise funds and recruits, causing major arguments.

**Burgis, Alexander.** Courier. Lodged with Mr Beezley of Panton Street. Regular financial go-between and witness of deeds executed by Strickland for clients 'beyond sea' until 1738. Strickland used him in June 1737 to take £192 3s 9d, 'a debt due to Mr Hansbie from Mr Wybarne'.[5]

**Carew, Margaret Delphina OSA** (d. 1770). WWTN LA 048. Choir nun, Louvain. Professed 1722.

**Carington, Anne, Viscountess** (d. 1748). Widow of Charles, 2nd Viscount Carington (d. 1706). Third daughter of William Herbert (c. 1626–96). Active Jacobite. Clandestine marriage in 1709 to Kenneth Mackenzie.[6]

**Carnaby, Robert?** Of Durham. Radclyffe family connection.

**Carnan, Thomas.** London agent of Sir Henry Englefield.

**\*Caryll, John,** of Harting and Ladyholt, Sussex (1666?–1736). Married Mary, sister of Kenneth Mackenzie. Friend of Alexander Pope. Godfather of Martha Blount of Mapledurham (1690–1763).

**Challoner, Richard** (1691–1781). Titular Bishop of Debra and Vicar Apostolic of the London District. Living at Mrs Bret's, Queens Square, Devonshire Street.

**Chilton, Ann (Mary Anna) OP** (1669–1741) WWTN BD 021. Choir nun, Dominicans, Spellikens, Brussels. Professed 1688; dowry 2,500 guilders. Prioress 1733–39. Second daughter of Christopher Chilton and Margarit Thompson:

> Receavd with Sister Mary Ann Chilton, tow thousand five hondred gilders; five hondred gilders was spent on her Cloathing & Profession, the tow thousand

---

4 Glickman (2009), pp. 22, 105. Brent's admission cannot be traced in the registers; a Robert Brent Lytcott was, however, admitted to Gray's Inn in 1729/30.
5 *Blount MSS, E* 50.
6 The date is given as 1709 in Antoin E. Murphy, *Richard Cantillon: Entrepreneur and Economist* (Oxford: Clarendon Press, 1986), p. 109, but as 1705 in ibid., p. 211. BL Add. MS 28251, fol. 221, dates it as January 1711.

gilders is on the parish of Borem ... The parish of Bornhem has paid in this many [money?], & its put on my Lord Ailesbury for 5 per cent in the year 1720. My Lord Ailesbury paid this money in the year 1721 ... Mistris Chilton promised to leave her Daughter 100 pound more at her death, to make her portion 350 pound, & recommended the performance to her son & heir Mr Christopher Chilton, who charg'd himself theirwith, & promis'd us kindly to make up for the Interest or Arreers: who at his death accordingly, & to be pray'd for after his Death, in his Will left our howse two Actions upon the India Company at Paris, which yealds yearly about 300 french Livers. These two Actions are in the hands of the Reverend Father, Fr. Peter Neville, Procurator of the Jesuits of the English Province at Paris, who hath undertaken to remitt us yearly the Accidents theirof which we have accordingly Receiv'd since Mr Chilton's death 1738 ... The yearly Payment is uncertain, according as the mony rises & falls which comonly produceth about half the vallue of our Currant Gildars ... The two Actions left us by Mr Christofer Chilton was sold at Paris by the consent of the Consell for 2191-07-3: Currant, which mony was put out as follows: Put out by Mr Nettine Banquier in Brussells for us 2000 Gilders Currant at Hannay the 9th of September 1743 at 4 per Cento Currant. Remainder of this Mony is 191-07-3 which is in the Cappitall Bag kept in the Depositume.[7]

**Cholmeley, Elizabeth Teresa (Monica) OSA** (1705–40). WWTN LA 049. Choir nun at Louvain. Daughter of Thomas Cholmeley of Bransby, Yorks. and Katherine Tunstall.

**Cholmeley, Margaret ('Peggy').** Milliner and dressmaker. Courier. A cousin of Cecily Tunstall.

**\*Cholmeley, Thomas (b. 1663).** Father of Elizabeth Cholmeley. Recusant. In 1736 his son Thomas married Elizabeth, only child of Thomas Walton of West Thorndon, Essex, Essex agent of Lord Petre.[8]

**Chorley, Richard,** of Hartwood Green. Lawyer for Henry and John Eyre; agent for Sir Marmaduke Constable. Related by marriage to Catherine Walmesley, widow of the 7th Lord Petre. Assumed responsibility for Petre family affairs following Strickland's death.

**Cleve, Jean de [Decleve].** Banker, used by the Spellikens.

**Collingwood, John.** Courier. Partner and son-in-law of John Mondehare, who were Strickland's London wine merchants and sometimes travelled to France on business.

**Collingwood, Mary Cornelia OSA** (1708?–75). WWTN LA 064. Choir

---

[7] 'Records of the Dominican Nuns of the Second Order (Vilvorde and Brussels), 1661–1697', in *Dominicana*, Catholic Record Society 25 (London: Catholic Record Society, 1925), pp. 15, 217.

[8] *Blount MSS, C* 130/14: marriage settlement.

nun at Louvain. Professed 1726. Sister of John Collingwood. Another brother, **Thomas**, was also associated with Louvain.

**Coleman, Anne (Anne Ursula) [Coalman] OP** (1667–1733). WWTN BD 022. Choir nun, Spellikens, Brussels. Professed 1685; dowry 3,500 guilders. Daughter of John Coleman.

**Conquest, Elizabeth (née Brent)**, of Bloomsbury Square (d. before 1743). A sister of Lady Lytcott.

***Constable, Cuthbert** (c. 1680–1746). Born Cuthbert Tunstall; changed his name in 1718 on inheriting Burton Constable from his cousin, the last Viscount Dunbar. Antiquary and physician. Married firstly Amy Clifford (d. 1731; three children, William, Cicely and Winifred), secondly Elizabeth Heneage (1711–post 1736), whose only son, Marmaduke, resumed the surname Tunstall on inheriting Wycliffe. Brother of Cecily Tunstall. Executor of Lady Mary Radclyffe.

***Constable, Sir Marmaduke** (1682–1746). Of Everingham, Yorks.

**Crathorn, Ralph** (b. c. 1634). Husband of Ann Tunstall (b. 1644).

**Crathorn of Ness, William [alias Yaxley]** (1670–1740). Secular priest. Studied at Douai College; ordained 1697. Editor of John Crathorne.

**Crathorne, Miss**. Possibly Anne Crathorne, niece of Lady Anne Radclyffe, who left her a £20 annuity in her will in 1699.[9]

**Crathorne (Crathorn), Barbara Agatha OSA** (d. 1743). WWTN LA 076. Choir nun at Louvain. Professed 1700. Cousin of Lady Anne Radclyffe, who left her a £20 annuity in her will of 1699, and of Cecily Tunstall. Daughter of Ralph Crathorne of Crathorne, Yorks., and Anne Tunstall of Scargill, Co. Durham. Sister of William Crathorne and Ralph Crathorne, both priests of Douai.

**Crispe, Lady Maria [Marie] OSB** (1687–1757). WWTN BB 050. Choir nun at the Benedictine convent, Brussels. Clothed 1686; professed 1687. Abbess 1719–57. Educated in convent school from 1680, when her mother, Mary Collins (WWTN BB 043), entered the novitiate. After Strickland's death, Lady Mary Crispe of the Benedictine Dames of Brussels resorted to a carefully worded letter of attorney to recover a debt from Michael Blount II of Mapledurham granted to her in a Chancery suit; it is noteworthy that the very cautious description of her is as a spinster 'now residing in Brussels'. She used John Staples of the Middle Temple as her attorney. She was the subject of a 1737 poem by Michael Blount I

---

9 *Blount MSS, C* 98/58.

of Mapledurham, celebrating her jubilee, which is printed in its entirety in *ECIE*, vol. 3, pp. 361–5.

**Culcheth, John** (d. 1733). Attorney for the Swinburne family of Capheaton. Strickland received payments through him for Dunkirk.

**Culcheth, Thomas SJ** (1654–1730). Born in Lancashire. Professed 1674; ordained 1686. His father, Thomas, was a non-juror in 1715, as was his uncle John, who practised law at Staples Inn and then Gray's Inn. Another brother was a Jesuit and four of his six sisters became nuns at various convents.

**Daly, Mary Power**, *See* Power, *alias* Daly, Mary.

**Daniel, Elizabeth (Mary) OSA**. WWTN LA081. Choir nun at Louvain. Professed 1723.

**Daniel, Robert**. Notary public, of Antwerp, 'His Majesty's Secretary' at the Brussels Court. Three notarial certificates of the life of Lady Catherine Radclyffe survive (1733–5), drawn up by the Imperial Notary John Anthony du Rij, certified by the burgomasters, sheriffs and council of Louvain, attested by J. B. du Chateau and bearing the wafer seal of Louvain. Daniel further sealed and certified its English version in 1733 and 1735.[10]

**Day, Thomas (Thomas Brown** alias **Day)** (1668–1748). Secular priest. Treasurer of the English Chapter and its Dean from 1732. Messenger who appears particularly to have overseen movements of Catholics between England and the Continent.

**Derwentwater**, *See* Radclyffe.

***Devereux (Shevereux), Elizabeth** (d. 1735). Only daughter and heir of Leicester Martin of Ipswich. Wife of Pryce Devereux, later 9th Viscount Hereford (1664–1740), who accused Strickland of conspiring with Edward Spelman and Robert Hoxton and forming a conspiracy against him to alienate her affections. MS drafted her will in 1732.

**Dicconson, Edward** (1670–1752). Of Wrightington, Lancs. Titular Bishop of Malla; Vicar Apostolic of the Northern District. Procurator of Douai College; became Vice-President in 1713. Left Douai 1720 to work on the English mission. Chaplain to Mr Giffard of Chillington.

**Dillon, Mr**. Banker, of Dublin. Lived near the church of St Peter's Poor,

---

[10] Essex Record Office, D/DP F290 (c. 1733); *Blount MSS, C* 157/23 (2 January 1733/4 OS); *Blount MSS, C* 145/63 (18 January 1734/5); *Blount MSS, C* 157/23 (1735).

London (St Peter le Poer, Broad Street, City of London). Traded with France and Holland.

**Draper, Mr Burgis**. Of Reading, gentleman. Merchant. In partnership with George Waters as bankers to James Bartholomew Radclyffe, 4th Earl of Derwentwater.

**Du Rij, Jean Antoine**. Imperial notary.

**Ellerker, Margaret Xaveria OP** (d. 1737). WWTN BD 028. Choir nun, Spellikens, Brussels. Professed 1711.

> The Interest of all the Capital mony we put out on the Estate of his Grace the Late Duke of Powis has been fully satisfyed, as hath been since by his Grace the Presant Duke, in the succession of his Father, in full, till he pay'd in the Principal mony the 14th of February 1734, to Mr Mannock Strickland Esquier who does Business for our Community since Mr Arthur has given over acting in that kind. Of this Capital which was 1040 pounds stirling, Mr Strickland lent 1000 p. at 4 per Cent to L. Peters [Lord Petre?] the 19 of March 1736 English Stile, our Stile 1737, which he pay'd in August the 9th 1739. This 1000 Capital Mr Strickland put out to Lord Arundel, the 29th Sept 1739, for 4 per cent.
>
> Sister Margaret Ellerker had one hundred pound which was put upon my Lord Ailesbury for six per cent 100. She had seven hundred bookes call'd *the Reformation, judged* worth a crowne a piece, and the brass plate to print the 'Tree of Life,' all of which is to make up her portion when they are sold. [11] My Lord Ailesbury has paid this hundred pound in the year 1720. Sister Margarit Ellerker dyed the 22nd of February 1737, aged 67, and 26 professed. She was only daughter to Mr … Ellerker, a Yorkshier family, and of his lawfull wife Mistress … Profession, the two thousand gilders is on the Parish of Borem. 2500. [12]

**Englefield, Betty**. Possibly Alice Elizabeth Englefield OSA (d. 1744). WWTN PA 049. Choir nun, Augustinians, Paris. Professed 1691. Daughter of Anthony Englefield of Englefield, Berks., and Alice Stokes of London.

**Englefield, Sir Henry [Harry]** (1706–80). Of Whiteknights, near Reading.

**Erington (Errington), Ann (Anne) OSA** (1667–1717). WWTN LA 087. Lay sister, Louvain. Professed 1667. May have been related to Thomas Errington, who accounted for cash returned 1720–29 on the Earl of Derwentwater's estate. [13]

---

11 Guilday, p. 418 (where she is not named). Both works are untraced.
12 ECIE, vol. 5, p. 174; 'Records of the Dominican Nuns of the Second Order (Vilvorde and Brussels), 1661–1697', in *Dominicana*, Catholic Record Society 25 (London: Catholic Record Society, 1925), p. 211.
13 *Blount MSS, C* 145/36.

**Eyre, John**, of Gray's Inn and Bures Hall, Norfolk (d. 1739). Second son of Thomas Eyre of Hassop (1624?–1688) by his second marriage, to Mary Bedingfeld, in 1644. Admitted to Gray's Inn 1701. Had a practice with his older brother, Henry Eyre (c. 1667–1719), which was later taken over by their pupil, MS (admitted to Gray's Inn 1696), following Henry's death.

**\*Eyre, Margaret (Peggy) Martina OSA** (1720–81). WWTN LA 089. Choir nun, Louvain. Clothed 1738; professed 1739; dowry 5,000 florins de change. Daughter of Thomas Eyre (1624?–1668) of Hassop, Derbys., and Maria Holman of Warkworth, Northumberland.

**Eyre, Mary Anne OSA** (b. 1730). WWTN LA 090. Choir nun, Louvain. Clothed 1748; dowry of 5,000 florins. Daughter of Thomas Eyre of Hassop (1624?–1668) and Maria Homan of Warkworth, Northumberland.

**Fell, Charles**. Predecessor of Gilbert Haydock as agent to St Monica's, Louvain. Lost the Louvain convent £300 on a bad investment, whose history can be traced in the letters. This sum was a gift in 1723/4 from Lady Mary Radclyffe, initially paid to Thomas Day and then transferred to Fell for the use of the Misses Hanford.[14] Notes from Lady Mary Radclyffe indicate that the payment was to be organised by Strickland through the London goldsmith Peter Wyke.[15]

**Fennick (Fenwick), Rodger**. Lawyer. Friend of 3rd Earl of Derwentwater; accompanied him on his return from France to England in 1709.

**Fletewood, Lady Mary Benedicta (Fleetwood) OSB** (1665–1748). WWTN DB 061. Choir nun, Benedictine Dames, Dunkirk. Professed 1686. Elected Prioress 1712. Became second Abbess 1712 in succession to Dame Mary Caryll (d. 1712). Died 10 October 1748. A Mrs Fleetwood (perhaps a relative) resided at Little Wild Street, Drury Lane in 1728.[16]

**Gage, Mrs**. Probably Delariviere Gage (née D'Ewes) (d. 1746), mother of Sir Thomas Gage, 3rd Baronet of Hengrave, Suffolk.

**Gage, Sir William, 2nd Viscount Gage**. Of Firle, Sussex. Guardian during his minority of Robert James Petre, 8th Baron Petre.

**Gerard, Lady Elizabeth** (c. 1680–1743). Only child of Digby, 5th Baron Gerard (1662–84), who died at the Rose Tavern, Covent Garden, aged twenty-two, from a drinking match. There were no male heirs.

**Giffard (Gifford), Peter (c. 1687–1746)**. Of Chillington, Staffs. Cousin

---

14  *Blount MSS, C* 145/70–1.
15  Anstruther 3, pp. 236–7.
16  *Blount MSS, C* 74/255.

of Henry Stonor. Barbara Petre, daughter of Robert James Petre, 8th Baron Petre, married his son Thomas Giffard.

**Gother, John** (d. 1704). Convert; secular priest and controversialist. Author of devotional works popular with the convents.

**Grymes [Grimes], Samuel**. Merchant in the City of London. London correspondent of Mme Broeta of Antwerp.

**Gyles, Thomas**. Scrivener. Used by Strickland to intervene in mortgage matters.

**Hacon, Mary OSA** (d. 1740) WWTN LA 118. Choir nun, Louvain. Professed 1686. Sister of Mr Bartley.

**Haggerston, William** (b. 1684). Second son of Sir Thomas Haggerston, 2nd Baronet (d. 1710), who married Anne, daughter of Sir Philip Mark Constable. His older brother Thomas was killed in the service of James II in Ireland. Three brothers became recusant priests. Estates sequestered 1649–53. Cousin of Cecily Tunstall.

**Hanford, Misses**. Intended recipients of £300 from Lady Mary Radclyffe in 1723/4, badly invested by Charles Fell in 1724 with the notorious Jacobites Lady Lytcott and Mrs Throckmorton, as well as a legacy of £2,000 from Colonel Thomas Radclyffe held for them by Thomas Day and only to be released if Day could be trusted.

**Hansbie, Morgan Joseph OP**, of St James', Middlesex (1673–1750). Younger son of Ralph Hansbie of Tickhill Castle, Yorks. Brought up near Antwerp. Dominican friar; ordained 1698. Lived in London near Dean Street, Holborn, and near Hendon, Middlesex; visited Lady Petre at Cheam. Chaplain to the Spellikens, Brussels, 1708. Vice-rector 1612, then fourth rector of the Dominican College at Louvain 1717. Provincial 1721. Prior of Bornhem 1728. Vicar-provincial for Belgium 1728, 1738–42; vice-provincial for England 1747. Died in London aged seventy-eight.

*****Haydock, Cuthbert** (1684–1763). Secular priest. Chaplain of the family home, Mawdesley, Staffs., from 1714. He served as chaplain to the Duke of Norfolk and then at the Euxton mission, where he succeeded Fr. Thomas Towneley (1669–1737) from 1733 to 1740, before going to Worksop Manor.[17]

*****Haydock, Gilbert (1682–1749)**. Secular priest who acted as a go-between for these communities. Distinguished himself academically at Douai College; ordained sub-deacon 1706 and priest 1708. Arrested in 1715 and imprisoned in Lancaster Castle. In 1716, while still a prisoner

---

[17] Anstruther 3, p. 96.

was appointed as Chaplain at St Monica's, Louvain. In contact with the Jacobite court in Rome.[18]

**Haydock, Hugh**. Secular priest, youngest brother of Gilbert and Cuthbert.

*****Heneage, Winifred**. Daughter and heir of John Moore the elder of Kirklington, Notts.; sister of Cecily More. Cousin of Cecily Tunstall. Married 1720 Thomas Heneage (b. 1677), non-juror, of Cadeby, Lincolnshire. Client of Strickland, whose Mannock grandmother was Mary Heneage, wife of Sir Francis Heneage.

*****Herbert, Lady Lucy (Teresa Joseph) OSA** (1669–1744). WWTN BA 101. Choir nun, English Convent, Bruges. Clothed 1692; professed 1683; Procuratrix 1699–1709; Prioress 1709–44. Sister of the 2nd Marquess of Powis. Her repeated interventions with her brother were crucial to getting him to pay up funding for her and other convents.

*****Herbert, William, 2nd Marquess of Powis and Jacobite 2nd Duke of Powis** (1665–1745). Powis was one of Strickland's two chief patrons (Strickland's house in Queen Square, Bloomsbury, was almost on the doorstep of Powis House in Ormond Street). Powis's revenues received a considerable boost with the discovery of lead on his Welsh estates at Mochnant and Llangynog,<?> but were savagely eroded by reckless speculation with the financier Joseph Gage on the French and Spanish exchanges by his wilful daughter Lady Mary Herbert (b. 1686), who drew into collusion with her Lady Anne Carington, her aunt. Powis's extensive Northamptonshire estates eventually had to be sold to meet the debts run up by Lady Mary, which she expected her father and brother to underwrite.

**Herbert, William, Viscount Montgomery, later 3rd Marquess (Duke) of Powis** (1693–1748). Succeeded his father in 1745.

**Howard, Hon. Philip** (1687–1750). Brother of Thomas, 8th Duke of Norfolk (1683–1732). Non-juror. He had four daughters.

**Hyde, Bernard**. Brother of Winefrid Hyde.

**Hyde, Catherine (Catherine Winifred) OP** (1698–1752). WWTN BD 044. Choir nun, Spellikens, Brussels. Professed 1716; dowry £120, paid by her aunt and godmother, Catherine Thorold. Youngest daughter of Francis Hyde of Pangbourne, Berks., and Frances Thorold of Lancashire.

> Sister Catherin Winefrid Hyde had first for portion 120 pound starling; 20 the Procuratrix had for her novice year's pention; the 100 pound is a life

---

18  Ibid.
19  See Murphy, *Richard Cantillon*, esp. chap. 7.

rent at Briges [Bruges] for 100 gilders a year. 100. Sister Catherin Hyde was cloathed and profest very hansomly, of the charges of her kinde relation, Sister M. Rosa Howard, of Norfolk, who procuer'd and lay'd out for her Cloathing & Profesion, fifty pounds starling. Mistress Catharin Thorold, aunt and Godmother to Sister Catharin Winifrid Hyde, to whom she gave the above said portion of 120 pound st. on which some she was receiv'd and profess., promis'd that if her circumstances better'd, so as to enable her, she would farthar extend her kindness to her. And accordingly at her death, left her neece a hundard & twenty-five pound, which made her fortun in all 295 pound. This last 125 pound was paid in the year 1735 Councellor Strickland, who put it out the same year with other of our capital mony, for perpetual rent, at 5 per cent, on Mr Paston's estate.<sup><?></sup>

**Hyde, Winefrid**. Of Hammersmith and Weston, near Bath. Frequently used contact. Not the same person as Catherine (Winifrid) Hyde.

**Ireland, Winefride**. A nun of this name (a relative of the Webbs of Great Canford) entered the Sepulchrines in Liege in 1694 (WWTN LS 126). None of that name appears at Louvain. Nothing is known of a second Miss Ireland, despite the account entries in the plural form.<sup><?></sup>

**Jenings, Veronica OSA** (d. 1737). WWTN LA 147. Choir nun, Louvain; a widow. Professed 1710.

**Jessup, Isabella Constantia OSA** (1721–83). WWTN LA 149. Choir nun, Louvain. Clothed 1743; professed 1744.

**Johnson, Catherine (Anna Catherine Justina) OSA**. WWTN LA 151. Choir nun, Louvain. Professed 1703.

**Jones, Frances? Prisca OSA** (1693/4–1770). WWTN LA 154. Choir nun, Louvain. Professed 1715. Her (twin?) sister Joanna Alipia Jones (d. 1767), WWTN LA 155, was also a choir nun at Louvain (also professed 1715).

**Kerby, Lancelot**. Attorney, of Winchester.

**Kingdon, Abraham** (d. before December 1743). Son of Abraham and Alice Kingdon. Merchant, of London and Bruges.

**Knight, Margaret Augustina Austin OSA** (1731–71). WWTN LA 160. Choir nun, Louvain. Professed 1731. Born at Kingerby, near Market Rasen, Lincs. The Knight family, staunch Catholics, owned the estate

---

[20] 'Records of the Dominican Nuns of the Second Order (Vilvorde and Brussels), 1661–1697', in *Dominicana*, Catholic Record Society 25 (London: Catholic Record Society, 1925), p. 100.
[21] See Louvain day books, receipts for 22 July 1736, 14 February 1736/7 and 17 February 1738/9.

from the seventeenth to the nineteenth centuries.<?> Kingerby became known as a hiding place for recusant priests.

**Lacon, Rowland**. Non-juror, of Linley Hall, Salop.

**Langdale, Marmaduke**, 4th Baron Langdale of Holme (1718–71). Married *Elizabeth Widdrington.

**Langdale, Miss**. One of the four children of the 4th Lord Langdale.

**Lathouse (Lettas), Grace Lucy OSA** (1719–1808). WWTN LA 166. Lay sister, Louvain. Clothed 1740; dowry 300 florins. Daughter of Richard Letes and Eleanor Helmes.

**Ledger, Mrs**. Sister of Catherine Johnson.

**Lee, John, and his wife Frances Lee**. In the household of Lord Teynham.

**Lytcott (Lithcot), Lady Anne (née Brent)**. A notorious Jacobite. Daughter of Robert Brent, James II's barrister. Widow of Sir John Lytcott. Her family sacrificed a £2,500 estate at Larkstoke in Gloucestershire and other land (which was shared between her and her four Brent sisters, Elizabeth Conquest and Margaret, Mary and Frances Brent) to follow James II into exile at St Germain-en-Laye.<?> Strickland may already have had good reason to beware of the lady, having had to write to her in 1729 accusing her of dishonest dealing:

> London Septr. 15th. 1729 / Madame / Lord Montgomery being in the Country, He has Sent me up your Ladyship's Letter, and desired me to Answer it for him. He saies he thinks it very unreasonable for Your Ladyship to Expect he should put a Stop to Pere Frecourts presentation, when you know, had those Twenty Six Actions [shares] and 8/10. been deliver'd by you to Mr Loftus as they ought to have been, and which he offer'd to take in Satisfaction of his whole Debt, My Lord would have saved £5,000 Sterling, that is to say £3,000 he has already paid him, and £2,000 more which he is to pay him at my Lord Duke's death. Besides Lord Montgomery cannot think the Letter he Writ your Ladyshipp a Sufficient Authority for Pledging or Pawning the Actions, of which or the Sume borrowed upon them you never before thought proper to Acquaint his Lordship, Nor to give him any particular Account of what you either Received or paid for him. So that he saies he must Insist upon your Ladyshipps giving a particular Account of those Actions, in which he's willing you should have all just allowance, and particularly of 4,004 Livres 4 Sols which Duddell in his Account Charges himself with as received from your Ladyshipp. But your Ladyshipp will remember Severall other things

---

22  On the Knight family, see J. S. Hansom, 'Addenda to Market Rasen, Lincs., Register, 1640–1780. Extracts from Kingerby and Other Parish Registers, 1640–1792', in *Miscellanea XII*, Catholic Record Society 22 (Leeds: Catholic Record Society, 1921), p. 351.
23  Glickman (2009), p. 72.

which his Lordshipp left in your Custody when he left Paris, of which also he Expects an Account.

The Affair of the 260 Actions pretended to be Deposited in your Ladyshipps hands for Indempnifying the Family against Edwin's Debt has always been a Mistery to me, and a Wonder that now the Debt is paid those Actions are not Ordered to be Sold that the money ariseing from them and the many Dividends in Arrears may be Applied toward payment of what has been borrowed on the Estate for the Discharge of that Debt. These Considerations make me imagine, as I have also been told, that there were no Actions really Deposited but only a bundle of Wast paper put into your Ladyshipps hands, which I'm rather induced to believe for that I See Lord Duke directs the paper to be delivered to Lady Mary [Herbert] Unopened, Sure no One before his Grace ever took so much Care & pains to deceive hisself & family. Please to Direct for me at my Chambers in Grays Inne / who am Madame Your Ladyshippes most Obedient humble Servant / Mannock Strickland / To Lady Lythcot[24]

**Lytcott, Robert Brent** (b. 1704). Son of Lady Anne Lytcott.

**Mackenzie, Kenneth** (d. 1730). Kinsman of the 4th Earl of Seaforth. Solicitor, of Grays Inn and of The Salterns, Portsea. Contracted a clandestine marriage in 1709 to Anne, Viscountess Carington.[25]

**McNenny, Mr**. Irishman. Lawyer in Brussels. Counsellor to the Archduchess.

**Magrath, Frances (Mary Louisa) OSA** (1703/4–86). WWTN LA 176. Choir nun, Louvain. Professed 1723.

**Maire, John**, of Lartington, Yorks. (1703–71). Admitted to Gray's Inn 1727. Leading Catholic conveyancer in succession to Strickland and preceding Matthew Duane. Some of Strickland's papers were passed after his death to Maire.

**Mannock, Anne**. Youngest daughter of Sir Francis Mannock (1675–1758), 4th Baronet of Giffords Hall, Suffolk. Cousin of Mannock Strickland.

**Manson**, *See* Monson.

**Marcham, Mrs**. Of Bruges.

**Martin, John**. Probably an alias.

**Meighan, Thomas** (d. 1753). The leading Catholic printer and bookseller of his era.

**Melling, John (Jean)** (1689–1745). Secular priest. Cousin of Mr Shephard.

---

[24] *Blount MSS, B* 25, p. 58 (letter book and precedent book of Henry Rogers Trubshaw), copy of letter from MS to Lady Lytcott.
[25] Murphy, *Richard Cantillon*, p. 109. Murphy is inconsistent about the date of this marriage: on p. 211 he dates it as 1705. BL Add. MS 28251, fol. 221, dates it as January 1711.

**\*Milborne, Clayton**, of St Giles-in-the-Fields and Ospringe, Kent (d. 1744). Son of Clayton (d. 1726) and Rebecca Milborne. Strickland was Rebecca Milborne's executor.[26]

**Monington, Frances (Phillothea) OSA** (1690–1742). WWTN LA 183. Choir nun, Louvain. Professed 1720; dowry 3,000 florins. Daughter of Thomas Monington and Maria Tijldon; sister of Gaynor Constantia Monington.

**Monington, Gaynor Constantia (Clare) OSA** (d. 1756). WWTN LA 182. Choir nun, Louvain. Professed 1726. Sister of Frances Monington.

**Monson [Manson** in the letters], **Lady Anne**. Wife of Sir William Monson (1693–1748).

**Montgomery, William Herbert, Viscount**, *See* Herbert.

**Moody, Captain**. Agent.

**More, Cecily (Mary Cecilia) OSA** (d. 1755). WWTN LA 186. Choir nun at Louvain. Professed 1690. Prioress 1733–55. Born Kirklington, Yorks. Sister of Winifred Heneage; another sister at Rouen (they were the last three members of that family).

**\*Mostyn, Lady Teresa (d. 1766)**. Sister of Christina Towneley. Second wife of Sir George Mostyn. Jacobite; member of the Oak Society founded in 1749 by John Caryll. Fellow members included Mrs Towneley, Lady Newburgh and Lady Mostyn (mother-in-law of the Society's founder, John Caryll).[27] All were clients of Strickland.

**Neesum, Mrs Mary**. Unidentified. Party to foreign exchange transactions.

**Nettine [Nettien], Mr**. Banker, of Brussels.[28]

**\*Newburgh, Charlotte Maria Livingston, 3rd Countess of** (c. 1694–1755). Wife of Charles, titular 5th Earl of Derwentwater.

**Norfolk**, *See* Howard.

**\*Norris, Teresa**. Widow. Agent in Norwich for Margaret Xavier Ellerker, Procuratrix of the Spellikens.

**Palmes, Grace [Grace Mary] OSA** (1701–71). WWTN LA 195. Choir nun, Louvain. Professed 1720; dowry 4,500 florins. Daughter of George Palmes and Anna Witham of Cliffe, Yorks.

---

26 *Blount MSS, C* 133/6.
27 Paul Kléber Monod, *Jacobitism and the English People 1688–1788* (Cambridge: Cambridge University Press, 1989), p. 83.
28 *Blount MSS, C* 129/50, 1740.

**Park, Mr.** Husband of Mrs Bennet.

**\*Paston, Edward** (b. 1726). Of Town Barningham, Norfolk.

**Peirson, Edward.** Goldsmith and banker at the Acorn in Fleet Street. His father, Richard Peirson, is on record as having traded 1672–1712, and Edward traded 1718–31.[29]

**Penson, Thomas.** Lawyer, of Gray's Inn and of St Andrew, Holborn. Admitted 21 May 1719, the same year as Strickland, with whom he worked closely on the affairs of Henry Eyre, Viscountess Carington, the Duke of Powis and others. Fourth son of Thomas Penson of Lilleshall, Staffs.

**\*Petre, Lady Anne (Anna Maria or Anne)** (1716–60). Also referred to as Lady Mary Petre. Daughter and heir of James Radclyffe, 3rd Earl of Derwentwater. Wife of Robert James Petre, 8th Baron Petre.

**\*Petre, Robert James, 8th Baron Petre** (1713–42). Succeeded posthumously, his father having died of smallpox. Scientist and horticulturist. In 1732 married Lady Anna Mary Radclyffe, daughter of James, 3rd Earl of Derwentwater. Elected a Fellow of the Royal Society at the age of nineteen. Strickland was his agent and adviser. Died 1742 of smallpox.

**Pigott, Nathaniel** (1661–1737). Barrister of the Middle Temple. The last Catholic to be called to the Bar for nearly 150 years. Represented many major clients, some of whom Strickland took over on Pigott's death. He was the author of the standard text on conveyancing, *A Treatise of Common Recoveries, their nature and* use (London, 1739), of which Strickland owned a copy.

**Plowden, Peter.** Correspondent, via Adlam's Coffee House, near Turnstile in Lincolns Inn Fields.

**Porter, Mrs.** Pensioners of this name were resident at Louvain in 1741 and 1742.[30]

**\*Power**, alias **Daly, Mary.** Wife of Thomas Power *alias* Daly of Ireland. Only daughter of John Coleman of St James', Westminster. On 10 February 1736 Strickland drafted a letter of attorney whereby he was empowered to demand an annuity and its arrears due with any other payments under her father's will.[31]

---

[29] F. G. H. Hylton Price, *A Handbook of London Bankers* (London: Simpkin, Marshall and Co., 1890–91), pp. 127–8; A. Heal, *The London Goldsmiths 1200–1800* (Cambridge: Cambridge University Press, 1935), p. 223 (Heal spells the name as Pierson but is aware of the variant spelling).
[30] *Blount MSS, C* 64/218 and 235.
[31] *Blount MSS, C* 127/56–7.

**Powis**, *See* Herbert.

**Primer (Primmer), Mary (Mary Dorothy) OSA** (d. 1778). WWTN LA 205. Lay sister, Louvain. Clothed 1734; professed 1735, aged 26; dowry 300 florins.

**Prudent, Mrs.** Courier.

**Radclyffe,**<sup><?></sup> **Lady Anne**. Fifth daughter of Sir Edward Radclyffe (1589–1663). Sister of Francis, 1st Earl of Derwentwater (1625–96). Living unmarried at Wycliffe 1705. Bequests in her will (3 October 1699) include £1,000 to the children of 'her nephew and niece Francis Tunstall of Wycliffe and Cicily his wife' and £20 annuities each to her niece Mrs Anne Craythorne and her cousin Barbara Craythorne; the residue was bequeathed to her executor and nephew Thomas Radclyffe.<sup><?></sup>

**Radclyffe, Arthur** (c. 1664–1728). Fifth son of Francis, 1st Earl of Derwentwater. Variously of Capheaton and Dilston, Northumberland.

**\*Radclyffe, Lady Catherine OSA** (c. 1651–1744). WWTN LA 209. Choir nun, Louvain. Professed 1688. Daughter of Francis Radclyffe, 1st Earl of Derwentwater; aunt of the executed (martyred) Jacobite James, 3rd Earl of Derwentwater. Various relatives in convents. Legatee of her brother Colonel Thomas Radclyffe and of her sister Lady Mary Radclyffe. She was entitled to an annuity of £100 from the family estates, sequestered after the execution of the 3rd Earl. The entailed portions of the estates were finally released following Mary's marriage to Strickland's patron the 8th Lord Petre. The annuity is first mentioned in 1733 after the success of the Earl's daughter in redeeming her entitlement to a portion of £20,000 from her father's estates with the help of Strickland from Greenwich Hospital, to which Sir Robert Walpole had given the lands. Four certificates of her life are known to exist.<sup><?></sup>

**Radclyffe, Charles, titular 5th Earl of Derwentwater** (1693–1746). Third and youngest son of Edward, 2nd Earl, by Mary Tudor, illegitimate daughter of Charles II by Moll Davies. Surrendered himself prisoner at Preston November 1715; escaped December 1715 from Newgate to France, where he lived for many years, serving as a general officer

---

[32] For the Radclyffe family, see F. J. A. Skeet, *The Life of the Right Honourable James Radcliffe Third Earl of Derwentwater, (Co. Northumberland), Viscount Radcliffe and Langley & Baron Tynedale (Co. Cumberland), and Fifth Baronet of Dilston; with an Account of His Martyrdom for the Catholic Faith & Loyalty to His Rightful King* (London: Hutchinson and Co., 1929).

[33] *Blount MSS, C* 98/58.

[34] Essex Record Office, D/DP F290 (c. 1733); *Blount MSS, C* 157/23 (2 January 1733/4 OS); *Blount MSS, C* 145/63 (18 January 1734/5); *Blount MSS, C* 157/23 (1735).

to the French king. Taken prisoner on his way to join Prince Charles Edward Stuart in 1745. Executed 1746 on Tower Hill on a charge of treason. Married Charlotte Maria Livingston, Countess of Newburgh, as her second husband.

**Radclyffe, Lady Elizabeth** (1654–1723). Third daughter of Francis, 1st Earl of Derwentwater. Professed at [St Monica's? convent] 1688.

**Radclyffe, James, 3rd Earl of Derwentwater** (1689–1716). Jacobite rebel leader; executed for treason to make an example and treated by the Jacobites almost as a martyr.

**Radclyffe, James Bartholomew, titular 6th Earl of Derwentwater** (1712–87). Also 4th Earl of Newburgh (title inherited through his mother).

**\*Radclyffe, Lady Mary**, of Old Elvet, City of Durham (d. 3 March 1725/6). Eldest daughter of Francis, 1st Earl of Derwentwater. Inherited the estates of her brother Colonel Thomas Radclyffe. Will written 1722; probate granted in London 29 March 1726 to Cuthbert Constable and John Bacon of Stawart.[35] Estate of £41,000.[36]

**Radclyffe, Sir Ralph**. Of Hitchin, Herts.

**Radclyffe, Colonel Thomas** (1658–1716). Variously of Capheaton, Dilston and Plessey, Northumberland. Third son of Francis, 1st Earl of Derwentwater. Went in the suite of Lord Castlemaine to Rome in 1685. Died at Douai; date of death usually given as before 24 February 1716. Note in *Blount MSS* states that he died after his executor Henry Eyre, who died 1719. Will not proved until 1734.

**Rivers, John Savage, 5th Earl Rivers** (1665–1737). Roman Catholic priest. Title inherited from his uncle Richard Savage, 4th Earl (c. 1660–1712), who supported William III.[37]

**Rodbourne, Henry** (d. 1740?). Lawyer. Agent to the Earl of Derwentwater at Dilston, Northumberland.

**Rodbourne, Isabella (Mary) OSA** (d. 1769). WWTN LA 210. Daughter of Henry Rodbourne. Choir nun, Louvain. Professed 1712. Her godfather was Sir John Webb. Name on database erroneously given as Redbourne.

**Segrave, Mary Frances OP** (1716–90). WWTN BD 058. Choir nun, Spellikens, Brussels. Clothed 1733; professed 1734; dowry £359. Served

---

35 *Blount MSS, C* 145/59.
36 *Blount MSS, C* 145/74c.
37 Anstruther 3, pp. 196–7.

as novice mistress and Sub-Prioress. Born in Bath, Somerset. Daughter of Henry Segrave of Scabbrough, near Dublin, and Anna O'Neal.

At Mistris Segrifs profession all the above said conditions [concerning payments, all to be in 'exchange money'] were performed by her father, & payd to Mr Strickland the above saide Summe. 350 placed by Mr Strickland on security of Mistress Devereux's estate at 5 per sent'.[38]

**Seldon, Mr**. Brother of Mrs Isabella Smith.

**Sheldon, Mr**. Of Winchester.

**Sheldon, Miss**. Pensioner.

**Shephard, Mr**. Cousin of the secular priest John Melling. Lodged with Mrs Heneage.

**Shevereux, Mrs**. *See* Devereux.

**Short, Margaritt [Margaret Mary Agnes] OP** (1715/16–80). WWTN BD 062. Choir nun, Spellikens, Brussels. Clothed 1733; professed 1734; dowry £300 (examination). Prioress 1770–79. Eldest daughter of Francis Short of Bury St Edmunds and Jane Harrison.

The Council agreed to receve Mistress Margrite Short upon tryal for a years noviciat upon the following conditions. That she is to have three hondert pounds portion if she lives to the age of one and twenty til wich time we ar to heve the interest there of besids twenti pound att clothing and twenti moure att the profession and is to pay for the year of her noviship fifteen pound wich we supose to be the interest of the abouve three hondert pounds. The 11 of Jun 1734 the Reverend Mother Cald her Councel on recieving Mistress Margerit Short to her Profession; & having reneu'd the Contract, wee find sum small changes in affairs on the account of her fathers death in her Noviship, so to ajust all maters wright, the Councel was pleased to determin as followes. [terms stated] Sister Margarit Mary Agness Short was profess'd the 22th of June, 1734. The eldest daughter to Mr Francis Short at Berey in Suffolk, & his lawfull wife, Mistress Joanna Harrisson. She had 200 permission gils for her Cloathing expences, and 3000 permission gilders for her portion, out of which was deducted 200 pern gilders for her profession expences: which 200 gils we added out of our capital mony, to make up again the full summe of 3000 pern gilders, to put out to rent, which accordingly was put out by Counceller Mannock Strickland Esquire, at 5 per cent to Mr Paston, 1736, on the 25th of February. Agreed by the Venerable Mothers of the Council that the legacy bequeathed to late S.M. Agnes & S.M. Ursula Short by their late uncle, Doctor P. Short, be applied to discharge the principal sum of one thousand glds. exchange, together with the interest due on the same, & the remainder to said legacy to be applied in purchasing deals & slates for the roof of the monastery etc.[39]

---

[38] *Blount MSS, C* 114/8. Mistress Devereux is a reference to Elizabeth Devereux.
[39] 'Records of the Dominican Nuns of the Second Order (Vilvorde and Brussels), 1661–1697',

**Short, Mary Ursula OP** (1716–41). WWTN BD 061. Choir nun, Spellikens, Brussels. Clothed 1734; professed 1735; dowry 1,000 guilders (examination). Second daughter of Francis Short of Bury St Edmunds and Jane Harrison; sister of Margaritt Short.

The 14 of July 1734 the Reverend Mother Mariana Chilton Cald the Councel to propose Mistress Ursula Short to her Clothing. Her temporal Conditions are Fifty pound starling in Mr Bostacks hands & fifty more promised at her Profession, payable to our orders by Mistress Dikison whose note in case of death wee have which is all wee can demand as agreed one, Mistress Dickison has paid the 50ll as promised. She had in al for her fortun 1000 gilders, and 100 pern gilders, given her for the expences of her profession. Of the 1000 gilders portion, 500 was joyn'd to make up 2000 pern gilders of ours, put out for us att Haynau, by Mr Nettine, at 4 per cent, the 12th of April 1738; which carry's intrest from the same day. This 500 pern gilders (or 50 pound) was pay'd by Mr Dicconson, by our appointment to Councellour Mannock Strickland in England for our orders, which we drew over to place as above. The other 500 pern gilders (or 50 pound) of her portion, in Mr Bostock's her uncle's hands, is not pay'd us as yet, to this presant year 1740.[40]

**Shrewsbury, Mary Talbot, commonly called Countess of**, *See* Talbot, Mary.

**Smith, Mrs Elizabeth and her sister Frances [Wells?]**. Elizabeth was nanny to Michael Blount II of Mapledurham's eldest son and daughter. Settled at Dunkirk.

**\*Smith, Elizabeth Mary Winefrid OSA** (1696–1752). WWTN LA 237. Choir nun, Louvain. Clothed 1738; professed 1739; dowry 10,000 florins. Daughter of Charles Smyth, 3rd Viscount Carington of Burford, Oxon. and Frances Pate of Sysonby, Leics. Her father's second wife was Lady Anne Herbert, daughter of the 1st Marquess of Powis. Lady Anne Herbert was deeply mired in the bubble of the Mississippi System (the French equivalent of the South Sea Bubble) through the gambling of her niece Lady Mary Herbert and Lady Mary's lover, the financier Joseph Gage. Strickland handled Carington affairs.[41] Perhaps this influenced her to be particularly cautious over the transmission of her own substantial fortune to her beneficiary, the Louvain convent. She was rightly very concerned to protect it against Strickland's son, the litigious and imprudent Dr Joseph Strickland (1724–90), who squandered his siblings' inheritance

in *Dominicana*, Catholic Record Society 25 (London: Catholic Record Society, 1925), p. 232.
40 'Records of the Dominican Nuns of the Second Order (Vilvorde and Brussels), 1661–1697', in *Dominicana*, Catholic Record Society 25 (London: Catholic Record Society, 1925), p. 214.
41 See Murphy, *Richard Cantillon*.

from his parents, such as it was, in unwise court disputes until and after the final payout in 1771.

**Smith, Isabella Cecilia Marina OSA** (1702–84). WWTN LA 238. Choir nun, Louvain; professed 1722. Prioress 1762–84. Daughter of Bartholomew Smith of Winchester, brother[-in-law?] of Mr Sheldon.

**\*Spelman** alias **Yallop, Edward** (d. 1767). Son of Charles Yallop of Bowthorpe Hall, Yorks. Later adopted his grandmother's surname of Spelman. Translator of Xenophon (Edward Gibbon was an admirer). The use for three generations of the additional surname Yallop may have been intended to deflect doubts about the legitimacy of his father's birth.

**Stafford, Edward** (1708–46). Son of John Stafford-Howard (Vice-Chamberlain to Queen Mary of Modena in succession to Robert Strickland, father of Mannock Strickland) and his second wife, Theresa Strickland (1687–1778), who was Maid of Honour to the Queen. Strickland was guardian to his nephew.

**Stapylton (Stapleton), Misses**. Pensioners; daughters of Nicholas Errington Stapylton. **Charlotte Caroline Stapylton OSA** WWTN LA 241. Clothed 1737, aged 17; professed 1738; dowry 4,000 guilders; died 1778. No other sister was at Louvain, though her sister **Mary Stapylton OSB** (d. 1797 aged 83) was a nun at the Benedictines in Brussels.

**Stapylton, Sir Miles**, of Myton, Yorks. (c. 1708–52). To guarantee £12,000 to Winifred Heneage, wife of Thomas Heneage and daughter of John More of Kirtlington, he raised a £400 mortgage on Kirtlington and other estates.[42]

**Stapylton (Stapleton), Nicholas Errington**. Father of Charlotte Stapylton.

**Stourton, Lady Catherine**, *See* Walmesley, Catherine.

**Strickland, Anne Winifred** (1690–99). Sister of Mannock Strickland. Born at St Germain-en-Laye; died in the royal convent of Chaillot.

**Strickland, Bridget** (d. October 1736). Mother of Mannock Strickland; fourth daughter of Sir Francis Mannock (d. 1686), 2nd Baronet of Giffords Hall, Stoke-by-Nayland, Suffolk. Bedchamber woman to Queen Mary of Modena, whom she accompanied into exile at St Germain-en-Laye. Her position had been considerable, as is evidenced by the codicil to the Queen's will leaving her '£1,000 part of the £20,000 owing by the King', by the Old Pretender's gift to her of one of Queen Mary Beatrice's clocks, and by the fact that during the Queen's lifetime Mrs Strickland had been one of the principal channels for the dispensing of royal pensions.

---

[42] *Blount MSS, C* 107–21 and *C* 196/30.

After the Queen's death she appears to have returned to England with her son Roger in 1718, but little is known of her time in England. Her pension from France appears to have been cut off in 1723 and she wrote appealing to the Old Pretender for its restoration, which produced only limited success. By 1731 she was back in France, at the convent of the Benedictine *Dames Anglaises* at Dunkirk, which her daughter Henrietta entered twenty years later in 1751.[43]

**Strickland, Elizabeth Mary ('Betty')** (1726–30). One of Mannock Strickland's daughters.

**Strickland, Francis Edward Joseph** (1691–1745). Younger brother of Mannock Strickland. Companion of Prince Charles Edward Stuart (the Young Pretender) and the only Englishman among the 'Seven Men of Moidart', who accompanied the Prince to Scotland in 1745. Died in Preston Gaol.

**Strickland, Jarrard, of Sizergh** (1704–91). Cousin of Mannock Strickland.

**Strickland, John ('Jack')** (1723–1802). Sent to school on the Continent, at Bornhem, in 1732; used *alias* of John Wright. Admitted to Douai 1735; ordained priest there 1747. Stationed at (successively) Paris, Rouen, Dunkirk and again at Paris 1747–56. Entered the Seminary of St Gregory's College, Paris, 1747. Took seminary oath as a priest 1748 and in same year 'had faculty for Confession'. In 1749 he 'pass'd master of arts', 'obtain'd a dispensation from writing his divinity for all the three years' and then left the seminary for Rouen 'to help the nuns who had dismiss'd Mr Ed: Daniel'. Returned to Rouen 1752; 1753 passed the three stages of his examinations, then went to Dunkirk as confessor to the Poor Clares, replacing Dr. Perry 1754–56, returning to St Gregory's College before returning to England where he followed an increasingly eccentric regime of strict fasting with repasts of gargantuan proportions. Became a member of the Chapter, and Archdeacon of Essex, Herts., and Bedford. In poor health in 1767.

**Strickland, Mary Eugenia** (1722–65). Mannock Strickland's eldest daughter. Married Michael Blount II of Mapledurham 1742.

**Swinburne, Sir John, 3rd Baronet** (1698–1745). Of Capheaton, Northumberland. Married to Mary Bedingfeld (d. 1761).

**Talbot, Mary, commonly called Countess of Shrewsbury** (d. 1752).

---

[43] Some of her correspondence was published in L. P. Wenham, *Roger Strickland of Richmond: A Jacobite Gentleman 1680–1749* (Northallerton: North Yorkshire County Record Office, 1982).

The 13th Earl, Gilbert Talbot (1672/3–1743), nephew of his childless predecessor, was a Jesuit priest and sometime chaplain to Lord Petre (possibly the source of the connection to Strickland) who never assumed the title. He was succeeded by his nephew George (1719–87), whose father, also George (d. 1733), was a younger brother of Gilbert. The father's family connections are of great interest. His wife, Mary, was a major source of funding for Strickland. The marriage settlement of her daughter states that she and her husband were 'commonly called' Earl and Countess of Shrewsbury. She was the daughter of Thomas, 4th Viscount Fitzwilliam of Merrion, and sister of Richard, 5th Viscount, himself a considerable source of funding for Strickland's clients. Mary's mother was the sister of George Pitt of Stratfield Saye, who acted as Protestant trustee for mortgage loans handled by Strickland.

**Tancred [Tanckred], Thomas**. Of Red Lion Square. Woollen draper. Married Frances Gazaigne. Grandson of Sir William Tancred, 2nd Baronet (d. 1703). Elizabeth, one of his daughters, lived in Liege. He was among Strickland's most frequent couriers.

**Thornburgh, Dr William** (1700–50). President of Douai College, 1738–50.[44]

**Tooker, James**. Of West Grinstead. Used frequently by Strickland as a trustee for loans to Viscountess Carington.

**\*Towneley, Ursula (Christina) OSA** (1712–71). WWTN LA 270. Choir nun, Louvain. Professed 1712. Procuratrix. Family connections included the Pastons. Her sister Teresa (d. 1766) was the second wife of Sir George Mostyn.

**Trapps, Mr**. Possibly Francis Trappes-Byrnand (b. 1697), whose daughter Elizabeth married George Crathorne of Ness Hall, Yorks. Father of Joanna Teresa Trapps. He had other daughters, Margaret and Elizabeth.

**Trapps, Joanna Teresa OSA** (d. 1735). WWTN LA 225. Choir nun, Louvain. Professed 1722.

**Trubshaw, Henry Rogers** (d. 1786?). Strickland's clerk. An attorney and a Protestant.

**Tunstall, Anne (Pulcheria) OSA** (1678–1758). Choir nun, Louvain. Professed 1686. Daughter of Francis Tunstall of Wycliffe, Yorks., and Cecily Constable of Burton Constable, Yorks.; sister of Cecily Tunstall.

---

[44] Godfrey Anstruther, *The Seminary Priests: A Dictionary of the Secular Clergy of England and Wales, 1558–1850. IV. 1716–1800* (Great Wakering, Essex: Mayhew-MacCrimmon, 1977), p. 278.

Francis changed his surname to Constable in 1718 as a condition of inheriting Burton Constable estate from the last Viscount Dunbar. His grandson Marmaduke resumed the name of Tunstall. The family was numerous; it is difficult to identify with certainty the relatives mentioned.

**Tunstall, Bryan.** Of York. He is one member of a particularly complicated set of names changed for inheritance purposes involving the Tunstalls of Thurland and the Constables of Burton Constable.

**Tunstall, Cecily (Monica) OSA** (c. 1687–1775). WWTN LA 281. Choir nun, Louvain. Professed 1704. Procuratrix. Daughter of Francis Tunstall of Wycliffe, Yorks., and Cecily Constable of Burton Constable, Yorks. Sister of three nuns and relative of nine more. Her brother Cuthbert Constable *alias* Tunstall was a client of Strickland.

**Tunstall, Marmaduke** (d. 1760). Younger brother of Cecily Tunstall and Cuthbert Tunstall *alias* Constable.

**Tunstall, Mary (Genoveva) OSA** (1692–1770). Choir nun, Louvain. Professed 12 June 1701. Sister of Cecily Tunstall.

**Tunstall, Winefrid.** Niece of Cecily Tunstall. Possibly a pensioner.

**Turville, Mr.** Of Antwerp.

*****Vannuffle, John Baptist.** Lace merchant in Brussels. Source of foreign exchange in collaboration with Samuel Grimes of London.

**Walker, Frances (Mary Catherine)** (1720–56). WWTN LA 291. Choir nun, Louvain. Clothed 1736; professed 1737; no dowry.

**Wallrad d'Alsace-Boussut de Chimay, Thomas Philip, Archbishop of Mechelen** ('His Eminence') (1679–1759). Cardinal 1719. There were no English cardinals at the time and the convent at Louvain would have fallen under the authority of the local bishop in any event.[45]

*****Walpole, Edward.** Of Dunston, Lincs. Petition of bankruptcy and will consisting largely of private instructions, 1740.[46]

**Walton, Thomas, the younger.** Son of Thomas Walton the elder. In 1736 married Elizabeth, only child of Thomas Cholmeley of West Thorndon, Essex, agent of Lord Petre.[47]

**Walmesley, Catherine, Lady Stourton** (1697–1785). Ardent Jacobite; brought a £50,000 dowry to her second marriage, in 1712, to Robert,

---

[45] I am grateful to James E. Kelly for this identification and this information.
[46] *Blount MSS, C* 134/16, C 1124/10 and 13.
[47] *Blount MSS, C* 130/14: marriage settlement.

7th Baron Petre. Left widowed by her husband's death from smallpox in 1713, she married as her third husband Charles, 15th Baron Stourton (1702–53), in 1744.[48]

**Walton & Boag.** Receivers of the estate, goods and chattels of the late 3rd Earl of Derwentwater.

**Ward, Mr.** Rumoured to have married Lady Lytcott. Refused to pay for the clothing and profession of his sister **Mary Anne Ward OSA** (d. 1746), WWTN LA 293, choir nun, Louvain; clothed 1734; professed 1735.

**\*Warpole, Mr.** Either Edward Walpole of Dunston, Lincs., or John Walpole of Grays Inn, who lamented in his will (1721) yet another reason for not supporting overseas exiles – that 'I did intend to give several legacies amongst my relations and friends but my losses have been so great in the unfortunate South Sea I can scarce do it with good conscience for fear of injuring my poor wife whose advice had I been so fortunate to follow I should have got enough for them and her too so hopes [*sic.*] they will forgive me'.[49]

**Waters, George** (d. 1752). Banker in Paris. Succeeded by his son, also George.

**Watson, George.** Agent to Lord and Lady Petre at Ingatestone and Thorndon, Essex.

**Webb, Edward.** Lawyer; admitted to Gray's Inn 1703. Second son of John Webb of St Andrew Holborn. (Not entirely honest) partner of Mannock Strickland in the South Sea Funds and other investments.

**Webb, Sir John.** Of Great Canford, Dorset (d. 1745). Married Barbara Belasyse (d. 1740). His daughter Anne Maria (d. 1723) was the wife of the 3rd Earl of Derwentwater, executed in 1716; their daughter Anna Mary (1716–60) married Robert James Petre, 8th Baron Petre (1713–42).

**Williams, Mr.** Supplier of drugs and medicines.

**Willoughby, Cassandra.** Sister of Elizabeth Willoughby; cousin of Cecily Tunstall.

**Willoughby, Elizabeth Placida OSA** (1716–56). WWTN LA 299. Choir nun, Louvain. Professed 1716. Daughter of Robert Willoughby and **\*Ursula Cholmeley** (source of investment via Strickland:[50] Francis

---

48 See L. A. Hardy, 'The Petre Family in Lancashire: A Study of a Catholic Family, Their Estate, Its Management and Operation 1700–1852', unpublished MA dissertation, Huddersfield Polytechnic, 1987.
49 *Blount MSS*, *C* 134/9: admission, 1680.
50 *Blount MSS*, *D* 4/6: deed of trust, endorsed 9 August 1719.

Croft to William Fitzherbert; includes £1,000 held by her). Niece of Elizabeth Teresa (Monica) Cholmeley.

**Wilson, George**. Of Symonds Inn, Chancery Lane. Looked after Lady Mary Radclyffe's affairs.

**Witham, cousin**. Several possible identifications, none conclusive, including Dr. Robert Witham.

**Witham, Dr. Robert** (1667–1738). President of the English College, Douai 1714–38.

**Wisiscote**. Also appears as Wisoscate. Untraced.

**Wollascott, Mary Xaveria OSA** (1716–71). WWTN LA 309. Choir nun, Louvain. Professed 1716. Daughter of Martin Wollascott of Woolhampton and Brimpton, Berks., and Mary Throckmorton of Coughton Court, Warwicks. Sister of William Wollascott.

**Wollascott, William**. Of Woolhampton, Berks.

**Worthington, Jane (Joanna) OSA** (1717–67). Choir nun, Louvain. Professed 1717. Daughter of Richard Worthington of Blainscough Hall near Chorley, Lancs., and Margaret Alcock of Lancs.

**Worthington, Mary Genoveva OSA** (1674–1733). WWTN LA 319. Choir nun, Louvain. Clothed 1672 aged 16; professed 1674; dowry 3,000 florins. Sixth Prioress 1727–33. Daughter of Thomas Worthington of Blainscough Hall near Chorley, Lancs., and Jane Plumpton of Yorkshire. Three of her sisters also became nuns.

**Worthington, Fr Thomas OP** (1671–1754). Brother of Mary Genoveva Worthington. Payment of Lady Catherine Radclyffe's annuity was routed from Henry Rodbourne via Worthington to Strickland.[51]

**\*Wright, Anthony**. Goldsmith-banker, head of The Golden Cup, Henrietta Street, Covent Garden. Cousin of Strickland's wife, Mary Wright (d. 1750) of Kelvedon Hatch, Essex. He had previously been in partnership with his father, Richard Wright.[52] The leading Catholic bankers, established 1699 by William Wright, goldsmith, until their collapse in 1840, they were heavily used by Strickland as a source of finance and as bankers.[53]

---

[51] *Blount MSS, C* 145/75.

[52] *Blount MSS, C* 129/9: agreement between Anthony Wright and his mother, Martha Wright, to terminate the partnership with her son carried on since her husband's death intestate with a personal estate of more that £18,000, to receive the £6,000 annuity to which she became entitled on her husband's death (1729). Draft by MS.

[53] *Blount MSS, C* 129/19: Anthony Wright's draft will of 1740; *C* 129/12: draft will of 1743.

**Wybarne [Wyborne], Charity**. Daughter of Lettis Wybarne and John Wybarne of Hawkwell. Boarded at Louvain. Debt owed for her pension and travelling.

***Wybarne, Lettis** (d. 1738). Née Tasburgh. Of Norwich. Widow of John Wybarne of Great Hawkwell, Kent. Source of much argument over payment of a legacy and debt (of £36 11s 6d) owing since 1700 and specified in her will (drafted in 1737 by Strickland, kinsman, executor and trustee).[54] Her son John died intestate in 1740.

**Wyke, Peter**. Goldsmith-banker, opposite Gray's Inn Gate, Holborn. Used frequently by Strickland for exchange transactions, and before him by Henry Eyre, Strickland's mentor, who used, among other goldsmith-bankers, Wrights, Edward Peirson (who went bankrupt in 1728) and the Bank of England.[55] He appears to have had a son, Francis Wyke (d. 1757).[56]

**Yates, Mary (Mary Catharine) OP** (d. 1773). Convert. Choir nun, Spellikens, Brussels. Clothed 1733; professed 1734; dowry £150 (examination). Prioress 1740–43. Daughter of William Yates of Yatebank, near Blackburn and Isabella Rishdon of Haslingden, Lancs.

---

[54] *Blount MSS, C* 133/43, *C* 133/58 and *D* 5/50.
[55] Wyke is obscure and does not appear in Price, *Handbook of London Bankers*.
[56] Heal, *London Goldsmiths 1200–1800*, p. 273 (for Francis Wyke, listed at the same address).

# LADY CATHERINE RADCLYFFE'S
# CERTIFICATE OF LIFE, 1730 AND 1734/5[1]

| *Original text* | *Translation* |
|---|---|
| Aujourd'hui le dix-huitieme Jour du mois de Janvier mil sept cent ans trente neuvieme Stile de Brabant et septieme jour dudit mois de janvier Stile d'Angleterre paru devant moi Jaques Antoine de Rij notaire admis par le Conseil Souverain de Sa Majeste Imperiale et Souverain et Catholique ordonné en Brabant et resident a Louvain present les temoins embas denommés comparirent le sieur Gilbert Haijdocke et le sieur Jean Melling amb[assa]deur Anglois lesquels jointement les d[eu]h temoins en bas denommés sous serment ont declares prece es mains de moi le dit notaire ont declaré attesté & affirmé ainsi que moi notaire de bien connoitre l'honorable Lady Catherine Radclyffe, seconde fille du tres honourable Francois feu Comte de Derwentwater decede & que la dite Honorable Lady Catherine Radclyffe est actuellement en vie pour s'etre aujourd'huij presentée en personne pardevant nous en sa demeure vié nous nous [sic] sommes [transportes?] en la paroisse de St | Today the eighteenth day of January 1739 [sic] Brabant style and the seventh day of the said month English style there appeared before me, Jacques Antoine du Rij, notary admitted by the Sovereign Council of His Imperial and Sovereign and Catholic Majesty qualified in Brabant and resident at Louvain, the witnesses named below comprising Gilbert Haydocke, gentleman, and John Melling, gentleman, English representative, who jointly as the two witnesses named below, have declared, attested and affirmed under oath before me the said notary that they well know the Hon. Lady Catherine Radclyffe, second daughter of the Rt. Hon. Francis late Earl of Derwentwater deceased, and that the said Hon. Lady Catherine Radclyffe is at present living in order to be presented in person before us in her dwelling in our presence and that we were taken to the parish of St |

[1] There are slight differences in wording between the 1730 and 1735 certificates. The text of the 1730 certificate is reproduced here, while the 1734/5 certificate is illustrated to demonstrate the slight variation in wording and dating. Certificates are held in the Essex Record Office, D/DP F290 (c. 1733) and at Mapledurham, *Blount MSS*, C 157/23 (2 January 1733/4 OS), C 145/63 (18 January 1734/5 NS) and C 157/23 (18 January 1734/5 NS).

Jaques audite Louvain de l'avoir vue et de l'avoir parlé La personnellement connoitre puisque elle a aussi jointement soussigné le present certificate de sa propre main que nous offerons de ratifier pardevant nous Juges et Justices que besoin pourroit etre sous le meme serment aussi fait et passé a Louvain en sa demeure de la dite Lady Catherine Radclyffe le jour mois et an que dessus en personne de Gaspar Popel et d'Adrien Berckmans temoins a ce requis [(]etant la minute originale de dette ecrite sur timbre de six sous) signee Gilbert Haydocke John Melling Catherine Radclyffe Gaspar Popel Adrianus Berckmans et de moi ledit notaire
    Quod Attestor
    J: A: du Rij + notaire

Jacques in Louvain aforesaid where we saw and spoke with her in person since she has also added her signature below to the present certificate in her own hand which we offer to ratify in front of us judges and justices as required before us under the said oath also taken at Louvain in her own residence of the said Lady Catherine Radclyffe the day month and year given above in the presence of Gaspar Popel and Adrien Berckmans, witnesses to this deed being the original minute of this writing over a stamp of six sous) Signed: Gilbert Haydocke, John Melling, Catherine Radclyffe, Gaspar Popel, Adrianus Berckmans and of me the said notary
    As attestor
    J. A. du Rij +

Nous Bourguemaistre echevins du Conseil de la Ville de Louvain Capitale de Brabant certifions et attestons que Jaques Antoine du Rij est notaire admis ... qualifié aux actes de quelles est ... tout en jugement que de hors en foi nous avons fait depecher la presente par un de nos Secretaires Jurés sous le Sceau ordinaire de cette Ville le septieme Mars 1735 stile de Brabant
    J H Buggenhout +

We the Mayor and Aldermen of the Town Council of Louvain, capital of Brabant, certify and attest that Jacques Antoine de Rij is admitted as notary qualified for the actions of which he is responsible and externally, that in good faith we have expedited the present deed by one of our secretaries sworn under the Ordinary Seal of this Town, 7 March 1735 Brabant style.

I do herby certify, that the here above Certificate of Life of the Honble Lady Catherine Radclyffe of Lovain, is genuine & in due form, the notary Du Ry's qualification being duly attested by one of the Secretaries of the Magistrate of Louvain & with their Town Seal, according to the Practice in these Austrian Low Countries. Given at Brussels under my hand & seal this 8th day of March 1734 & five
[Seal] Rob: Daniel
His Majesties Co, at Brussels

# THE ENGLISH CARTHUSIAN COMMUNITY AT NIEUPORT, FLANDERS

## Editor's note

The documents here published for the first time (*Blount MSS, D* 9/19–23) are five in number and are kept in the archives at Mapledurham House, accompanied by an impressive manuscript history of the English branch of the order (*Blount MSS, E* 32, not transcribed here). Although the financial arrangements of nuns are the primary subject of this volume, the attempt to rescue the Nieuport Charterhouse sheds further light on the precarious financial position of English religious houses.

The Sheen Anglorum Charterhouse was a community in Flanders of English Carthusian monks driven out of England into exile in 1539. They settled in Nieuport in Flanders in 1626, remaining there until 1783. The Prior at the time of the fundraising efforts of Michael Blount II of Mapledurham (1719–92) was Dom Gilbert Jump (1712–74), who succeeded Thomas Yate as Prior in 1743 and had previously held the office of Procurator. The establishment was always small. It seems to have been financed by charitable donations, with a large proportion coming from London tradesmen, whereas a large element of convent funding came from the families of the nuns themselves. It is noteworthy that some contributions to the Charterhouse fund are indicated as being from Protestant donors (including a few clergy); no such indication appears with the convents.

Michael Blount's preface to his account book well explains the context of the attempt to rescue the establishment. His younger brother Walter (name in religion: Maurus) was a monk there. He was born in 1727 and died at the age of eighteen, a Benedictine monk at Douai, on 14 October 1746, according to Croke; the transition from one order to another and one establishment to another is unexplained.

The text presented here is a transcript of the fair copy bound record of donors (*Blount MSS, D* 9/19), in the hand of Michael Blount II, the prime mover in this initiative. The remaining items consist of the documents used by Blount in compiling the fair copy; they are:

1. *Blount MSS, E* 32: 'A history of the English Carthusians or Charter monkes …With an appendix of the dignitie of a monasticall life'. Handwritten copy of a printed book(?). Late seventeenth century (c.

1670–80), contemporary leather binding. 21 cm × 16 cm. Coloured frontispiece, [6], 1–17, [1], 18–124, [1], 125–211, [1], 212–272, then 35 blank leaves. Copy of an engraving as frontispiece. A few marginal notes in another hand. Bookplate and signature: 'Michael Blount [1740]'.

2. *Blount MSS, D* 9/19–23: Subscriptions for the English Carthusians: 1747–48: Booklet with list of subscribers to the relief fund for the English Carthusians at Nieuport.

1748: List of subscribers to a fund collected by Michael Blount II for the benefit of Dom Gilbert Jump and his monastery. Total amount subscribed: £50, mostly by Catholic London tradesmen.

1752: Obit list of subscribers to the fund for relief of English Carthusians at Nieuport, headed by the Dowager Countess of Shrewsbury (d. 1752).

May 1755: Account of money received by Michael Blount II for the relief of the English Carthusians at Nieuport.

1755–57: 'An Account of Money received by me Michael Blount for the use of the Carthusians at Nieuport in Flanders since the 19th of November 1755 when I began my 2d Collection'.

## Blount MSS, E 32

The substance of the case of the English Carthusians at Nieuport in Flanders, and of their humble petition to all charitable persons, particularly to their native friends.

The English Carthusians were Founded at Schene [Sheen] (now call'd Richmond) by King Henry 5th, King Henry 8th put many of them to death, & the Rest unable to withstand the Fury of the Times Left England in a Body and Settled at Nieuport, where they have continued ever since, having a small Revenue, tho' Sufficient to support their Frugal and Abstemious way of Life.

But the unhealthy Air of the Place, the extream Poverty of it's Natives, and the frequent Wars in the Netherlands, have at all times so distress'd them, that they had reason to Fear a future Subvertion, either for want of Members, or of Means to Support them; for some of the Profess'd Monks generally Labour under Continual Infirmities, and Young Men have been often, either deterr'd from Entering amongst them, or after Tryal, obliged to abandon their Vocation; But in time of War (which the Country they are Situated in has been frequently the Seat off) their little Revenue was not Sufficient to give them bread, & much less to Enable them to Keep their House in due repair, or releive the wants of the famish'd Inhabitants.

In these Melancholy Circumstances they Lived when the late War began to Infest their Neighbourhood: the French were no sooner Masters of Ipres and Furnes, when, besides the exorbitant Exactions these good Gentlemen were made liable to, Three Fourths of their small Subsistance, which are payable to them from those Towns, were Stop'd; the Austrians at ye same time open'd the Sluces and ruin'd their Farms by Inundation; Their usual Pentions were no longer paid, and the Walls of their Convent, being Crack'd in Several places from Top to Bottom, threaten'd to fall on their Heads and Bury them in the Ruins:

T'was happy for them that the Town of Nieuport Surrender'd some time after upon Summons, for in Case of a real Seige, they must inevitably have been destroy'd, being Situated at the Foot of the Rampart under two Batterys, and the great Magazine of Powder, faceing the Enemies Attacks.

Being thus reduced to Live upon Allms, they humbly Casted themselves at the Feet of their Brethren, particularly those of their own Teutonick Province, but were rejected as being Strangers, and positively required to repair their House, or Suffer Alienation. This Severity happily United all the English Houses in the Netherlands in favour of the Distress'd: they Advised an Address to the Subjects of Great Brittain, and promised to recommend it, but on Express Condition of their Removeing from Nieuport to a more healthy Place, and where they should be less Exposed to the Calamities of War.

Upon this the General of the Order was Consulted, and being assur'd that the Building a new Convent would not Cost much more then to duely Repair their Habitation at Nieuport, he Approved their Design, and Promised to Grant his Licence and Leave for their Removal as soon as they should be Enabled to Purchase a small Tract of Land, and Build.

The perfecting their Undertakeing and Re-establishment depends therefore wholy on the Zeal & Charity which still shines in great Brittain however Oppress'd, and which was never known to fail when justly Call'd upon; To this Charity they most humbly recommend themselves as to their last hope, beging, they will not Suffer them to be dispersed whom their Ancestors united, and the End of whose Union is to Love and Serve God, and Avert his Wrath from their Native Country: But as Charity is Confounded with Injustice unless directed and Govern'd by Prudence, they ernestly desire their Friends to weigh well their own Circumstances, and give them no more than may be consistent with the wellfare of themselves and Familys. On these and no other Terms they hope to Perpetuate the Name of English Carthusians, and the Memory of their kind Benefactors to the Latest Posterity, to the End that no Blessings may be wanting to them or their Progeny, which the Prayers of a Gratefull Community can procure: But if, after all their honest Endeavours for a Re-establishment, they should fail of Success, they are prepar'd to receive the will of Heaven with an Humble Submission, And to Offer up in Sacrifice the Final Dissolution of the only English Charter-House on Earth.

N.B. The Original Case and Petition is Sign'd by most of the Superiours of Our English Houses in Flanders as Recommending this Charity.

[*Index follows*]

An Alphabetical List of the Names of those who have Charitably Contributed towards the Support and Re-establishment of this worthy Religious Family.

'He Lendeth our Lord that hath Mercy on the Poor; and He will Repay him the like.'

Proverb. Chapter 19. Verse 17.

Key to the following List of Benefactors
+      Those Names that are Mark'd with a Cross are Priests.
P      Protestants
P.P.      Parsons
D      Dead since they Contributed

Charity Covers a Multitude of Sins.

A

| | | | | £ | s | d |
|---|---|---|---|---|---|---|
| Mrs: Mary Allwyn | widow | | Hampshire | 3 | 3 | 0 |
| Mr: William Andrews | | | London | 0 | 2 | 6 |
| Mr John Arden + and Collected by him at Edgbaston &c in all | | | Worcestershire | 1 | 14 | 6 |
| Mrs: Isabella Arnold | widow | | London | 0 | 2 | 0 |
| The Right Honble Ann Lady Dowager Arundel | | D | | 1 | 1 | 0 |
| The Right Honble Mary Lady Arundel | | | Wiltshire | 1 | 1 | 0 |
| Mr: Thomas Attwood | physitian | | Worcestershire | 2 | 2 | 0 |
| Mr: Philip Andre | | + | London | 0 | 10 | 6 |

B

| | | | | £ | s | d |
|---|---|---|---|---|---|---|
| Mrs: Bamber | | D | Hampshire | 0 | 1 | 0 |
| Mr: John Barker | Sadler | | London | 0 | 2 | 6 |
| Mr: Walter Barns | Apothecary | | Dorsetshire | 0 | 5 | 0 |

| | | | | | | |
|---|---|---|---|---|---|---|
| Mrs: Frances Barns | | D | Dorsetshire | 0 | 2 | 6 |
| Mr: Joseph Barr | Innkeeper | P | Hampshire | 0 | 1 | 0 |
| Mr: Bryant Barrett | Laceman | | London | 5 | 5 | 0 |
| Basil Bartlett | | | Worcestershire | 2 | 2 | 0 |
| Sir Henry Bedingfeld Bart | | | Norfolk | 20 | 0 | 0 |
| Mrs: Bedingfeld | widow | | Suffolk | 1 | 1 | 0 |
| Mrs: Elizabeth Bedingfeld | | | Suffolk | 0 | 10 | 6 |
| Mr: Thomas Berington | | + D | | | | |
| Mr: Francis Petre | | + | London | 5 | 5 | 0 |
| Mr: John Typper | | + | | | | |
| Robert Berkeley Esqr | | | Worcestershire | 2 | 2 | 0 |
| A Collection gather'd by Mr John Betts in & about Winchester | | + | Hampshire | 3 | 8 | 0 |
| Mr: Beverley | China & Glass Seller | | London | 0 | 2 | 6 |
| Richard Biddulph Esqr | | | Sussex | 5 | 5 | 0 |
| Mrs: Hannah Blackburne | Widow | | London | 0 | 1 | 0 |
| Mrs: Mary Agnes Blount | Widow | | Hampshire | 2 | 12 | 6 |
| Mr: Henry Tichborne Blount | | + | London | 0 | 15 | 0 |
| Mrs: Mary Eugenia Blount | | | London | 1 | 2 | 0 |
| Michael Blount | | | London | 1 | 15 | 6 |
| Mr: Henry Bolney | Perruke maker | | London | 0 | 2 | 6 |
| Mr: James Bowen | Butcher | P | London | 0 | 3 | 6 |
| Mrs: Bowles | | | Dorsetshire | 0 | 2 | 6 |
| Mr: John Boys | Taylor | | London | 0 | 5 | 0 |
| Mrs: Boys | | | London | 0 | 5 | 0 |
| Mr: James John Bradley | | + | London | 0 | 5 | 0 |
| Ralph Brandling Esqr: | | D | London | 2 | 2 | 0 |
| Sir Charles Brown Bart: | | D | London | 1 | 1 | 0 |
| George Bruning Esqr: | | D | Hampshire | 0 | 5 | 0 |
| Mrs: Buttlar | | | London | 0 | 2 | 6 |
| Mr: James Butler | Haberdasher | | London | 0 | 10 | 6 |
| Mrs: Elizabeth Byerley | Widow | | London | 0 | 10 | 6 |

| | | | | £ | s | d |
|---|---|---|---|---|---|---|
| Mr: Thomas Byerley | | | London | 0 | 5 | 0 |
| Mrs: Jane Bond | Widow | D | | 2 | 2 | 0 |
| Mr: Pacificus Baker | | + | London | 0 | 10 | 6 |
| Mr: Samuel Bishop | Malster | | Oxfordshire | 0 | 2 | 6 |
| Mr: John Beaumont | | | Hampshire | 0 | 3 | 6 |
| Mr: Peter Birt | Mercer | P | Berkshire | 0 | 10 | 6 |
| Mrs: Martha Berington | | | Berkshire | 0 | 1 | 0 |
| Mrs: Frances Bishop | | | Oxfordshire | 0 | 2 | 6 |
| Master Michael Blount | | | Oxfordshire | 0 | 2 | 6 |
| Mrs: Eleanor Bayley | | | London | 0 | 10 | 6 |
| Mr: George Bishop Junr | | | London | 0 | 2 | 6 |
| Mrs: Elizabeth Butler | | | Berkshire | 0 | 5 | 6 |
| Mr: John Barnwell | | + | Hampshire | 0 | 2 | 6 |
| Mr: Robert Beaumont | | | London | 0 | 2 | 6 |
| Mr: Nicholas Butler | Upholsterer | | London | 0 | 2 | 6 |

## C

| | | | | £ | s | d |
|---|---|---|---|---|---|---|
| Mrs: Ann Cameron | | | Worcestershire | 0 | 2 | 6 |
| Francis Canning Esqr: | | | Warwickshire | 5 | 5 | 0 |
| Mrs: Carew | Widow | D | Hampshire | 0 | 2 | 6 |
| Mr: Joseph Carpue | Shoe-maker | | London | 1 | 1 | 0 |
| Mr: Francis Carpue | Silk-dyer | | London | 0 | 2 | 6 |
| Mr: Charles Carpue | Shoe-maker | | London | 0 | 13 | 0 |
| Mr: Francis Carpue being part of a Charitable Legacy deposited in his hands to dispose off | | | London | 1 | 1 | 0 |
| Edward Carryl Esqr: | | | Hampshire | 2 | 2 | 0 |
| Mrs: Alice Cattaway | | D | London | 0 | 2 | 6 |
| Mrs: Margaret Cattaway | | D | London | 0 | 2 | 6 |
| Mrs: Teresa Charlton | | | Northumberland | 1 | 1 | 0 |
| Mr: William Charlton | | P | Northumberland | 1 | 1 | 0 |
| John Chichester Esqr: | | | Devonshire | 50 | 5 | 0 |

| | | | | | | |
|---|---|---|---|---|---|---|
| Mrs: Margaret Cholmeley | Milliner | D | London | 0 | 2 | 6 |
| Mrs: Barbara Cholmeley | China-Seller | | London | 0 | 2 | 6 |
| Mr: Christopher Clark | | D | London | 1 | 11 | 6 |
| Ralph Clavering Esqr: | | | Northumberland | 1 | 1 | 0 |
| Mr: John Cleveland | Coal-merchant | P | London | 0 | 2 | 0 |
| Cuthbert Clifton Esqr: | | D | Surry | 5 | 5 | 0 |
| Mr: Major. Cockburne | Coachman | D | London | 0 | 5 | 0 |
| Mr John Collins | Joyner | | London | 0 | 2 | 6 |
| Mr: George Collingwood | | | Northumberland | 0 | 10 | 6 |
| Mr: Colgrave Junr: | | | London | 0 | 2 | 6 |
| Sir William Compton Bart: | | D | Gloucestershire | 5 | 5 | 0 |
| Dennis Compton Esqr: | | D | Wiltshire | 1 | 1 | 0 |
| Collected from Wilton & Callaley congregations | | | Northumberland | 2 | 13 | 6 |
| A Collection made by Mr: Charles Cordel | | + | Sussex | 0 | 10 | 0 |
| Mrs: Elisabeth Constable | | | London | 1 | 1 | 0 |
| Mr: Constable | | + | Norfolk | 0 | 18 | 0 |
| Mary Lady Conyers | | D | Huntingtonshire | 5 | 0 | 0 |
| Mr: Charles Cordel | | + | Sussex | 1 | 1 | 0 |
| Mr: James Cook | Tanner | | Hampshire | 0 | 2 | 6 |
| Mr: Thomas Cornforth | | + D | Dorsetshire | 0 | 5 | 0 |
| Mr: John Cotes | | + | Northumberland | 1 | 1 | 0 |
| Mr: John Cottingbelt | Watchmaker | | London | 0 | 2 | 6 |
| Mrs: Elizabeth Cottingbelt | | D | London | 0 | 2 | 6 |
| Mr: Cossens | Staymaker | D | London | 0 | 2 | 0 |
| Mr: Samuel Cox | | | Worcestershire | 1 | 1 | 0 |
| Mrs: Alicia Cox | | | Worcestershire | 0 | 5 | 0 |
| Mr: Peter Croce | Vintner | | London | 0 | 2 | 6 |
| Mr: Charles Cruse | Merchant | | London | 1 | 1 | 0 |
| Mr: Romanus Chapman | | + | London | 0 | 2 | 6 |
| Mr: Thomas Cox | | + | Berkshire | 0 | 2 | 6 |
| Mr: Samuel Clark | Tanner | P | Buckinghamshire | 0 | 2 | 6 |

# D

| | | | | £ | s | d |
|---|---|---|---|---|---|---|
| Mr: John Darrel | | + | Northumberland | 9 | 10 | 6 |
| Mr: Robert Delamotte | Fan-maker | | London | 0 | 5 | 0 |
| Mr: Bento Demages | Wine Merchant | D | London | 1 | 1 | 0 |
| Mr: De Witte | Merchant | | London | 1 | 1 | 0 |
| Mr: Robert Dillon | Merchant | | London | 1 | 1 | 0 |
| John Doncastle [Dancastle?] Esqr: | | | Berkshire | 1 | 1 | 0 |
| The Right Honble: Elizabeth Lady Dormer | | D | Shropshire | 2 | 2 | 0 |
| The Honble: John Dormer | | | Buckingham-shire | 5 | 5 | 0 |
| Henry Doughty Esqr: | | | Berkshire | 1 | 1 | 0 |
| Mrs: Frances Doughty | Widow | | London | 0 | 10 | 6 |
| Mrs: Ann Doughty | | D | Middlesex | 0 | 5 | 0 |
| Mr: George Doughty | | | Berkshire | 0 | 5 | 0 |
| Mathew Duane Esqr: | | | London | 0 | 10 | 6 |
| Mr: Isaac Dudley | Fish-monger | P | London | 1 | 1 | 0 |
| Mr: Francis Dunn | Wine merchant | | London | 0 | 5 | 0 |
| Mr: Thomas Daniel | | | Lancashire | 0 | 1 | 0 |
| Mr: John Duthy | Attorney | P | Hampshire | 0 | 10 | 6 |
| Mr: Joseph Demages | Wine Merchant | | London | 1 | 1 | 0 |
| Miss Frances Doughty | | | London | 0 | 5 | 0 |
| Miss Charlott Doughty | | | London | 0 | 4 | 0 |
| Mr: John De La Forse | Staymaker | | London | 0 | 5 | 0 |
| Mr: James Doughty | | | London | 0 | 2 | 6 |
| Mr: Robert Doughty | | | London | 0 | 2 | 6 |
| Mr James Douglas | | | London | 0 | 0 | 6 |

## E

|  |  |  |  | £ | s | d |
|---|---|---|---|---|---|---|
| Mr: Edwards | Tobacconist |  | London | 0 | 1 | 0 |
| Mrs: Sophia Edwards |  |  | London | 0 | 1 | 0 |
| Mrs: Egan |  |  | London | 1 | 1 | 0 |
| Mr: Grey Elliott |  |  | London | 0 | 5 | 0 |
| Mr: Richard Elliott | Apothecary |  | London | 0 | 5 | 0 |
| Miss Frances Ellis |  |  | Northumberland | 0 | 5 | 0 |
| Mr: William Ellis |  |  | Sussex | 1 | 1 | 0 |
| Mr: William Errington |  | + | London | 0 | 2 | 6 |
| Mr: William Errington |  |  | Northumberland | 1 | 1 | 0 |
| Mr: Edward Eyre | Linnen-Draper |  | London | 1 | 1 | 0 |
| James Eyre Esqr: |  | D | Norfolk | 2 | 2 | 0 |
| Mr: William Eyston |  |  | London | 0 | 2 | 6 |
| Mr: Charles Felix Englefield |  | + | Berkshire | 1 | 1 | 0 |
| Mrs: Eyre | widow |  | London | 2 | 2 | 0 |

## F

|  |  |  |  | £ | s | d |
|---|---|---|---|---|---|---|
| James Farrel Esqr: |  |  | London | 2 | 2 | 0 |
| Mr: Peter Farrer |  |  | Northumberland | 0 | 2 | 6 |
| Mr: Anthony Featherstone |  | + D | Hampshire | 0 | 5 | 0 |
| Mr: James Fenwick |  |  | Northumberland | 0 | 10 | 6 |
| Mrs: Fermor |  |  | Yorkshire | 3 | 3 | 0 |
| George Fitzgerald Esqr: |  |  | London | 10 | 0 | 0 |
| Richard Fitzgerald Esqr: |  |  | London | 1 | 1 | 0 |
| Mr: Richard Frazer | Apothecary | D | London | 0 | 2 | 6 |
| Mr: Thomas Fryer | Hosier | P | London | 0 | 1 | 0 |
| Mr: Thomas Field | Taylor |  | London | 0 | 1 | 0 |
| Mr: John Fletcher | Laceman |  | London | 0 | 2 | 6 |
| Mr: William Freebody | Fisherman | P | Oxfordshire | 0 | 1 | 6 |

| | | | | £ | s | d |
|---|---|---|---|---|---|---|
| Monsieur Le Comte De Furstenberg General of the Hessian Troops now in England | | | Hampshire | 1 | 1 | 0 |
| Mr: James Fleming | Brazier | | London | 0 | 0 | 6 |
| Mrs: Mary Fisher | | D | London | 0 | 0 | 6 |

## G

| | | | | £ | s | d |
|---|---|---|---|---|---|---|
| The Right Honble: Lady Viscountess Gage | | D | London | 1 | 1 | 0 |
| Mrs: Mary Giffard | Widow | D | Staffordshire | 100 | 0 | 0 |
| The Honble: Lady Giffard | | D | London | 1 | 1 | 0 |
| Mr: Thomas Gilpin | Goldsmith | | London | 0 | 10 | 6 |
| Mrs: Christiana Gold | | D | London | 1 | 1 | 0 |
| Mrs: Ann Goodwin | | | Hampshire | 0 | 1 | 0 |
| Mr: John Gordon | | | London | 2 | 2 | 0 |
| Mr: Henry Graham | | | Hampshire | 1 | 1 | 0 |
| Mrs: Elizabeth Green | Fruiterer | | London | 0 | 1 | 0 |
| Mr Greenwell | Upholsterer | | London | 0 | 5 | 0 |
| Mr: Richard Grene | | + D | London | 0 | 2 | 6 |
| The Right Honble: Thomas Lord Viscount Gage | | P D | London | 5 | 5 | 0 |
| Mr: Henry Goore | | | Lancashire | 0 | 5 | 0 |
| Thomas Rookwood Gage Esqr: | | | Suffolk | 3 | 3 | 0 |
| John Gauntlett | Wine Merchant | P | Hampshire | 0 | 10 | 6 |

## H

| | | | | £ | s | d |
|---|---|---|---|---|---|---|
| Mrs: Catherine Hales | | | Northumberland | 2 | 2 | 0 |
| Mr: William Halloran | Merchant | | London | 2 | 2 | 0 |
| Mr: Edward Harlee | Coachmaker | | London | 0 | 10 | 6 |
| Miss Mary Harold | | | London | 1 | 1 | 0 |
| Mr: Peter Hasert | Cabinet-maker | D | London | 0 | 10 | 6 |

| Mr: Hatton | Watch-maker | | London | 0 | 5 | 0 |
|---|---|---|---|---|---|---|
| Thomas Havers Esqr: | | | Norfolk | 2 | 2 | 0 |
| Mr: William Havers | | | London | 0 | 10 | 6 |
| Mrs: Ann Hawkes | | | Worcestershire | 0 | 10 | 6 |
| Mrs: Catherine Heneage | Widow | | London | 0 | 10 | 6 |
| Mr: Henry Heneage | | | Lincolnshire | 1 | 1 | 0 |
| Mr: Dominick Hernon | Grocer | | London | 0 | 13 | 0 |
| William Hesketh Esqr: | | D | Lancashire | 45 | 0 | 0 |
| Mrs: Mary Hesketh | | D | Lancashire | 45 | 0 | 0 |
| Mr: Thomas Hodson | Apothecary | | London | 0 | 18 | 0 |
| Mr: David Horne | Perruke-maker | P | London | 0 | 2 | 6 |
| Mr: John Hornyold | | | Worcestershire | 0 | 10 | 6 |
| Mr: Anthony Hornyold | | | Worcestershire | 0 | 10 | 6 |
| Mrs: Hornyold | | | London | 0 | 10 | 6 |
| From a Person in Lancashire by the Hands of John Howard | | + | London | 4 | 4 | 0 |
| Mr: Thomas Hoy | | | London | 0 | 1 | 0 |
| Sir Windsor Hunloke Bart: | | D | Derbyshire | 20 | 0 | 0 |
| Mr: Francis Hunt | Laceman | D | London | 0 | 2 | 6 |
| Mr: Gyles Hussey | | | London | 1 | 7 | 6 |
| Mrs: Mary Hussey | | | Dorsetshire | 1 | 1 | 0 |
| Mr: Edward Hussey | | + | Essex | 0 | 10 | 6 |
| Mr: James Hussey | | | London | 0 | 2 | 6 |
| John Hussey Esqr: | | D | Dorsetshire | 0 | 10 | 6 |
| Mrs: Susanna Hussey | | | Dorsetshire | 1 | 1 | 0 |
| Mr: Peter Hussey | Merchant | | London | 2 | 2 | 0 |
| Mrs: Hussey | | | London | 0 | 5 | 0 |
| Miss Hussey | | | London | 0 | 5 | 0 |
| Master James Hussey | | | London | 0 | 5 | 0 |
| The Honble: Charles Howard | | | Cumberland | 10 | 10 | 0 |
| Mrs: Jane Harrison | | | Lancashire | 0 | 1 | 0 |
| Mr: Joseph Howse | | D | London | 0 | 2 | 6 |

| | | | | £ | s | d |
|---|---|---|---|---|---|---|
| Mr: James Horne | | + | London | 0 | 2 | 6 |
| Mr: James Hewson | Bookseller | D | London | 0 | 2 | 0 |
| Mr: James Hutton | Inn Keeper | | London | 0 | 5 | 0 |
| Mr: Philip Hanson January 1756 | | P | London | 0 | 1 | 0 |
| Mr: James Hill | Stone Cutter | P | Berkshire | 0 | 2 | 6 |
| Mr: James Hughes | | | London | 0 | 2 | 6 |

## I, J

| | | | | £ | s | d |
|---|---|---|---|---|---|---|
| Mr: Abraham Ibbotson | Grazier | | Sussex | 0 | 5 | 0 |
| Mr: John Jones | Whipmaker | P D | Hampshire | 0 | 2 | 6 |
| Mr: James Julian | Wine Merchant | | London | 0 | 10 | 6 |
| Mr: Joachim Ingram | | + | London | 0 | 2 | 6 |

## K

| | | | | £ | s | d |
|---|---|---|---|---|---|---|
| Anthony Kemp Esqr: | | D | Sussex | 1 | 1 | 0 |
| Miss Barbara Kemp | | | Sussex | 1 | 11 | 6 |
| Miss Ann Kemp | | | Sussex | 1 | 11 | 6 |
| Mr: John Kempson | Druggist | | London | 0 | 2 | 6 |
| Mr: Joseph King | Watch-maker | | Dorsetshire | 0 | 5 | 0 |
| Mr: Robert Knowles | | | London | 1 | 1 | 0 |
| Mr: Frederick Kandler | Silver Smith | | London | 0 | 10 | 6 |

## L

| | | | | £ | s | d |
|---|---|---|---|---|---|---|
| Mr Brereton Lacy | | D | London | 0 | 10 | 6 |
| Mr William Lacy | | D | Hampshire | 0 | 5 | 0 |
| The Right Honble Marmaduke Lord Langdale | | | London | 10 | 0 | 0 |
| Mr Thomas Langdale | Distiller | | London | 1 | 1 | 0 |
| Mrs: Susanna Lane | | | Sussex | 0 | 2 | 6 |
| Sir Henry Lawson Bart. | | | Yorkshire | 3 | 3 | 0 |

| | | | | £ | s | d |
|---|---|---|---|---|---|---|
| Mr: Samuel Lasingham | Shoemaker | P | London | 0 | 1 | 0 |
| Mrs: Apollonia Lee | | | Worcestershire | 0 | 10 | 6 |
| Mrs Leyburn | | | Durham | 0 | 10 | 6 |
| Mrs: Dorothy Lloyd | | | Essex | 0 | 10 | 0 |
| Mr: James Ludgater | Shoemaker | | Sussex | 0 | 1 | 0 |
| Mrs: Catherine Ludgater | | | Sussex | 0 | 1 | 0 |
| Mr: Isidore Lynch | Merchant | | London | 1 | 1 | 0 |
| Lady Lawson Dowager | | | Yorkshire | 10 | 0 | 0 |
| Mrs: Elenanor Lacy | | | Hampshire | 1 | 1 | 0 |

## M

| | | | | £ | s | d |
|---|---|---|---|---|---|---|
| Alexander Maccarty Esqr. | | | London | 1 | 1 | 0 |
| Mr: Henry Mackworth | Apothecary | | London | 0 | 10 | 6 |
| Mr: Timothy Macnamara | Merchant | | London | 1 | 1 | 0 |
| Mr: John Megenis | Apothecary | | Middlesex | 0 | 5 | 0 |
| Thomas Maire Esqr | | D | | 3 | 3 | 0 |
| Mr: Thomas Maire junr | | | | 1 | 1 | 0 |
| Mr: John Maire | | | London | 1 | 1 | 0 |
| Mr: James Malo | Cambrick Merchant | | London | 0 | 10 | 6 |
| Mrs: Ann Mannock | | D | London | 1 | 1 | 0 |
| Sir Francis Mannock Bart | | | Suffolk | 25 | 0 | 0 |
| The Three Miss Meads Five Shillings Each | | | London | 0 | 15 | 0 |
| Mr: Thomas Meighan | Bookseller | D | London | 0 | 10 | 6 |
| Mr: Milan | | D | London | 2 | 2 | 0 |
| Mr: Mitchel | | | London | 0 | 1 | 0 |
| Mrs: Monington | Widow | D | Herefordshire | 1 | 1 | 0 |
| Mr: Henry Moody | Warrener | | Hampshire | 0 | 1 | 0 |
| Mrs: Frances Morey by her Will | | D | Berkshire | 100 | 0 | 0 |
| Mrs: Sarah Mortershut | | | Hampshire | 0 | 1 | 0 |
| Sir Edward Mostyn Bart | | D | Flintshire | 5 | 5 | 0 |

| | | | | £ | s | d |
|---|---|---|---|---|---|---|
| Mr: Thomas Mounteney | Stay-maker | | Hampshire | 0 | 2 | 6 |
| Mr: John Mumford | Salesman | P D | London | 0 | 3 | 0 |
| Mrs Mary Moorcroft | | | Lancashire | 0 | 2 | 0 |
| Mrs: Mounteney | | P D | London | 0 | 2 | 6 |
| Mr Edward Madew | | + | Oxfordshire | 0 | 2 | 6 |
| William Middleton Esqr. | | | Yorkshire | 1 | 1 | 0 |
| Mr John Monkhouse | Watchmaker | | London | 0 | 2 | 6 |
| Mrs: Mary More | | | London | 0 | 1 | 0 |
| Miss Ann Monington | | | London | 1 | 1 | 0 |
| Miss Hannah Madoe | | | London | 0 | 2 | 6 |
| Mr: Thomas Martin | | + | Berkshire | 0 | 5 | 0 |
| Miss Frances Manby | | | London | 1 | 1 | 0 |
| Miss Mary Manby | | | London | 1 | 1 | 0 |

## N

| | | | £ | s | d |
|---|---|---|---|---|---|
| Mrs: Elizabeth Needham | Bookseller | London | 0 | 2 | 6 |
| Mr: James Nelson | Apothecary | London | 0 | 5 | 0 |
| Mr: Thomas Newel | Shoemaker | Hampshire | 0 | 1 | 0 |
| Mr: James Newman | Gardiner | Sussex | 0 | 1 | 0 |
| Mr: James Nicholas | Jeweller | London | 0 | 10 | 6 |
| Mr: Thomas Norris | | Hampshire | 0 | 2 | 6 |
| His Grace Thomas Duke of Norfolk | | Nottinghamshire | 50 | 0 | 0 |

## O

| | | £ | s | d |
|---|---|---|---|---|
| Mr: Edward Orpwood January 1756 | London | 0 | 2 | 0 |

## P

| | | | £ | s | d |
|---|---|---|---|---|---|
| Mrs: Panton | | London | 0 | 2 | 6 |
| Mr: Christopher Parker | Lamp Furnisher | London | 0 | 2 | 6 |

| | | | | £ | s | d |
|---|---|---|---|---|---|---|
| Mrs: Ann Patrick | | | Sussex | 0 | 1 | 0 |
| Mrs: Mary Penniend | | | Sussex | 0 | 1 | 0 |
| Mr: Henry Perrin | Cabi-net-maker | D | London | 0 | 2 | 6 |
| The Right Honble Earl of Peterborough | | P | Berkshire | 1 | 1 | 0 |
| The Right Honble Ann Lady Petre | | | Essex | 10 | 10 | 0 |
| Mrs: Teresa Petre | Widow | | London | 4 | 4 | 0 |
| Miss Mary Plastid | | | London | 0 | 10 | 6 |
| Edmund Plowden Esqr | | D | Shropshire | 1 | 1 | 0 |
| Mrs: Plowden | | D | Shropshire | 1 | 1 | 0 |
| Mr: Poyntz January 1756 | | + | London | 0 | 1 | 0 |
| Mr: James Price | | + | Berkshire | 1 | 2 | 6 |

## R

| | | | | £ | s | d |
|---|---|---|---|---|---|---|
| Mr: Henry Racket | | | London | 0 | 10 | 6 |
| Thomas Riddle Esqr. | | | Northumberland | 1 | 1 | 0 |
| Mr: William Runciman | Woollen-draper | | London | 0 | 10 | 6 |
| Mrs: Runciman | Widow | | London | 0 | 1 | 0 |
| Mrs: Mary Russel | | | Worcestershire | 1 | 1 | 0 |
| Mr: Thomas Rice | Shoemaker | | London | 0 | 1 | 0 |
| Mr: James Rogerson January 1756 | | + | London | 0 | 2 | 6 |
| Mrs: Mary Rogers | | | Hampshire | 0 | 10 | 6 |

## S

| | | | | £ | s | d |
|---|---|---|---|---|---|---|
| Bryan Salvyn Esqr | | | Durham | 2 | 2 | 0 |
| Mr: John Selbye | | | Northumberland | 0 | 5 | 0 |
| Edward Sexton Serle Esqr: | | | London | 0 | 10 | 6 |
| Mr: Ralph Seton | Upholsterer | | London | 0 | 2 | 6 |
| Mr: John Seton | Upholsterer | | London | 0 | 2 | 6 |

| | | | | | | |
|---|---|---|---|---|---|---|
| John Shaftoe Esqr: | | | Northumberland | 1 | 1 | 0 |
| Mr: Shakleton | Painter | P | London | 0 | 2 | 6 |
| Mr: Jeremy Shaw | | + | London | 0 | 10 | 6 |
| William Sheldon Esqr: | | | Worcestershire | 5 | 0 | 0 |
| Mr: Shepheard | | | Dorsetshire | 0 | 1 | 0 |
| Miss Elizabeth Shepheard | | | London | 0 | 1 | 0 |
| Mr: Nicholas Sherwood | Surgeon | | London | 0 | 10 | 6 |
| The Right Honble George Earl of Shrewsbury | | | Oxfordshire | 5 | 5 | 0 |
| The Right Honble Mary Countess Dowager of Shrewsbury | | D | | 5 | 5 | 0 |
| Mr: George Silvertope | | | Northumberland | 1 | 1 | 0 |
| Mr: Joseph Silvertope | | | Northumberland | 0 | 5 | 0 |
| Sir Edward Simeon Bart | | | Oxfordshire | 10 | 0 | 0 |
| Mrs: Bridget Sinnott | | D | Hampshire | 0 | 10 | 0 |
| Sir Edward Smith Bart: | | | London | 5 | 5 | 0 |
| Mr: William Smith | | + | London | 0 | 2 | 6 |
| Mr: William Smith | | P D | Oxfordshire | 0 | 2 | 6 |
| Mr: Charles Smith | Bricklayer | | London | 0 | 2 | 6 |
| Mr: Smith | | + | Suffolk | 1 | 7 | 0 |
| Mr: Thomas Smith | | | Northumberland | 0 | 10 | 6 |
| Mr: Joseph Smithson | Apothecary | | London | 0 | 5 | 0 |
| Sir Edward Southcote Bart | | D | Essex | 20 | 0 | 0 |
| Lady Southcote | | D | Essex | 5 | 0 | 0 |
| Philip Southcote Esqr: | | | Surry | 5 | 5 | 0 |
| Mr: Edward Spicer Woodward | | | Sussex | 0 | 1 | 0 |
| Francis Stafford Esqr: | | | Hampshire | 1 | 1 | 0 |
| John Stapylton Esqr: | | D | London | 1 | 1 | 0 |
| Mr: Thomas Stapylton | | + D | London | 0 | 10 | 6 |
| William Stourton Esqr: | | | London | 0 | 10 | 6 |
| Mr: Andrew Streeke | Syder Merchant | P D | London | 0 | 0 | 6 |

| | | | | £ | s | d |
|---|---|---|---|---|---|---|
| Mrs: Mary Strickland by her Will | | D | London | 10 | 0 | 0 |
| Mr: Suffield | Wine Merchant | | Norfolk | 0 | 10 | 6 |
| Mrs: Mary Swinburne | | | Northumberland | 1 | 1 | 0 |
| Mr: William Swinburne | | P | Northumberland | 0 | 10 | 6 |
| Miss Helena Suzzeker | | | Lancashire | 0 | 2 | 0 |
| Mr: Charles Strickland | | | London | 0 | 0 | 6 |
| Mr: Henry Stonor | Grocer | | London | 0 | 2 | 6 |
| Miss Winefride Strode | | | London | 0 | 1 | 0 |
| Mr: William Smith | Coal Merchant | | London | 0 | 10 | 6 |
| Mr: Joseph Strickland | | + | London | 1 | 1 | 0 |
| Mr: John Strickland | | + | Paris | 1 | 1 | 0 |
| Mrs: Hannah Stapler | | | London | 0 | 2 | 6 |
| Mr: William Sterck | Watchmaker | | London | 0 | 2 | 6 |
| Mr: John Smith | Coffee House Keeper | | London | 0 | 2 | 6 |
| Mr: Philip Sherlock | | | London | 0 | 0 | 6 |
| Edward Sheldon Esqr: | | | Hampshire | 3 | 3 | 0 |

## T

| | | | | £ | s | d |
|---|---|---|---|---|---|---|
| Timothy Taffe Esqr: | | P | London | 1 | 1 | 0 |
| The Honble Charles Talbot | | | Oxfordshire | 2 | 2 | 0 |
| Mrs: Frances Tanckred | | D | London | 1 | 1 | 0 |
| Miss Mary Tasburgh | | | London | 1 | 1 | 0 |
| Stephen Tempest Esqr: | | | Yorkshire | 10 | 10 | 0 |
| Mr: Thomas | | | London | 0 | 5 | 0 |
| Mr: George Thornburgh and Mrs: Thornburgh his Wife | Druggist | | London | 0 | 10 | 6 |
| James Thornton Esqr: | | | Northumberland | 5 | 5 | 0 |
| Mrs: Elizabeth Thornton | | | Northumberland | 2 | 2 | 0 |
| Mrs: Margaret Thornton | | | Northumberland | 0 | 15 | 0 |
| Miss Margaret Thornton | | | Northumberland | 0 | 5 | 0 |

| | | | | £ | s | d |
|---|---|---|---|--:|--:|--:|
| Miss Ann Thornton | | | Northumberland | 0 | 5 | 0 |
| Miss Mary Thornton | | | Northumberland | 0 | 2 | 6 |
| Mrs: Dorothy Thorold | Widow | | London | 0 | 10 | 6 |
| Mr: Peter Tompson | | | Northumberland | 0 | 10 | 6 |
| Mr: Charles Tootell | | + | Lancashire | 0 | 10 | 0 |
| Mr: Wm: Tourville | Inn-keeper | | London | 0 | 10 | 6 |
| Mr: Thomas Tozer | Brewer | P | London | 0 | 2 | 6 |
| Mr: Nicholas Tuite | Merchant | | London | 5 | 5 | 0 |
| Marmaduke Tunstall Esqr: | | | Yorkshire | 21 | 0 | 0 |
| Mr: John Turberville | Miller | | Hampshire | 1 | 1 | 0 |
| Mr: William Townsend | Undertaker | P | London | 0 | 2 | 6 |
| Mr: Stephen Turner | Surgeon | | London | 1 | 1 | 0 |
| Mr: Alexander Taylor | | + | Oxfordshire | 0 | 5 | 0 |

### U, V

| | | | | £ | s | d |
|---|---|---|---|--:|--:|--:|
| Mr: Joseph Vanhacken | Painter | D | London | 0 | 10 | 6 |
| Mr: Thomas Vaughan | | P | London | 0 | 5 | 0 |
| Mr: Charles Umfreville | | + | London | 0 | 5 | 0 |
| Unknown hands | | | | 32 | 11 | 0 |
| Unknown hands | | P | | 21 | 3 | 0 |
| Mrs: Elizabeth Uthwatt | | | London | 0 | 10 | 6 |

### W

| | | | | £ | s | d |
|---|---|---|---|--:|--:|--:|
| William Wakeman Esqr: | | | Gloucestershire | 2 | 2 | 0 |
| Mr: James Walmsley | Upholsterer | | London | 0 | 2 | 6 |
| Mrs: Wareham | | D | London | 0 | 2 | 6 |
| Sir Thomas Webb Bart: | | | Wilshire | 20 | 0 | 0 |
| Eleanor Lady Webb | Widow | | Berkshire | 1 | 1 | 0 |
| Edward Webbe Esqr: being part of a Sum Bequeathed for Charitable Uses by Sir John Webb Bart: deceased | | D | London | 10 | 10 | 0 |
| Edward Weld Esqr: | | | Dorsetshire | 10 | 0 | 0 |

| | | | | | | |
|---|---|---|---|---|---|---|
| The Honble Lady Mary Wells | | | Hampshire | 1 | 1 | 0 |
| Mr: John West | Frame-maker | | London | 0 | 2 | 6 |
| John White Esqr: | | D | London | 0 | 15 | 16 |
| Ralph Widdrington Esqr: | | D | Northumberland | 1 | 1 | 9 |
| Edward Horseley Widdrington Esqr: | | | Northumberland | 1 | 1 | 0 |
| Mr: Thomas Williams | Druggist | | London | 0 | 2 | 6 |
| Mrs: Elizabeth Williams | | | Worcestershire | 0 | 5 | 0 |
| Mrs: Wills | | P | London | 0 | 2 | 0 |
| Mrs: Sarah Wilkinson | | | London | 0 | 2 | 6 |
| Mrs: Wolf | Widow | D | London | 0 | 2 | 6 |
| John Wolf Esqr: | | | Oxfordshire | 7 | 7 | 0 |
| William Wollascott | | D | Berkshire | 3 | 3 | 0 |
| Mr: Thomas Wollascott | | D | London | 0 | 2 | 6 |
| Mrs: Mary Woods | | | Suffolk | 0 | 10 | 6 |
| Mr: William Wrege | | P.P. | Northumberland | 0 | 10 | 0 |
| Mr: Anthony Wright | Banker | | London | 5 | 5 | 0 |
| Mrs: Constantia Wright | | | Essex | 0 | 5 | 0 |
| Mr: Henry Wyborne | | + | Norfolk | 4 | 1 | 0 |
| Mr: William Wyatt | Shoemaker | D | Hampshire | 0 | 0 | 6 |
| Mr: Peter Whittell | | D | Middlesex | 0 | 10 | 6 |
| Mrs: Elizabeth Whittell | | | Middlesex | 0 | 5 | 0 |
| Mr: George Webbe | Upholsterer | | London | 0 | 2 | 6 |
| Mr: James Wheble January 1756 | | | London | 0 | 0 | 6 |
| Mr: Thomas West | Woollen-draper | P | Berkshire | 0 | 3 | 0 |
| Mr: John White | Wine Merchant | | London | 0 | 10 | 6 |
| Mr: Robert Westby | | | London | 3 | 3 | 0 |
| Mr: John Westbrooke | Bell Hanger | | London | 0 | 2 | 6 |
| Mrs: Eleanor Willis | Widow Cutler | | Berkshire | 0 | 2 | 6 |
| Mr: William White | Mercer | P | Hampshire | 0 | 10 | 6 |

| Mr: Thomas Walsh | Perrukemaker | | Berkshire | 0 | 2 | 0 |
| Mr: John West | Surgeon | P | Hampshire | 0 | 2 | 6 |
| Mr[s]: Cecily Watson | | | London | 0 | 0 | 6 |

## Y

| | | | | £ | s | d |
| Mr: Charles Young | | | | 0 | 5 | 0 |

# BIBLIOGRAPHY

## Manuscripts

The British Library, London
Add. MSS 28228–28230, 28251, Caryll Papers
Mapledurham House, Oxfordshire
Blount Manuscripts, including Strickland Papers
The National Archives, Kew
PROB 11/682/124

## Printed sources

Anstruther, Godfrey, *The Seminary Priests: A Dictionary of the Secular Clergy of England and Wales, 1558–1850. II. Early Stuarts, 1603–1659* (Great Wakering, Essex: Mayhew-MacCrimmon, 1975)
———, *The Seminary Priests: A Dictionary of the Secular Clergy of England and Wales, 1558–1850. III. 1660–1715* (Great Wakering, Essex: Mayhew-MacCrimmon, 1976)
———, *The Seminary Priests: A Dictionary of the Secular Clergy of England and Wales, 1558–1850. IV. 1716–1800* (Great Wakering, Essex: Mayhew-MacCrimmon, 1977)
Bellenger, Dominic Aidan. *English and Welsh Priests 1558–1800: A Working List* (Bath: Downside Abbey, 1984)
Blount, Michael, *A Congratulatory Poem presented to the Right Reverend Lady, Lady Mary Crispe of the Isle of Tenet, Abbess of the RR. Benedictin Dames at Brussells. On the Occasion of celebrating her Jubilie, the fifth day of June, 1737* (Brussels: Printed by Peter Foppens, 1737)
Bowden, Caroline (ed.), *English Convents in Exile, 1600–1800*, 6 vols (London: Pickering and Chatto, 2012–13)
[Butler, Charles], *Historical Account of the Laws against the Roman Catholics of England* ([London]: Printed by Luke Hansard & Sons, for Keating, Brown, & Co.; Booker and Faulder; Ridgeway; Budd; and Fitzpatrick & Coyne, Dublin, 1811) [Copy at Mapledurham has MS attribution of authorship; no other copies traced]
Campbell, R., *The London Tradesman. Being a Compendious View of all the Trades, Professions, Arts, both Liberal and Mechanic* (London: T. Gardner, 1747)
Cantillon, Richard, *Dictionary of Political Economy*, ed. R. H. Inglis Palgrave (London: MacMillan, 1915)

Corp, Edward T., *L'Autre Exil: les Jacobites en France au Début du XVIIIe Siècle: Actes du Colloque 'la Cour des Stuarts à Saint-Germain-en-Laye au Temps de Louis XIV'* (Toulouse: Les Presses du Languedoc, 1993)

——, *A Court in Exile: The Stuarts in France 1689–1718* (Cambridge: Cambridge University Press, 2004)

*La Cour des Stuarts à Saint-Germain-en-Laye au Temps de Louis XIV* (Paris: Musée des antiquités nationales de Saint-Germain-en-Laye, 1992)

Croke, Sir Alexander, *The Genealogical History of the Croke Family. Originally Named Le Blount*, 2 vols. (London: John Murray; Oxford: Joseph Parker, 1823)

Estcourt, Edgar, and Payne, John Orlebar (eds), *The English Catholic Nonjurors of 1715: Being a Summary of the Register of Their Estates* (London: Burns and Oates, 1885)

Gillow, Joseph, *A Literary and Biographical History, or Bibliographical Dictionary of the English Catholics*, 5 vols (London: Burns and Oates, 1885–1902)

Glickman, Gabriel, *The English Catholic Community 1688–1745: Politics, Culture and Ideology* (Woodbridge: Boydell Press, 2009)

Guilday, Peter, *English Catholic Refugees on the Continent, 1558–1795. I: The English Colleges and Convents in the Catholic Low Countries* (London: Longmans, Green and Co., 1914)

Hansom, J. S., 'Addenda to Market Rasen, Lincs., Register, 1640–1780. Extracts from Kingerby and other Parish Registers, 1640–1792' in *Miscellanea XII*, Catholic Record Society 22 (Leeds: Catholic Record Society, 1921)

Heal, Ambrose, *The London Goldsmiths 1200–1800* (Cambridge: Cambridge University Press, 1935)

Hoppitt, Julian, *A Land of Liberty? England 1689–1277* (Oxford: Oxford University Press, 2000)

Hornyold, Henry, *Genealogical Memoirs of the Family of Strickland of Sizergh* (Kendal: T. Wilson and Son, 1928)

Kirk, John, *Biographies of English Catholics in the Eighteenth Century* (London: Burns and Oates, 1909)

Langford, Paul, *A Polite and Commercial People: England 1727–1783* (Oxford: Oxford University Press, 1989)

Melton, F. C., *Sir Robert Clayton and the Origins of English Deposit Banking, 1658–1685* (Cambridge: Cambridge University Press, 1986)

Monod, Paul Kléber, *Jacobitism and the English People 1688–1788* (Cambridge: Cambridge University Press, 1989)

Murphy, Antoin E., *Richard Cantillon: Entrepreneur and Economist* (Oxford: Clarendon Press, 1986)

Parmiter, Geoffrey de C., *Elizabethan Popish Recusancy in the Inns of Court* (London: Institute of Historical Research, 1976)

Price, F. G. H. Hylton, *A Handbook of London Bankers* (London: Simpkin, Marshall and Co., 1890–91)

'Records of the Dominican Nuns of the Second Order (Vilvorde and Brussels), 1661–1697', in *Dominicana*, Catholic Record Society 25 (London: Catholic Record Society, 1925)

Rumbold, Valerie, *Women's Place in Pope's World* (Cambridge: Cambridge University Press, 1989)

Ruvigny, A. H. D. H. de la C. de Melville, Massue de (Marquis of Ruvigny and Raineval), *The Jacobite Peerage, Baronetage, Knightage and Grants of Honour* (Edinburgh: T. C. and E. C. Jack, 1904)

Skeet, F. J. A., *History of the Families of Skeet, Somerscales, Widdrington, Wilby, Blake, Murray, Grimshaw and others* (London: n.p., 1906)

Skeet, F. J. A., *The Life of the Right Honourable James Radcliffe Third Earl of Derwentwater, (Co. Northumberland), Viscount Radcliffe and Langley & Baron Tynedale (Co. Cumberland), and Fifth Baronet of Dilston; with an Account of His Martyrdom for the Catholic Faith & Loyalty to His Rightful King* (London: Hutchinson and Co., 1929)

Wenham, L. P., *Roger Strickland of Richmond: A Jacobite Gentleman 1680–1749* (Northallerton: North Yorkshire County Record Office, 1982)

Whelan, Basil, 'Our Historic English Convents: English Cloisters in Flanders in the Penal Times. VI – The Seventeenth and Eighteenth Centuries', *The Tablet*, 5 November 1921, p. 24

Williams, Richard G., 'Pigott, Nathaniel (*bap.* 1661, *d.* 1737)', in *ODNB*, online edition, http://www.oxforddnb.com/themes/theme.jsp?articleid=92738, accessed 2 July 2010

Williams, Richard G., 'Strickland, Mannock John (1683–1744)', in *ODNB*, online edition, http://www.oxforddnb.com/view/article/64936, accessed 2 July 2010

Young, Francis (ed.), *Rookwood Family Papers, 1606–1761* (Woodbridge: Suffolk Records Society, 2016)

**Unpublished theses**

Hardy, L. A., 'The Petre Family in Lancashire: a Study of a Catholic Family, Their Estate, Its Management and Operation 1700–1852', unpublished MA dissertation, Huddersfield Polytechnic, 1987

Williams, Richard G., 'Mannock Strickland (1683–1744): The Life and Professional Career of a Catholic Jacobite Counsellor-at-Law', unpublished PhD thesis, University of London, 2000

**Online sources**

*The History of Parliament*, online edition: http://www.historyofparliamentonline.org

*Oxford Dictionary of National Biography*, online edition: http://www.oxforddnb.com

'Who Were the Nuns?' database: http://wwtn.history.qmul.ac.uk

# INDEX

Letters to MS are indexed under name of sender and convent of origin. Letters to others are listed under sender, recipient and convent of origin, as appropriate.
Financial matters are discussed throughout the text and are not fully itemised.
Page spans may indicate repeated mentions rather than continuous discussion.

## The Catholic Record Society

The Catholic Record Society was established in 1904 in order to publish editions of primary sources relating to Catholic individuals and ecclesiastical institutions in the British Isles, including registers, chronicles, letters and diaries. The Society's motto, *Colligite fragmenta ne pereant* ('Gather up the fragments lest they perish'), reflects the aim of the Society to make primary sources available to posterity and a general readership.

Over ninety volumes have been published so far and they form a unique collection of primary source material indispensable to all those with an interest in the history of Catholic dioceses, parishes, religious communities, schools and colleges. The Society has also published a number of scholarly monographs dealing with particular topics or with Catholic individuals prominent in public life.

*British Catholic History*, formerly titled *Recusant History*, is the official journal of the Catholic Record Society, published twice annually in May and October by Cambridge University Press. The journal acts as a forum for innovative, vibrant, transnational, inter-disciplinary scholarship resulting from research on the history of British and Irish Catholicism at home and throughout the world. It publishes peer-reviewed original research articles, review articles and shorter reviews of works on all aspects of British Catholic history from the fifteenth century up to the present day. Central to its publishing policy is an emphasis on the multi-faceted, national and international dimensions of British Catholic history. The journal welcomes contributions on all approaches to the Catholic experience.

The Catholic Record Society welcomes new members, whose membership entitles them to receive *British Catholic History* as well as new Catholic Record Society volumes. The Society hosts an annual conference.

catholicrecordsociety.co.uk